Social Accounting and
Public Management

Routledge Critical Studies in Public Management

EDITED BY STEPHEN P. OSBORNE

The study and practice of public management has undergone profound changes across the world. Over the last quarter century, we have seen

- increasing criticism of public administration as the over-arching framework for the provision of public services,
- the rise (and critical appraisal) of the 'New Public Management' as an emergent paradigm for the provision of public services,
- the transformation of the 'public sector' into the cross-sectoral provision of public services, and
- the growth of the governance of inter-organizational relationships as an essential element in the provision of public services

In reality these trends have not so much replaced each other as elided or co-existed together—the public policy process has not gone away as a legitimate topic of study, intra-organizational management continues to be essential to the efficient provision of public services, whist the governance of inter-organizational and inter-sectoral relationships is now essential to the effective provision of these services.

Further, whilst the study of public management has been enriched by contribution of a range of insights from the 'mainstream' management literature it has also contributed to this literature in such areas as networks and inter-organizational collaboration, innovation and stakeholder theory.

This series is dedicated to presenting and critiquing this important body of theory and empirical study. It will publish books that both explore and evaluate the emergent and developing nature of public administration, management and governance (in theory and practice) and examine the relationship with and contribution to the over-arching disciplines of management and organizational sociology.

Books in the series will be of interest to academics and researchers in this field, students undertaking advanced studies of it as part of their undergraduate or postgraduate degree and reflective policy makers and practitioners.

1. Unbundled Government
A Critical Analysis of the
Global Trend to Agencies,
Quangos and Contractualisation
Edited by Christopher Pollitt
and Colin Talbot

2. The Study of Public Management in Europe and the US
A Competitive Analysis of National
Distinctiveness
Edited by Walter Kickert

3. Managing Complex Governance Systems
Dynamics, Self-Organization and
Coevolution in Public Investments
Edited by Geert Teisman, Arwin van
Buuren and Lasse Gerrits

4. Public Services Management
Edited by Graeme Currie, Jackie Ford,
Nancy Harding and Mark Learmonth

5. Social Accounting and Public Management
Accountability for the Common Good
Edited by Amanda Ball and Stephen P.
Osborne

Social Accounting and Public Management

Accountability for the Common Good

Edited by Amanda Ball and Stephen P. Osborne

Routledge
Taylor & Francis Group
New York   London

First published 2011
by Routledge
711 Third Avenue, New York, NY 10017

Simultaneously published in the UK
by Routledge
2 Park Square, Milton Park, Abingdon, Oxon OX14 4RN

First issued in paperback 2012
Routledge is an imprint of the Taylor & Francis Group, an informa business

© 2011 Taylor & Francis

The right of Amanda Ball and Stephen P. Osborne to be identified as the authors
of the editorial material, and of the authors for their individual chapters, has been
asserted by them in accordance with sections 77 and 78 of the Copyright, Designs
and Patents Act 1988.

Typeset in Sabon by IBT Global.
Printed and bound in the United States of America on acid-free paper by IBT Global.

Library of Congress Cataloging-in-Publication Data
Osborne, Stephen P., 1953–
    Social accounting and public management : accountability for the common good / by
Stephen P. Osborne and Amanda Ball.—1st ed.
        p. cm.—(Routledge critical studies in public management ; 5)
    Includes bibliographical references and index.
    1. Social accounting.   2. Public administration.   I. Ball, Amanda.   II. Title.
    HD60.O83 2010
    352.3—dc22
    2010005792

ISBN13: 978-0-415-65421-0 (pbk)
ISBN13: 978-0-415-80649-7 (hbk)
ISBN13: 978-0-203-84607-0 (ebk)

Contents

PART II
Accountabilities

PART III
Social Accounting and Sustainability

PART IV
Social Accounting, Social Capital, and the Social Economy

PART V
Social Accounting, Accountability, and Ethics

Figures

Tables

Acknowledgements

The value of Emily Kate Hewitt's and Isobel Speedman's kindly manner and contributions as editorial assistants cannot be overstated. The support of Laura Sterns and Terry Clague at Routledge, and their initial sponsorship of the Prague workshop that instigated this volume, is also acknowledged. This original workshop was also jointly sponsored by the International Research Society on Public Management (IRSPM) and the Third Sector Study Group of the European Group on Public Administration (EGPA).

1 Introduction: Accounting—For the Common Good?

Amanda Ball and Stephen P. Osborne

Within the disciplines of public management in general, and accounting in particular, the study of social accounting is gaining significant momentum. This book aims to contribute to the momentum. It explores concepts of social accountability and innovations in the related practices of social accounting and social audit in the public services and third sector. It considers both what contribution this development can have to our understanding of accountability within the public sphere and how social accounting can impact accounting practice in the field.

WHAT IS "SOCIAL ACCOUNTING"?

"Social accounting" refers to organisational information disclosures (financial or non-financial) which significantly extend the scope of traditional financial accounting. It implies wide accountabilities to societal interest groups beyond the traditional model of financial reporting (via the profit and loss account and balance sheet). An often-cited explanation is that provided by Gray (2002, 687):

> Social accounting is . . . a generic term . . . to cover all forms of "accounts which go beyond the economic" . . . —social responsibility accounting, social audits, corporate social reporting, employee and employment reporting as well as environmental accounting and reporting.

A considerable body of academic literature investigates the accounting practices and motives of *businesses* that report on their social, environmental, or sustainability impacts (Deegan and Soltys 2007; Gray 2002; Matthews 1997, 2004; Milne 2007; Parker 2005; Owen 2008). The more normative and philosophical writing (see, for example, Gray 1992, 2002) in support of such socially related disclosures argues that social accounting should have enabling potential and lead to action and change for the better—for instance, in the relationship between an organisation and its stakeholders and/or the natural environment. Indeed, a number of surveys amongst top international firms demonstrate a steady rise in such disclosure practices, if not their efficacy in changing society (Milne, Ball, and Gray 2008). Perhaps surprisingly, such developments have not had the impact upon the public sphere that one might have anticipated, especially given the current high profile of the climate change debate (Ball 2005). One recent review of the theoretical underpinnings of the public management discipline and the paradigmatic implications of public governance for this argued that the question of sustainability and social accounting was one of the core "new questions" that the discipline had to address if it was to meet the challenge of supporting responsive and effective public services in the new millennium (Osborne 2010b).

SOCIAL ACCOUNTING IN THE PUBLIC AND THIRD SECTORS

This book aims to contribute empirical and theoretical insights as to the state, utility, and potential of social accounting and accountability in the public and third sectors. Researchers specialising in social accounting have tended to largely overlook these fields in favour of issues impacting business and the accounting profession (Ball and Grubnic 2007; Matthews 1997; Milne 2007; Owen 2008)—although Marcuccio and Steccolini (2005) is one recent, and welcome, exception to this. Conversely, there are indications that the concepts, accounts, audits, and metrics of social accounting are becoming increasingly significant across a broader pallet, addressing issues of importance not just for for-profit, business organisations, but also for public policy and management more broadly. These include the issues of the nature of accountability in the contemporary plural state (Osborne 2006), environmental and societal sustainability (Ball 2005), the ethical management and governance of public services and resources (Lawton 1998), and the creation and sustenance of social capital as an essential element of the modern plural state (Lowndes and Pratchett 2008; Rossteutscher 2008). This book is intended to address this nexus of issues and disciplines and, through this, make a contribution to the development of both the disciplines of social accounting and public management. It draws together not only leading researchers from the field of accounting who are striving to address this issue, but also scholars from the broader field of public management and third sector studies who are also struggling to make sense of accountability in the contemporary fragmented state (Haveri 2006).

We believe that this book is opportune in the aftermath of a global financial and economic crisis and as governments worldwide contemplate deep spending cuts in the public and third sectors. We anticipate an intensification of the use of (conventional) financial management and accounting technologies as part of a discourse of savings, value, and profit and loss in both sectors. Although a considerable body of "alternative" public sector accounting research contests such developments, accounting requirements, often modelled on private sector practice, continue to proliferate under modern managerial styles of governance and strategy increasingly adopted in both sectors (Broadbent and Guthrie 1992). Yet, as Anderson-Gough and Brown argue:

> we *know* accounting is not the perfect measuring device; we *know* it has assumptions and power effects; we *know* it shapes and even distorts behaviour. (2009, 97; emphasis added)

We contend that, although the NPM discourse is predicated at the policy and managerial levels on the "three E's", this does not necessarily mean that the mainline staff of public service organisations and other stakeholders necessarily *identify* with this discourse. We argue here for public management and social accounting researchers to take up some of the concerns of an "alternative" public sector accountability and accounting agenda through critical engagement with the dominant discourse of economic rationality—and the managerial and accounting practice that it engenders. We also contend the need to explore social accounting in the context of new bases for public management in the twenty-first century—predicated on such values as the common good, social justice, social and ecological sustainability, and ethical public management—even as the social legitimacy of public and third sector organisations' claims on government resources is severely tested (Osborne 2010a).

Certainly, public bodies and third sector organisations can be observed to produce socially oriented qualitative and quantitative disclosures. Organisations in these sectors have not only had to meet corporate, for-profit standards of accountability (that is, demonstrating proper financial stewardship), but also have long had "an additional dimension of accountability in respect of their not-for-profit objectives" (Perrin 1985, 22). A key question, however, is whether and how existing commitments and obligations for *social disclosure* provide any basis for advancing our understanding and the practice of *social accounting and accountability*. By this we mean accountings which are socially significant—that is, they are planned to render visible, challenge, or confront changing patterns of social, political. and economic control and "those factors that are shaping the social roles which information is serving" (Hopwood 1978, 63).

This alternative narrative of accounting and accountability also has significance beyond the confines of the accounting field alone. As we have suggested, the accounting discourse that has long dominated accountability within the public sphere has been one rooted firmly in the traditional financial model of profit and loss, with a focus for public services on their economy and efficiency—often to the exclusion of their effectiveness and equity (Broadbent and Guthrie 2008). However, the increasingly fragmented public sphere, together with the shock waves for public finances and public services produced by the recent global recession, present a challenge to this hegemony.

Whilst politicians have competed to take the (immoral) high ground of public spending cuts and "efficiency savings" as a response to the latter crisis, we would argue that such an approach is profoundly short-sighted and likely, in the longer term, to exacerbate the fragility of the public sphere. Many of the traditional financial accounting models simply cannot cope with the sophistication of the public governance of the fragmented state, whilst enduring global economic recovery will require a more sustainable approach to accountability than "simple" profit and loss accounts (Osborne 2010a). This book will explore this complexity and suggest new directions in the theory and practice of accountability that can take this debate forward.

CROSS-DISCIPLINARY PERSPECTIVES

In order to advance both the concept and the practice of social accounting, and its contribution to public management, this book for the first time brings researchers from a range of disciplines together (including accounting, political science, management, third sector studies, sociology, and policy studies) to discuss and develop our knowledge and theory of social accounting and accountability in the public and third sectors.[1] Indeed, authoritative reviews of the extant social accounting literature are candid in their admissions that the field has been dominated by a coterie of senior academics, whose work, unfortunately, is most frequently cited by each other (Parker 2005; Deegan and Soltys 2007; Ball and Milne 2007). These same reviews also bemoan a dearth of academic work on the building of models and tools to foster social accounting disclosures (Matthews 1997; Gray 2002). As we argue here, social accounting and accountability exist at the nexus of a number of disciplines—accounting, political studies, and management, for example—all of which have important perspectives on the topic but which are usually dealt with in isolation. The attempts by some economists to provide cost-benefit analyses of public policy proposals, for example, can be construed as a form of social accounting (Matthews 1997), yet it is rarely discussed in this context or the combinatory potential acknowledged across these disciplines. The cross-disciplinary focus of this volume is, we believe, a unique contribution to the body of knowledge across the disciplines embraced by it.

OVERVIEW OF THE BOOK AND HOW TO READ IT

The contribution of this book to the fields of social accounting and public management lies in exploring five core questions. These five questions, in turn, motivate the five substantive parts of the book:

Part I presents a number of critical discourses on social accounting and audit in order to address our first core question: *What social accounting* concepts and practices have evolved over the recent past in order to meet the challenges facing contemporary public and third sector organisations?

Part II presents an interdisciplinary examination of the nature of accountability and approaches to its evaluation in different public and third sector contexts. Here our core concern is in understanding: *What is the nature of "accountability" in contemporary (global) society and what challenges does this pose for public policy and management?*

Part III considers the development of social accounting for social and ecological sustainability in public and third sector bodies. Here we ask: *Can social audit and accounting contribute to sustainable development in our contemporary (global) society, and what might this contribution be?*

Part IV reviews emerging models to account for social capital in this society. Our core question is: *To what extent is it possible to account for social capital in contemporary (global) society, and what technologies are evolving to enable this?*

Part V explores the nexus of social accounting, ethics, and accountability in public services. We ask: *Can social audit and social accounting be mobilised as an input into ethical public management?*

By way of conclusion, our final chapter reflects holistically upon these five core concerns.

The volume is intended as a resource both for the inquisitive student and practitioner and for the researcher across a number of fields—social and environmental accounting (and accounting more broadly), public policy and public management, third sector studies and social policy. A systematic reading will provide an overview and multidisciplinary perspective of the contribution of social accounting to key contemporary cross-cutting themes—such as the changing nature of accountability in the fragmented state, evaluating the import of the social capital, sustainability, and public service ethics in contemporary public services, and, of course, the contribution of social accounting to these important debates. Alternatively, the book can be treated as a resource, with each individual chapter offering a new and novel perspective on key public management and accounting debates in theory and in practice. The choice, as they say, is yours.

NOTES

1. The genesis of this volume was in a workshop on "Social Accounting, Social Audit, and Accountability in the Public and Third Sectors" held at the Charles University in Prague, the Czech Republic, in May 2008. This workshop was sponsored by the International Research Society for Public Management (IRSPM) and the Third Sector Study Group of the European Group for Public Administration (EGPA). The majority of the chapters in this volume were presented for the first time at that workshop and have subsequently been extensively revised. They are supplemented here by a number of specially commissioned chapters exploring specific aspects of accountability and social accounting in the public and third sectors.

REFERENCES

Anderson-Gough, F., and R. Brown. 2009. "University Management Practices, Accounting, Gender and Institutional Denial." *Pacific Accounting Review* 20 (2): 94–101.

Ball, A. 2005. "Environmental Accounting and Change in UK Local Government." *Accounting, Auditing and Accountability Journal* 18 (3): 346–373.

Ball, A., and S. Grubnic. 2007. "Sustainability Accounting and Accountability in the Public Sector." In *Sustainability Accounting and Accountability*, ed. J. Unerman, J. Bebbington, and B. O'Dwyer, 243–265. London: Routledge.

Ball, A., and M. J. Milne. 2007. "Talking to Ourselves? The Intellectual and Activist Failure of Social Accountants and What to Do about It." Presented at the 6th Australasian Conference on Social and Environmental Accounting Research (CSEAR 2007), Sydney, Australia, 2–4 December.

Broadbent, J., and J. Guthrie. 1992. "Changes in the Public Sector: A Review of Recent 'Alternative' Accounting Research." *Accounting, Auditing and Accountability Journal* 5 (2): 3–31.

———. 2008. "Public Sector to Public Services: 20 Years of 'Contextual' Accounting Research." *Accounting, Auditing and Accountability Journal* 21 (2): 129–169.

Deegan, C., and S. Soltys. 2007. "Social Accounting Research: An Australasian Perspective." *Accounting Forum* 31 (1): 73–89.

Gray, R. 1992. "Accounting and Environmentalism: An Exploration of the Challenge of Gently Accounting for Accountability, Transparency and Sustainability." *Accounting, Organizations, and Society* 17 (5): 399–425.

———. 2002. "The Social Accounting Project and *Accounting, Organizations and Society*: Privileging Engagement, Imaginings, New Accountings and Pragmatism over Critique." *Accounting, Organizations, and Society* 27 (7): 687–708.

Haveri, A. 2006. "Complexity in Local Government Change: Limits to Rational Reforming." *Public Management Review* 8 (1): 31–46.

Hopwood, A. 1978. "Social Accounting—The Way Ahead?" In CIPFA, *Social Accounting*, 53–64. London: The Chartered Institute of Public Finance and Accounting.

Lawton, A. 1998. *Ethical Management for the Public Services*. Milton Keynes: Open University Press.

Lowndes, V., and L. Pratchett. 2008. "Public Policy and Social Capital." In *Handbook of Social Capital*, ed. D. Castiglione, J. Van Deth, and G. Wolleb, 677–707. Oxford: Oxford University Press.

Marcuccio, M., and I. Steccolini. 2005. "Social and Environmental Reporting in Local Authorities: A New Italian Fashion?" *Public Management Review* 7 (2): 155–176.

Matthews, M. R. 1997. "Twenty-Five Years of Social and Environmental Accounting Research: Is There a Silver Jubilee to Celebrate?" *Accounting, Auditing and Accountability Journal* 10 (4): 481–531.

———. 2004. "Developing a Matrix Approach to Categorise the Social and Environmental Accounting Research Literature." *Qualitative Research in Accounting and Management* 1 (1): 30–45.

Milne, M. J. 2007. "Downsizing Reg (You and Me)! The 'Real' Sustainability Agenda." In *Social Accounting, Mega Accounting and Beyond: A Festschrift in Honour of M. R. Mathews*, ed. R. Gray and J. Guthrie, chapter 6. St. Andrews: CSEAR.

Milne, M. J., A. Ball, and R. Gray. 2008. "Wither Ecology? The Triple Bottom Line, the Global Reporting Initiative and the Institutionalization of Sustainable Development Reporting." Presented at the American Accounting Association Annual Meeting, Anaheim, California, 3–6 August.

Osborne, S. P. 2006. "The New Public Governance?" *Public Management Review* 8 (3): 377–388.

———. 2010a. *The New Public Governance? Emerging Perspectives on the Theory and Practice of Public Governance.* London: Routledge.

———. 2010b. "Public Governance and Public Services Delivery: A Research Agenda for the Future." In *The New Public Governance? Emerging Perspectives on the Theory and Practice of Public Governance,* ed. S. Osborne, 413–428. London: Routledge.

Owen, D. 2008. "Chronicles of a Wasted Time? A Personal Reflection on the Current State of, and Future Prospects for, Social and Environmental Accounting Research." *Accounting, Auditing and Accountability Journal* 21 (2): 240–267.

Parker, L. D. 2005. "Social and Environmental Accountability Research: A View from the Commentary Box." *Accounting, Auditing and Accountability Journal* 18 (6): 842–860.

Perrin, J. R. 1985. "Differentiating Financial Accountability and Management in Governments, Public Services and Charities." *Financial Accountability and Management* 1 (1): 11–32.

Rossteutscher, S. 2008. "Social Capital and Civic Engagement." In *Handbook of Social Capital,* ed. D. Castiglione, J. Van Deth, and G. Wolleb, 208–240. Oxford: Oxford University Press.

Part I

Social Audit and Social Accounting

Cross-Disciplinary Perspectives

2 A Brief Re-Evaluation of "The Social Accounting Project"

Social Accounting Research as if the World Matters

Rob Gray, Jesse Dillard, and Crawford Spence

Ever tried. Ever failed. No matter. Try again. Fail again. Fail better.
(Beckett 1983)[1]

INTRODUCTION

To try and talk about "social accounting" as a singularity is probably to invite confusion. "Social accounting" embraces a diversity of practices—from (for example) environmental management accounting to habitat inventories; from Multinational Corporation stand-alone "sustainability" reports to dialogue-based third sector syntheses (Schaltegger and Burritt 2000; Jones 1996; Kolk 2003; Pearce 2003; Ball and Seal 2005; Marcuccio and Steccolini 2005). It is to this diverse notion of social accounting that we wish to direct our attention here. More particularly, though, we will speak about that academic community of social accounting with which we are most familiar—that community which, to a greater or lesser extent, draws its orientations, methods, and concerns from the world of accountants. In doing so, we will try to provide the beginnings of a critique of (what we see as) "our" academic community—but one especially informed by some of the experiences we observe in the public management community. (What the public management community can maybe learn from us is quite another matter.)

Social accounting in the academy, as we understand it here, tends to be concerned with issues of accountability, business and non-business organisations, institutions, society, and the state. The motivation tends to be a concern to contribute to a better life—and never forgetting that for many a better life is any life at all. But to take such a position (especially in accounting, business, and management) has been to invite resistance and repression from colleagues, politicians, and the business community. We approach this chapter in the belief that all informed conversations must be encouraged.

Consequently, this chapter explores some of the possibilities of social accounting—but with a clear eye upon one's place and one's duty in a world of privilege—confronted with a world of the oppressed, a vandalised nature, and a wounded planet. We approach this chapter as accountants whose literature and research has been largely dominated by a concern for Anglo-Saxon, private sector organisations. It is this literature that we try to revaluate here, but in the explicit recognition that other readers may not be familiar with it. This chapter emerges from our epistemic community's shared assumptions about such matters as professionalism, recording and information, accountability, disclosure, and business. It is this (loosely defined) epistemic community that we principally refer to in what follows[2] and whose assumptions we are seeking to re-examine.

Social accounting in this literature has attracted a range of criticisms for its: quietism (Tinker, Lehman, and Neimark 1991); masculism (Cooper 1992); managerialism (Neu, Warsame, and Pedwell 1998); attachment to modernity (Everett and Neu 2000; Andrew 2000) and liberalism (Shenkin and Coulson 2007); its (incorrectly alleged) attachment to voluntarism (Gallhofer and Haslam 1997); its (correctly alleged) attachment to proceduralism (Lehman 2001; Ball and Seal 2005); and its under-theorised nature (Puxty 1991). Many of these challenges have substance and various attempts have been made to respond directly to them and/or to redirect social accounting accordingly.

More constructive critiques have been offered by (for example) Cooper et al. (2005). Their work illustrates an entirely different type of social account which mounts a substantial challenge to the potentially conservative, organisationally based exploration of social accounting with which academic social accountants are more usually concerned. Perhaps equally telling are the long-overdue reminders that social accounting is not only a private sector—but also a public and third sector—phenomenon (Ball 2002). More recently there have been a series of formal and informal discussions around the possibility that "the social accounting project" as generally understood in the accounting literature might have failed and Milne (2007) has challenged social accountants to consider the narrowness of their enterprise. These challenges resonate with the growing interest in shadow, silent, and counter-accounts in offering a challenge to potentially autistic academic pursuits (see, for example, Gray 1997; Adams 2004; Gallhofer et al. 2006).[3]

The chapter is organised as follows. Following this introduction, the next section continues our preface and reflects upon our notion of social accounting. The following section considers the (radical) potential of social accounting before we evaluate in the next section what (if anything) has been achieved. The final sections of the chapter explore how we might move forward and what (other or "other"?) sorts of social accounting we might pursue and embrace.

SOCIAL ACCOUNTING (IN) CONTEXT

Social accounting,[4] in both the for-profit and not-for-profit sectors, is (broadly) concerned with control of the entity and its responsibility and accountability to ranges of stakeholders. But social accounting in the two sectors has largely developed independently.[5]

The private sector development of social accounting has nearly always been a voluntary act undertaken by (typically) the larger corporations, (see Gray, Bebbington, and Collison 1996 for a summary). Explanations for these efforts have tended towards image management and a concern with legitimating the organisation. As organisations have grown, so such legitimation has been more systematic and more crucial. Indeed, if it is the case that Multinational Corporations (MNCs) are the dominant force on the planet, the accountability of these creatures is a *sine qua non* of a civilised and free civil society (see, for example, Korten 1995; Bakan 2004). Social accounting, in our judgement, becomes a concern with conflict: as long as there is a major difference between what a corporation willingly tells society, what corporations actually do, and what society has a right to know, social accounting information is crucial.

By contrast, it seems to us that social accounting in the public and third sectors has developed slightly differently. In the absence of any analogue for "profit", much early effort was expended in the examination of key performance indicators which might capture the principal activities of the organisation (Booth and Paterson 1982). Although this continues as a focus of interest (Wall and Martin 2003; Galera, Rodriguez, and Hernandez 2008), something more systematically like social accounting emerged as public and third sector organisations began to feel the pressure to justify their social and environmental existence—particularly in economic terms.

Simply put: We could speculate that private sector social accounting is a response by principally economic organisations to demonstrate that they are not purely economic; whilst not-for-profit organisations might be thought to have developed social accounting to justify their pursuit of social and environmental goals in economic terms. Both developments could be hypothesised as consequences of the increasing distances between individuals and organisations (as a contrast here with Rawls's notion of closeness) coupled with the rise of the neo-liberal agenda and its attendant focus on economics and markets (Evans 2000; Gray, Bebbington, and Collison 2006).

One key difference which emerges from this speculation lies in how the accountable organisation is viewed. In the private sector, the corporation seeks to justify its activities whilst many stakeholders (including researchers) question the very existence of the organisation within alienating global financial markets. Social accounting (in its normative intention if not its actual practice) for private sector organisations therefore often exhibits a combative element to deal with the conflict of power and responsibility. For the public/third sector organisation, the central place of the epistemic community on which the organisation is based is clearly recognised. Its raison d'être is not in question and social accounting is developed to justify the entity and its primary tasks. The similarity of this expression of interests in social accounting is, if nothing else, ironic.

Despite the efforts of a few (Ball and Grubnic 2007), these concerns and their attendant literatures have not intersected as much as they might. This chapter is our tentative attempt in this direction.

SOCIAL ACCOUNTING AND ITS RADICAL INTENT?

Social accounting within the accounting academy has been predominantly concerned to develop corporate accountability in the name of some democratic ideal motivated by a concern over the power and influence of the corporation (Porritt 2005; Korten 1995). Enquiry into social accounting offers, *inter alia*, the promise of holding the international corporate and financial complex accountable to civil society. Such accountability could expose much duplicity and make transparent the essential conflicts that a global, astonishingly successful capitalism generates. Such accountability would allow for the possibility of clarifying the social injustice and environmental degradation imbedded in production, consumption, and expansion—indeed, in modern financial capitalism. Such an accountability (Owen 2008) would demand that both civil society and the state act in a manner which has the potential to produce a very different world from the one in which we now live. It could have a considerable impact on our world: challenging many current notions of the success of late financial capitalism and exposing uncontrolled financial markets for what they are (Gray 2002). Such an accountability would allow debates about organisational sustainability and responsibility to be held with evidence rather than entirely through assertion (Milne, Kearins, and Walton 2006).

This sense of the potential of (private sector) social accounting and accountability might be thought of as a means through which different visions about social, environmental, and economic organisation might emerge. To do this, it is normally assumed, there is a need to reintroduce some explicit ethic to the practice of capitalism. Such an introduction might (of course) not be possible and would, in all probability, beg the question as to whether we need to adopt a reformist or a revolutionary vision. However, at this point we are less concerned by this than we are in recognising that the creation and communication of accounts in the broad sense is a ubiquitous human activity (Arrington and Francis 1993), and social accounting can offer both new accounts and some of the ways in which the essential changes to conventional accounting might be brought about. However, there remains the very real empirical concern that the only (social) accounting change that is likely to be possible under present conditions will be anodyne whereas a full accounting (however specified) *must* expose conflicts through which current debates within political economy might be better informed.

WHAT HAS SOCIAL ACCOUNTING ACHIEVED?

Despite the challenges that social accounting has attracted, and despite the fact that it has not succeeded in reforming practice, social accounting is neither all failure nor all success. Having had to fight (especially in academe) for much of its life to have any existence at all, social accounting's survival itself is an achievement (Laine 2006). Social accounting has produced a healthy and diverse network of scholars, teachers, and practitioners; it has advanced the subject in teaching and research; and it has generated a range of experiments, engagements, and challenges with practice (see, for example, Unerman, Bebbington, and O'Dwyer 2007).[6]

Despite this, social accounting may have failed to maintain a creative energy between the world as it is and the world as it should be (Everett 2007). Milne's (2007) reassessment of social accounting research concludes that the dominant concern with (corporate) disclosure studies suggests something fundamentally unhealthy about an area of study that has infinite potential and yet seems to exhibit so relatively limited an imagination. Has the initial revolutionary fervour of private sector social accounting given way to the interests of publication and research assessment? Has acceptability triumphed over complexity? Is there something that encourages conformity in academe and the inability/reluctance to escape the "epistemology of modernity" (Lehman 2006; Tuttle and Dillard 2007)?

Social accounting does not seem to possess the capacity to research absence (Choudhury 1988) or silence (Hines 1992). Speculation and proposals for practice in the literature seem unlikely to sit too far from what is currently considered to be the art of the possible. So the literature contains relatively few genuinely radical and innovative proposals. Is this self-discipline or perhaps a fear that the journals would treat such attempts as incoherent assertion?

This leads to a significant point: Social accounting academe is so often limited to being a function of current social accounting practice. Research, in the private sector at least, is largely limited by an activity that is a function of international financial capitalistic hegemony. In a remarkable sense, we find ourselves only able to study that which power will allow us to study. This is not a new phenomenon—nor is it limited to social accounting. But it certainly offers a challenge to any project which wishes to be both innovative and reformist (perhaps even revolutionary) when the empirical terms of the work must be negotiated in unfairly balanced contracts with the very organisations one wishes to change.

There are limits, of course, but social accounting *has* achieved a great deal. The social and environmental language of business, accounting, and finance has changed; claims for accountability by capital have been shown to be empty; voluntary disclosure has been exposed as cherry-picking; the claims for responsibility and sustainability are exposed as hollow; and we *do* now know how to undertake substantial social, environmental, and sustainability reporting. That business in particular—and most of business academe—chooses to ignore these developments in social accountability is not entirely the fault of social accounting.

IMAGINATION, SOCIAL ACCOUNTS, AND THE FUTURE

Despite the struggle with ways to produce a literature of imagination and engagement (Adams and Larrinaga-González 2007), much important work takes place in social accounting. The experimentation with accounting for (un)sustainability (Bebbington 2007; Spence and Gray 2008), the innovative use of a social account by Cooper et al. (2005), and the work on social audits and empowering "stakeholder" groups have a long and noble history (see, for example, Harte and Owen 1987; Owen 2007), and initiatives such as the silent and shadow accounts (Gibson et al. 2001; Adams 2004; Gallhofer et al. 2006) offer very considerable opportunities for alternative accountings in a variety of settings. These successes can encourage us to cast our net yet wider. For example, Collison et al. (2007) and Gray (2006) offer ways in which global- or national-level data may be employed to change the focus of how we conceive of the accounting entity and thereby challenge much empty rhetoric in corporate modernity. The dialogic accounting suggested by Thomson and Bebbington (2005) offers a new decentred approach to accounts. What we have here, in all probability, are the emergent threads of new conceptions of what a social account might become.

But it may well be in the public and the third sectors where the most vibrant examples of, and opportunities for, new accountings reside. Seeking out the contours of values-based organisations—whether social enterprise or NGO, for example—and working actively with them offers considerable promise (Capron and Gray 2000; Young and Tilley 2006). Beyond this lies the tantalising prospect of seeking the transformation of conventional organisations to "new models", whatever that might be (Young and Tilley 2006). Many of the ingredients will lie in values-based organisations and in NGOs and community businesses.

What we are driving towards here are accountability regimes that are more actively normative (see, for example, Osborne 2008; Klijn 2008) and that perhaps, at least initially, start to look more like, and may indeed act in partnership with, (say) the better forms of journalism.

Consequently, we cautiously propose a range of areas in which social accounting—at least as we have tended to understand it here—has yet to develop. So, in the interest of moving towards a more productive conclusion to this chapter we could see social accounting in the academy giving more attention to such matters and tasks as:

- Systematically analyse social enterprise and charity accountings.
- Respond to the literatures of public sectors' forays into social accounting (see, especially, Marcuccio and Steccolini 2005; Ball 2002; Ball and Seal 2005).
- Start to describe, illustrate, and draw out the parameters of less procedural and/or more horizontal accountability mechanisms (see, for example, Lehman 2001, 2006; Klijn 2008). What would "enacted accounts" look like and how might the research community help them to develop (Ball and Seal 2005)?
- Explore and develop what social accounting must look like in non-western contexts.
- Further develop notions of social bookkeeping and management information systems (see, for example, Dey 2007; Dey, Evans, and Gray 1995; Brown, Dillard, and Marshall 2005).
- Reconsider accounts for specific stakeholder groups such as the employees and the unemployed; suppliers in uneven relationships versus fair trade; communities and so on.
- Reconsider social accounts for the dispossessed and/or the excluded.
- Exploring what accounts of social justice might look like.
- Develop accounts of human rights.
- How might academic social accountants develop the idea of accounts of (say) industry groupings or geographically determined collections of organisations? What information would this produce and what might be done with it?
- Is it possible and useful to increase research into taxation and offer a wider range of narratives about taxation, its incidence and avoidance?
- How might academic social accountants begin to learn how to consider more multiple accounts and their interplay?
- New accounts are needed to develop the work of Jones (1996) and Pallot (1997) on biodiversity—but further, how might social accounts of air, land, water, and other categories of human and non-human experience be articulated?
- What sorts of accounts would speak more directly to policy makers and, if at all, to what extent would such accounts require dangerous compromise and the silencing of other voices?
- Inevitably the further expansion of the "accounting for the other by the other"[7]—silent and shadow accounting as has been developed but which offers so very many more possibilities (see, for example, Gibson et al. 2001).

Such a list could—and probably should—be a great deal longer. After all, the universe of all possible accountings is unlikely to be quite so finite as our imaginations. The substantive point here, though, is that within the academy of social accountants and accounting there is a great deal of work that needs to be done: and much of it will not be done whilst convention, normal science, and the whim of capital holds sway.

CONCLUSIONS

Social accounting needs to become more vibrant, irreverent, mischievous—angry. It needs to become (as Ghandi suggests) the change it wishes to be. How imaginative can it become? Can social accounting learn how nature accounts—if at all? Maybe the academy more broadly must learn how humans account, person-to-person; how market-alien values (Thiellemann 2000) are the stuff of human existence; and how commerce is valuable but dangerous. Maybe social accounting can stretch towards a new empowerment of accountability and accounting as language—perhaps even trying to study social accountability as a multiplicity, as the very glue that binds persons together and which separates persons from their nature. As authors, we are convinced that the academy more widely needs to learn new ways to authentically grant *warranty* in debate and deny all suppression from others. The academy should abandon that which cannot be seen as commensurate with a good life and expose all of our taken-for-granted assumptions more explicitly—despite the discomfort that this will bring.

Social accounting may learn to transform old organisations or to build a "new model" of entity. It may very well enjoin an abandonment of organisations as entities altogether. Perhaps researchers can respond to the analysis of Albrow and Glasius (2008) and focus on a new global civil society imbedded in new and better-understood forms of communication and democracy. Maybe then society will face the conflicts and decide who will suffer in the transition to a less unjust world. As authors, we speculate—and hope—that closeness and authenticity will become our criteria, community our potential, and a recognition of absurdity our chief weapon.

NOTES

1. We are grateful to Hugh McBride for this reference as a motto for social accounting!
2. This community shares some commonality with the community that makes up The Centre for Social and Environmental Accounting Research (CSEAR), a membership-based organisation comprising at the time of writing over seven hundred members in over forty countries. More detail can be found at www.st-andrews.ac.uk/management/csear.
3. For more information, see the CSEAR web site.
4. We are using *social accounting* here as the usual generic term to cover, *inter alia,* social responsibility accounting; social, sustainability, and environmental accounting; reporting, disclosure, and audit; and so on.

5. We recognise that this is a predominantly Anglo-Saxon review: we apologise unreservedly if this is too parochial or narrow.

6. Successful engagements by the social accounting academic community include: the leading-edge reporting by "values-based" organisations like Traidcraft and Landcare; the experiments in accounting for sustainability in Landcare and BP; the engagement and support of socially responsible investment (SRI) and its community; work with trades unions; the considerable progress in social accounting in third sector organisations; the policy developments of GRI, Institute of Social and Ethical Accountability (ISEA) and, especially, the ACCA (and now worldwide) reporting awards; the Environmental Management Accounting Network (EMAN) project; and so on.

7. This is a direct quote from a paper being developed by Colin Dey and Ian Thomson on the role of shadow accounting—we are unable to reference it but we can acknowledge it!

REFERENCES

Adams, C. 2004. "The Ethical, Social and Environmental Reporting–Performance Portrayal Gap." *Accounting, Auditing and Accountability Journal* 17 (5): 731–757.

Adams, C. A., and C. Larrinaga-González. 2007. "Engaging with Organisations in Pursuit of Improved Sustainability Accountability and Performance." *Accounting, Auditing and Accountability Journal* 20 (3): 333–355.

Albrow, M., and M. Glasius. 2008. "Democracy and the Possibility of a Global Public Sphere." In *Global Civil Society 2007/8*, ed. M. Albrow, H. Anheir, M. Glasius, M. Price, and M. Kaldor, 1–18. London: Sage.

Andrew, J. 2000. "The Accounting Craft and the Environmental Crisis: Reconsidering Environmental Ethics." *Accounting Forum* 24 (June): 197–222.

Arrington, C. E., and J. R. Francis. 1993. "Giving Economic Accounts: Accounting as Cultural Practice." *Accounting, Organizations, and Society* 18 (2/3): 107–124.

Bakan, J. 2004. *The Corporation: The Pathological Pursuit of Profit and Power.* London: Constable and Robinson.

Ball, A. 2002. *Sustainability Accounting in UK Local Government: An Agenda for Research.* London: ACCA.

Ball, A., and S. Grubnic. 2007. "Sustainability Accounting and Accountability in the Public Sector." In *Sustainability Accounting and Accountability*, ed. J. Unerman, J. Bebbington, and B. O'Dwyer, 243–265. London: Routledge.

Ball, A., and W. Seal. 2005. "Social Justice in a Cold Climate: Could Social Accounting Make a Difference?" *Accounting Forum* 29 (December): 455–473.

Bebbington, J. 2007. *Accounting for Sustainable Development Performance.* London: CIMA.

Beckett, S. 1983. *Worstward Ho.* London: John Calder.

Booth, P. J., and H. M. Paterson. 1982. "External Financial Reports: Necessary but not Sufficient for the Accountability of Non-Business Organisations." *Accounting Forum* (March): 13–21.

Brown, D. L., J. F. Dillard, and R. S. Marshall. 2005. "Strategically Informed, Environmentally Conscious Information Requirements for Accounting Information Systems." *Journal of Information Systems* 19 (Fall): 79–103.

Capron, M., and R. H. Gray. 2000. "Experimenting with Assessing Corporate Social Responsibility in France: An Exploratory Note on an Initiative by Social Economy Firms." *European Accounting Review* 9 (1): 99–109.

Choudhury, N. 1988. "The Seeking of Accounting Where it is Not: Towards a Theory of Non-Accounting in Organizational Settings." *Accounting, Organizations, and Society* 13 (6): 549–557.

Collison, D. J., C. Dey, G. Hannah, and L. Stevenson. 2007. "Income Inequality and Child Mortality in Wealthy Nations." *Journal of Public Health* (March): 1–4.

Cooper, C. 1992. "The Non and Nom of Accounting for (M)other Nature." *Accounting, Auditing and Accountability Journal* 5 (3): 16–39.

Cooper, C., P. Taylor, N. Smith, and L. Catchpowle. 2005. "A Discussion of the Political Potential of Social Accounting." *Critical Perspectives on Accounting* 16:951–974.

Dey, C. 2007. "Social Accounting at Traidcraft Plc: A Struggle for the Meaning of Fair Trade." *Accounting, Auditing and Accountability Journal* 20 (3): 423–445.

Dey, C., R. Evans, and R. H. Gray. 1995. "Towards Social Information Systems and Bookkeeping: A Note on Developing the Mechanisms for Social Accounting and Audit." *Journal of Applied Accounting Research* 2 (December): 36–69.

Evans, R. 2000. *Corporate Ethical Accounting: (How) Can Companies Tell the Truth?* Cambridge: Grove Books.

Everett, J. 2007. "Fact, Desire and Lack in Deegan and Soltys's 'Social Accounting Research: An Australasian Perspective.'" *Accounting Forum* 31:91–97.

Everett, J., and D. Neu. 2000. "Ecological Modernization and the Limits of Environmental Accounting." *Accounting Forum* 24 (March): 5–29.

Galera, A. N., D. O. Rodriguez, and A. M. L. Hernandez. 2008. "Identifying Barriers to the Application of Standardized Performance Indicators in Local Government." *Public Management Review* 10 (2): 241–262.

Gallhofer, S., and J. Haslam. 1997. "The Direction of Green Accounting Policy: Critical Reflections." *Accounting, Auditing and Accountability Journal* 10 (2): 148–196.

Gallhofer, S., J. Haslam, E. Monk, and C. Roberts. 2006. "The Emancipatory Potential of Online Reporting: The Case of Counter Accounting." *Accounting, Auditing and Accountability Journal* 19 (5): 681–718.

Gibson, K., R. Gray, Y. Laing, and C. Dey. 2001. *The Silent Accounts Project: Draft Silent and Shadow Accounts Tesco plc 1999–2000.* Glasgow: CSEAR.

Gray, R. H. 1997. "The Silent Practice of Social Accounting and Corporate Social Reporting in Companies." In *Building Corporate Accountability: Emerging Practices in Social and Ethical Accounting, Auditing and Reporting*, ed. S. Zadek, R. Evans, and P. Pruzan, 201–217. London: Earthscan.

———. 2002. "Of Messiness, Systems and Sustainability: Towards a More Social and Environmental Finance and Accounting." *British Accounting Review* 34 (December): 357–386.

———. 2006. "Social, Environmental, and Sustainability Reporting and Organisational Value Creation? Whose Value? Whose Creation?" *Accounting, Auditing and Accountability Journal* 19 (3): 319–348.

Gray, R., J. Bebbington, and D. J. Collison. 2006. "NGOs, Civil Society and Accountability: Making the People Accountable to Capital." *Accounting, Auditing and Accountability Journal* 19 (3): 319–348.

Harte, G., and D. L. Owen. 1987. "Fighting De-Industrialisation: The Role of Local Government Social Audits." *Accounting, Organizations, and Society* 12 (2): 123–142.

Hines, R. D. 1992. "Accounting: Filling the Negative Space." *Accounting, Organizations, and Society* 17 (3/4): 313–342.

Jones, M. J. 1996. "Accounting for Biodiversity: A Pilot Study." *British Accounting Review* 28 (December): 281–303.

Klijn, E. H. 2008. "Governance and Governance Networks in Europe: An Assessment of Ten Years of Research on the Theme." *Public Management Review* 10 (4): 505–525.

Kolk, A. 2003. "Trends in Sustainability Reporting by the Fortune Global 250." *Business Strategy and the Environment* 12 (September–October): 279–291.

Korten, D. C. 1995. *When Corporations Rule the World.* West Hatford and San Francisco: Kumarian/Berrett-Koehler.

Laine, M. 2006. "Still the Kiss of Death: A Personal Reflection on Encountering the Mainstream Paradigm as a PhD Student." *Social and Environmental Accounting Journal* 26 (September): 9–13.

Lehman, G. 2001. "Reclaiming the Public Sphere: Problems and Prospects for Corporate Social and Environmental Accounting." *Critical Perspectives on Accounting* 12 (December): 713–733.

———. 2006. "Perspectives on Language, Accountability and Critical Accounting: An Interpretative Perspective." *Critical Perspectives on Accounting* 17:755–779.

Marcuccio, M., and I. Steccolini. 2005. "Social and Environmental Reporting in Local Authorities." *Public Management Review* 7 (2): 155–176.

Milne, M. 2007. "Downsizing Reg (Me and You)!: Addressing the 'Real' Sustainability Agenda at Work and Home." In *Social Accounting, Mega Accounting and Beyond: A Festschrift in Honour of M. R. Mathews,* ed. R. H. Gray and J. Guthrie, 49–66. St. Andrews: CSEAR Publishing.

Milne, M. J., K. N. Kearins, and S. Walton. 2006. "Creating Adventures in Wonderland? The Journey Metaphor and Environmental Sustainability." *Organization* 13 (6): 801–839.

Neu, D., H. Warsame, and K. Pedwell. 1998. "Managing Public Impressions: Environmental disclosures in Annual Reports." *Accounting Organizations and Society* 23 (April): 265–282.

Osborne, S. 2008. "Ten Years of *Public Management Review.*" *Public Management Review* 10 (4): 451–452.

Owen, D. 2007. "Social and Environmental Accounting: Celebrating a Silver Jubilee of Engagement and Community." In *Social Accounting, Mega Accounting and Beyond: A Festschrift in Honour of M. R. Mathews,* ed. R. H. Gray and J. Guthrie, 67–76. St. Andrews: CSEAR Publishing.

———. 2008. "Chronicles of Wasted Time? A Personal Reflection on the Current State of, and Future Prospects for, Social and Environmental Accounting Research." *Accounting, Auditing and Accountability Journal* 21 (2): 240–267.

Pallot, J. 1997. "Accounting for Infrastructure Assets: Technical Management and Political Context." *Financial Accountability and Management* 13:225–242.

Pearce, J. 2003. *Social Enterprise in Anytown.* London: Calouste Gulbenkian Foundation.

Porritt, J. 2005. *Capitalism: As If the World Matters.* London: Earthscan.

Puxty, A. G. 1991. "Social Accountability and Universal Pragmatics." *Advances in Public Interest Accounting* 4:35–46.

Schaltegger, S., and R. Burritt. 2000. *Contemporary Environmental Accounting: Issues, Concepts and Practices.* Sheffield: Greenleaf.

Shenkin, M., and A. B. Coulson. 2007. "Accountability through Activism: Learning from Bourdieu." *Accounting, Auditing and Accountability Journal* 20 (2): 297–317.

Spence, C., and R. Gray. 2008. *Social and Environmental Reporting and the Business Case.* London: ACCA.

Thiellemann, U. 2000. "A Brief Theory of the Market—Ethically Focused." *International Journal of Social Economics* 27 (1): 6–31.

Thomson, I., and J. Bebbington. 2005. "Social and Environmental Reporting in the UK: A Pedagogic Evaluation." *Critical Perspectives on Accounting* 16 (July): 507–533.

Tinker, T., C. Lehman, and M. Neimark. 1991. "Corporate Social Reporting: Falling Down the Hole in the Middle of the Road." *Accounting, Auditing and Accountability Journal* 4 (1): 28–54.

Tuttle, B., and J. Dillard. 2007. "Beyond Competition: Institutional Isomorphism in US Accounting." *Accounting Horizons* 21 (December): 387–409.

Unerman, J., J. Bebbington, and B. O'Dwyer, eds. 2007. *Sustainability Accounting and Accountability*. London: Routledge.

Wall, A., and G. Martin. 2003. "The Disclosure of Key Performance Indicators in the Public Sector." *Public Management Review* 5 (December): 491–509.

Young, W., and F. Tilley. 2006. "Can Business Move beyond Efficiency? The Shift toward Effectiveness and Equity in the Corporate Sustainability Debate." *Business Strategy and the Environment* 15:402–415.

3 Participatory Governance and Social Audit in the Third Sector

Giulio Citroni and Sabina Nicolella

This chapter describes the role that participation and participatory governance may have in social accounting and auditing in third sector organisations. After an introductory section describing the relevance of third sector organisations in the planning and implementation of social and other policies, the second section outlines a model for participatory governance that may respond to many of the challenges that these organisations face in terms of transparency, legitimacy, and effectiveness of operations. The third section describes three instances where this model was tentatively implemented by the authors, while the following sections point to the open issues and conclude on the perspectives of the participatory model.

THREATS AND OPPORTUNITIES IN THE NEW SOCIETAL ROLE OF THE THIRD SECTOR

Third sector organisations are becoming essential participants in defining local, national, and international social agendas, and in developing joint social projects. They also play an important role as partners of public agencies as well as international organisations, large private corporations, and small and medium enterprises (SMEs). The proliferation of multi-stakeholder forums (for example the European Multi-Stakeholder Forum on CSR, EU Water Initiative Multi-Stakeholder Forum, and the Global Reporting Initiative) indicates the importance attributed to third sector organisations by institutional as well as profit-making bodies.

In addition, third sector organisations are progressively establishing a new role in society due to their increased ability to secure high-quality services in areas where welfare systems are not fully covered by governments, especially concerning minority needs. Furthermore, by virtue of their proximity to social and environmental needs, third sector organisations are emerging as valid representatives of specific needs, thus holding a special place in the debate on inclusiveness and democratisation of globalisation (Evers and Laville 2004). This new role in formulating and implementing the "welfare mix", however, imposes new responsibilities upon the third sector, increasingly called to answer for instances of transparency and representativeness.

Indeed, the issue of representativeness is strongly posed by the relatively narrow nature of the issues and the interests that third sector organisations pursue, preventing them from being representative of wider societal needs. Furthermore, wider societal interest might be interpreted by third sector organisations from a particular (local, ideological, sectoral) point of view, not necessarily mirroring a more general set of interests or perspectives.

Closely interconnected with the issue of representativeness stands the challenge of transparency and accountability.[1] As third sector organisations become an increasingly important social actor, their economic relevance grows: Some of the largest international NGOs, for instance, receive millions of dollars of donations every year,[2] while the scope of the social economy grows larger every year. The very reasons why the third sector exists demand that the economic and financial resources it generates are devoted to serve societal needs in the most efficient and effective way. In addition, in most western countries third sector organisations enjoy special tax schemes and other benefits by virtue of the purposes they serve. Therefore, their capability to pursue their declared intentions in good faith and effectively, and to demonstrate this to donors and to contracting public agencies as well as to beneficiaries, is becoming a fundamental asset for third sector organisations.

Opening up the organisation to stakeholder contribution and scrutiny can be an effective answer to these issues of representativeness and transparency/accountability. Engaging both internal and external stakeholders in the formulation of organisational strategies, policies, and actions that affect them brings the concept of representativeness to a more concrete level. While maintaining the integrity of their specific mission and identity, organisations that engage stakeholders in their decision processes are challenged with real needs and expectations that might affect the outcome of their actions, as well as the way the same actions are co-ordinated and organised. As Preston and Post highlight, "internal and external participativeness raise serious issues about the traditional legitimacy and autonomy of managerial organisations" (1974, 483), but such issues can be dealt with on the basis of a shared definition of the boundaries of participation and the rules that guide it.

Furthermore, participation of stakeholders in the evaluation of the consistency between the organisation and its strategic objectives (which in the third sector should meet the needs and interest of stakeholders) boosts transparency. The adoption of adequate accountability and assurance tools can ensure access to reliable, complete, and material information, necessary to evaluate the performance of any organisation. Transparent sustainability reporting and stakeholder panels are only two of the many possible solutions.

PARTICIPATORY GOVERNANCE AND
ORGANISATIONAL RESPONSIBILITY

The debate on organisational responsibility, and the action and policies that follow, stems from the recognition that organisations hold responsibilities to society that exceed their legal liabilities, either because of incompleteness of applicable legislation (Ruppolo 1991), or due to a mismatch between the law and general moral perception (Sapelli 2007). However, the limits and content of such responsibility are difficult to define a priori. What is clear is that organisational responsibility concerns the sphere of ethics, since its voluntary nature implies the autonomous (not derived by law) definition of what is good and what is bad. In a climate of incertitude, driven by the growing complexity of society where ethics is becoming increasingly difficult to define univocally, the concept of organisational responsibility has to be narrowed down to be operationalised. While the content and extent of responsibility might differ from one sector to another, and according to normative and social contexts, organisational responsibility as a whole can be seen as a process of sense-making (Basu and Palazzo 2008). In this situation, the organisation draws cognitive maps of its environment, connecting the internal perception of external pressures with the external perception of what the organisation is, that is, reading the environment where the organisation operates with stakeholders. Values, organisational culture, as well as materiality of the action to the stakeholders and stakeholder engagement are key elements of this approach to organisational responsibility whether applied to private enterprises, public agencies, or third sector organisations.

Amongst the driving factors that lead third sector organisations to adopt organisational responsibility tools, the most likely to matter are the preservation or the acquisition of legitimacy, the attraction of economic resources, the continuous improvement of reputation, and the development of management systems and quality. The case studies discussed in the following also show that change management is a relevant factor, too, insofar as the definition of organisational responsibility policy and tools coincides with the definition of values and culture (what we do and how we do it are consequences of who we are). Sustainability reporting and stakeholder engagement can serve this purpose, respectively giving accurate evidence of the actions taken and of the relative figures, and creating the opportunity to open strategic planning to stakeholders' input through the adoption of a participatory approach to governance.

Participatory governance brings stakeholders to the centre of strategic and functional planning: It is a set of processes that involve stakeholders in the definition of the organisation's strategic goals, in the evaluation of the extent to which these goals are met, and in the planning and carrying out of possible specific activities needed to meet the goals themselves. It is a model of organisational governance that embraces several crucial aspects of organisational responsibility at once, such as accepting one's responsibility towards stakeholders and materiality policies regarding stakeholders' expectations, transparency, and accountability. Participatory governance can be efficiently set in a wider organisational responsibility program that holds sustainability, production, and organisation in one strategic concept.

Particularly, participatory governance puts strong demands on organisational responsibility instruments, in that they must be conducted following principles of information, stakeholder engagement, and stakeholder empowerment, which are not always easily met. At the same time, however, it helps to find innovative solutions and guarantees that sustainability strategies and innovations in organisational responsibility are accepted and implemented throughout the organisation, and with the support of external stakeholders, in ways that performance/management-oriented forms of organisational responsibility do not guarantee.

Within this framework, social auditing and reporting become fundamental tools to achieve the goals of participatory governance, by:

• reducing relevant information gaps between the organisation and its stakeholders;
• making public the organisation's commitment towards goals agreed with concerned stakeholders;
• creating opportunities to set strategic goals with the co-operation of stakeholders;
• evaluating the performance in meeting agreed goals with the active participation of concerned stakeholders; and
• creating a fertile ground for the planning of improvement projects with concerned stakeholders.

EVIDENCE FROM THREE CASE STUDIES

The issues raised and the tools described in the preceding paragraphs can be further investigated with reference to three organisations in which a participatory, stakeholder-driven approach to social auditing and reporting was experimented with by the authors of this chapter. In fact, similar experiments have been made in Italy with varying degrees and types of stakeholder involvement, but this is a process often limited to the gathering of data on given issues, and to the rather conventional "advertising" that follows the publication of reports; in some cases, internal stakeholders (those contributing their resources to the core activities of the organisation: employees, managers, volunteers) are involved in some form of diffuse "collective writing" when narrative or indicator-based reports of single projects and activities are included in the main social/environmental report. Quite rarely, however, is an *explicit* connection between organisational responsibility tools and participation drawn, as was analytically described earlier.

The three cases, from which some considerations and ideas for further research and practice will be drawn, are non-profit organisations in the region of Friuli-Venezia Giulia, in north-eastern Italy:

- The United World College of the Adriatic (henceforth UWCAD), founded in Duino, near Trieste, in 1982, is a scholarship-based international school, part of a wider "United World Colleges" movement; just under two hundred students, sixteen to eighteen years old and coming from eighty different countries, benefit from a full scholarship and spend two years at UWCAD, where they are engaged in academic activities (leading to the International Baccalaureate diploma) as well as other sorts of activities (sports, social services, music and arts, etc.). The school hires teachers, administrative and technical staff on a commercial basis, and runs on a budget of about four million euros a year, most of the income being provided by public (national and regional) funding. The social audit was first carried out in 2003, then again in 2005, leading to the publication of two Social Reports.

- Comunità di San Martino al Campo ("Comunità" in the following) mainly carries out voluntary work including several activities of a social work nature: meals and accommodation for the poor and the homeless especially, but also "street-level" counselling, prevention of deprivation and marginalisation in schools, social rehabilitation of ex-convicts, and so on. The Comunità was founded in 1970 in Trieste, where it now runs dormitories, homes, and flats for short- to long-term stays; it runs projects with schools and prisons. It has a budget of about 1.1 million euros a year, mainly derived from the fees paid by the municipality and the health care authority for assistance to the poor and the homeless. The social audit was first carried out in 2006, resulting in the publication of the first Social Report, then in 2007 with the publication of a second edition of the Social Report.

- Centro di Formazione Professionale Opera Villaggio del Fanciullo (CFP) is a vocational training centre for young people, based in Opicina, near Trieste. It was founded in 1950 and now trains graphic designers, mechanics, constructional ironwork fitter-machinists, and ship-joiners. It is part of Opera Villaggio del Fanciullo, a Christian-Catholic organisation which also runs, on the same premises, a printing works and an asylum for young offenders and marginalised or deprived youths. The financial resources of CFP mainly derive from student fees and special projects developed with local authorities, and sum up to just under two million euros a year. The social audit process started in late 2007 and resulted in the publication of a social audit report about a year later.

These three cases share some features particularly concerning the driving forces that led to the adoption of organisational accountability tools. These include:

- The recent or forthcoming change in organisational leadership: Charismatic founders and their staff had either recently left the organisation (UWCAD) or were growing old and laying grounds for takeover by a younger generation of leaders (Comunità and CFP). Issues and problems that used to be settled by use of "moral suasion" and charismatic authority progressively need to be tackled through formal and explicit channels of conflict transformation. In the case of CFP this also includes inter-organisational governance, in that the overarching structure of "Opera Villaggio del Fanciullo" was and is planned to be reformed according to clearer boundaries and more formalised relationships.
- A "window of opportunity" was generated in all cases by the funding provided by Solidarietà Trieste, an agency set up by the local Industrial Association to support management innovation in the third sector: Part of their effort towards innovation was oriented to favour an improvement in effectiveness and efficiency, and a change in sources of funding for the three organisations, which, following the change in leadership, would have to abandon some of the "political" channels of funding and turn to private funding based on accurate accounting and reporting of their activities and impacts.
- A feeling of misperception and/or misrepresentation by the local community and the local press was felt in all three organisations: Their activities were more commonly perceived as basic help for the "underclass" (be it "drug addicts" at the Comunità, juvenile delinquents at CFP, or students from the "third world" at UWCAD) than as qualified social and educational services; this phenomenon was perceived as problematic in external relations with donors and institutions and in the motivation and commitment of employees and volunteers.

The combination of these factors indicates that internal and external drives were present in all three initiatives, so that none of them were undertaken on a merely "communicative" or "marketing" basis. The balance among these factors also varied over time within each experiment, as actors came to realise the implications of the work they were doing.

In each of the three organisations, a process was designed and implemented that would lead to the publication and diffusion of a Social Report (*Bilancio Sociale*), describing the activities of the organisation, their use of (economic, social, environmental) resources, and their (economic, social, environmental) impacts. The Social Reports were going to be structured according to the Gruppo di Studio per il Bilancio Sociale Standard (2001), the most widespread in Italy, which consists of three sections—which, with the partial exception of the second one, are defined loosely enough to allow for contents best fitted for the aims and purposes of the auditing and reporting effort:

1. Corporate identity: A definition of corporate structure, values, mission, strategies. and policies sets the framework for the definition of the audit and evaluation process, allowing for the identification of goals and of responsibilities thereof.
2. Creation and allocation of added value: Statutory financial statements are "translated" into a readable, understandable structure highlighting the economic impact of corporate activities on different categories of stakeholders.
3. The social account: Indicators are defined and measured which describe the non-economic impact of corporate activities on different categories of stakeholders.

The process that was implemented is rather similar to what evaluation theory describes as "constructivist evaluation" (Guba and Lincoln 2001), where the "evaluand", the object of the evaluation, is not given in advance and must be defined through a hermeneutic process involving stakeholders. This model fits our concerns in that the symmetry that was postulated in the preceding paragraphs as a basis for interaction between third sector organisations and their environment implies that no unilateral interpretation of stakes and performance can be adopted.

In each organisation, a combination of the following activities was (and is) being carried out in different forms:

1. Identification of the mission, vision, values, and policies of the organisation: This had already been done through a recent participatory process of collective writing in the Comunità, while at UWCAD it was done by the consultants on the basis of a wide range of existing documents (articles of association, mission statement of the UWC movement, advertising materials, and so on); at CFP, the top management held a series of meetings to address the issue and reformulate the mission and vision statements which dated back to the 1950s, also on the basis of recent collective-writing efforts, which, however, had not resulted in a definitive text.
2. Identification of critical areas of performance: Based on the results of the first phase, a survey was carried out whereby stakeholders were asked to identify inconsistencies between stated values and actual practices, or between performance and perception, so that auditing and reporting activities could be focused on what matters to stakeholders; in this phase, traditional and more innovative tools of social enquiry were employed, such as expert interviews, focus groups, observation, and participant observation,[3] as well as participatory

action research techniques and deliberative workshops, including—
in the case of CFP—two "open-space technology"[4]-type workshops
involving the teachers and employees.

3. Definition of social and economic indicators and textual/narrative
contributions to be included in the auditing and reporting process in
order to cover the critical areas of performance identified: This was
done through the combined involvement of management, consultants,
and stakeholders, both internal and external, depending on the relevance, complexity, and sensitivity of issues at stake.

4. Data collection and reporting: Data for the indicators and the narrative contributions were gathered with the involvement of a large part
of the organisations, so that the reports tended to be the result of a
collective effort co-ordinated by the consultant (UWCAD) or by an
internal working group (Comunità and CFP).

5. Communication and evaluation: Public presentations of the report
were organised, where several categories of stakeholders took part in
a rather informal assessment of the results and outcomes of the audit
process. No formal evaluation process was carried out.

Along the social auditing process, however, some issues arose that pose further challenges to the model. These are outlined in the following sections.

GOAL SETTING AND SUSTAINABILITY

Contrary to ingenuous, and ultimately normative, expectations that "all
stakeholders are good stakeholders", sustainable development, civic engagement, or philanthropy might not be on everybody's agenda. Let alone
individual interests and economic interests—which must be the object of
conflict transformation efforts and be construed as an essential part of
the bottom line of a social audit and report—the local community or specific groups within it may have a much more down-to-earth or downright
opportunistic attitude towards a third sector organisation, and "phase 2",
the definition of critical issues in performance, may take surprising turns.
This was the case with UWCAD, where the municipal administration was
involved in the definition of critical issues in the management of the college
premises: Environmental concerns were just *not* perceived as an issue at all
("The local wastewater treatment plant is insufficient for the local population, so an extra three hundred inhabitants don't really make a difference",
were the words of an executive officer during an interview), while the fact
that the college could raise money from regional and central government
to build sports facilities or other infrastructure which may be used by local
people as well was perceived as a much more enticing prospect.

The involvement of stakeholders in the case of Comunità was deeper.
The issues and proposals which emerged from interviews and focus groups,

with both internal and external subjects, were then discussed by the top management and considered and integrated into the formulation of strategic goals for the following year, which were then published in the first Social Report. This process set the basis for a virtuous cycle of engagement, commitment, evaluation, and assurance. Indeed, the second Social Report.

A very narrow line separates participation and manipulation in the political and in the market context, where the implications of power relations may affect the way participation is perceived and implemented (see, for example, Katznelson 1972). In the third sector, however, persuasion, "conversion", and even some form of mild proselytism may be an important factor in the commitment and effort that people dedicate to voluntary as well as remunerated work. Thus, a balance must be struck between the organisation's idea of sustainability/social good and that of stakeholders, whereby the organisation decides autonomously and freely but finds ways to determine whether and how their actions are understood, how well they perform, and how they can improve.

In the cases examined, the "open mindset" necessary for this step was not consistently present. It may be shared by only some of the managers, or only with respect to some specific issues but not to others. When this is the case, participation will be rather limited, and for those who do participate the experience may be a very negative one, leading to increased mistrust and discontent.

The issue of representativeness is at stake here, as we outlined it in the preceding paragraphs: Third sector organisations may hold a partial perspective, but must make this clear and be open to scrutiny as to *whether* and *how* they act according to it, so that at least those who share it (or are willing to accept or benefit from it) are somehow represented. Taking other points of view into account may be part of the process of understanding one's own personal—or organisational—stances (Sclavi 2003).

THE INVOLVEMENT OF BENEFICIARIES

Participatory governance in organisations may involve different sets of stakeholders: employees, volunteers, partner organisations, donors, governments, and contracting bodies were engaged in some form of "active listening" or participation. However, beneficiaries of social and educational services were not an active part of any of the projects: Their involvement in the auditing process was either implicit in the general endeavour to communicate effectively to all stakeholders *including* beneficiaries in a passive role (Comunità), or else was the done through the participant observation on the part of the consultant for the early phases of the auditing process and through limited involvement in the phase of data collection via a questionnaire survey (UWCAD); at Comunità and CFP, the stories and comments of students and beneficiaries were included in the report as testimonies to the complexity or efficacy of organisational action, but did not influence the overall structure or content of the accounting and auditing process.

This exclusion does not simply arise from a malaise or worry that beneficiaries may not be satisfied with levels or quality of service, since much more complicated and conflicting relationships were handled in the auditing process: For example, at the Comunità, interviews and focus groups were held that let members of the organisation discuss rather sore issues with the two co-operatives that respectively supply maintenance services and professional social workers to the Comunità itself.[5]

The exclusion of beneficiaries derives at least partly from a more subtle problem, that is, the vagrant nature of many third sector activities; definition and categorisation of beneficiaries as a set of stakeholders is complex and quite unstable, their stories and conditions are not easily generalised; there may be a large share of people among them—as was the case at the Comunità—who are not easily involved due to their psychological or mental condition, or due to their extremely brief contact with the organisation. Some of these difficulties also apply to market-oriented and political organisations, but the concepts and organisational tools that these two sectors have developed to "make sense" of differences are much more complex and include institutions like parties and party systems and tools like advertising and marketing.

THE INVOLVEMENT OF THE TECHNOSTRUCTURE

Commitment of the top management in the organisation is a necessary but not sufficient condition to implement an effective auditing process. Administrative and other staff must also be committed to the underlying logics of the participatory approach to social auditing so that information can be gathered and processed effectively and the process carried out smoothly.

This was the case at the Comunità, where the organisational climate was quite positive from the start and the general aims of the auditing process were widely shared: A previous participatory process had been effectively carried out for the formulation of a "charter of values"; at UWCAD, on the other hand, a previous effort of "self-evaluation" had been perceived as a burdensome and immaterial endeavour, and many of the problems that the social audit was meant to solve (lack of motivation, poor administrative performance) were an obstacle to the process itself; similarly, a strongly hierarchical style of management at the CFP was a serious problem at the outset of the process. Hermeneutical and creative tools of debate and active listening may help to overcome some of these problems, letting each member of staff find their own objectives and rewards in the process; in the case of CFP, an anonymous online "wall" was set up where members of staff were called to contribute to a mapping of stakeholders and of critical issues, after small "open-space-type" workshops had been held to set off sufficient understanding of the process.

The consequences of a lack of understanding, motivation, or involvement of staff proved to be decisive: A delay in the process, a snowball effect of decreased motivation of other stakeholders, difficulties in gathering and interpreting data, and most of all, an inability to make the social auditing process an ongoing endeavour, building the capabilities within the organisation for a recurring (for example, annual or biannual) update and upgrade of the social audit and report. Even the communication of results—usually one of the pillars of motivation to start a social audit process—may be left unattended if staff are not willing to take initiative to support and promote it.

THE INVOLVEMENT OF CONSULTANTS

Internal capacity-building may be an important objective of a participatory approach to social auditing and reporting. It may lead to a much less expensive process in following years, and to an improved "fit" of auditing and reporting tools to the organisation. However, an initial input from an outside source may be of great value in conflicting or otherwise problematic environments. Mediation of contrasting views on several issues may be decisive: There may be conflicting and apparently incompatible perceptions (external communication and propaganda versus organisational management tool) on what the social audit is and ought to be in the first place or on what the mission of the organisation is, and on which stakeholders are to be contacted and involved, for example. Mediation will most likely consist in letting members of the organisation, and participants in a "working group" doing the paperwork for the social audit, understand there is no "one best way" but rather some sets of criteria to be applied to their own needs and aspirations. Similarly, the relationship between internal and external stakeholders may need to be mediated in order to minimise misunderstandings about the nature of the auditing process and overt conflict.

In addition to mediation, however, actual transmission of knowledge from the consultant to the organisation is vital to favour an ongoing effort in regular auditing processes. The techniques for social and hermeneutical enquiry, abilities in the construction of indicators, data analysis and reporting, and at least some degree of awareness of the auditing practices allow the organisation to proceed to subsequent cycles of social auditing and to seek support from consultants only when needed—for example, in the case of conflicts or when innovative design of a process is deemed necessary. On the other hand, a fully "contracted-out" approach to social auditing seems to insulate the process from internal ownership and responsibility, and members of the organisation may feel that the issues that are dealt with, or the method that is used, are not relevant or appropriate to what they experience in the organisation itself.

CONCLUSIONS

As was stated at the outset, third sector organisations are a relevant part of the policy-making chain, and as such must be included in the evaluation and accounting efforts that are more commonly oriented to the public sector. In the absence of an established chain of democratic accountability, and also of market mechanisms, accountability in the third sector must find its own ways and tools, so that corporate action and its (economic, social, environmental) impacts—which cannot be measured against votes or consumer decisions—can be measured against declared values and individual and collective expectations. The three cases examined, where a hermeneutical approach to the definition of a social audit process was experimented with, have helped highlight some of the opportunities and risks of a "participatory governance" approach to social auditing and reporting: A procedural approach to reporting, underlying the importance of stakeholder engagement and leaving the contents and structure of the audit and report to negotiation and deliberation, may help construct a shared definition of the goals and capabilities of the organisation and may be part of a strategy addressing problematic issues.

However, some problems remain unsolved: the definition of the boundaries of the organisation (and the subsequent inclusion/exclusion of specific stakeholders in the auditing process), the credibility of a process that has no prior definition of the output it is to produce, the paradox of motivation and accord that must pre-exist in order to be elaborated upon and reinforced in the process.

NOTES

1. Significantly, the major International Non-Governmental Organisations (INGOs) have recently signed the "International Non-Governmental Organisations Accountability Charter" (http://www.ingoaccountabilitycharter. org/), which contains, amongst the other principles, a specific framework for social reporting.
2. For example, in 2007 Oxfam International received, just in the form of donations, US\$8,283,401 (Oxfam International 2007), Greenpeace International €204,892 (Greenpeace International 2007), and International Save the Children Alliance almost US\$125,000,000 (International Save the Children Alliance 2008).
3. Participant observation was experimented at UWCAD, where a consultant lived in the college for several weeks while working on the social audit.
4. Workshops held with open-space technology are self-organised seminars where participants are free to introduce and select issues for the common agenda. Several working groups spring out of the initial general assembly where the agenda is defined. Each working group discusses a single topic that will be added to the works of the other working groups in the end. Facilitators smooth the works of the groups and of the assembly, but the time schedule and the issues discussed are mainly driven by the participants.

5. In a nutshell: The co-operatives were established as "spin-offs" of the Comunità, and the present relationships between the three subjects suffered from unclear definitions of boundaries and mutual responsibilities. The issue was only partly cleared out over the auditing process, but quite directly, and positively, faced.

REFERENCES

Basu, K., and G. Palazzo. 2008. "Corporate Social Responsibility: A Process Model of Sense-Making." *Academy of Management Review* 33 (1): 122–136.

Evers, A., and J. L. Laville, eds. 2004. *The Third Sector in Europe.* Cheltenham: Edward Elgar.

Greenpeace International. 2007. Annual Report. http://www.greenpeace.org/international/about/reports.

Gruppo di Studio per il Bilancio Sociale. 2001. *Milan: Social Reporting Standard.* http://www.gruppobilanciosociale.org/allegati/GBSAssets/   standard_inglese.pdf.

———. 2001. *Guidelines and Checklist for Constructivist (a.k.a. Fourth Generation) Evaluation, Evaluation Checklists Project.* www.wmich.edu/evalctr/checklists.

International Save the Children Alliance. 2008. Annual Report. http://www.savethechildren.net/alliance/about_us/mission_vision/index.html.

Katznelson, I. 1972. "Antagonistic Ambiguity: Notes on Reformism and Decentralization." *Politics and Society* (Spring): 329–330.

Oxfam International. 2007. Financial Statement. http://www.oxfam.org/en/about/annual-reports.

Preston, L., and J. E. Post. 1974. "The Third Managerial Revolution." *Academy of Management Journal* 17 (3): 476–486.

Ruppolo, G. 1991. *La grande impresa.* Turin: Giappichelli Editore.

Sapelli, G. 2007. *Etica d'impresa e valori di giustizia.* Bologna: il Mulino.

Sclavi, M. 2003. *Arte di ascoltare e mondi possibili.* Milan: Bruno Mondadori.

4 Budget and Social Capital System Theory
Empirical Research Tools

Cynthia E. Lynch and Thomas D. Lynch

INTRODUCTION

This chapter explains how to do empirical research using the concepts of budget systems and social capital. We believe researchers can use both concepts as theoretical research tools to greatly enhance understanding of social auditing, social accounting, and accountability. In this chapter, we explain a previously developed budget system model and demonstrate how it can be used as a model to calculate social capital.

Both models enable those who do empirical research to greatly strengthen their understanding of how to achieve greater accountability and trust in government and non-profit organisations. Our recommended systems model permits the measurement of both organisational accomplishments and social capital. This chapter articulates a practical research agenda that explains how researchers and policymakers can use these models to create, enhance, and sustain co-operation as well as judge effectiveness and efficiency in our governments and non-profit organisations.

The chapter is divided into six sections with this introduction being the first section. The second section presents a short review of the familiar modernist concept of theory. The third section summarises the budget system theory model and explains its relevance to social auditing, social accounting, and accountability. The fourth section introduces "social capital" as a concept. The fifth section presents the social capital systems theory model. The final section offers some concluding thoughts.

MODERNIST CONCEPT OF THEORY

Although remarkably important, the modernist concept of theory is commonly misunderstood by many. A good example in the US is the recurring debate over the subject of creationism versus evolution. Advocates of creationism say that evolution is *merely* a theory, as is creationism. Therefore, they argue, creationism should hold at least equal standing in the classroom and society as the theory of evolution. However, not all theories are equal. Some merit little if any credibility from serious researchers and society.

To understand why some theories should be given more credibility than others we must first understand the purpose of empirical theory or what some call scientific theory. Theories help us to conceptually organise knowledge of the physical and social world. Theories are frameworks to organise abstract concepts and often provide explanations of causality among phenomena. More powerful and useful theories define interrelationships among known concepts and facts so that we can grasp causal relationships. Thus, researchers can use such knowledge to predict and even recommend how governments and non-profit organisations can constructively intervene in our physical and social world to accomplish desired end purposes.

Theories that merit more serious credibility must provide means by which an independent third party can "test" or refute the theory itself. For example, if XYZ theory explains a phenomenon called ABC, then an objective observer should be able to see ABC happening as predicted by theory XYZ. If the theory cannot be tested by another researcher, then it is merely a model, a framework, an approach, a perspective, or an ideological concept. Thus, it might be useful, but it does not rate the status of a strong theory, and perhaps it should not even be called a theory. Such a non-theory concept might be useful to explain something like religious views but researchers should not consider it a theory unless it can earn some standing within the research community as testable.

Even the best of theories are always subject to question and doubt as they can never be proven. Theories can never be accepted on faith. For example, the theory of evolution has evolved further since Darwin first stated it. Scientists consider its current version as a very good theory but it is always subject to more questioning. Why? Because, if it is considered true science, the researchers accept that some future research might be able to disprove the theory at some future time. To say creationism is a theory is highly questionable because it has not yet gained enough credibility in the world of empirical research with the appropriate, rigorous testing to properly refer to it as a "theory".

BUDGET SYSTEM THEORY

One approach to empirical theory building that is used in public administration as a study is to use the concepts found in the systems theory literature. As a conceptual tool, historians of systems theory can trace it back to Aristotle, but it was primarily developed in the 1950s, 1960s, and 1970s by authors such as Ludwig von Bertalanffy in his book *General Systems Theory*; D. I. Cleland and W. R. King in *Management: A Systems Approach*; Norbert Wiener in *Cybernetics*; and Anatol Rapoport and W. J. Horvath in "Thoughts on Organization Theory", which appeared in *General Systems*

Theory (von Bertalanffy 1968). Probably the best case against the use of systems theory concepts was made by Ida R. Hoos in her 1972 book titled *System Analysis in Public Policy: A Critique.* A complete discussion of the system theory concepts is beyond the scope of this chapter.

This chapter focuses on the use of systems theory as it applies to public budgeting. For many decades public budgeting used a common version of systems theory. This system version used the simple framework of input/output. Martin Knapp, David Easton, Karl Deutsch, Frederick J. Lyndon, Ernest G. Miller, and Jesse Burkhead developed the model further by adding "process" to the interrelated parts (Lynch and Lynch 1998a). They posited that there were casual links running from input, to process, to output in the budget process. Inputs were factors such as money and resources needed to run an organisation. Processes were what happened within the organisational workplace, such as answering phones and writing reports. Outputs were the products produced by the work effort in process.

By definition, a system is an array of interrelated parts. The previous budget system models understood these interrelated parts to be input, process, and output with input causing process to occur and process causing output to occur. With the advance of computing technology and another generation of thinking about this model, Thomas D. Lynch, one of the authors of this chapter, argued three items should be added to the list of interrelated parts (Lynch 1989) discussed previously. First, the notion of outcomes was added to the causal chain as a separate concept, which now became inputs-process-outputs-*outcomes*. In public service, providing programs is necessary but insufficient for the justification for public expenditures. There must be an impact on the target population or the program has wasted the public's tax dollars. Thus, the concept of outcomes goes well beyond the earlier notion of simply measuring programs or activities and is critical to justifying any budget request.

Outcomes are the impacts of the governmental outputs (programs and activities) on individuals and society. In other words, outcomes are the consequences or results that happened because of the government actions. Reasoning like Aristotle, the budget system has an end purpose that Aristotle called the *telos.* In the budget system, the *telos* enables decision-makers to make authoritative allocation of public resources in order to intervene

Figure 4.1   Burkhead et al. budget system model.

actively as an organisation in the ongoing activities of society and achieve desired public policy impacts.

Second, this conceptual contribution brought three imbedded feedback loops into the budget systems model. The three feedbacks are (a) reporting on accomplished outcomes, such as using an evaluation report; (b) reporting on accomplished outputs, such as using progress reports on program accomplishments; and (c) reporting and monitoring on the processes in the program, such as using accounting and financial information related to the program.

The third concept Lynch added to the older system model was the notion of intervening variables, such as external social events, technological advances, 1/100 year weather events, unexpected economic upheavals, and so on. The intervening variables concept recognised the openness of the social system and that outside factors, often beyond the control of policymakers, could influence the system at any point along the causal chain of input to process to output to outcome. The importance of this version of the budget system model is that it requires researchers and policymakers to recognise the budget can be and is influenced by factors outside the control of government. Once understood, then such factors can be modelled with computer simulations much like what is done with chaos theory.

The environment in which the budget system exists impacts what takes place in the budget system itself and the theory, therefore, must reflect that situation. Thus, this model shows that intervening variables influence the system along the causal chain of input to process to output to outcome. This theoretical approach permits researchers to isolate and measure the intervening variables and their influence on the causal chain using established analytical investigation tools.

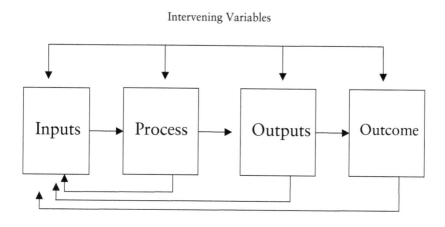

Figure 4.2   Lynch budget system model.

The advantages of this more sophisticated version of system theory are real. The earlier version of system theory gave awareness that a budget might permit leaders of government or a non-profit organisation to direct their efforts to accomplish desired goals and objectives. However, there was analytical confusion if the analysis required a clear differentiation of output or outcome. Given that efficiency is the ratio of input to output and effectiveness is the ratio of input to outcome, the earlier budget system model resulted in analytical nonsense when addressing matters of effectiveness and efficiency because output and outcome were not differentiated.

In budgeting, a government agency asks for money from the executive and the legislature or a non-profit organisation asks donors to give it money so that it can accomplish something important in society. Both argue that with money they will make a positive difference in society. Prior to the revised version of the system model, there was an array of specific theories to demonstrate causal connection between an agency's budget and some of their impacts on society. For example, there was a medical theory that a polio vaccine would cure polio and thus a government program to supply and administer that vaccine would eliminate polio in a country. However, no general theory existed that analysts could use across the board in every government or non-profit program. With these additions to the budget system model, a more general approach to theory was possible, and thus the theory became much more powerful and useful.

With this theoretical advancement, analysts could use research design and assign measures to inputs, outputs, and outcomes in order to empirically measure performance. Before this more fully developed theory, assessment of the so-called bottom line of government was impossible except in special programs that were grounded on specific causal theories linked to the particular programs. In the private sector, the so-called bottom line or *telos* is profit. In the public sector, the bottom line or *telos* is public service that improves the quality of life in the nation and world. Before this revised system theory, there was no way to assert that progress was being made toward achieving its *telos* in government or the non-profit sector. With the revised model it is not only possible, but questions regarding comparative efficiency and effectiveness can be examined empirically.

This theoretical advance changed the practice of budgeting. Although government reformers have frequently attempted to use performance-based budgeting since 1907, those efforts often failed because their theoretical understandings did not permit the needed analyses nor was the technology adequate for the required level of analysis. Nevertheless, administrative reforms wished to instil some type of performance budgeting in the Franklin D. Roosevelt, Lyndon B. Johnson, Jimmy Carter, and Richard M. Nixon administrations. The reforms were different in detail, but at the core of each was a desire to use performance measures to make rational budget decisions rather than use pure political compromises based on power relationships. Each reform effort in turn faded into history as the next president ignored the reforms of his predecessor. In each reform, the subsequent president noticed the previous reform took a lot of work that bore little positive and useful analytical results because the theoretical models were inadequate.

The latest attempt at reforming the American federal budget occurred in 1993 at the beginning of the Clinton administration. In addition, the same type of performance budget reforms occurred at state and local levels of government in the United States as well as in governments around the world. A critical difference with the performance budget reforms of the 1990s is that the incoming George W. Bush administration did not drop the Clinton budget reform but rather built on it. The current Obama administration is also continuing to use these reforms. This was and is unique in American administrative history as previous administrations have usually abandoned their predecessor's budget reforms once they gained power.

The budget reforms were not perfect. For example, practical problems still exist, such as difficulty in selecting the correct performance measures for each element in the theory and getting policymakers attuned to the value of using the system model in their often very political decision-making context. Nevertheless, the Clinton/Bush performance budget reform was successful.

This discussion is important to the theme of this book. If social auditing, social accounting, and even the notion that a funding group can hold government or a non-profit organisation accountable, then there must be some rational and analytical means to measure so-called progress and conceptually understand the assumed linkages between resources and desired outcomes. There must also be some means to expose those assumed linkages to the rigor of empirical investigation. The upgraded budget system model does that.

This discussion is also important at another level because systems theory has the strong possibility of also providing a theoretical advance in understanding the concept of social capital. A version of this theoretical construct was first presented in 2002 in an article titled "Productivity and the Moral Manager" published in *Administration and Society* (Lynch, Lynch, and Cruise 2002). This chapter builds on that article.

THE SOCIAL CAPITAL CONCEPT

We assume social capital can occur in one or more social organisations. We also assume that a positive working relationship among participants of governments and non-profit organisations enhances their interventions in society and makes them more effective. Where capital exists and can be quantified, there is a need for thorough accounting and auditing. Thus, social capital is closely related to effective social auditing and accounting.

Coleman explains, social capital is "facilitating the achievement of goals that could not be achieved in its absence" (Coleman 1988, 302). But, how and to what degree do specific features and relationships constitute social capital? Coleman identifies types of social capital in pairs, including: (a) obligations and expectations and (b) norms and sanctions that differ in varying circumstance and relationship involving institutions and groups of individuals (Edwards and Foley 1997).

Currently, there is a lack of consensus on what "social capital" is in the literature and this chapter addresses that problem. Robert Putnam (1995a) suggests that co-operation arises out of trust, but never defines how to conceptualise trust. The normal evolution of new ideas among researchers leads us to expect such vagueness and lack of consensus while the scholarly community assimilates this new and complex concept. For example, many discussions of social capital confuse norms, values, social networks, and outcomes (Eastis 1998; Newton 1997). Eastis points out:

> when the pundits refer to the value of social capital do they mean the norms of co-operation that my neighbours and I agree to form a neighbourhood crime watch? Do they mean the networks that are broadened when I meet people down the street for the first time? Or, do they mean the value of social capital lies in the actual reduction in crime that results from the group's actions? (Eastis 1998: 66–67)

Since the inherent nature of social capital is multidimensional, this is an inescapable conundrum. To give order to the concept of social capital, we suggest using a holistic conceptual approach using systems theory. Our purpose in doing so is to allow the professional community to use social capital as a concept that expands our understanding of co-operation and collaboration in significant ways. First, we want to link co-operation to the concept of "capital" and thus signal the importance of investment or growth potential of the group's ability to work together. Second, we want the concept identified with the *structure* created from this collaborative effort that we call *capital* (Fountain 1998). For example, we agree with Burt (1992: 9), "well functioning partnerships, consortia, and networks are in and of themselves a form of social capital".

Social capital is a sharable resource held by the participating individual institutions and in the overall relationships among the institutions within the network. For example, with the successful completion of a small project, the group may decide to apply the already established collaborative process to another project. This makes sustainable development possible in communities and governments. They expand the original small network to include more partners and take on more ambitious projects as the parties learn how to collaborate productively and develop solid reputations for trustworthiness.

Social capital is neither good nor bad but rather functional or dysfunctional, just like its constituent elements of trust, relationships, and norms. We argue here that social capital can be used simply as a tool for social auditing and social accounting. Social capital allows the analyst to understand and predict rational action that can perhaps lead to long-run growth in enhanced co-operation with a community and an organisation. As Jane Fountain (1998) points out, trust allows actors to engage in productive collaboration and norms decrease transaction costs and regulate behaviour. The important point here is that social capital is a powerful conceptual tool.

Our proposed social capital model, which is parallel in structure to the budget systems model discussed earlier, consists of a causal chain starting with trust, then relationships, then norms, and finally achieving or approximating a sense of oneness. This is a systems model with intervening variables, such as technology, or other external factors that can and do influence and change trust, relationships, norms, and a sense of oneness. In addition, our model (discussed later in this chapter) has three nested feedback loops that provide information to the participants. They involve participation, the sense of civil society, and meaningful social and economic growth in the target community.

With this model, policy analysts can address research questions such as: What needs to be built up in order to increase trust among participants? Conversely, we may ask: What factors need to be torn down in order to enhance trust? Other possible research questions are: How can improved trust create stronger relations? How does weakening trust diminish relationships? What positive norms are created when relationships are strong? What norms are weakened when relationships are weak? What is the positive sense of oneness that is created when norms are strong? What are the signs of a weakening sense of oneness when norms are weakened? What intervening variables seem to strengthen trust, relationships, norms, and a sense of oneness? What intervening variables seem to weaken trust, relationships, norms, and a sense of oneness? Each of these researchable questions can help us strengthen our understanding of social capital and how it can be used to strengthen our communities and how to get more positive results from our communities when tension levels make co-operation very difficult.

SOCIAL CAPITAL SYSTEMS THEORY

As noted earlier, the social capital systems theory is quite parallel to the budget systems model. In the budget systems model, the key causality chain is input, process, output, and outcome. In the social capital systems model, the key causality chain is trust, relationships, norms, and oneness. Each element of this model is selected for its causal explanatory value when considering the interrelated parts of the system and the desired outcome we have called "oneness".

In the budget system model, the three nested feedback loops are financial reporting, progress reporting, and program evaluation reporting. In the social capital model, the three nested feedback loops are reporting on participation (from relationships to trust), reporting of civility (from norms to trust), and reporting on growth (from oneness to trust). Figure 4.3 presents the system elements of the social capital model and the relationship of each to the others.

In the social capital system theory, trust is the starting point for nothing in the system can move without this key element. If trust is present, relationships can flourish, social norms will move in a positive direction, and, finally, a sense of oneness or harmony among the participants will result. Trust, which is necessary to hold modern society together, requires strong institutions capable of overcoming the diverse and often competing interests of groups, who are keenly interested in their short-term and possible long-term benefits rather than the larger public good (Berman 1997). Unless our social structures are specifically and consciously oriented toward promoting a strong sense of social oneness that brings benefits to the whole, they will contribute to divisiveness and dysfunctional behaviour for that society. Edwards and Foley (1997, 533) noted that "social structures, in other words, must be filled with certain 'content' before it can fully perform the functions usually attributed to it in the current discussion."

Russell Hardin (1993), in his article "The Street-Level Epistemology of Trust", examined the rationality of trust. In his view, there are two central elements in applying a rational choice account of trust. First, there is the incentive of the trusted to fulfil the trust. Second, there is sufficient

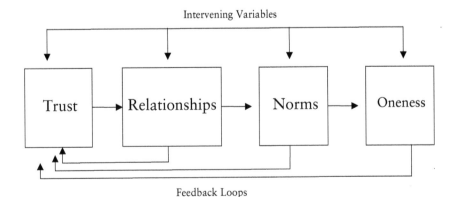

Figure 4.3   Social capital system model.

knowledge to allow the participants to trust. That is to say, we trust some-one if we have adequate reason to believe that person's trustworthiness is furthered by his or her own interest. One's trust turns not on one's own interest but on the interest of the trusted (Hardin 1993).

Trust involves giving discretion to another to affect one's interests. This is inherently risky as the trusted participant may abuse the power of discre-tion. Hardin (1993, 507) noted that most writers suppose "trust is by far the more productive option. Distrust leads to forgone opportunities, trust can lead to successful and mutually beneficial interactions." For Hardin (1993, 521), trust per se is not the collective good but trustworthiness is: "Creating institutions that help secure trustworthiness thus helps support or induce trust." He is quite insistent that we should consider them sepa-rately in any analysis. He says, "There is no *a priori* reason to suppose that either trust or trust worthiness is the dominant consideration in general" (1993, 512).

Relationships represent how things get done between and among partici-pants in organisations or society. Relationships, which are connections or networks of individuals, groups, and organisations, are a crucial element of the social capital system theory because they represent the ability to mobilise a wide range of personal social contacts that are possibly essential for the effective functioning of social and political life (Kolankiewicz 1994; Newton 1997). In its positive form, we call this "networking". In its nega-tive form, we call this "the good old boys system".

Over time (often only a short period of time), relationships produce norms of behaviour. Norms represent a range of values and attitudes that influence or determine how individuals and groups relate to each other. We can understand and define this element of the system in terms of group attitudes, values, and behaviour. Trust, relationships, and norms are closely related, but we must conceptually separate them to prevent confusion or unwarranted assumptions. If Aristotle and Hardin are correct, then trust and trustworthiness are cognitive virtues. This means that we can design behavioural interventions to teach and direct relationships toward creating norms of virtuous behaviour (Hardin 1993; Lynch and Lynch 1998a).

Reciprocity in a relationship needs to address consequences associated with the relationship. Reciprocity need not be a tit-for-tat calculation that each person in the relationship is ensured an automatic repayment for a deed. Rather, the age-old concept of Karma (or, in the American lexicon, "what goes around comes around") is the basis of reciprocity. Thus, those engaged in reciprocity assume that good turns done to them by others shall be returned by them in some unspecified time in the future (Lynch and Lynch 1998b; Sahlius 1972).

Oneness is the final key element in the social capital systems theory. Oneness or harmony, which is the often an expected or desired social change among the participants, is a jointly felt sense of unity and shared being. Thus, the relative presences of a common sense of unity and shared identification are how a researcher can measure oneness. It occurs when the participants emotionally and mentally move from using the pronoun "I" to "we" when discussing their actions. Changing pronouns may not only be a "matter of the heart", as Putman (1995b) explained the concept, but also an economic and biological need to preserve the species.

The concept of oneness is provocative and even unsettling for some because they feel that oneness comes at the expense of personal identity and individuality. For some, the nature of humankind is to see and even hold everything separately. For example, instead of seeing others and themselves as part of one system or one whole, they see the parts and consider them as separate independent elements. People who think in that manner celebrate unique personalities, differences of opinions, individual ethnicity, fragmented faith, and structured social status as ways to describe their individuality. Their devotion to their individuality serves to foster fear, anxiety, pride, vanity, frustrations, and desires (Chinmoy 1974, 1985). Such an individuality creates disappointment, anger, aggressiveness, conspicuous consumption, depression, hostility with others, arguments, and misunderstanding among individuals and peoples.

Oneness is a concept that applies to individuals as well as to groups. Oneness does not and cannot mean an extinction of individuality. When an individual or group starts thinking more inclusively, then some sense of oneness among the participants begins to occur. At this point, the participants begin to think on a deeper, vaster, and higher realm than before (Chinmoy 1974, 77) and the notion of "I" starts to become "we". When each participant thinks in terms of "we", the "I" is no longer paramount in the minds of the participants.

SYSTEM DYNAMICS: FEEDBACK LOOPS AND INTERVENING VARIABLES

As in the budget systems model, a researcher can measure each of the previously described elements of the social capital system model. This ability to measure means that a researcher or an analyst working for a policy leader can use the system's nested feedback loops to monitor the progress of each key element. Thus, policy leaders can adjust their behaviour and actions to maximise the likelihood of achieving their desired sense of oneness. The three feedback loops, moving from the inner to the outer, are called participation, civility, and growth.

Participation is the inner feedback loop from relationship to trust. Participation is conscious involvements in a collective action that to a lesser or greater extent can help the participants create positive norms or relational habits. By definition, Youniss, McLelland, and Yates (1998, 628) claim that participation "implies a sense of collective agency and acceptance of social responsibility. These actions can have a positive or negative direction in reinforcing established behaviours or they can be a conscious effort to challenge or overturn a prevailing system."

Knowledge of participatory action as feedback reporting on relationships helps the parties understand if their relationships are to some greater or lesser extent effective. Thus, greater trust is built among the parties. If the feedback informs the parties that the relationships are working, then this helps them form norms of behaviour that are likely to create continuing behaviour patterns that will more firmly establish positive relationships over time. Feedback that reports working relationships allows the participants to see that co-operation is constructive and might further individual or group political and moral goals. If the feedback on participation is particularly positive, the participants feel empowered competency and they see themselves as responsible for the society and the well-being of all its members (Youniss, McLelland, and Yates 1998).

Civility is the middle feedback loop from norms to trust. Thus, in this model, it is information back to the participants that informs them on the acceptance and workability of the existing interrelationship norms among the participants. If the participants perceive the formal and informal norms as effect, then the participants increase their trust in the joint relationships, their relationships grow stronger, and ultimately the good feedback concerning civility feeds their joint feeling that oneness does exist among them.

Essentially, the civility feedback loop tells the participants that the existing norms regarding their relationships do or do not contribute to their overall sense of oneness. Typically, if norms increase the joint sense of equity, justice, and fairness, then the norms are functional to the relationship. Thus, researchers can use the feelings about equity, justice, and fairness to develop proxy measures of civility.

Growth is the outer feedback loop of oneness to trust. As mentioned before, oneness is an expansion of the participants' understanding and consciousness from the "I" to the "we". When this occurs, the participants think on a deeper, vaster, and higher realm. Growth is feedback that informs the participants on the increase or decrease of the sense of oneness among them. For example, participants examine their growth in size (for example, their gross national product), their profits, and their market share. If there is growth, they interpret that as a growth in oneness and a measure of success in their relationship with the other participants. Although such measures are useful, they are insufficient. Performance measures of all the participants, including such factors as the conditions (for example, health, education, income) of the least among the participants must be included. We believe the oneness of the whole also needs to be judged by the status or condition of the least within the whole.

Intervening variables exist in both the budget system model and the social capital system model. The primary focus of each model is upon the causal chain. However, because each system is open, outside variables will inevitably influence what happens in the causal chain. Such variables can be natural disasters, economic realities such as inflation and recession, political instability, wars or other conflicts, and new technologies. Often, researchers can use chaos theory to understand the impact of intervening variables on the causal chain and in particular the sense of oneness among the participants. In any sophisticated research design looking at the causal chain, researchers will need to examine and test possible intervening variables to sort out the causal implications.

RESEARCH AND POLICY-MAKING IMPLICATIONS OF THE SYSTEMS MODEL

In this chapter, we presented two theoretical tools for considering social audits, social accounting, and accountability. Both permit researchers to approach the challenge of advancing knowledge using empirical research methods. Both use systems theory as the theoretical means to organise concepts that have wide research applications. Both require researchers to develop performance indicators of the elements in their respective system models if they wish to move beyond broad generalisations to more specific causal understandings.

In the case of the more advanced budget systems model, researchers can see if inputs such as money allocated in budgets have the desired impacts on society. This model is particularly helpful in establishing accountability in government and non-profit organisations.

In the case of the social capital systems model, researchers can go beyond resource allocation to see if social interactions among sets of participants are essentially working. Beyond monitoring the viability of social interactions, researchers can investigate what policymakers can do to improve social interactions so that joint efforts are more likely to be successful.

REFERENCES

Berman, S. 1997. "Civic Society and Political Institutionalization." *American Behavioral Scientist* 40 (5): 562–547.
Burkhead, J. 1967. *Government Budgeting.* New York: John Wiley and Sons.
Burt, R. S. 1992. *Structural Holes: The Social Structure of Competition.* Cambridge, MA: Harvard University Press.
Chinmoy, S. K. G. 1974. *The Inner Promise: Paths to Self-Perfection.* New York: Simon and Schuster.
———. 1985. *Beyond Within.* NY: Agni Press.
Cleland, David I., and William R. King. 1975. "The Design of Management Information Systems: An Information Analysis Approach." *Management Science* 22(3): 286–297.
Coleman, James. 1988. "Social Capital in the Creation of Human Capital." *American Journal of Sociology* 94, S95–S120.

Eastis, C. M. 1998. "Organizational Diversity and the Production of Social Capital." *American Behavioral Scientist* 42 (1): 66–67.

Edwards, R., and M. Foley. 1997. "Escape for Politics: Social Theory and Social Capital Debate." *American Behavioral Scientist* 40 (5): 550–561.

Fountain, J. E. 1998. "Social Capital: Its Relationship to Innovation in Science and Technology." *Science and Public Policy* 25 (2): 103–115.

Hardin, R. 1993. "The Street-Level Epistemology of Trust." *Politics and Society* 21 (4): 505–529.

Hoos, I. R. 1972. *System Analysis in Public Policy: A Critique.* Berkeley: University of California Press.

Kolankiewicz, K. G. 1994. "Elites In Search of a Political Formula." *Daedalus* 123:143–157.

Lynch, T. D. 1989. "Budget System Approach." *Public Administration Quarterly* 13 (3): 321–341.

———. 1998a. "Twenty-First Century Philosophy and Public Administration." In *Handbook of Organization Theory and Management: The Philosophic Approach,* ed. T. D. Lynch and T. J. Dicker, 463–478. New York: Marcel Dekker Inc.

———. 1998b. *Word of the Light.* Seattle: Hara Publishing.

Lynch, T. D., C. E. Lynch, and P. L. Cruise. 2002. "Productivity and the Moral Manager." *Administration and Society* 35 (4): 347–369.

Lynch, T. D., and R. Smith. 2005. *Public Budgeting in America.* 5th ed. Englewood, NJ: Prentice Hall.

Newton, K. 1997. "Social Capital and Democracy." *American Behavioral Scientist* 40 (5): 575–586.

Putnam, R. 1995a. "Bowling Alone: American's Declining Social Capital." *Journal of Democracy* 6 (1): 65–78.

———. 1995b. "The Strange Disappearance of Civic America." *The American Prospect* 6:35–42.

Sahlius, M. 1972. *Stone Age Economics.* Hawthorne, NY: Aldine.

Von Bertalanffy, L. 1968. *General Systems Theory.* New York: Braziller.

Youniss, J., J. McLelland, and M. Yates. 1998. "What We Know about Engendering Civic Identity." *American Behavioral Scientists* 40 (5): 620–63.

5 What Is It Worth?

Social Accounting for Membership Organisations

Laurie Mook, Femida Handy,
and Meenaz Kassam

INTRODUCTION

A growing literature suggests valuation of unpaid labour should be included in financial statements of organisations that utilise volunteer labour (Razek, Hosch, and Ives 2000). There is also extended debate in the literature on whether non-market activities should be monetised, and the methods to do this are debated (Brown 1999; Hodgkinson and Weitzman 1996; Handy and Srinivasan 2004). This chapter embraces the viewpoint that non-market activities should be included in organisational accounting, and specifically builds upon the techniques presented by Mook and her colleagues (Mook, Quarter, and Richmond 2007; Mook, Richmond, and Quarter 2003) in developing the Expanded Value Added Statement (EVAS).

This chapter discusses volunteering in a membership organisation and illustrates one method, the EVAS, that allows us to measure the impact of volunteer member participation in a religious congregation within a social accounting framework. The chapter also highlights the need for social accounting in understanding the social economy, which includes non-profits, co-operatives, and social enterprises, and which has primarily social or socio-economic purposes (Quarter, Mook, and Armstrong 2009).

Highlighting the value of unpaid labour in the production of goods and services, national surveys now document the amount of volunteering that takes place. The Current Population Survey in the US for 2008 found that about 61.8 million people (26.4 percent of the population) were volunteers (Bureau of Labor Statistics 2009). The Canadian national survey of Giving, Volunteering and Participating shows that in 2007, 12.5 million Canadians (46 percent of the population aged fifteen and over) volunteered (Hall et al. 2009).

Research to date has attached a monetary value to volunteer time within national contexts to further highlight its value to society (Independent Sector 2009). Monetising volunteer labour has allowed researchers to do a cost-benefit analysis of the use of unpaid labour in organisations—highlighting both the contribution of volunteers and making donations of time and money comparable (Handy and Srinivasan 2004; Cnaan 2009).

By expanding value added statement to include the value added by volunteers, we capture a more complete picture of the impact of organisations in the social economy that rely on unpaid labour. In this respect, our research provides a practical framework which contributes to the discussion of the social economy.

Given the heterogeneity of the not-for-profit sector, our contribution lies in providing a case that provides insights into the value of social accounting and its applicability. Although the substantive findings of our study cannot be generalised to all types of non-profit organisations, the EVAS method can be applied to other types of organisations, with modifications.

ORGANISATION: CHOICE AND BACKGROUND

Non-profit organisations lie along a continuum in terms of benefits they provide; at one end, organisations producing benefits largely geared towards members, such as professional associations, sports associations, labour unions, recreational and sport clubs, and religious congregations. On the other end of the spectrum, there are those organisations producing benefits to third parties, such as hospitals, shelters, food pantries, and environmental organisations. Between the two ends of this spectrum are those non-profit organisations producing benefits to their members and third parties such as advocacy groups, museums, and some religious activities. Volunteers respond according to differing opportunities and personal constraints: and volunteer labour supply will differ by sector, sub-sector, and type of organisation.

In this exploratory study, we chose to examine an organisation that is closer to one end of the spectrum—that is, one producing benefits largely for its membership. Our case study organisation is used to introduce the concept of social accounting using the EVAS and to illustrate the practicality and limitations of using the EVAS. Although EVAS methodologies may be contested, a strong defence lies in the pragmatic benefits of rendering visible a more complete picture of not-for-profit performance.

The Islamic mosque ABC[1] is a relatively young non-profit religious organisation that exudes a "collective desire to be your neighbour's keeper" in addition to carrying out religious functions. The congregation grew steadily from ten members in the 1960s to a count of two thousand current members.

Members pay fees to belong to the organisation; in addition, some members volunteer time or make monetary donations. Unpaid member contributions of time are an important part of the organisation's human resources and lead to a reduction in the membership fee. The worship and non-worship services of the ABC appear to be widely appreciated by the membership, but what was unknown prior to this study is what portion of the members donate volunteer contributions; how much these contributions add to the organisation's total human resources; what the value added of these unpaid member contributions is; and how volunteers perceive volunteering.

There are almost two thousand voting members of the ABC. Membership costs range from $125[2] for students to $450 per year per family. According to ABC, the membership comprises 838 families, 363 students, and 389 seniors. Due to the family memberships, the actual numbers rise to about five thousand individual members. A large majority of the members are Indian Muslims originating from East Africa. A fourteen-member board of directors (nine elected officers and five appointed from interest groups) oversees the twenty-three subcommittees of volunteer that provide services ranging from social assistance via family support network and seniors groups, to theological counselling and teaching, to administration via the finance committee and media relations. Although the value of the various services may differ, they combine to allow for a functional community. ABC has four full-time paid staff.

Given that most of the community is comprised of immigrants from East Africa who value education and hard work, and given the proclivity of such communities towards entrepreneurship, we assume that a large percentage of the community will comprise entrepreneurs and professionals (Khanna 2007, 177). Moreover, given that this is a religious congregation that espouses "doing good", actively participating in the ABC and holding offices gains volunteers community approval (Abdul-Rahman 2003).

DATA COLLECTION AND FINDINGS

Data was collected by reviewing documents including audited financial statements and through an online survey administered to members. The survey was sent out at the end of January 2007 to 661 ABC members with valid e-mail addresses, and a link to the survey was also sent out weekly in a newsletter and posted on the ABC web site. In total, 435 useable responses were collected. Of these, 213 reported that they had volunteered for ABC in the year ending 31 December 2006. Estimates of hours volunteered by area were also received from the president of the mosque and several program leaders.

The majority of respondents (n = 435) were men (56 percent); born outside of Canada (81 percent); and had an average of sixteen years of membership at ABC. Relative to the overall pool of respondents, ABC's 213 currently active volunteers (those who had volunteered in the last fiscal year) were 54 percent men, 75 percent born outside Canada, with an average membership of sixteen years.

Of those 213 reporting they had volunteered, 172 responded to the question of how many hours. In total, they reported contributing 26,188 hours for the year ending 31 December 2006. About 48 percent of this group also volunteered for other organisations (n = 182). Respondents who had never volunteered for ABC were 65 percent men, 94 percent born outside Canada, and had been members of the association for an average of fourteen years.

The total hours reported by the survey respondents were then compared to the estimate prepared by ABC leaders. This estimate amounted to a total of 54,030 hours. It took into account that in some areas, members did not respond to the survey. For instance, some women may not use computers, or relegate the task of responding to the survey to their husbands or children. The leadership also felt that many respondents did not consider certain aspects of what they were doing as volunteering, for instance, preparatory work. One member was surprised that making phone calls and driving to pick up supplies for an event counted as volunteering. For the purposes of the expanded value added statement that follows, the average of these two totals (26,188 from the survey and 54,030 from the estimate made by mosque leaders), or 40,109 hours, is used.

VALUE ADDED BY VOLUNTEERS

Value added is a measure of wealth that an organisation creates by "adding value" to raw materials, products, and services with labour and capital. It is equal to the value of outputs minus the cost of externally purchased goods and services (Mook, Quarter, and Richmond 2007). Although value added statements have generally been applied to for-profit businesses, they can also be applied to non-profits (Mook, Quarter, and Richmond 2007).

A challenge in adapting the value added statement to non-profits is that volunteers generate a portion of the organisation's value added. However, volunteer contributions normally do not involve monetary transactions and so are excluded from the financial statements. A key challenge in creating a value added statement for non-profits is attributing a market value to volunteering. Another challenge is to value any benefits of volunteering that are received by volunteers. As well, there is a larger issue of attributing value to the social impacts of non-profits since these are difficult to quantify and not generally monetised.

INTRODUCTION TO THE EXPANDED
VALUE ADDED STATEMENT

Non-profit organisations are different from business enterprises in significant ways: they operate for purposes other than to earn a profit; their efficiency and effectiveness cannot be determined through information in financial statements only; and they may receive large amounts of resources from providers (for example, donors, government) who do not expect monetary benefits in return (Razek, Hosch, and Ives 2000). Non-profit organisations are also different in that they acknowledge the contribution of multiple stakeholders (for example, funders, clients, and community), involve volunteers, and have both social and economic goals.

The EVAS recognises the uniqueness of non-profits by focusing on both economic and social impacts, instead of just the financial "bottom line" (Mook, Quarter, and Richmond 2007). For instance, the EVAS analysis of a housing co-operative identified key aspects of the organisation's functioning that were not apparent in the financial statements (Richmond and Mook 2001). These included: providing employment; skills development and personal growth for members; the impact of unpaid labour and other contributions; and a contributing to society through services and payment of taxes.

The EVAS also emphasises the collective effort needed for an organisation to achieve its goals, viewing each stakeholder as important to its viability as a socially and economically responsible organisation. Including volunteers and society as stakeholders presents an alternative perspective of an organisation to focusing solely on its ability to earn a financial surplus.

There are two parts to a value added statement:

1. the calculation of value added by an organisation
2. its distribution to the stakeholders

For an expanded value added statement, the value added is broadened from including only financial transactions to including non-monetised social contributions such as those made by volunteers. Therefore, in the EVAS, volunteers become one of the stakeholders and a portion of the value added is distributed to them.

Determining the market value for the outputs of a for-profit firm is relatively straightforward—it is the amount of revenue received through sales, or in other words, the amount people have paid for those goods or services in the market. However, for some non-profit organisations revenues are seen as inputs and the term *outputs* is generally used to mean the direct products of its activities; for example, such services as free counselling for a given number of clients. Determining the market value for the outputs of a non-profit organisation presents unique challenges because its goods and services may not involve market transactions, and non-financial inputs such as contributions of volunteer labour are generally ignored, as are indirect outputs such as the increase in the human capital of volunteers or increasing safety in neighbourhoods. Yet it is possible to assign a comparative market value (a reasonable rate if it were exchanged in the market) to some inputs and outputs, such as the labour provided by volunteers or free meals in soup kitchens, in order to produce a partial EVAS. In order to do this, we look to the market rate for similar activities to impute value.

ESTIMATING THE VALUE ADDED BY VOLUNTEERS

To estimate the monetary value of the unpaid services contributed by ABC members, three values were used: (a) an hourly rate based on occupation and skill; (b) an hourly rate based on the type of organisation; and (c) an hourly rate based on survey responses. The first two values assume a replacement value methodology, where unpaid labour is valued at what it would cost the organisation to replace its volunteers with paid staff and continue the services currently provided by a volunteer, whereas the third is a modified version of the opportunity cost method. A brief elaboration of each approach follows.

Valuation Based on Occupations and Skill

For an hourly rate based upon occupation or skill, we used values based on Human Services and Social Development Canada data. For ABC, there were a variety of occupations requiring differing skill levels and spanning seven occupation types. Using these rates, the value of the 40,109 hours of volunteer contributions for ABC was estimated at $997,520—an average of $24.87 per hour.

Valuation Based on NAICS

For an hourly rate based on the North American Industry Classification System (NAICS),[3] the category applicable to ABC is sub-sector 6241, Individual and Family Services. The hourly rate for those involved in this category for the year 2006 was $12.67, and was used for low-skill activities. The salaried rate was used for high-skilled activities and was $18.96. A mid-point rate of $15.82 was used for those activities requiring a medium level of skill. Using these rates, the comparative market value of volunteer contributions for the year would be estimated as $681,097—an average of $16.96 per hour.

Valuation Based on Opportunity Costs

Opportunity costs are the wages volunteers would earn in the labour market if they chose to remain there instead of volunteering. We follow Handy and Srinivasan (2004) and use modified opportunity cost values based on survey responses to the following question: "To estimate a value of your efforts imagine you were to be paid for your volunteering time with ABC, what would you consider as a reasonable *compensation per hour*? If you do more than one task then take an average. Please choose your currency and insert the estimated amount in the space beside it."

This is not a typical survey question and individuals are not often asked to value their volunteer time. As there is no upper boundary to how much they are willing to accept for the hours donated, this response may be biased upwards, as is the case in many willingness-to-accept compensation responses (Coursey, Hovis, and Schulze 1987). We chose the median response to exclude some inflated responses as well as those who responded zero. For ABC, the median reported rate was $15.00, which suggests the comparative market value of volunteer contributions for the year would be $601,635.

Given the possible upward and downward biases in the three methods chosen, we calculated the average of the three methods to value the volunteer hour, $18.95 for ABC. Where it is difficult for organisations to replicate these methods, we suggest using the valuation based on organisation type for salaried workers, that is, the NAICS rate of $18.96, which is sufficiently close to the value arrived on averaging. The example of the EVAS shown in Table 5.1 uses this valuation of volunteer hours, as well as data from the financial statements for the year ended 31 December 2006. For the 40,109 hours contributed, this works out to an estimated value of $760,600.

Table 5.1 presents the partial value added by ABC, and refers to different types of value added:

Table 5.1   Partial Expanded Value Added Statement for ABC

Expanded Value Added Statement (Partial) *		*Financial Accounts*	*Social Accounts*	*Combined Accounts*
One-year period				
Outputs		$2,336,890	$760,600	$3,097,490
Less: Externally purchased goods and services		$2,096,635		$2,096,635
Total Value Added		$240,255	$760,600	$1,000,855
Distribution of Value Added				
Employees	Wages and benefits	$240,255		$240,255
Members/Community	Volunteer contributions		$760,600	$760,600
Total Value Added Distributed		$240,255	$760,600	$1,000,855

* The Expanded Value Added Statement shown here is partial in that it focuses only on the value added from volunteer contributions of hours, not the value of all impacts of the organisation.

- Financial, which represents information from audited financial statements only (what you would also find on a conventional value added statement).
- Social, which represents information about non-monetised contributions for which a market comparison is estimated.
- Combined, which represents the total of the financial and social value added.

Table 5.1 is referred to as partial value added as we only consider the volunteer contributions, rather than an extensive analysis of all the outputs of the organisation (see Cnaan's contribution to this volume, Chapter 20).

The first step in calculating the amount of value added is to assess the total outputs of the organisation and assign a comparative market value to them. The primary outputs of ABC include worship services, education, and social assistance. Because conducting a market comparison of all the organisation's outputs is beyond the scope of this study, the amount that the organisation spends on providing these services is taken as a measure of their value. For the fiscal year under consideration, the amount was $2,336,800 for ABC (Table 5.1, "Financial" column). This is what this organisation spent in order to provide its services or outputs.

For the primary outputs in the "Social" column, we include the market comparison leading to the dollar value of the hours contributed by volunteers ($760,600).

The value of volunteer contributions is added to the amount that the organisation spends on its services in order to arrive at a closer approximation of the total cost, as if the goods or services had been offered through the market. To arrive at the total value of the organisation's outputs, the expenditures ($2,336,890) are added to the social contributions ($760,600) to arrive at a total of $3,097,490 (see "Combined" column).

Then, in order to measure the value added by the organisation, the goods and services that are purchased externally, $2,096,635 (see Table 5.2), are subtracted from the total outputs of $3,097,490 (as per the definition of value added),[4] leading to a total of value added of $1,000,855 (see "Combined" column).

The value added by the organisation is distributed to the stakeholders in its entirety in the EVAS. The lower rows of Table 5.1 present the distribution of value added, with three stakeholders, employees, members, and the

Table 5.2 Reconciliation of Expenditures on Audited Financial Statements to Purchases of External Goods and Services on Value Added Statement

Total expenses	$2,336,890
Less: Employee wages and benefits	$240,255
Equals: Purchases of external goods and services	$2,096,635

organisation receiving shares. For example, the value added distributed to employees represents their wages and benefits of $240,255.

The stakeholder referred to as society receives value added of $760,600, equivalent to the value of volunteer contributions. In total, the value added distributed corresponds to the value added created.

SUMMARY AND OBSERVATIONS

The EVAS (Table 5.1) indicates that $1,000,855 of value added was created for ABC. If the audited financial accounts only were considered, ABC appeared to create value added of $240,255 for the year. The EVAS shows that the financial information without the social value added does not tell the organisation's whole performance story. Including volunteer contributions in the calculation of value added led to an increase of about 317 percent.

When considering the financial and in-kind resources received by the organisation in the fiscal year, volunteer hours account for 24 percent of the total (Figure 5.1). This figure shows that volunteer contributions, both monetary and non-monetary, provide the organisation with a significant resource that should be counted in its overall performance.

The significance of ABC's volunteer contributions is evident when examining the proportion that volunteers contribute to the overall human resources of the organisation. Based on the estimate of 40,109 volunteer hours and a workweek of thirty-five hours (1,820 per year or thirty-five multiplied by fifty-two), volunteers contributed twenty-two full-time equivalent (FTE) positions for the fiscal year. If you add this to the FTE of the paid staff of four, the total then becomes twenty-six FTEs. This means that, including volunteer contributions, more than five times the labour is required in the production of ABC's goods and services than the traditional accounting statements show (Figure 5.2).

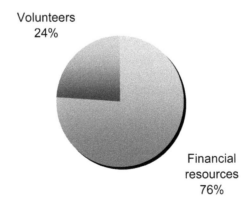

Volunteers
24%

Financial
resources
76%

Figure 5.1   Monetary and non-monetary contributions.

FTEs

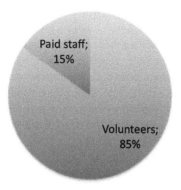

Figure 5.2 Proportion of total activity hours by volunteers and staff.

Social goods and services, those not given a monetary value, are often a large part of a non-profit organisation's operations. Without taking these goods and services into account, there is neither a clear picture of a non-profit's performance, nor the contributions made by its members.

In the case of ABC, the EVAS tell a different story than the financial statements alone—and to a different audience. The EVAS helps various stakeholders, particularly members in the case of ABC, see what value they have added to their organisation. For ABC, this amount is 85 percent. The EVAS may help members to understand better what value they have received and to appreciate that without substantial unpaid member contributions it would not be possible for ABC to provide the same level of service at current membership rates.

The strengths of the EVAS model lies in its ability to take a broader look at the organisation and the role of members, and to put this in a larger social-economic perspective. The challenges of the EVAS are shared by other forms of alternative accounting and economics—quantifying and placing a value on goods and services that are seen as "free". Yet, as the EVAS undertaken for ABC shows, free goods and services are utilised and produced in large measures by the organisation, and therefore need to be accounted for if the whole performance story of the organisation is to be told. The EVAS model attempts to integrate financial information, for which there are accepted methods of accounting, with non-financial or social information—and to develop a methodology that supports this.

The limitations of the EVAS affect the non-profit sector as a whole: there are few resources to track free goods and services. The EVAS method attempts to place a reasonable market value on items and activities that do not pass through the market. More research will be required to refine this process. However, the EVAS in this case study currently captures and displays information that other forms of accounting do not. The organisation and its stakeholders can use this information to understand the integral role and value of its members who contribute services without payment.

Whereas the EVAS presented here begins to capture the impact of volunteers upon the organisation, these estimates are probably understated because there are additional externalities associated with volunteering that were not assessed in this study. The work of volunteers in the area of theological teachings, dissemination of educational materials, and social assistance for ABC can serve to expand the base of support for the organisation by making the work of the organisation transparent. They also provide their organisation with word-of-mouth promotion and have the potential to cultivate a broader base of supporters. This may result in increasing organisations' networks and capacity to attract more members.

Another positive externality is the role modelling of volunteers, for example, to other members who may be willing to donate and or volunteer if their colleagues volunteer, thereby increasing the future pool of volunteers and donations (Toppe, Kirsch, and Michel 2002; Solberg 2003). Such positive externalities of volunteering are not captured in the EVAS statement, hence our findings need to be understood as an under-estimate of the benefits of volunteering.

CONCLUSIONS

This case study of ABC demonstrates how volunteer services by members can be presented within a social accounting framework. The work is experimental, but the technique is transferable. The technique is important because, unlike the conventional accounting statements, it captures the value that volunteers add to the organisation within a framework that addresses the value added of ABC.

Although it would be reasonable to argue that there is a difference between volunteering in a membership association where the benefits largely accrue to the membership and similar volunteering in a publicly oriented non-profit such as hospitals, the distinction is not as categorical as it may seem at first glance. ABC does serve a large membership and only half of the respondents reported that they volunteered for the organisation, suggesting that there may be many who benefit from the labour of a few. Therefore, volunteering seems like an appropriate label for unpaid labour contributions to membership organisations even though there is a financial benefit for all members resulting from the volunteering undertaken by some. The EVAS statement highlights the distribution of financial returns to the stakeholders and provides a way to assess what portion of the returns accrue to members.

There are methodological challenges in doing the EVAS. Notwithstanding issues of valuing volunteer time, difficulties exist regarding the proper selection of items included and imperfections in the methods available to assign them a monetary value do pose some challenges to the use of EVAS. Such limitations are not unique to EVAS, however, and are shared by other forms of alternative accounting, which struggle to accurately identify, measure, quantify, and value social, environmental indicators and sustainability impacts and performance (Ranganathan 1999).

The narrow focus of most policymakers on easily understood effects of organisations (both for-profit and non-profit), structures (for example, new performing arts centres and sports stadiums), and events (for example, arts festivals and sports tournaments) on regional or national GDP, employment, personal income, and tax revenues also explains the popularity of economic impact studies that focus on largely short-run regional spending flows—in contrast to broader measures of economic contribution. This tension between primarily instrumental economic impacts versus more intrinsic economic rewards has been at the heart of the long-simmering debate as to how to properly measure economic impact. While economists and others adapt their own tools to provide some measure the economic impact of non-profit organisations where significant positive externalities exist, social accounting methods such as the EVAS can be viewed as the social accounting profession's attempt to confront the similar limitations of its own traditional framework in answering the question "What is it worth?"

To the extent that the EVAS makes visible the contribution of volunteer labour, both private and public funders are able to see that the return to their investment is multiplied by volunteer labour. Donors of money can see that the impact goes much farther when combined with volunteer labour. This return to their investment is largely hidden in traditional accounting statements; an area for further research is the synergies between donations of money and time for an organisation.

Environmental and societal sustainability requires us to pay keen attention to the impact of organisations on a scale hitherto ignored. The impact of organisations, often measured solely in financial terms, leaves out issues of sustainability. The monetary metrics of measurement are so ingrained in society that using other metrics results in the findings being ignored—not thereby garnering the attention they deserve among policymakers. The EVAS and social accounting frameworks address this issue by using traditional monetary measures and imbedding the social impact into the well-established framework of value added statements. We envisage that the further developments along this route of social accounting will perforce gain attention as it will appear in the bottom line of statements, traditionally regarded as metrics for management decisions. This, we hope, will beget questions on the social impact of the work organisations engage in. There are those who would eschew playing the monetary numbers game, asking that attention be paid to multiple bottom lines which use different metrics even though they are not integrated into traditional accounting statements. We encourage the plurality of discourse in a field where our end goal is convergent—our routes may be different, but these efforts are to make visible the environmental and social impacts of management decisions. With heterogeneity of organisations operating in different sectors in varying cultural contexts, with multiple stakeholders, and using a range of accounting methods, no one way is salient in envisioning social impact.

NOTES

1. This is an assumed name.
2. All monetary figures are in Canadian dollars.
3. See US Census Bureau web site at http://www.census.gov/epcd/naics02/ and the Statistics Canada web site at http://www.statcan.ca/english/Subjects/Standard/naics/2002/naics02-menu.htm.
4. Value added is a measure of the value added to external goods and services through the use of labour and capital.

REFERENCES

Abdul-Rahman, M. S. 2003. *To Make the Heart Tender (Ar-Riqaq)*. Adobe eBook: MSA Publication Ltd.
Brown, E. 1999. "Assessing the Value of Volunteer Activity." *Nonprofit and Voluntary Sector Quarterly* 28 (1): 3–17.
Bureau of Labor Statistics. 2009. http://www.bls.gov/news.release/volun.nr0.htm.
Cnaan, R. A. 2009. "Valuing the Contribution of Urban Religious Congregations." *Public Management Review* 11 (5): 641–662.
Coursey, D. L., J. L. Hovis, and W. D. Schulze. 1987. "The Disparity between Willingness to Accept and Willingness to Pay Measures of Value." *Quarterly Journal of Economics* 102 (3): 679–690.
Hall, M., D. Lasby, S. Ayer, and W. D. Gibbons. 2009. *Canadians: Highlights from the 2007 Canada Survey of Giving, Volunteering and Participating*. Catalogue No. 71-542-XPE. Ottawa: Minister of Industry.
Handy, F., and N. Srinivasan. 2004. "Improving Quality while Reducing Costs? An Economic Evaluation of the Net Benefits of Hospital Volunteers." *Nonprofit and Voluntary Sector Quarterly* 33 (1): 28–54.
Hodgkinson, V. A., and M. S. Weitzman. 1996. *Dimensions of the Independent Sector: A Statistical Profile*. 2nd ed. Washington, DC: Independent Sector.
Independent Sector. 2009. *Value of Volunteer Time*. http://www.independentsector.org/programs/research/volunteer_time.html#value (accessed 6 October 2009).
Khanna, T. 2007. *Billions of Entrepreneurs: How China and India Are Reshaping their Futures and Yours*. Boston: Harvard Business School Press.
Mook, L., J. Quarter, and B. J. Richmond. 2007. *What Counts: Social Accounting for Nonprofits and Cooperatives*. 2nd ed. London: Sigel Press.
Mook, L., B. J. Richmond, and J. Quarter. 2003. "Integrated Social Accounting for Nonprofits: A Case from Canada." *Voluntas* 14 (3): 283–298.
Quarter, J., L. Mook, and A. Armstrong. 2009. *Understanding the Social Economy: A Canadian Perspective*. Toronto: University of Toronto Press.

Ranganathan, J. 1999. "Signs of Sustainability: Measuring Corporate Environmental and Social Performance." In *Sustainable Measure*, ed. M. Bennett, and P. James, 475–495. Sheffield: Greenleaf Publishing.

Razek, J. R., G. A. Hosch, and M. Ives. 2000. *Introduction to Governmental and Not-for-Profit Accounting*. 4th ed. Upper Saddle River, NJ: Prentice Hall.

Richmond, B. J., and L. Mook. 2001. *Social Audit for WCRI*. Toronto: Authors.

Solberg, H. A. 2003. "Major Sporting Events: Assessing the Value of Volunteers' Work." *Managing Leisure* 8 (1): 17–27

Toppe, C. M., A. D. Kirsch, and J. Michel. 2002. *Giving and Volunteering in the United States Findings from a National Survey*. Washington, DC: Independent Sector.

6 Exploring the Potential of Shadow Accounts in Problematising Institutional Conduct

Colin Dey, Shona Russell, and Ian Thomson

INTRODUCTION

Within the extensive social and environmental accounting literature (Thomson 2007) there are reports of a particular form of social accounting produced by external organisations, including campaigning NGOs,[1] on *their* representation of the social and environmental impacts of others (see, for example, Moerman and Van der Laan 2005; Gallhofer et al. 2006; Dey 2007). The intended audience for these reports was not simply the organisation associated with the problematic impacts, but also included political institutions, the media, and sections of the general public (Gray 1997; Harte and Owen 1987; Medawar 1976; Cooper et al. 2005; Collison et al. 2007). Given that the reports attempted to challenge, problematise, and de-legitimate those currently in a dominant position of power, implicitly we understand that these accounts will be prepared by, or on behalf of, less powerful social groups. They may therefore be thought of as an "accounting for the other, by the other" (cf. Shearer 2002), or more concisely, "shadow accounts" (Dey 2007). In this chapter, we consider the role of shadow accounts in systematically creating alterative representations, new visibilities, and knowledge of existing situations in order to problematise, act as a catalyst for intervention, and typically represent the views of oppressed social groups or ecological systems.

Shadow accounting can be viewed as a technology that measures, creates, makes visible, represents, and communicates evidence in contested arenas characterised by multiple (often contradictory) reports, prepared according to different institutional and ideological rules. Any evaluation of shadow accounting should recognise this contest for power and the intention to influence decisions. From a theoretical perspective, shadow accounting possesses significant emancipatory potential (Gallhofer et al. 2006; Shenkin and Coulson 2007; Spence 2007; Bebbington and Thomson 2007). At the same time, however, there are also concerns over how shadow accounts problematise, and the intention and intervention strategies of shadow accountants. Shadow accounting is a voluntary activity and shadow accountants are self-selecting individuals or organisations seeking to bring about change in line with their belief structure, which need not be emancipatory. This raises the questions as to what characteristics shadow accounts should possess if they are to fulfil their emancipatory potential or whether they are merely a political device for imposing one worldview over others. Researching shadow accounting requires a systemic investigation of the assemblage of engagements and contextual factors that constitute the governing network within which any reports are located, in particular, the power relationships and dynamics. The next section of this chapter draws on academic studies that have applied the Foucauldian concept of governmentality to accounting to develop an analytical framework to explore the potential of shadow accounting to enable emancipatory social and ecological change.

GOVERNMENTALITY INSIGHTS ON ACCOUNTING

Prior research on accounting within a governmentality framework provides a number of insights into our attempt to understand shadow accounting as a governing technology. Accounting is recognised to represent, construct, problematise, and measure the vision, conduct, and practices of social organisations. Accounting, through the application of systematic calculative rationality, renders entities visible through numerical representation in centres of calculation facilitating "regimes" of governing and political rationalities to be operationalised (Hoskin and Macve 1986; Jones and Dugdale 2001; Miller and Rose 1990). These entities can include individual workers, products, places, programs, social groups, organisations, or nation-states (Rose 1991; Miller and O'Leary 1993). Dean (1999) discusses numerous examples of governing technologies that rely on accounting techniques. These include the establishment of statistical norms, demonstrating regulatory compliance, taxation, subsidies, market incentives, budgetary control, audit, surveillance, and governing by measurable objectives. Thus, accounting practices can be employed in the government of others (Miller and O'Leary 1987; Miller and Rose 1990) and of the self (Willmott 1996).

Accounting forms part of the knowledge construction processes within organisations and is used to measure and judge the effectiveness of other governmental technologies (Boland and Schultze 1996). While there are many forms of knowledge within organisations, accounting often legitimates knowledge by granting it power within governing discourses. Accounting can be used to make processes "thinkable" and "governable", but it also can make other processes "unthinkable" and "ungovernable". Accounting therefore possesses definitional powers and operates as a dividing practice (Rose 1991) establishing institutional norms of acceptable behaviour and thinking (Russell and Thomson 2009). Accounting's ability to classify actions as "unacceptable" and "exceptional", and thus requiring some form of intervention, makes it a powerful and adaptable technology that can operate in different contexts.

Shadow accounting could be conceptualised as making "thinkable" and "governable" those issues currently regarded by organisations as "unthinkable" and "ungovernable". This contrasts with criticisms of voluntary, self-authored corporate social and environmental reports. These criticisms include: inability to problematise and challenge dominant institutional thinking; falsely legitimating businesses' belief in the sustainability of their operations (Brown and Deegan 1998; Campbell 2000; O'Donovan 2002); promoting a "business as usual" agenda (Larrinaga-Gonzalez and Bebbington 2001); conveying weak versions of sustainable development (Bebbington and Thomson 1996); and corporate and/or managerial capture of the social and environmental agenda. Bebbington and Thomson (2007) argue that future development of social and environmental accounting must recognise the importance of developing alternative accountings that offer different conceptions of "nature", "society", and "business success" that are aligned with emancipatory change. One technique with such potential is shadow accounting.

PRIOR EXPERIMENTS IN SHADOW ACCOUNTING

Gray (1997) proposed that social and environmental reports (silent accounts) could be compiled using information disclosed by companies in their annual reports. These "corporate silent accounts" were claimed to represent the corporation's own voice. Gray also proposed the shadow account, similar in content to the silent account, but using information beyond the control of the company juxtaposed with the corporate silent account. Shadow accounts of corporate impacts are drawn up from external sources, such as newspaper articles, direct testaments from workers, ex-employees, individuals living near plants, trade unions, suppliers, public pollution registers, NGO reports, scientific reports, court prosecutions, and health and safety breaches. A corporate shadow account is drawn from independent, though not necessarily objective, sources and control over content does not remain with the corporation.

Corporate shadow accounts are intended to reveal contradictions between what companies choose to report and what they suppress, problematising their activities and providing new insights into their social and environmental impacts. The shadow account represents a shift from an organisation-centred perspective towards more independent and stakeholder-driven approaches (Dey 2007; Gibson et al. 2001; Gray et al. 1997).

We build our analysis from Gray's original notion of corporate shadow accounting through a review of reports of external problematising accounts, as well as our own experience in constructing experimental shadow accounts. Using the analytics of government framework (Dean 1999), we identified common aspects between these apparently diverse accounting techniques. These shadow accounts shared a common objective of problematising a particular dimension of an organisation's conduct. The focus of these shadow accounts ranged from multinational corporations, nation-states, industrial plants, individual projects, government policies, river pollution and student poverty (for example, Collison et al. 2007; Cooper et al. 2005; Harte and Owen 1987; Solomon and Thomson 2009). These shadow accounts had a defined teleology and typically were part of a political campaign by the shadow accountants, who acted as representatives of oppressed social groups (Medawar 1976) or ecological systems (Solomon and Thomson 2009). These problematising external accounts have been referred to by a number of different terms, including social audits (Medawar 1976), deindustrialisation audits (Harte and Owen 1987), silent accounts (Gray 1997), shadow accounts (Gray 1997; Gibson et al. 2001), reporting-performance portrayal gap analysis (Adams 2004), social accounts (Cooper et al. 2005), and counter accounts (Gallhofer et al. 2006). Despite the variety of terms used to describe them, we observed that these accounts systematically created alterative representations, new visibilities, and knowledge of contested situations in order to problematise and act as a catalyst for change.

Harte and Owen (1987) discussed UK local authorities' use of social cost analysis to measure the impact of plant closure decisions and problematise deindustrialisation in order to justify government intervention (see also Clark et al. 1987). Unfortunately, despite providing compelling evidence, many shadow accounts were deemed ineffective in bringing about change arguably due to contemporary political dynamics. However, notions of effectiveness can be difficult to evaluate—see, for example, Dean's (1999, 11) definition of governing with its "diverse set of relatively unpredictable consequences, effects and outcomes". In a further example, Carroll and Beiler (1975) described the purpose of social auditing in 1940 in the US not as an accurate, evidence-based process, but as a powerful check against problematic government behaviour: "While the measuring stick may not be trustworthy, it is nevertheless useful for the purposes of castigation" (Temporary National Economic Committee, quoted by Carroll and Beiler 1975, 591).

Cooper et al. (2005) demonstrated the political power of systemic, evidence-based external social audit methodology in problematising student poverty and higher education financing plans in Scotland. What was noticeable in this study was how the shadow accountants made use of parliamentary processes to present their evidence to bring about reform. Bebbington and Thomson (2007) discussed the potential of shadow accounting in risk conflicts where individuals or collectives collect data and develop theories that draw attention to defects in official accounts of events, constructing alternative accounts; problematising official accounting assumptions; questioning the origins, presentation, and interpretation of costs, statistics, and other evidence; and uncovering creative accounting techniques. Adams's (2004) discussion of portrayal gap analysis on a single company demonstrated the potential power of this form of external problematising through creating new knowledge and visibilities of an organisation's conduct. The power of Adams's alternative account was evident in the organisation's reaction to it and their problematisation of her account. A number of other shadow accounts have been similarly problematised by those criticised, in their attempts to regain social legitimacy (Campbell and Beck 2004; Power 2004; Georgakopoulos and Thomson 2008).

We suggest that these shadow accounts rendered visible certain phenomena in numeric form, problematised current policies, programs, and actions, and presented and justified intervention in pursuit of an idealised vision held by the shadow accountants. The nature and content of these accounts, the problematisation processes, and desired future states were seen to be reflexively interconnected. Shadow accounting, therefore, has the potential to establish or impose norms of acceptable behaviour and to divide actions into "good" or "bad" as a precursor to intervention. Despite the use of statistics, numbers, costs, and values, shadow accounting remains fundamentally a social process that constructs social realities rather than neutrally reflecting reality (Hines 1988). Intervention strategies are often predicated by problematisation through quantification (Rose 1991). Rendering specific issues visible and amenable to problematisation is therefore crucial in the legitimation of programs of intervention (Miller 1990) and intervention requires both engaging with and disrupting dominant discourses. Accounting-based technologies can problematise current policies, programs, and actions and justify some form of intervention in context of a new idealised image of a better state. The new visibilities offered by numerical, quantified accounts of harm mean that they are a powerful technology in engagement processes, particularly in contexts that privilege this form of knowledge.

An example of this is the shadow account produced by Action on Smoking and Health (2002) challenging British American Tobacco's claim to be a socially responsible organisation, re-presenting them as an organisation profiting by harming the health of millions, creating social costs, and shortening the life of addicted smokers. This shadow account can be seen as a wider program of activism by Action on Smoking and Health to prohibit tobacco smoking. Another such example was the report by Collison et al. (2007) which sought to expose the claim that Anglo-American capitalism was a superior mode of governing by reporting on the paradoxical correlation between certain developed countries' increasing GDP per capita and increasing child mortality rates.

SHADOW PRACTICES, PROGRESSIVE CHANGE, AND DIALOGIC ENGAGEMENT

It is important to consider how shadow accounting might facilitate progressive social change, how it could lead to change (Boyce and Davids 2004), or whether it possesses the power to do any more than legitimate existing forms of institution or organisational activity (Bebbington and Thomson 2007). The ability of various parties to engage effectively thus becomes crucial in this analysis (Boyce 2000). We argue that how shadow accounts are used to engage is as significant as the content of these shadow accounts (Thomson and Bebbington 2005). Further, we suggest that if shadow accounts are to be emancipatory rather than oppressive, then they should be part of a dialogic process (Bebbington et al. 2007) and avoid anti-dialogic engagements.

Anti-dialogic engagements are associated with maintaining existing social and environmental inequalities and oppressive forms of government, or one group attempting to replace existing forms of government with their own system that merely replaces one set of inequalities and oppression with another. Freire (1970) suggests that oppressors maintain their power by the promotion of the myths of their superiority and the oppressed's inferiority through a process described as anti-dialogics. The oppressors design and operate systems that deny the oppressed the opportunity to critically perceive the "reality" of these myths; they remain ignorant of their transformative abilities or the possibility of any other way of being. Anti-dialogic engagement programs, therefore, need to isolate different members of society, to artificially create and deepen rifts. This divisive process is often portrayed as improving the conditions of the oppressed by partially rewarding some of the oppressed whilst perpetuating systemic injustice. Anti-dialogics is premised on manipulating the oppressed to conform to the oppressor's objectives. These organisations, rather than challenging the structural problems of oppression, enrol small groups of the oppressed into maintaining their oppressive regime for them, tempting "leaders" with access to power and improved material circumstances. This power and improved lifestyle is, however, conditional on a partial alliance with their dominators and subservience to their wider aims and objectives.

Key to this manipulation is a widespread social ignorance and the need to stop the oppressed from thinking. A fundamental characteristic of anti-dialogics is the destruction of the oppressed's worldview and its replacement with a worldview conducive to their continued oppression. This cultural invasion inhibits the oppressed's natural creativity by curbing their existing forms of expression. It is also designed to ensure that the oppressed perceive their reality through the lens constructed for them by the oppressors, confirming the oppressed's inherent inferiority and the impossibility of change.

If shadow accounts are intended to bring about emancipatory change then they should expose and reflect on "invisible" or "silenced" factors that oppress specific groups, re-examining situations in light of new understandings, problematising existing situations, re-presenting and re-narrating existing situations and identifying solutions in contested areas. Shadow accounts should recognise Freire's (1970) notion that it is possible to resolve the contradiction of different worldviews, not by denying their differences but by denying the invasion of one worldview by the other.

Given that shadow accounting is premised on the assumption that something is wrong, its initial concern is problematisation. However, there are a number of ways that issues can be problematised. We suggest that emancipatory problematisation should create spaces for potential change by opening up the dialogue, if only to explain why the organisation is as it is (Calton and Payne 2003). By including more individuals in the problematisation, more voices can be heard. Shadow accounts should "refigure the terms of the story" in order to "re-narrate" (Olson 1996, 3; Adams 2004) an existing story. Emancipatory shadow accounts should not create one dominant story, but rather "widen the number and kinds of stories that get told and the actors who tell them" (Olson 1996, 3). Shadow accounting allows the possibility of representing different voices from within and external to organisations. This heteroglossia of "many voices" can help level the playing field (Mitra 2001, 38) and enable a critique of power by drawing attention to excluded voices (Brown, Stevens, and Maclaran 1999) and different ways of thinking. Shadow accountants must recognise that dialogue with the powerful requires "oppositional" forms of talk, for example, the development of counter-narratives articulated with social movements and subaltern groups (Everett 2004; Cooper et al. 2005). As Everett (2004, 1079) observes, "the voices of those most affected by damaging corporate activities" have too often been absent from social and environmental accounting.

The shadow accounting projects reviewed in this chapter are examples of ways of "talking back", exposing contradictions, destabilising the taken for granted, and addressing the silences and absences of conventional financial reporting. Shadow accounting can develop capacity for critical reflection, surfacing of social and political tensions and contradictions, emergence of new discourses (Bokeno and Gantt 2000), and expose the taken-for-granted and normalised nature of social arrangements (White 1994). Shadow accounting should be aware of stakeholders' participation rights, dialogic entitlements, political institutions, and power dynamics (Bebbington et al. 2007; Lehman 2001) if they are not to be "as useful as an anchor on a bicycle" (Ormonde 1985, 4).

Feldman (2000, 559) notes that "stories alone are not enough, for effective stories need 'already willing listeners' . . . [they rely] upon a willingness on the part of the audience to participate, to be changed, or at least to acquiesce to the telling". Even when shadow accounts provide convincing financial and/or statistical evidence this will not bring about desired changes, especially if there are no willing listeners. Shadow accounting without concern for strategies for reforming systems of governing is likely to be ineffective. Shadow accountants should be aware of the possibility of confrontation and action, but this should be a synthesis of action and reflection. Shadow accounts should raise consciousness as to why a problem exists, but also consider whether its cause is a structural problem that requires wider social reform.

CONCLUSIONS

In this chapter, we considered the role of shadow accounts in systematically creating alterative representations, new visibilities, and knowledge of existing situations in order to problematise, act as a catalyst for intervention, and represent the views of oppressed social groups or ecological systems. Shadow accounting has significant potential to critique and challenge undesirable institutional conduct because it appears to be effective in the production of new knowledge and the creation of new visibilities. Shadow accounting can challenge dominant institutional knowledge and visibilities and reform organisational activities and certain technologies of government. Shadow entities are always constructed by the negative consequences of the targeted organisation and typically challenge the right of individuals, consumers, companies, and "the market" to be privileged over the rights of wider populations. As long as conventional accounting is powerful within institutions, then shadow accounting has the potential to be powerful as it emulates the dominant rationality within the institution.

Whilst there were conceptual similarities between the accounts examined in this chapter, there was considerable variation in the choice of entity, content, media, dissemination, accounting methods, and techniques. There is clearly a need to comprehensively study prior shadow accounts to systematically map the practice and motivations of shadow accountants, as well as to gain insights into their evaluations of the effectiveness of different shadow accounting technologies. For example, to what extent shadow accounts rely on calculative techniques/monetary values and what the perceived impact of this type of knowledge in bringing about change was.

The published research in this area would suggest that if shadow accounting is to promote emancipatory social change, then it should be educative, promote debate, change collective knowledge of contested situations, identify feasible alternative actions, and create space to enable action (Lehman 2001; Dillard, Brown, and Marshall 2005; Thomson and Bebbington 2005; Bebbington et al. 2007). Shadow accounts should allow a meaningful critique of the reporting entity, a questioning of decision-makers, and monitoring compliance with internal or external standards. They also should allow for a critique of these standards, social norms, regulations, and legislation. However, simply providing new accounts or evidence will not necessarily bring about change; social realities cannot be changed just by "changing their dialogues". If shadow accounting is to achieve the emancipatory role implicitly or explicitly attached to it, we argue that it must engage with other shadow practices and dialogues, such as shadow marketing, shadow public relations, and shadow health and safety. However, consideration has to be given to the voluntary, self-selecting, self-referential nature of shadow accounting. Anyone can produce a shadow account using their own shadow accounting methods, prepared according to their own standards. The prior research has reported on shadow accounts that represented oppressed groups, but shadow accounts could easily be prepared by (or on behalf of) the powerful and oppressive in society to perpetuate ecological and social inequalities. Issues such as motivation and underlying purpose, as well as the reliability, verifiability, and trust in the evidence, costs, and narratives presented in shadow accounts require further research and consideration. In this respect, further consideration should be given as to when an activist's intervention in a contested arena becomes a shadow account and when this shadow account could be considered emancipatory. In addition, there is a need for institutional frameworks that enable dialogic engagements arising from shadow accounts to take place, as well as consensus by participants not to abuse their power.

While understanding the urgency for action by shadow accountants, the radical changes they seek will emerge from a long-term reform process rather than from a single shadow account. Prior shadow accounting projects strengths lay in their success in exposing and reflecting on "invisible" or "silenced" factors, re-examining situations in light of new understandings, problematising existing situations, re-presenting and re-narrating existing situations, and presenting solutions. However, many shadow accounts have lacked an awareness of how to overcome any obstacles to change. Unless shadow accounts and shadow accountants are sensitive to these governmentality dimensions, they will not change the reality of social groups and our natural ecology.

NOTES

1. See, for example, Friends of the Earth (2003); Action on Smoking and Health (2002).

REFERENCES

Action on Smoking and Health. 2002. *British American Tobacco: The Other Report to Society.* London: ASH.
Adams, C. 2004. "The Ethical, Social and Environmental Reporting–Performance Portrayal Gap." *Accounting, Auditing and Accountability Journal* 17 (5): 731–757.
Bebbington, J., J. Brown, B. Frame, and I. Thomson. 2007. "Theorizing Engagement: The Potential of a Critical Dialogic Approach." *Accounting, Auditing and Accountability Journal* 20 (3): 356–389.
Bebbington, J., and I. Thomson. 1996. *Business Conceptions of Sustainability and the Implications for Accountancy. Research Report 48.* London: ACCA.

———. 2007. "Social and Environmental Accounting, Auditing and Reporting: A Potential Source of Organizational Risk Governance?" *Environment and Planning* 25 (1): 38–55.

Bokeno, R. M., and V. W. Gantt. 2000. "Dialogic Mentoring: Core Relationships for Organisational Learning." *Management Communication Quarterly* 14 (2): 237–270.

Boland, R. J., and U. Schultze. 1996. "Narrating Accountability: Cognition and the Production of the Accountable Self." In *Accountability: Power, Ethos and the Technologies of Managing*, ed. R. Munro and J. Mouritsen, 62–81. London: International Thomson Business Press.

Boyce, G. 2000. "Public Discourse and Decision Making: Exploring Possibilities for Financial, Social and Environmental Accounting." *Accounting, Auditing and Accountability Journal* 13 (1): 27–64.

Boyce, G., and C. Davids. 2004. "The Dimensions of Governmentality Studies in Accounting: Complementary and Critical Potentials." Presented to the 4th Asia Pacific IPA Conference, Singapore.

Brown, N., and C. Deegan. 1998. "The Public Disclosure of Environmental Performance Information—A Dual Test of Media Agenda Setting Theory and Legitimacy Theory." *Accounting and Business Research* 29 (1): 21–41.

Brown, S., L. Stevens, and P. Maclaran. 1999. "I Can't Believe It's Not Bakhtin! Literary Theory, Postmodern Advertising, and the Gender Agenda." *Journal of Advertising* 28 (1): 11–24.

Calton, J. M., and S. L. Payne. 2003. "Coping with Paradox: Multi-Stakeholder Learning Dialogue as a Pluralist Sense-Making Process for Addressing Messy Problems." *Business and Society* 42 (1): 7–42.

Campbell, D. 2000. "Legitimacy Theory or Managerial Reality Construction: Corporate Social Disclosure in Marks and Spencer Corporate Reports 1969–1997." *Accounting Forum* 24 (1): 80–100.

Campbell, D., and C. Beck. 2004. "Answering Allegations: The Use of the Corporate Website for Restorative Ethical and Social Disclosure." *Business Ethics: A European Review* 13 (2/3): 100–116.

Carroll, A., and G. Beiler. 1975. "Landmarks in the Evolution of the Social Audit." *Academy of Management Journal* (September): 589–599.

Clark, N., R. Critchley, D. Hall, R. Kline, and D. Whitfield. 1987. "The Sheffield Council Jobs Audit—Why and How?" *Local Economy* (February): 3–21.

Collison, D. J., C. R. Dey, G. M. Hannah, and L. A. Stevenson. 2007. "Income Inequality and Child Mortality in Wealthy Nations." *Journal of Public Health* 29 (2): 114–117.

Cooper, C., P. Taylor, N. Smith, and L. Catchpowle. 2005. "A Discussion of the Political Potential of Social Accounting." *Critical Perspectives on Accounting* 16 (7): 951–974.

Dean, M. 1999. *Governmentality: Power and Rule in Modern Society*. London: Sage Publications.

Dey, C. 2007. "Developing Silent and Shadow Accounts." In *Sustainability Accounting and Accountability*, ed. J. Unerman, J. Bebbington, and B. O'Dwyer, 307–327. London: Routledge.

Dillard, J., D. Brown, and R. Marshall. 2005. "An Environmentally Enlightened Accounting." *Accounting Forum* 29 (1): 77–101.

Everett, J. 2004. "Exploring (False) Dualisms for Environmental Accounting Praxis." *Critical Perspectives on Accounting* 15 (8): 1061–1084.

Feldman, A. 2000. "Othering Knowledge and Unknowing Law: Oppositional Narratives in the Struggle for American Indian Religious Freedom." *Social and Legal Studies* 9 (4): 557–582.

Freire, P. 1970. *The Pedagogy of the Oppressed.* New York: Seabury.
Friends of the Earth. 2003. *Failing the Challenge: The Other Shell Report 2002.* London: FoE.
Gallhofer, S., J. Haslam, E. Monk, and C. Roberts. 2006. "The Emancipatory Potential of Online Reporting: The Case of Counter Accounting." *Accounting, Auditing and Accountability Journal* 19 (5): 681–718.
Georgakopoulos, G., and I. Thomson. 2008. "Social Reporting, Engagements, Controversies and Conflict in Scottish Salmon Farming." *Accounting, Auditing and Accountability Journal* 21 (8): 1116–1143.
Gibson, K., R. Gray, Y. Laing, and C. Dey. 2001. "The Silent Accounts Project: Draft Silent and Shadow Accounts 1999–2000." Presented to BAA Scottish Group Conference, Stirling.
Gray, R. 1997. "The Silent Practice of Social Accounting and Corporate Social Reporting in Companies." In *Building Corporate Accountability: Emerging Practices in Social and Ethical Accounting, Auditing and Reporting*, ed. S. Zadek, R. Evans, and P. Pruzan, 201–217. London: Earthscan.
Gray, R., C. Dey, D. Owen, and S. Zadek. 1997. "Struggling with the Praxis of Social Accounting: Stakeholders, Accountability, Audits and Procedures." *Accounting, Auditing and Accountability Journal* 10 (3): 325–364.
Harte, G. and D. Owen. 1987. "Fighting De-Industrialisation: The Role of Local Government Social Audits." *Accounting, Organizations, and Society* 12 (2): 123–141.
Hines, R. 1988. "Financial Accounting: In Communicating Reality, We Construct Reality." *Accounting, Organizations, and Society* 13 (3): 251–261.
Hoskin, K., and R. Macve. 1986. "Accounting and the Examination: A Genealogy of Disciplinary Power." *Accounting, Organizations, and Society* 11 (2): 105–136.
Jones, C., and D. Dugdale. 2001. "The Concept of an Accounting Regime." *Critical Perspectives on Accounting* 12 (1): 35–63.
Larrinaga-Gonzalez, C., and J. Bebbington. 2001. "Accounting Change or Institutional Appropriation?—A Case Study of the Implementation of Environmental Accounting." *Critical Perspectives on Accounting* 12 (2): 269–292.
Lehman, G. 2001. "Reclaiming the Public Sphere: Problems and Prospects for Corporate Social and Environmental Accounting." *Critical Perspectives on Accounting* 12 (3): 713–733.
Medawar, C. 1976. "The Social Audit: A Political View." *Accounting, Organizations, and Society* 1 (4): 389–394.
Miller, P. 1990. "On the Interrelations between Accounting and the State." *Accounting, Organizations, and Society* 15 (3): 315–338.
Miller, P., and T. O'Leary. 1987. "Accounting and the Construction of Governable Person." *Accounting, Organizations, and Society* 12 (3): 235–265.
———. 1993. "Accounting Expertise and the Politics of the Product: Economic Citizenship and Modes of Corporate Governance." *Accounting, Organizations, and Society* 18 (2/3): 187–206.
Miller, P., and N. Rose. 1990. "Governing Economic Life." *Economy and Society* 19 (1): 1–31.
Mitra, A. 2001. "Marginal Voices in Cyberspace." *New Media and Society* 3 (1): 29–48.
Moerman, L., and S. Van der Laan. 2005. "Social Reporting in the Tobacco Industry: All Smoke and Mirrors?" *Accounting, Auditing and Accountability Journal* 18 (3): 374–389.
O'Donovan, G. 2002. "Environmental Disclosures in the Annual Report: Extending the Applicability and Predictive Power of Legitimacy Theory." *Accounting, Auditing and Accountability Journal* 15 (3): 344–371.

Olson, G. 1996. "Writing, Literacy and Technology: Toward a Cyborg Writing." *Journal of Composition Theory* 16 (1): 1–36.

Ormonde, P. 1985. "Opening the Books: Meeting the Needs of Shop Stewards." *Work and People* 2 (3): 3–5.

Power, M. 2004. *The Risk Management of Everything: Rethinking the Politics of Uncertainty*. London: Demos.

Rose, N. 1991. "Governing by Numbers: Figuring out Democracy." *Accounting, Organizations, and Society* 16 (7): 673–693.

Russell, S., and I. Thomson. 2009. "Analysing the Role of Sustainable Development Indicators in Accounting for and Constructing a Sustainable Scotland." *Accounting Forum* 33 (3): 225–244.

Shearer, T. 2002. "Ethics and Accountability: From the For-Itself to the For-the-Other." *Accounting, Organizations, and Society* 27:541–573.

Shenkin, M., and A. Coulson. 2007. "Accounting through Activism: Learning through Bourdieu." *Accounting, Auditing and Accountability Journal* 20 (2): 297–317.

Solomon, J., and I. Thomson. 2009. "Satanic Mills and Braithwaite's 'On the Rise and Fall of the River Wandle; its Springs, Tributaries, and Pollution': An Example of Victorian External Environmental Auditing?" *Accounting Forum* 33 (1): 74–87.

Spence, C. 2007. "Social and Environmental Reporting: A Hegemonic Discourse." *Accounting, Auditing and Accountability Journal* 20 (6): 855–882.

Thomson, I. 2007. "Accounting and Sustainability: Mapping the Terrain." In *Sustainability Accounting and Accountability*, ed. J. Unerman, J. Bebbington, and B. O'Dwyer, 19–37. London: Routledge.

Thomson, I., and J. Bebbington. 2005. "Corporate Social Reporting: A Pedagogic Evaluation." *Critical Perspectives on Accounting* 16 (5): 507–533.

White, L. G. 1994. "Policy Analysis as Discourse." *Journal of Policy Analysis and Management* 13 (3): 506–525.

Willmott, H. 1996. "Thinking Accountability: Accounting for the Disciplined Production of Self." In *Accountability: Power, Ethos and the Technologies of Managing*, ed. R. Munro and J. Mouritsen, 23–39. London: International Thomson Business Press.

Part II
Accountabilities

7 Czech Elites and Citizens as Part of a Public Accountability System

Pavol Frič

INTRODUCTION

In terms of their formal institutions, the post-communist countries of Central Europe are reasonably accountable. The last eighteen years has seen the introduction of an ample system of formal accountability institutions, mechanisms, and procedures including: free elections, parliaments, controlling systems, freedom of the press, a growing number of civil society organisations, and special legislative background (for example, acts on the conflict of interests, public procurement, free access to information, the institution of ombudsman, and reporting rules).[1] It has become difficult for official authorities to openly dispute the principle of accountability. Paradoxically though, many post-communist scholars and the general public do not usually view political and public institutions in these countries as being accountable. The quality of formal institutions is usually thought to be much lower than that of similar institutions in Western European countries. The Central European post-communist countries have experienced formal Europeanisation, but their institutions have yet to achieve European operating standards. Why is this so? What is behind the formal façade of these institutions? What is the cause of the "accountability paradox" of Central Europe? The most readily accepted explanation ascribes to a widespread culture of informality, perpetuated by a complex "ecosystem" of informal networks, which can be seen as the standard-bearers of an "anti-accountability system".

The attention of academic scholars and policy practice is usually focused on the level of preparedness of various actors (officials, politicians . . .) to display accountability in the conditions given by the quality of formal or institutional accountability infrastructure (parliament, courts, media . . .), accountability legislative background, and bureaucratic control mechanisms. Our analysis builds on the so-called relational approach to the phenomenon of public accountability. Authors within the realm of this approach understand accountability as a relationship between two counterparts: the accountor and the accountee (Pollitt 2003), the actor and the significant other (Day and Klein 1987), or the accountor and the public accountability forum (Bovens 2005). In this case, accountability is seen as a system of relations among actors in a certain institutional arrangement (Day and Klein 1987; Mulgan 2003; Goodin 2003; Bovens 2005).

In this chapter, the Czech elites[2] play the role of actor/accountor and the Czech general public play the role of accountee/accountability forum. Public accountability is studied as a set of vertical relations between elites and citizens. The authors just mentioned focused their attention mainly on the question of whether accountors "are or can be held accountable *ex post facto* by accountability forums" (Bovens, Schillemans, and 'T Hart 2008, 227). In light of this perspective, public accountability should not be viewed asymmetrically, as only the duty of one party to answer to the other party for its actions. On the contrary, public accountability presupposes that the accountee (significant other, accountability forum) is also obliged to fulfil a certain role in the accountability system. The accountee is not a passive accountability consumer.

In this sense, we understand accountability as a complex system of obligations. The fulfilment or breach of these obligations by one party will cause the other party to react accordingly. We postulate that this interactive system can only function if both parties, that is, the elites and the general public, abide by their respective roles. Not only the elites, but also the members of the general public have to act in an accountable manner and actively respond to the elites' behaviour in order to make the system work. This, however, is not automatic. In a democratic system, citizens should be actively involved in the public accountability discourse (Maravall 1999; Schmitter 1999), or in dialogue with public servants (Harmon 1995), and consequently demand (by making grievances and claims) public elite accountability. They should react flexibly to the elites' anti-accountable defensive strategies (Maravall 1999) and enforce sanctioning of the elites for their non-accountable behaviour. If citizens do not fulfil these democratic obligations within the public accountability system, they lose their moral right to expect the elites to be accountable. In other words, the functioning of the accountability system depends on the elites' willingness to be accountable as well as on citizens' moral qualities and abilities to fulfil the accountee role.[3] The goal of this chapter is to show that the Czech public accountability system is not working well because neither the elites nor the citizens fulfil their respective roles in the system.

INFORMAL NETWORKS IN THE POST-COMMUNIST WORLD

Informal networks[4] can have both a positive and negative influence on society. However, the extent of these positive and negative effects can differ from one society to another. Bright sides prevail in some and dark sides in others. Traditionally, western societies have been viewed as those where informal networks have a predominantly positive effect, as the morals of their informal networks are usually not found to conflict with the formal order; formal institutions and informal networks, rather, complement each other (in mutually exclusive or substitution relationships) and are dynamically balanced. Informal networks with negative program orientations are either kept within due limits or pushed to the margins of society. In contrast, post-communist countries are considered stereotypically as having informal networks with a strong negative influence. These countries are portrayed as societies with high levels of corruption, whose public administration institutions are largely under the influence of these informal networks.[5] Formal decision-making procedures are thought to be manipulated by behind-the-scenes agreements or collusions of interconnected subjects, forging their informal contracts beforehand (Sajó 1998). Informal networks have "made themselves at home" in these societies to such an extent that they are deemed to constitute parallel power structures. Events in formal institutions take place *pro forma*, in order to meet formal requirements; however, it is "everybody's secret" that all important public-interest decisions are made within informal networks for the benefit of their members. A review of the literature on the political and economic transition of post-communist countries suggests that these countries are safe havens of informal networks, whether inherited from communism or formed under the new regime.

As indicated earlier, the different impacts of informal networks in the western and post-communist worlds are often explained with reference to the extent to which the informal networks are imbedded in the communist past (path dependence), or the specific historical heritage of the post-communist countries that they cannot quickly recover from (regardless of whether or not they intend to). Many authors (Bowser 2002; Kabele 1992; Karklins 2002; Ledeneva 1998, 2003; Možný 1991; Rose 1999; Tucker 2000) direct our attention to the fact that the countries in the former "communist bloc" have faced something that could be called a "regulatory conversion"—an actual takeover of control of formal institutions by informal networks. The communist past of the Central and Eastern European countries suggests that the effect of the informal economy and informal relationships on the functioning of a society can be quite pronounced. So pronounced, in fact, that it can completely take over formal institutions and then, according to Mungiu-Pippidi, the whole society becomes an informal system, that is, an "informal society".[6]

Government institutions in post-communist countries often become private agencies under the influence of informal networks. Post-communist informal networks are characterised as parasitic formations that exist within the formal bodies of public administration, draining the resources needed for society's development (Tucker 2000). The authors who conceptualise informal networks within the theories of social capital write about the weakness of civil society in post-communist countries and the weak support of non-governmental organisations (be it through membership or volunteering). They point out that everyday problems are still frequently being solved within informal networks of "acquaintances". While this strategy was quite efficient for totalitarian regimes, it prevents spreading vital trust among citizens and instead cements the elements of anti-social capital, comprising of purely instrumental, exploitative relations (Bowser 2002; Ledeneva 2004; Uslaner 2004, 2).

Venelin Ganev discusses the prevalently negative connotations of the concept of "network" in the eyes of post-communist countries' citizens. Say the word in a post-communist social context and you will often face hostile reactions and cynical remarks about egoistic power elites (Ganev 1998, 3). The opinion that informal networks have benefited the overall development of post-communist societies by filling the transition vacuum in the business sphere by lowering uncertainty of economic transactions, helping restructure the industry (Stark and Bruszt 1998), and shifting these societies into the next stage of development is quite rare within the current debate.

THE CONSPIRATORIAL VIEW FROM BELOW

As suggested earlier, there is a crucial distinction between a formal institutional accountability arrangement (Bovens 2005) and informal elite networks that exist within formal institutions. The latter may undermine the accountability of these institutions or even form an informal anti-accountability system, transforming the formal accountability arrangement into a mere fiction. The prevailing opinion is that informal networks do harm to post-communist societies, undermining the accountability of elite and state institutions. The use of the term "informal networks" in public discourse in the Czech Republic is closely connected with the proliferation of conspiracy theories about the hidden misconduct of national elites. The public is suspicious that elites only fake accountability in order to build an image of accountability without being really accountable.

Clientelism or corruption enhanced through informal networks is anathema to accountability. Informal connections and systems of mutual favours can obviously have a dysfunctional effect on accountability systems where elites are constrained within in a relatively narrow circle of people. In this case, networks "kill the competition" and sacrifice quality and accountability on the altar of complicity and elite cohesion. The inclination of informal networks to easily slide into cronyism and corruption is also well known in the Czech Republic. Most Czechs believe that the Czech elites are confined and interlinked by a dense network of mutual favours (Frič 2007, 68). This makes a mere dummy democracy out of the ideological competition and its rules. Czech citizens have a suspicion that their democracy is too elitist (oligarchic) and that elites are just playing the formal accountability game.

Citizens, together with the media, love to create and disseminate conspiracy theories about the elite members of society. For example, the following conspiracy theory emerged in the Czech public discourse during the privatisation of national property in the early 1990s. Václav Klaus, then federal minister of finance and later prime minister and president, was quoted as saying that he does not know how to tell dirty money from clean. Tomáš Ježek, one of main architects of the voucher privatisation scheme[7] and then president of the National Property Fund,[8] attempted to exclude the privatisation process from moral evaluation by repeatedly and publicly asserting that standard laws and norms cannot be applied to the privatisation process and standard laws should only begin to apply *after* the process is over (Reed 1999). Ježek and Klaus thus helped in taking the Czech government's tolerance for corruption for granted. Such public remarks fuelled a widespread conspiracy theory about "the lights having been turned off during the privatisation". According to the latest data from 2008, the majority (65 percent) of citizens believe that the voucher privatisation was a planned fraud by a small group of individuals. This suspicion about an economic collusion of the elites was the favoured conspiracy theory circulated in the Czech Republic in 2008 (Frič 2008, 13).

As shown in the following table, anti-elitist conspiracy theories are widespread throughout Central Europe, while the situation in the Czech Republic is better than in the rest of the region.

The vast majority of Czech citizens harbour serious doubts about the elites' moral qualities and believe that the elites are conspiring against the ordinary citizens. Eighty-four percent of citizens believe that elites owe their positions to connections and corruption, and 85 percent of them believe that elites are only interested in protecting their privileges (Frič 2007, 68).

Table 7.1   Corrupt Politicians, Public Officials, and Business People Create Interconnected Network and Support to Each Other

	strongly/fairly agree
1. Croatia	93
2. Slovenia	92
3. Poland	91
4. Ukraine	91
5. Slovakia	91
6. Bulgaria	90
7. Romania	88
8. Russia	88
9. Lithuania	87
10. Estonia	84
11. Serbia and Montenegro	82
12. Hungary	81
13. Czech Republic	77

84   *Pavol Frič*

The frequent corruption scandals of members of the elite do not have a cathartic impact on public life because their actors usually escape punishment and retain assets that were acquired through illicit activities. Citizens do not perceive corruption scandals as proof of a functioning accountability system but rather as targeted provocations, which are part of a broader competition between informal elite networks. Moreover, most citizens believe that the revealed scandals are only the tip of the iceberg and the elites do not want to allow them the see the rest.[9] In other words, they believe that elites are bad account givers.

CITIZENS FAIL TO BECOME AN INTEGRAL PART OF THE PUBLIC ACCOUNTABILITY SYSTEM

It is no surprise that Czech elites take an equally critical approach to citizens. Elites believe that citizens are not fulfilling their role in the accountability system. This is validated by the finding that most (68 percent) respondents from the ranks of elites accuse citizens of dodging the law whenever possible, and that they are no longer willing to make sacrifices so that our shared future is better (62 percent; see Frič 2007, 71).

The elites point out the citizens' failure as an accountability forum. They question the citizens' right to hold their elites accountable and tell them: "Do not judge our actions because you are just like us". Public respect of the law is the core pillar of the functions of every law-abiding state and also an important indicator of the accountability system standards in society. The nagging question is whether it is possible to interpret the fact that citizens circumvent the law as the moral failure of individuals, or the failure of a system controlled by elites, or indeed even the failure of the elites alone, as they fail to act as role models and act instead as a privileged group above the law, providing a bad example to the common citizen. On the other hand, there is another explanation, which is fairly typical of the Czech Republic.

Table 7.2   To What Extent Do You Agree with the Following Statements Regarding Czech Citizens?

	strongly/fairly agree	
	the citizens	*the elites*
1. People in the Czech Republic only obey the law when it suits them.	81	69
2. Citizens are no longer willing to make sacrifices because of a better common future.	61	60
3. Czechs are keeping mouse and are afraid to raise their voice publicly.	59	60
4. Citizens sometimes slightly rebel but finally they always do what elites asked them to do.	63	68

Czech citizens seem to have adapted to the informal, clientelistic, unaccountable practices of their elites. A majority (59 percent) of citizens consider bribery to be a normal social practice. Most citizens (69 percent) agree that one is best "having a good friend in the right places" (CESES 2008); a patron who can help them to solve problems effectively. This is not surprising because citizens were used to this kind of informal network in the socialist era when elites and the government ensured their political stability by corrupting the general public, buying their loyalty with money and various perks. This "unwritten agreement" between the communist elites representing the state and the citizens could be paraphrased: "You will let us govern quietly and we will let you steal from the state". Further conventional wisdom was, "One must steal from the state or else one steals from one's own family". The level of the Czech Republic's current law enforcement problems suggests that this unwritten pact is still being upheld.

The two-way public–elite complicity was revived in the early 1990s when civic involvement was traded for consumerism. However, the current level of the general public's dissatisfaction with elites suggests that the silent agreement is not working smoothly. While almost everyone could steal in the socialist period, it is not the case in the new system of democracy and market economy. The ordinary citizen cannot become rich through petty offences, such as tax evasion, but elites can still amass a fortune through illicit activities. In socialist times there was a very small gap between the elites and the general public in terms of income or personal property.

Nowadays the number of people with access to unearned income from privatisation and public procurements may seem large, but it is not large enough. The fact that too many people are excluded from these possibilities makes the elites unable to corrupt the citizens the way they did during the socialist era. On the other hand, Czechs are not fearless followers of their leaders in civil society organisations, making these leaders look like generals without armies rather than respected leaders of social movements. Their potential for protest is limited. Citizens are not considered to be a valid part of the accountability system, and neither do they want to be. The courage that is necessary to hold elites accountable is absent. In an unpublished survey in fall 2008, out of a representative random sample of 2,353 Czech Republic citizens aged fifteen to seventy-nine, most of the citizens (56 percent) follow the rule: "One lives best quietly, without standing out, in order to avoid unnecessary trouble" (CESES 2008). This opportunistic attitude to public issues and the acceptance of clientelism as a normal social practice makes the Czech citizen an accomplice to the elites in sustaining an informal anti-accountability system, even if most people would not admit this. As clients, they cannot expect public accountability from their patrons. Indeed, clients should be faithful, believe in their patrons, and not hold them publicly accountable. For this they receive "secured" support from their patrons in case they need it.

CONCLUSIONS

The perspective which focuses our attention on the subjective dimension of accountability as a system of relations and interactions between elites and the general public leads to the surprise finding that not only elites but also citizens themselves are largely responsible for the poor efficiency of the Czech accountability system. They are not strong accountability claimants, nor do they enforce an accountability forum which can successfully deliver a smoothly operated accountability system. Czech citizens feel powerless face-to-face against the unaccountable behaviour of their elites. They do not perceive their correction to be a civic duty, but tend to be impassioned onlookers.[10] Therefore, a large majority of citizens stay away from the accountability system. Generally they have a strong suspicion that their state is corrupt, but on the other hand, they believe that it is not they, the state, that should fight corruption (Šindelářová 2004, 21, esp. 30). Citizens like to criticise their elites for unethical behaviour, but so far they have not taken any dramatic steps to change the situation. They themselves are not accountable because of their acceptance of violations of the law.

It is obvious that the aforementioned "unwritten pact" between the Czech elites and citizens undermines the accountability principles and is a trap from which it is difficult to escape. On the other hand, both the elites and the citizens feel relatively comfortable in this trap. Both sides have invested too much in the system of informal relations, and constructing a real accountability system seems too risky. Respecting the hidden rules of the corrupt game is safe and advantageous for the elites and also, to an extent, for the general public. The elites are not accountable and citizens do not abide by formal rules. Both sides limit their demands on the other side. The fact that the formal accountability system does not work causes little concern. The elites can merely pretend to be accountable, while the general public can excuse their transgressions by pointing to the elites' bad example. It is a comfortable, undemanding environment for both parties. Scandals widely publicised in the media involving corruption and clientelism among the elites, promises by the elites to bring an end to corruption, and emotional public criticisms are hardly more than empty rituals. As both sides, in Ortega y Gasset's (1969) words, fail to fulfil their "historic task", they lose the moral right to criticize the other party for doing the same. By avoiding the obligations that arise from their respective roles within the accountability system, neither side is in a position to hold the other party accountable.

In these conditions, the culture of account giving and account demanding is spreading very slowly. Elites can continue to play their accountability games and not expect any drastic sanctions for exposed misconducts. They remain bad account givers because the citizens remain bad account claimants. This makes a mockery of democracy. Citizens are aware of this, and "democratic" elites are losing legitimacy in their eyes. This increases the chances of a plebiscite leader riding the crest of populist anti-elitism and rallying the general public against their elites. No one can tell whether the plebiscite leader that the masses could "enthrone" will be an enlightened democrat or an extremist, prepared to bury democracy once elected.

NOTES

1. For example, Zdenka Mansfeldová in her description of Czech conditions said: "In the Czech Republic, conditions have been created for social accountability and civil engagement. There is state support for civic engagement in the legislative framework as well as in funding" (Mansfeldová 2006, 32).
2. Understood as people who occupy the top institutional positions at different spheres of societal life (i.e., political, economic, cultural).
3. Therefore, for us the term "accountability" has two basic connotations: "answerability" as the duty of elites, and "enforcement" as the duty and capacity of citizens (Schedler 1999, 14–19).
4. By *informal networks* we understand a set of interpersonal ties that are not sanctioned by a written normative system in an organisation or society.
5. See, for example, the state capture index (Hellman, Jones, and Kaufman 2000).
6. In an informal society: "informal institutions of power and power relationships are stronger and produce different outcomes from what one would expect by observing formal ones" (Mungiu-Pippidi 2002, 84).
7. Voucher privatisation was the main method of privatisation and hallmark of economic transformation in the Czech Republic during the first half of the 1990s.
8. A government body established for the purpose of privatisation of huge assets left behind by the communist state.
9. According to the CVVM survey, 83 percent of citizens are convinced that many scandals are kept under the lid, and 73 percent of them believe that corruption scandals are only the outcome of conflicts between informal networks (Škodová 2008).
10. Most Czechs do not even know what "accountability" means. The same applies to their elites—see Konopásek et al. (2002, 7).

REFERENCES

Bovens, M. 2005. "Public Accountability." In *The Oxford Handbook of Public Management*, ed. E. Ferlie, L. Lynne, and C. Pollitt, 182–208. Oxford: Oxford University Press.

Bovens, M., T. Schillemans, and P. 'T Hart. 2008. "Does Public Accountability Work? An Assessment Tool." *Public Administration* 86 (1): 225–242.

Bowser, D. 2002. "Corruption, Trust, and the Danger to Democratisation in the Former Soviet Union." http://www.transparency.org.ru/CENTER/DOC/article_18.doc.

CESES. 2008. "General Public as a Modernization Actor II." Unpublished survey.

Day, P., and R. Klein. 1987. *Accountabilities: Five Public Services*. London: Tavistock.

Frič, P. 2007. "How to Catch-Up the West: The Confrontation of the Czech Public and Elite Strategies." In *Popular Opposition and Support for Different Types of*

EU Integration, ed. L. Gatnar and D. Lane, 57–74. Prague: Sociologický ústav AVČR.

———. 2008. *Konspirační teorie: Jak vznikají, jakou mají strukturu a proč jim věříme?* Prague: GfK Praha.

Ganev, V. I. 1998. "Notes on Networking in Post-Communist Societies." *East European Constitutional Review* 9 (1/2): 1–7.

Goodin, R. E. 2003. "Democratic Accountability: The Distinctiveness of the Third Sector." *Archives Européenes de Sociologie* XLIV (3): 359–396.

Harmon, M. M. 1995. *Responsibility as Paradox*. Thousand Oaks, CA: Sage.

Hellman, J. S., G. Jones, and D. Kaufman. 2000. "Size the State, Size the Day: State Capture, Corruption and Influence in Transition." The World Bank, Policy Research Working Paper 2444.

Kabele, J. 1992. "Československo na cestě od kapitalismu ke kapitalismu. Pokus o participativní sociologii." *Sociologický časopis* XXVIII (1): 1992.

Karklins, R. 2002. "Typology of Post-Communist Corruption." *Problems of Post-Communism* 40 (July–August): 22–32.

Konopásek, Z., Z. Kusá, T. Stöckelová, T. Vajdová, and L. Zamykalová. 2002. *Public Accountability: Czech National Profile. Interim Report (Workpackage 1), European Research Project CT2001–00076*. Prague: Charles University and Academy of Sciences of the Czech Republic.

Ledeneva, A. V. 1998. *Russia's Economy of Favours*. Cambridge: Cambridge University Press.

———. 2003. "Informal Practices in Changing Societies: Comparing Chinese Guanxi and Russian Blat." London, Centre for the Study of Economic and Social Change in Europe, Working Paper No. 45.

———. 2004. "Ambiguity of Social Networks in Post-Communist Contexts." London, Centre for the Study of Economic and Social Change in Europe, Working Paper No. 48.

Mansfeldová, Z. 2006. "Political and Administrative Accountability in the Czech Republic." In *Participation of Civil Society in New Modes of Governance. The Case of the New Member States*, ed. H. Pleines, 22–34. Bremen: Research Centre for East European Studies.

Maravall, J. M. 1999. "Accountability and Manipulation." In *Democracy, Accountability, and Representation*, ed. A. Przeworski, S. C. Stokes, and B. Manin, 154–196. Cambridge: Cambridge University Press.

Možný, I. 1991. *Proč tak snadno . . . : Některé rodinné důvody sametové revoluce*. Prague: SLON.

Mulgan, R. 2003. *Holding Power to Account: Accountability in Modern Democracies*. Basingstoke: Palgrave.

Mungiu-Pippidi, A. 2002. "Culture of Corruption or Accountability Deficit?" *East European Constitutional Review* 11/12 (Winter/Spring): 80–85. http://www.law.nyu.edu/eecr/vol11_12num4_1/special/pippidi.htm.

Ortega y Gasset, J. 1969. *Úkol naší doby [The Modern Theme]*. Prague: Mladá fronta.

Pollitt, C. 2003. *The Essential Public Manager*. London: Open University Press/McGraw-Hill.

Reed, Q. 1999. "Korupce v privatizaci českou cestou." In *Korupce na český způsob*, ed. P. Frič, 159–204. Prague: GplusG.

Rose, R. 1999. "Living in an Antimodern Society." *East European Constitutional Review* 8 (1/2): 68–75.

Sajó, A. 1998. "Corruption, Clientelism, and the Future of the Constitutional State in Eastern Europe." *East European Constitutional Review* 7 (Spring): 54–63.

Schedler, A. 1999. "Conceptualizing Accountability." In *The Self-Restraining State: Power and Accountability in New Democracies*, ed. A. Schedler, L. Diamond, and M. F. Flatner, 13–28. Boulder, CO: Lynne Rienner Publishers.

Schmitter, P. C. 1999. "The Limits of Horizontal Accountability." *In The Self-Restraining State: Power and Accountability in New Democracies,* ed. A. Schedler, L. Diamond, and M. F. Flatner, 59–62. Boulder, CO: Lynne Rienner Publishers.

Šindelářová, M. 2004. *Corruption Climate in Central and Eastern Europe.* Prague: GfK Prague.

Škodová, M. 2008. "Postoje k aférám v politickém a veřejném životě." http://www.cvvm.cas.cz/upl/zpravy/100673s_ps70402.pdf.

Stark, D., and L. Bruszt. 1998. *Postsocialist Pathways: Transforming Politics and Property in East Central Europe.* Cambridge: Cambridge University Press.

Tucker, A. 2000. "Networking." *East European Constitutional Review* 9 (Winter/Spring): 107–112.

Uslaner, E. M. 2004. "Coping and Social Capital: The Informal Sector and the Democratic Transition." Paper prepared for the Conference on "Unlocking Human Potential: Linking the Formal and Informal Sectors," Helsinki, Finland, 17–18 September.

8 Non-Profit Organisations, Democratisation, and New Forms of Accountability
A Preliminary Evaluation

Taco Brandsen, Mirjan Oude Vrielink,
Thomas Schillemans, and Eelco van Hout

INTRODUCTION

Many non-profit organisations that work with public funding are subject to accountability mechanisms imposed by national or local governments. This is the traditional type of accountability in which the non-profit organisation is accountable to a single principal. Recent years have seen the rise of various new forms of accountability, which, though known by various names (for example, "social", "horizontal", "downward"), share the notion that the non-profit organisation is responsible to various principals or stakeholders. These new forms are seen as more democratic and more in keeping with the non-profit character of the organisations involved. Specifically, they are thought to give citizens a direct influence on service delivery by these organisations, whereas they would otherwise only be able to influence them indirectly through representative democratic institutions.

In this chapter, we examine whether this potential for democratisation is effectively realised. Do citizens really get a voice in service delivery? Our findings are the result of an extensive comparative research project in seven policy fields (higher education, health care, elderly care, social housing, welfare, child care, and care for the handicapped) where services are primarily delivered by the non-profit sector. On the basis of both qualitative and quantitative material, we describe how new forms of accountability take shape on the ground and whether they can fulfil the significant promise with which they are imbued. Our disciplinary backgrounds are in public administration and this perspective will inform our findings.

The evidence suggests that, while many new forms of accountability have been adopted with enthusiasm, their effects are limited. They offer useful input for organisational learning and give clients a greater say in day-to-day affairs of service providers, but on the whole they tend to strengthen the influence of already powerful interests in the providers' environment. This means that accountability can make a useful contribution to current systems of governance, but that ambitions should be modest.

CONCEPTUALISING ACCOUNTABILITY

The notion of accountability defies easy interpretation. The academic literature features a variety of different conceptual approaches of accountability. However, at a basic level of analysis, many authors agree upon a minimal definition.

In a narrow sense, accountability can be understood as the interaction between an accountor (person or organisation) and accountee (Pollitt 2003, 89; Kumar 2003), in which the former's behaviour is evaluated and judged by the latter, in light of possible consequences (see Day and Klein 1987; Scott 2000; Mulgan 2003). Accountability, as it is understood here, refers to the *process* by which actors provide reasons for their actions (Dunn 1999, 335). Such a process can be deconstructed as follows (Schillemans 2007):

1. There is a relationship between the accountor (X) and one or several accountees (Y).
2. X needs to explain him- or herself to Y.
3. Information about the performance of X passes to Y, either because X offers it freely or Y seeks out the information him- or herself.
4. Y passes judgement on the basis of the available information.
5. Y acts accordingly.

Starting from that basic conceptualisation, various interpretations are possible, depending on how each of the elements is defined:

1. Following the traditional conceptualisation of accountability in theories of public administration, Y tends to be equated with government, a single actor with hierarchical power over X. In the debate over alternative types of accountability, Y is often conceived as a set of multiple stakeholders who are in a non-hierarchical relationship with X.
2. According to some interpretations, one can only properly speak of accountability when the need for justification is based on mandatory requirements, for example, within a system of formal supervision. Others also include informal and voluntary expressions of justification, based on social compulsion (reputation), market position, and/ or inner feelings of moral responsibility.
3. Interpretations of accountability can range from broad ones that include any form of information passed on to Y, to narrow ones, where only a certain type of information is considered. Some authors include only institutionalised forms of information exchange in the definition, whereas others also incorporate informal processes. Another issue is whether accountability is restricted to exchanges of information that take the form of a dialogue (that is, two-sided communication) with a known and visible audience, or is taken to include

92   *Taco Brandsen, et al.*

any form of exchange, including the dispersal of information to a general public that includes "hidden stakeholders".

4. Different normative criteria can be applied to the performance of X. These can range from the realisation of precisely defined intentions (for example, the effectiveness in delivering the promised volume of services) directly to the anticipation of broad external effects (for example, the ways in which the organisations contribute to global social justice).

5. In case of failure, sanctions may vary from formal disapproval to tightened regulations, fines, discharge of management, or even the termination of the organisation. As Hood et al. (1999, 47) indicate: "It emanates with the 'ability to shame', escalates to lighter weapons such as certificates or formal (dis)approvals and culminates in the 'nuclear weapon' of liquidation". From a legal perspective, it is imperative that Y has sufficient investigative and sanctioning powers to hold X to account. The literature on accountability often focuses on the "heavy weapons" amongst the formal sanctions and the adoption of performance standards (see Przeworski, Stokes, and Manin 1999; Strøm 2000; Paul 1992; Broadbent, Dietrich, and Laughlin 1996; Besley and Ghatak 2003).

BROADENING ACCOUNTABILITY

Recent years have seen a surge of interest in alternative forms of accountability. These have been described with such diverse terms as *downward accountability* (Verschuere et al. 2006), *citizen accountability* (Paul 1992), and *societal accountability* (Smulovitz and Peruzzotti 2003). These of course overlap with the concepts of social audit and social accounting central to this book. Although each concept means something slightly different, two threads seem to run through all of these concepts.

Multiple Stakeholders

In the context of public administration, accountability has usually been interpreted through the lens of economically inspired principal–agent theories. The assumptions behind such theories is that one actor, the principal, needs instruments to encourage another actor, the agent, to act in the principal's interests because the interests of the principal and agent diverge. Accountability is seen as the process through which the agent accounts to the principal. As the agent almost invariably has more information than the principal, additional mechanisms are needed to uncover the necessary information. In more advanced theoretical work, the option of multiple principals has been proposed, which does more justice to the complex environments of non-profit organisations delivering services.

Rather than assuming that an actor X is responsible only to one principal (for example, central government), it is suggested that there are *multiple stakeholders* who are affected by the activities of the organisation and to whom the organisation therefore has a responsibility. These are not just governments or clients, but governments and clients and others. Of course, this makes the relationship between principals and agents far more complex. When the interests of principals diverge, the actor is expected to follow the principal whose incentives are the strongest. The implication is that issues of accountability cannot be solved simply by strengthening the position of one principal: The overall configuration must be taken into account.

Performance Criteria

A second element of alternative forms of accountability is the *extension of the range of performance criteria*, towards "new" ethical concerns such as social equality and environmental concerns. This touches upon the broader issue of the normative content of accountability, a subject on which principal–agent theory tells us very little. Steinberg (2008, 57) notes that:

> PA theory is positive, not normative. There are many principals involved in nonprofit organizations and contracts with outsiders. Principals in some roles or locations within chained problems are agents in other roles and locations. Positive theories are assessed by determining whether they are internally-consistent and consistent with empirical observations. By these criteria, PA theory is developing nicely, and the growth of applications to nonprofit settings is commendable. But for normative questions like "who should nonprofits be accountable to?" or "who should have the power to act as a principal, setting contract terms?" we apply different criteria. PA theory can at best identify structures of control and communication networks that are socially efficient, but efficiency is a limited guide in this normative setting.

Broadening the accountability concept raises questions about the relative distribution of power between stakeholders. As Steinberg (2008, 59–60) observes:

> Should the organization be accountable to all its legitimate stakeholders in the same way, or should accountability take different forms for different classes of stakeholders? What does accountability mean—is the organization accountable for delivering promised outputs, sharing appropriate information, providing a meaningful member voice in managerial decisions, or following processes that reward certain behaviors and punish others?

Changes in governance impact upon the relative distribution of power, which in turn affects the use of performance criteria. For instance, when funding is provided on a contract basis, this may imply a shift of power in favour of contract managers, perhaps to the detriment of trustees and clients. In turn, if the range of performance criteria is to be extended, that may require a change in the underlying structure of power.

Expectations

The expectations attached to new forms of accountability are huge. Its proponents regard them as an improvement over traditional, "vertical" accountability for two reasons. First, regular democratic processes are too slow and distant to convey their judgement on the quality of services (Goetz and Jenkins 2001; McCandless 2001). New kinds of accountability can be organised closer to home and lead to more direct feedback. Second, the growth in size and complexity of public administration has led to a fragmented system of public governance, which is ill-adapted to hierarchical models of accountability and calls for an accountability regime that is more decentralised (Braithwaite 1999), features more mutual relations between accountors and accountees (Behn 2001; Roberts 2001) and/or operates on the basis of a network (Harlow and Rawlings 2007; Papadopoulos 2007).

The assumption is that new kinds of accountability will empower stakeholders, including citizens, and usher a more direct form of democracy. But these are theoretical arguments. It is clear what new kinds of accountability could do, but does it actually happen? It is this question that we have addressed in our project.

CONTEXT AND METHODOLOGY

The Context: Welfare State Services in the Netherlands

The context of our project was the Dutch non-profit sector, which is among the largest in the world (Burger and Dekker 2001). The Netherlands have a welfare state where for historical reasons non-profit organisations have traditionally played a major role in service delivery. Especially from the second half of the twentieth century onwards, massive public funds were channelled into the sector, which as a result grew exponentially (Brandsen and Van de Donk 2009). Not surprisingly, public funding came with regulation and control, bringing service-delivering non-profits within the public sector. As such, they were later also subject to public management reforms that introduced (quasi-) market elements into the governance of service delivery, for example, by allocating funding on a contract basis and increasing the degree of competition over funding. Consequently many organisations are now best described as "hybrids", because they have elements of civil society, the state, and the market (Dekker 2004; Brandsen, Van de Donk, and Putters 2005). This applies to a broad range of providers in fields such as health care, elderly care, education, and social housing.

This process of hybridisation is a context in which the issue of accountability has moved centre stage. During the 1990s, there was a resurgence of interest in traditional accountability as government grappled with the multitude of arms' length agencies and quasi markets which it had itself created. Later, the debate became more complex as the design of accountability became one of the arenas where issues over governance were played out. Many of the organisations in question argued that they could organise accountability in ways that were far more effective than traditional, vertical accountability. The implication was that, if it could be proven those alternatives were equally or more effective, government supervision could be relaxed and they could operate with a greater degree of autonomy. That raises the question of how new kinds of accountability function not only as a technical but also a political issue.

Methodology

The aim of our project was to describe and compare the ways in which service providers make themselves accountable to their stakeholders. The project therefore proceeded over three stages:

1. We carried out a literature review on non-profit organisations in the fields of social housing, hospital care, elderly care, domiciliary care, social work, vocational education, higher applied education, and child care. This included both official documentation and previous studies into these fields (a number of them conducted by the present authors themselves). At the time, various studies were beginning to emerge which examined accountability in the various fields. However, these tended to focus on single fields and/or specific instruments. The aim of the literature review was to bring all the available evidence together. The texts were scanned on the basis of the previously developed categorisation of instruments and were used to see which instruments were used by whom and for what formal purpose.

2. We conducted twelve interviews, which mapped different manifestations of accountability within the different fields, as well as the historical and strategic motives behind their use. The respondents were both board members of federations of service providers and managers of service-providing organisations. These were transcribed, then coded and analysed on the basis of the previously developed categorisation of instruments. The interviews had a twofold purpose. First, they were intended to add missing information about which instruments were used. Second, and more importantly, they were used to understand the context in which these instruments

were used. With this information, it became possible to construct a comprehensive picture of the total configuration of instruments within each policy field.

3. Based on these data, we analysed the results of a survey of 137 service providers across all fields. The respondents were managers or their deputies. The survey measured the statistical distribution of different instruments (given that they were in a policy field, by how many organisations?). In addition, we asked respondents about their attitudes and beliefs regarding the instruments they used: Why did they use them, did they have added value, what were their effects? It must be stressed that this does not amount to measurement of the actual effects of the instruments, only their perceived effects. Although it would have been fascinating to measure the actual effects, this is methodologically complicated and, given the breadth of our study, it was a challenge for which we had insufficient resources.

THE EMPIRICAL EVIDENCE: A SUMMARY OF RESULTS

In this section we will discuss the nature of new kinds of accountability as it emerged from the literature review, interviews, and survey. We will describe the findings by way of the five elements of accountability described earlier:

1. the relationship between accountor and accountees
2. the extent to which justification is formally required
3. the nature of the information exchange
4. performance assessment
5. sanctions

Manifestations of the Accountability Relationship

The relationship between accountor and accountees is manifested through certain instruments. According to our sources, new kinds of accountability were manifested through the following means:

- Codes of conduct: signed statements detailing rules of expected behaviour and procedures in case of violation. For example, they may require signatories to establish a formal complaints procedure for their clients.
- Statements produced by the organisation describing its performance, for example, in annual reports, web sites, and newsletters.
- Comparative analysis in which the organisation's performance is compared to that of others, for example, through benchmarking.
- Stakeholder panels: These can be restricted to clients and their representatives (for example, patients and parents of the mentally

handicapped); alternatively, they represent a wide variety of interested parties (for example, all residents and business interests in a neighbourhood).

- Peer review: Organisations write self-evaluations, which are then assessed by colleagues or at least by people in a similar profession. The committee points out flaws and presents recommendations to improve performance.
- Independent internal bodies capable of critical assessment, such as an internal supervisory board or ombudsman.

Formal Requirements

Some instruments were mandatory in all policy fields. Codes of conduct had been included as compulsory elements of membership in the leading umbrella organisations of non-profit service providers. Having independent internal supervisory boards was a common element in the codes, making them mandatory by implication, as refusal to sign the code would result in suspension of membership. Other instruments were obligatory only within specific policy fields. In some instances, such instruments explicitly replaced supervision by the responsible ministry and were therefore mandatory. The prime example was in higher education, where universities and vocational schools were required to submit to peer reviews on a fixed-term basis (usually every four years).

Generally, however, instruments were adopted without any formal obligation. As a result, there was a lot of variation within policy fields or even within large organisations in which local branches partially organised their own processes of accountability. A number of service providers indicated that accountability at the organisational level was inextricably linked to their market position. This was clearest in vocational training, where schools depended strongly on the co-operation of employers for traineeships and input in the curriculum. The opportunities offered by employers before and after training are vital to the schools' reputation and indirectly to its market position. It has therefore been customary for them to engage in dialogue, well before this was associated with accountability. Generally, the dependence of service providers on partners in local networks has made the exchange of information a natural part of their production process.

What clearly emerged was that manifestations of accountability are linked to the dominant mechanisms of co-ordination to which the organisations are subject. We will explore the implications of this in the following.

The Nature of the Information Exchange

Nearly all organisations studied invested both in dialogues with their stakeholders and in communication of information to the general public. Some pressing issues arose out of the available data:

- While some stakeholders were easy to access (other service providers, local authorities), it proved more difficult to get in touch with others, because they were unknown to the organisation and/or were not capable of communicating at the more abstract level at which professionals wished to address them.
- It is doubtful whether the representatives of clients were actually in touch with their constituency. There are documented cases where it turned out that the majority of clients were unaware of, or violently disagreed with, commitments made on their behalf by their supposed representatives.
- It has been noted that stakeholders felt burdened by continually being involved in decisions over service delivery. Attendance at stakeholders meetings tended to be low, except at moments of public outrage. Certain types of stakeholders were systematically under-represented.
- Many organisations accounted for themselves by informal means, taking the form of chats, phone calls, and chance meetings. A number of respondents expressed concern that governments would not recognise such unstructured and unregistered processes as valid.

The Assessment of Performance

There is a host of criteria against which the performance of an organisation could be tested: efficiency, effectiveness, reliability, technical quality, democratic quality, integrity, sustainability, and many more. Each of these criteria is open to different interpretations and can have different meanings at different levels of analysis. Sometimes these are all lumped together under the label of "good governance". Certain types of stakeholders tended to emphasise different sets of criteria. For example, internal supervisory boards were inclined to stress financial considerations, while clients tend to be interested primarily in the practical aspects of service delivery relating to personal experience.

Sanctioning Power

Only a relatively small number of instruments used by the organisations were tied to formal sanctioning powers. Internal supervisory boards can ultimately suspend or fire managers. Violations of codes of conduct can be punished by the suspension of membership. However, the use of such drastic sanctions is quite rare. They apply to outright scandals, but they appear to be too blunt to sanction "regular" mismanagement. At least, sanctions were very rarely used and we must assume that this does not simply reflect the excellence of management.

An alternative mechanism for sanctioning is the power to "name and shame". Transparency about performance would cause a loss of reputation for bad performers and encourage them to improve their act. Alternatively, good performance can be rewarded through "name and fame" procedures that allow organisations a top spot in the rankings. Reports about the effectiveness of this mechanism have been contradictory: Some deny it, some do not. It has been noted that, although such reputation mechanisms are designed to be targeted at single organisations, the effect of negative publicity is often to discredit the entire field. However, what clearly emerges is that the instruments of accountability are most powerful when connected to other mechanisms of co-ordination. Specifically, this occurs when governments or markets intervene, for example, when the information is picked up by formal supervisors or when it encourages exit by clients.

Rather than step back, it appears that the introduction of new forms of accountability has in some cases *intensified* efforts by authorities to intervene in the affairs of autonomous service providers. The availability of more and better structured information about performance increases the knowledge of all stakeholders, including government. What makes government different is that it actually has the means to enforce its views. While new forms of accountability can theoretically be divorced from traditional ("vertical") accountability, this is often not the case in practice. This is a positive disincentive for service providers to release sensitive information.

In fields with a high extent of competition, information released to stakeholders can have a significant effect on market shares. This was most noticeable in higher and vocational education, where good ratings translated directly into higher student numbers. This mechanism of course depends on clients having a real choice—not the case, for instance, in social housing—and whether the information about performance is presented in an intelligible format. In higher education, national media have taken it upon themselves to publish annual rankings and make available data on performance more accessible. This is effective because it piggybacks on the market mechanism, through which the bulk of public funding is distributed: When students choose the school of their choice, the money goes with them.

CONCLUSIONS

New kinds of accountability potentially constitute an avenue towards democratic renewal and the possibility of rectifying the flaws of traditional accountability to governments, potentially even acting as a substitute. They could theoretically give citizens more control over the services they receive.

On the basis of the empirical evidence in this study, we have reached the following conclusions:

- New kinds of accountability come in many different forms, ranging from raw data on performance to comparative analysis, from communication towards a general public, to a dialogue with known partners.

- Most have been adopted voluntarily, some on a mandatory basis as part of a system of enforced self-regulation. There is a striking variety among organisations within policy fields.
- Much of the activity associated with accountability is informal, disorganised, and unrecorded. Attempts to involve stakeholders in institutionalised settings are only partially successful.
- Accountability mostly relies on informal powers of sanction, which are most effective when connected to other mechanisms (notably hierarchy or competition).

It is unlikely that alternative forms of accountability will ever be accepted as a substitute for traditional, vertical accountability. Some of the most significant communication with stakeholders (especially with individual citizens) takes place in schoolyards, on streets, in corridors, and in the margins of meetings. Such processes are unstructured and unrecorded. This does not make them any less effective, perhaps the more so, but it implies that such forms of accountability are also opaque and that their efficacy is largely a matter of faith. To compensate for this, organisations tend to supplement them with formal procedures modelled on traditional associational democracies (for example, an official stakeholder forum with an agenda and minutes) in order to satisfy bureaucratic requirements. These formal procedures usually complement (rather than substitute) other kinds of accountability. The net result is that rather than relieving the pressure for accountability, new kinds of accountability tend to make it worse.

Many of the organisations we examined indicated that they felt burdened by an increasing amount of paperwork. Staff members were required to comply not only with more but also with increasingly contradictory criteria. These are symptoms of what Koppell has aptly termed "multiple accountabilities disorder" (Koppell 2005). The fatigue of staff members was mirrored by stakeholders, especially individual clients, who showed increasing disinterest in being consulted and involved.

Another difficulty with new forms of accountability stems from the asymmetry of information between professional staff members and citizens. Individual clients face a knowledge gap when issues are discussed about which they have virtually no expertise. This is why their input generally concerns practical aspects of service delivery, related to personal experience, which managers tended to consider relevant as expressions of their clients' attitudes, but only of marginal relevance to decisions which they felt were more important. This confirms the findings of earlier research that distinguished between expert and experiential knowledge. The stakeholders who offer the most valuable input, in the eyes of professionals, are other professionals. The latter usually represent government departments, other non-profits, or commercial businesses. Not only do they speak the language of their counterparts, they also have the power to impose sanctions by withholding resources. For instance, local authorities can withhold permits and funds; other non-profits can refuse to collaborate where their co-operation is needed to make projects successful; businesses can withdraw training positions and funds. In other words, they can back up voice with exit or hierarchy. By comparison, citizens often have little to offer. As a result, new forms of accountability intended to strengthen the position of citizens may actually weaken it. However, they do have certain benefits compared to traditional accountability. Clients can express themselves more directly, even if it is about practical issues that professionals look down upon. Since more information on performance is generated and more stakeholders are giving feedback, there is potential for organisational learning.

Whether one considers new forms of accountability a success or a failure is, quite simply, a question of expectations. New forms of accountability have been invested with highly idealistic conceptions of democratisation and citizen involvement. Many people assume that stakeholders will jump at the chance of being involved. Against such high expectations, new instruments were bound to disappoint, especially when they were expected to have an impact immediately after their introduction. Our evidence shows that more modest and realistic ambitions may be in order. Reinventing accountability will take time.

REFERENCES

Behn, R. D. 2001. *Rethinking Democratic Accountability*. Washington, DC: Brookings Institution Press.
Besley, T., and M. Ghatak. 2003. "Incentives, Choice and Accountability in the Provision of Public Services." *Oxford Review of Economic Policy* 19:235–249.
Braithwaite, J. 1999. "Accountability and Governance under the New Regulatory State." *Australian Journal of Public Administration* 58:90–93.
Brandsen, T., and W. Van de Donk. 2009. "The Third Sector and the Policy Process in the Netherlands: A Study in Invisible Ink." In *Handbook on Third Sector Policy in Europe: Multi-Level Processes and Organised Civil Society*, ed. J. Kendall, 140–158. Cheltenham: Edward Elgar.
Brandsen, T., W. Van de Donk, and K. Putters. 2005. "Griffins or Chameleons? Hybridity as a Permanent and Inevitable Characteristic of the Third Sector." *International Journal of Public Administration* 28 (9/10): 749–765.
Broadbent, J., M. Dietrich, and R. Laughlin. 1996. "The Development of Principal–Agent, Contracting and Accountability Relationships in the Public Sector. Conceptual and Cultural Problems." *Critical Perspectives on Accounting* 7:259–284.
Burger, A., and P. Dekker. 2001. *The Nonprofit Sector in the Netherlands*. The Hague: Social and Cultural Planning Bureau.
Day, P., and R. Klein. 1987. *Accountabilities: Five Public Services*. London: Tavistock Publications.
Dekker, P. 2004. "The Netherlands: From Private Initiatives to Non-Profit Hybrids and Back?" In *The Third Sector in Europe*, ed. A. Evers and J.-L. Laville, 144–165. Cheltenham: Edward Elgar.

102   *Taco Brandsen, et al.*

Dunn, D. D. 1999. "Mixing Elected and Non-Elected Officials in Democratic Policy Making: Fundamentals of Accountability and Responsibility." In *Democracy, Accountability, and Representation*, ed. A. Przeworski, S. Stokes, and B. Manin, 297–325. Cambridge: Cambridge University Press.

Dunn, J. 1999. "Situating Democratic Political Accountability." In *Democracy, A Accountability, and Representation*, ed. A. Przeworski, S. Stokes, and B. Manin, 329–344. Cambridge: Cambridge University Press.

Goetz, A. M., and R. Jenkins. 2001. "Hybrid Forms of Accountability. Citizen Engagement in Institutions of Public-Sector Oversight in India." *Public Management Review* 3:363–383.

Harlow, C., and R. Rawlings. 2007. "Promoting Accountability in Multilevel Governance: A Network Approach." *European Law Journal* 14 (4): 542–562.

Hood, C., O. Scott, O. James, G. Jones, and T. Travers. 1999. *Regulation inside Government: Waste-Watchers, Quality Police, and Sleazebusters.* Oxford: Oxford University Press.

Koppell, J. 2005. "Pathologies of Accountability: ICANN and the Challenge of 'Multiple Accountabilities Disorder.'" *Public Administration Review* 65 (1): 94–108.

Kumar, S. 2003. *Accountability: A Qualitative Study of Relationships between the Public Sector, the Voluntary Sector and Users of Health and Welfare Services in the Context of Purchase of Service Contracting.* Birmingham: University of Aston.

McCandless, H. E. 2001. *A Citizen's Guide to Public Accountability. Changing the Relationship between Citizens and Authorities.* Victoria, BC: Trafford.

Mulgan, R. 2003. *Holding Power to Account. Accountability in Modern Democracies.* Basingstoke: Palgrave MacMillan.

Papadopoulos, Y. 2007. "Problems of Democratic Accountability in Network and Multilevel Governance." *European Law Journal* 14 (4): 469–486.

Paul, S. 1992. "Accountability in Public Services: Exit, Voice and Control." *World Development* 20:1047–1060.

Pollitt, C. 2003. *The Essential Public Manager.* London: Open University Press/ McGraw-Hill.

Przeworski, A., S. Stokes, and B. Manin. 1999. *Democracy, Accountability, and Representation.* Cambridge: Cambridge University Press.

Roberts, J. 2001. "Trust and Control in Anglo-American Systems of Corporate Governance: The Individualising and Socialising Effects of Processes of Accountability." *Human Relations* 54:1547–1572.

Schillemans, T. 2007. *Verantwoording in de Schaduw van de Macht.* The Hague: Lemma.

Scott, C. 2000. "Accountability in the Regulatory State." *Journal of Law and Society* 27:38–60.

Smulovitz, C., and E. Peruzzotti. 2003. "Societal and Horizontal Controls. Two Cases of a Fruitful Relationship." In *Democratic Accountability in Latin America*, ed. S. Mainwaring and C. Welna, 309–331. Oxford: Oxford University Press.

Steinberg, R. 2008. "Principal-Agent Theory and Nonprofit Accountability." Indiana University Purdue University Indianapolis (IUPUI), Department of Economics Working Paper Series, Working Paper No. 2008–03, 1–70.

Strøm, K. 2000. "Delegation and Accountability in Parliamentary Democracies." *European Journal of Political Research* 37:261–289.

Verschuere, B., K. Verhoest, F. Meyers, and B. G. Peters. 2006. "Accountability and Accountability Arrangements in Public Agencies." In *Autonomy and Regulation: Coping with Agencies in the Modern State*, ed. T. Christensen and P. Laegreid, 268–300. Cheltenham: Edward Elgar.

9 An Accountability Model and Self-Assessment Initiative for Third Sector Organisations in Hungary

Monika Molnár

INTRODUCTION

Civil society can be viewed as a composition of people who are connected neither for profit making nor for governmental power, but for some public purpose. In the last decades civil society has undergone a "global associational revolution" (Salamon et al. 1999), meaning that its non-profit and non-governmental organisations have grown in number, significance, and visibility. Moreover, civil society and its activities have become essential factors in democratisation, and its actors are expected to keep both public and private institutions accountable and promote their "good governance". However, it is argued in this chapter that voluntary organisations (VOs) are themselves not yet properly transparent and accountable for their own actions and operations, which questions the legitimacy and effectiveness of their watchdog activities, as well as their ability to act as a strong public voice.

Political change in the early 1990s brought about a "rebirth" of the Hungarian third sector. Since then, the sector has faced various challenges in the form of changing governmental regulations, transformation of the local and global market environment, and changing expectations concerning their operations, management, and governance practices. The so-called "non-profit accountability movement" is a recent phenomenon inside the Hungarian non-profit world, leaving the actors and organisations of the sector puzzled; nevertheless, they are being urged to make preparations to meet these new challenges.

Accession to the European Union, contracting out of public services, access to foreign funds, non-profit engagement in watchdog and advocacy activities, and spoiled public trust all have contributed to the changes and continuous developments of the Hungarian third sector. Accordingly, accountability has become a critical issue in the management and governance of the sector's organisations; however, there are still no frameworks or initiatives either in theory or in practice to address this issue. So, it is argued that the Hungarian third sector should develop and adapt its own accountability standards, and that the organisations should align their activities with the recommendations of these initiatives in order to meet both local and international requirements. Therefore, the author developed and tested an accountability tool that is introduced in this chapter. The implications of the model for theory, policy, and practice are also considered.

THE GENERAL NON-PROFIT ACCOUNTABILITY STANDARDS (GNAS): A HUNGARIAN INITIATIVE

The traditions of civil society in Hungary reach back to the 1800s. However, after the Second World War—during the socialist era—the state demobilised the real self-organising processes of society and the number of VOs fell. At the end of the 1980s more and more VOs were established, gradually becoming the primary agents of transformation, and the sector's huge expansion in the beginning of the 1990s shows that society always had a vital need to self-organise.

There has been significant quantitative and qualitative development in the Hungarian third sector since then, along with the improvement of policymaking regarding the civil sphere. The growing numbers of VOs and their increased engagement in activities related to the public sphere show that the third sector has found its place in the Hungarian society. However:

> the gradual process of decentralization and partnership is still in an early phase in Hungary. The system of redistribution is not transparent and there is no democratic control. The sharing of knowledge forms, the monitoring system and practice do not work. There is no strong and independent civil sector, most of the civil associations belong to local or national governments. All the development projects depend on political decisions. (Kelemen, Kovách, and Kristóf 2006, 51)

Well-designed accountability mechanisms act as checks against abuses of power; they increase openness and professionalism and enhance ethical conduct that are all crucial in order for VOs to gain and maintain public trust. In transitional societies such as Hungary VOs, in contrast to similar organisations in western countries, are considered not as a "symptom or mechanism of the existence of civil society, but rather as essential agents of its creation" (Osborne et al. 2005, 771), so enhancing accountability may have even greater significance in societal development. Moreover, as far as the function of civil society is concerned, VOs play the role—in addition to mediating between the citizens and the state or participating in policymaking, for instance—of maintaining the mechanisms that hold the government and the market accountable by the public (Cohen and Arato 1992; Osborne et al. 2005). This crucial role may only be fulfilled if VOs are themselves accountable. Accordingly, introducing accountability mechanisms into the Hungarian third sector, like the one presented in this chapter, may result in significantly strengthening the sector and civil society itself. This is explored further in this chapter.

The GNAS Framework and its Factors

In the development of the proposed accountability tool a methodology based on triangulation (including extensive document analyses, series of interviews and testing with VO representatives supplemented by interviews with other experts of the field, and observations) applying iterations has been used.

The development of the general non-profit accountability standards (GNAS) tool was accomplished in two stages. During the first stage, which lasted for a year, a global analysis was carried out by the author, including a study of international accountability initiatives and applicable Hungarian legislation. This was supplemented by a number of in-depth interviews with experts in the field. Based on the expert analysis of these various existing legal frameworks and other related mechanisms governing VOs, and also investigation into the numerous international accountability guidelines and standards (both non-profit and for-profit), the GNAS framework was worked out (depicted in Figure 9.1) for Hungarian VOs. As the sector is heterogeneous and its organisations vary considerably, the starting point in drafting the GNAS tool was that it should not aim to regulate the organisations' operations in detail. In other words, the elaborated initiative is principle-based. Moreover, as the sector can be characterised by diversity, and as each organisation creates value through its distinctive features, these differences have been taken into consideration as well. The second stage of the investigation, which was again carried out by the author, lasted for several months and included the testing of the initiative (outlined later in the third section of this chapter), the evaluation of the testing, and the revision and finalising process of the tool.

The GNAS framework can be categorised as one that aims to evaluate an organisation as a whole. As for the type of evaluation, it tends to focus on processes by making the implicit assumption that if they are performed well, then certain outcomes will follow. Data collection for the evaluation includes both quantitative and qualitative methods, and the standards applied are primarily absolute ones (Cutt and Murray 2000). The GNAS framework defines six main prescriptive standards of non-profit accountability with corresponding criteria and guidelines that show how the standards can be met. These standards are a set of core requirements with fundamental principles that define what may be considered as sound practice for accountable operations. Therefore, the extent to which an organisation is accountable to its stakeholders can be "measured" by how well, if at all, the different standards and their criteria and guidelines are met. On the other hand, given the heterogeneity of the sector, the GNAS naturally cannot be followed in the same manner in all of their parts by all of the sector's organisations. Considering, for example, the size of an organisation, its maturity and character, whether its operations are conducted as a foundation or as an association, its financial resources, or any other aspects relevant in this context, partial compliance or non-compliance may be justified by organisational peculiarities. However, moral considerations require that the standards and their guidelines be applied, which implies that an organisation must generally comply with the standards or explain any deviations (see later in this section the GNAS self-assessment questionnaire).

The GNAS briefly are as follows (see also Molnár 2008):

1. *Mission and Program—Organisational Integrity.* The corresponding criteria and guidelines address issues such as the organisation's mission statement (its form, accessibility, revision); organisational and operational regulations (existence, publicity, enforcement); strategic planning and goals; conformity with local and international laws, regulations, and guidelines; regulation of activities and programs, consistency, and effectiveness (monitoring); ensuring equity, equal opportunity, diversity, participation, and sustainability.
2. *Governance—Governing Board.* The corresponding criteria and guidelines address issues such as composition of the governing board (elected, volunteer, independent, active members, serving without compensation); responsibilities and duties of the board; conduct of

Figure 9.1   Framework of the general non-profit accountability standards (GNAS).

the board (policies, regular meetings having a quorum, preventing conflicts of interest); responsible, impartial, and fair governance.

3. *Finances—Financial Management.* The corresponding criteria and guidelines address issues such as regulating the financial management and administration (various policies, rules, formalities, restrictions); compliance with a diverse array of legal and regulatory requirements (for example, conducting reviews and reports); financial planning (for example, preparing the budget); structure of revenues and expenditures (for example, regulating the overhead and administration costs); supervision (monitoring, auditing).

4. *Fundraising.* The corresponding criteria and guidelines address issues such as fundraising planning and policies; consistency with the mission, goals, and organisational capacities; accurate and written agreements and recordings; activities and information disclosure maintained on a foundation of truthfulness, accurateness, and responsible stewardship; good donor relationship, privacy, adequate registration, and recording of funds.

5. *Human Resource Management Practices.* The corresponding criteria and guidelines address issues such as human resource policies (its form, principles, scope, contents); clear, performable, and communicated expectations, and corresponding performance evaluation and appraisal systems; adequate incentives; promoting volunteering and employee participation.

6. *Public Policy and Affairs—Communication to the Public.* The corresponding criteria and guidelines address issues such as communicational activities and information disclosure (external–internal communication, PR, communicational channels, and materials); accessibility, responsiveness, and openness; public benefit, interest representation, public policy, and advocacy activities (and their regulations); and stakeholder participation.

THE SELF-ASSESSMENT QUESTIONNAIRE

With the aim of designing a self-assessment tool that tests the compliance or non-compliance with the proposed accountability standards and their criteria, a structured questionnaire together with a methodology for its assessment were developed (see GNAS Questionnaire, GNAS Scoresheet, and GNAS Star).

The compilation of the complex questionnaire, the determination of its structure, and the number of questions, along with the composition of questions, followed the principles and requirements listed here:

- The questionnaire was designed to test the compliance or non-compliance with the accountability standards, should be applicable to audit the operations of VOs on the basis of the given criteria and guidelines (GNAS framework).

- The questionnaire should assess all the requirements comprised in the accountability standards and guidelines.
- When assessing the compliance with each of the accountability standards, the number and the type of questions should reflect the relative importance of each standard in the relation system of accountability (see Ebrahim 2003; Farkas and Molnár 2005).
- Given the heterogeneity of the sector, flexible application of the questionnaire should be ensured by providing space for explaining deviations justified by organisational peculiarities.

While constructing the questionnaire, the requirements of standardisation and measurability were also taken into consideration. The questionnaire is altogether ten pages long, listing mainly closed questions assessing the compliance with the specific criteria and guidelines. The questions include multiple-choice questions (definitive response), and Likert scale questions ranging from 1 to 5 aiming to determine the extent to which an organisation has complied with the accountability guidelines. Moreover, the questionnaire has three pages to gather general information about the organisations and seven pages testing the compliance with the standards. The latter part of the questionnaire has six sections in accordance with the accountability standards. In each section there are fifteen to twenty closed questions, plus an open-ended question asking for an explanation of organisation-specific deviations or non-compliances.

In the section serving to gather general information about the organisations, the questions correspond to questions in national non-profit statistical surveys aiming to get an overview of the characteristics and operations of the organisations in general. In addition, this section includes questions that gather supplementary information for interpreting an organisation's accountability data, and also for the sake of benchmarking. In the sections testing the compliance with the standards, the questions are assessing the realisation (and in some cases also the extent) of the specific guidelines.

THE METHODOLOGY OF ASSESSMENT: THE SCORING SYSTEM

For the assessment of the results/answers of the questionnaire, the following methodology was determined.

The section of the questionnaire gathering general information about the organisations was not assessed (at least not in points), as the purpose of this section was to compile the basic, neutral information and data of the organisations. Some data—the amount of the revenues, the number of the employees and volunteers, the existence of the public benefit status, and the pursuance of advocacy activities, for instance—was reinterpreted to provide profound meaning with respect to the answers given in the second, specific part of the questionnaire (as this information could help to explain the emergence of certain non-compliances). Additionally, in the research, the compilation of this information helped to evaluate the obtained results and complete qualitative analyses (by comparison) of the assessed organisations (for more detail and further references, see Molnár 2008).

Those sections of the questionnaire that tested the compliance with the standards were, on the other hand, assessed using a scoring system (except for the explanations of the organisation-specific deviations). The following requirements were set when designing the methodology of assessment:

- The assessment of the results/answers should not require special competencies or expert knowledge.
- A computer-based assessment of the results/answers should be made possible (see the online questionnaire and its assessment at the www. gnas.hu home page).
- The elaborated assessment methodology with respect to both the scores (values) of the GNAS and the total scores should be adequate to differentiate meaning in conformity with reality to distinguish between the accountability of the respective organisations.
- The results/outcomes of the assessment should be easily interpreted, both on the organisational level and in the comparison of the organisations (benchmarking).
- At the scoring of the questions, and also at the assessment of the accountability standards, their importance in the relation system of accountability should be taken into account, meaning they should be weighted accordingly.
- The methodology should be simple.

Taking all of the aforementioned requirements into account, the questions testing the compliance with the standards are assessed in a one-hundred-point score system (GNAS scoresheet) that is suitable for the self-assessment of the organisations. In the score system the subtotal scores of each GNAS standards are as follows:

- Mission and Programs: 26 (percent)
- Governance: 16 (percent)
- Finances: 15 (percent)
- Fundraising: 15 (percent)
- Human Resources: 14 (percent)
- Public Affairs: 14 (percent)

Due to the one-hundred-point score system (as indicated in the brackets) the accountability of the organisations can be expressed by percentage.

Moreover, it is quite simple to compare the scores of each standard or the scores of the various organisations.

It is important to emphasise in connection with the elaborated accountability initiative that the methodology focuses on the best practices, recommended general operational standards, and criteria, and therefore does not evaluate the organisations on a value basis: There are no "good" or "bad" practices, instead there are "less good", "good", and "more good" practices. Applying measure of value would forfeit the universality of the GNAS framework.

In order to facilitate the comparisons and the illustration of the results/scores, the so-called GNAS star was worked out (see Figure 9.2). The branches of the GNAS star correspond to the accountability standards; therefore, with the marking of the subtotal scores on each branch and with their star-like linking, the accountability of the organisations can be graphically displayed.

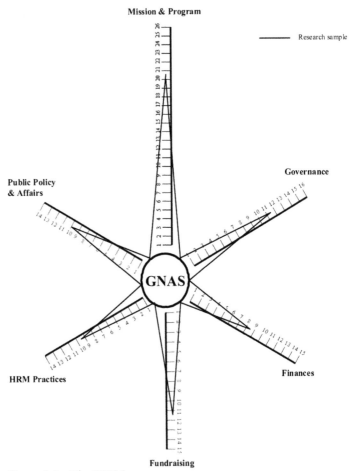

Figure 9.2   The GNAS star.

THE TESTING OF THE PROPOSED SELF-ASSESSMENT ACCOUNTABILITY INITIATIVE

In order to test and improve the GNAS framework and its assessment methodology, field research was carried out. The nature of the research and the attainment of the goals required that the applied methodology was flexible and close to or imbedded in real life and social conditions (see "grounded theory", Glaser and Strauss 1967). Therefore, the methodology of the research was qualitative.

Sample selecting tactics identified by Miles and Huberman (1994) were applied (see Table 9.1, where the numbers of the small stars indicate the significance of the tactics in the selection of the research sample). Given the qualitative nature of the testing, a small sample of thirty-five VOs as potential respondents was selected—out of which twenty-eight organisations eventually participated in the research obtaining a response rate of 80 percent—that could be identified as "typical" organisations of the Hungarian third sector with respect to the research.

The participation of potential respondents in the research was ensured by utilising various compliance principles (Dillard and Hale 1992; Groves, Cialdini, and Couper 1992; Groves and Couper 1998). The main message communicated to the organisations was that as carefully selected members of a small group, they would be participating in the testing and enhancement of a socially relevant tool that involved the on-site conduction and testing of a questionnaire, supplemented by semi-structured interviews (invoking compliance principles of commitment, scarcity, and prosocialness). Also tailoring or composing the approach based on the perception of

Table 9.1 Applied Sample Selecting Tactics

Sample selecting tactics	Characteristics
Theoretically based**	Suitable for the searching, analysis, and improvement of the examples of a given theoretical construction
Snowballing*	Based on personal relations, contacts, and introductions
Typical cases***	Searching and selection of normal, average, ordinary cases
Intensity***	Information-rich cases that intensively but not exaggeratedly represent the phenomenon under survey
Criteria**	Based on the fulfilment of specific prerequisites, for the sake of quality
Convenience*	For the sake of saving resource (e.g., time and money), but the validity weakens

Source: Miles and Huberman (1994).

the respondents and the situations (for example, tailoring the introduction rather than following a script) helped to improve compliance. As for the time frame concerned, the organisations were informed that the testing could be completed in an hour, but surprisingly, most of the actual testing lasted for almost two hours on average. As respondents gained insights and new views about their organisations, they found the experience of participating in the testing to be beneficial and thus the interviews became significant events for them. As the surveys were not anonymous, at each successfully completed testing occasion the participants were asked to provide reference (and more direct contact information) to those organisations that were selected for the sample but not yet interviewed in case they had any contacts there. Utilising this social validation compliance principle also proved to be very useful. Non-despondence resulted mainly from non-contacts, while explicit refusal occurred only in one occasion of all contacts with potential respondents.

The responding organisations were diverse with respect to their sizes (revenues): They ranged from the small (sometimes informal) organisations to the "biggest" local organisations. Moreover, they were also diverse in respect of their geographical locations, public benefit statuses, number and ratio of employees and volunteers, and their scopes of activities. Taking into account the characteristics of the Hungarian third sector (more specifically, the development and maturity of the organisations), on the one hand, the sample had to include the most significant VOs of the sector (theoretically based, information-rich cases, see group A of the respondents). On the other hand, these organisations were selected for the research sample in order to assess the current best practices and the prospective future benchmarks of the phenomenon under survey. The other part of the sample was comprised of small and middle-sized VOs (typical cases, see group B) and also a few "special" organisations (see group C). A primary objective at the selection of these organisations was to assure their diversity (in aspects such as their forms, public benefit statuses, scopes and ranges of activities, sizes of the revenues, and workers). An additional objective was that as far as possible these organisations should be simple and easy to access with respect to their geographical locations or connections. Moreover, at the selection of the sample the focus was on organisations that were suitable for testing the elaborated tool; therefore, the organisations included in the sample could be considered more institutionalised than the average.

The organisations participating in the research can be grouped into three categories:

- Group A: the "big ones", meaning the significant VOs of the sector (mainly charities and associations). Altogether thirteen organisations.
- Group B: small and middle-sized VOs. Altogether twelve organisations.
- Group C: "special" organisations (public funds/charities, public benefit companies). Altogether three organisations.

The research was carried out using a series of semi-structured interviews with the organisations in the sample. At these interviews, besides the testing of the GNAS tool involving the conduction of the questionnaire, the respondents were also asked additional questions in order to enhance the effectiveness of the research and to get the overall picture of the operations, existing accountability mechanisms, and possible biases. The main objective of the research was to test the elaborated initiative examining the applicability of the accountability standards, completing the questionnaire, and the methodology for assessment. In addition to that, an objective was also to get a qualitative picture of the situation and readiness of the selected "typical" VOs to adapt to the guidelines of the GNAS standards (for more detail on the findings of the testing and assessment, see Molnár 2008).

Based on the survey and the received feedback, grounded revision (and if required, modifications in the questionnaire and its assessment methodology) could be carried out. Detailed description of the alterations in the structure of the questionnaire and in its scoring is not necessary, as there were no substantial modifications. Only small changes were carried out, which included (a) amending, correcting, and rewriting expressions or parts of questions, (b) altering the positions of certain questions, (c) inserting sub-questions, and (d) modifying the assessment scores accordingly. A brief summary of the findings from the testing will be outlined.

As highlighted before, one purpose of the proposed accountability initiative is to strengthen confidence in the sector and in its organisations by contributing to increased professionalism and quality in the operations. The GNAS define what may be considered as sound practice for operations by identifying and defining the common values and structures, which the organisations should incorporate. The usefulness of these standards and guidelines has been unanimously confirmed by the organisations participating in the research. As expressed, the legitimacy of VOs is based upon the confidence in and quality of their work, and the support received from parties interested in them. The organisations may maintain their legitimacy by taking the requirements of their stakeholders into consideration and through obligating themselves to achieving their objectives in all operations. This requires the organisations to employ the right people, invest resources strategically, and ensure efficiency in their operations, which are well-defined in the GNAS.

In connection with the applicability and use of the elaborated methodology it was also found out that, as assumed, the GNAS naturally cannot be followed in the same manner in all of their parts by all of the sector's organisations. As a principle-based initiative with a general-universal scope, however, it is required that an organisation must generally comply with the standards or explain any deviations. Well-justified deviations from the guidelines do not, therefore, mean that an organisation does not meet the requirements for sound practice or that its overall accountability should be questioned. The assessment of small and practically not institutionalised organisations, for instance, may be distorted by special organisational attributes (for example, lack of specific regulations and policies, limited fundraising activities), and therefore their scores should be interpreted accordingly. In any case, further empirical work and more research needs to be done concerning the use of the GNAS and its evaluation system when they are applied.

CONCLUSIONS

This chapter has introduced an accountability tool that was developed and customised for Hungarian VOs. The proposed model, not being a pure top-down initiative but rather a collaborative one, might be considered applicable to the Hungarian third sector. Based on the results of the testing and the assessment of the sample organisations, the GNAS model proved to be an adequate tool for assessing and evaluating the accountability of VOs. On the organisational level, accountability requires a culture shift (Cutt and Murray 2000), and the standards can help build capacity by providing a common self-assessment tool that gives a definitive model and provides guidance (Farkas and Dobrai 2009). On the level of the stakeholders, the standards give a common framework to help set expectations and to get a better understanding of how VOs (should) work. Finally, on the sectoral level and for the whole practice, the standards create opportunities for dialogue and collaboration, which support the further enhancement of the standards, or the creation of other systems, and the exchange of best practices.

Accountability is becoming a common practice worldwide, and therefore the increased accountability of the third sector is a key element in its sustainability in Hungary. At the beginning of the research it was assumed that the greatest obstacle for enhancing the accountability of the Hungarian VOs was that its importance is not recognised. The research revealed that the real obstacle can be found in the lack of elaborated accountability initiatives. Therefore, it is argued that the Hungarian third sector and its organisations need their own accountability mechanisms that are adjusted to the local circumstances. They need "general" accountability standards and systems that assess them. Moreover, the effectual application of the accountability initiatives requires the "simplification" of the existing laws and regulations governing VOs. An adequate, unambiguous, and easily interpretable legal regulatory system is a necessary and indispensable condition for enforcing accountability in Hungary.

At a more theoretical level, the author does not assume that the concept of enhanced accountability of VOs is desirable per se (for more detail, see Molnár 2010). There is still debate concerning the concept and implementation of accountability. Issues of contention include the overburden of VOs with accountability requests, increased levels of bureaucracy, tensions in stakeholder prioritisation, balancing the short-term and strategic uses of accountability, and internal or pure external provenance of accountability mechanisms, to name just a few. Ideally, the significance of accountability mechanisms lies in the organising principle of accountability for better results, compared to accountability for minimum standards. To achieve better results, accountability must be a democratic process through which shared goals are explicitly established, progress is measured, and work to improve performance is motivated and guided.

One possible implication of the research could be the framing and developing of the conditions required for the introduction of such an accountability initiative to practice. It could be executed in various ways and levels. The proposed initiative would join the organisations to the "accountability movement" on a voluntary basis. On the other hand, if a regulatory, supervised, and controlled execution is considered, various problems can be identified (see, for example, "coercive isomorphism", DiMaggio and Powell 1991). The introduction of the accountability mechanisms to the practices of the Hungarian VOs is not easily achievable and might trigger resistance. It will take time for the sector to adopt this approach and apply its practices. It could be argued that in the formal sense accountability might remain an aspiration for Hungarian VOs rather than a reality. However, during the field research, an inner drive was identified that is already present in most of the organisations, striving for greater professionalism and hopefully enhanced accountability. In this context, being accountable might be considered as being driven less by isomorphism and more from within the organisations themselves.

Opinions vary with respect to the effectiveness and the impact of the various accountability initiatives on civil society and its organisations:

There are legitimate concerns about too much accountability, which can result in co-optation or goal deflection of NGOs by donors and a loss of sectoral innovation and diversity. Within the broader perspective on accountability, however, it becomes clear that these concerns are about too much external and upward accountability rather than accountability as a whole. The challenge of accountability lies not in a binary relationship between oversight and independence but in a more complex dynamic between external, internal, upward and downward mechanisms that are differential across NGO types and are embedded in organizational relationships. (Ebrahim 2003, 208)

The challenge of the non-profit world is to move away from accountability as a spectacle, as it is practiced in most events, useful as they are, to accountability as a norm (Newell and Bellour 2002). However, the difficulties still lie in the customisation, implementation, and enforcement of the proposed non-profit accountability mechanisms.

REFERENCES

Cohen, J., and A. Arato. 1992. *Civil Society and Political Theory*. London: MIT Press.
Cutt, J., and V. Murray. 2000. *Accountability and Effectiveness Evaluation in Non-Profit Organizations. Routledge Studies in the Management of Voluntary and Non-Profit Organizations*. New York: Routledge.
Dillard, J. P., and J. L. Hale. 1992. "Prosocialness and Sequential Request Compliance Techniques: Limits to the Foot-in-the-Door and The-Door-in-the-Face?" *Communication Studies* 43 (Winter): 220–232.
DiMaggio, P. J., and W. W. Powell. 1991. *The New Institutionalism in Organizational Analysis*. Chicago: University of Chicago Press.
Ebrahim, A. 2003. "Making Sense of Accountability: Conceptual Perspectives for Northern and Southern Nonprofits." *Nonprofit Management and Leadership* 14 (2): 191–212.
Farkas, F., and K. Dobrai. 2009. "Tudásalapú nonprofit szolgáltatások" ["Knowledge-Based Non-Profit Services"]. In *A szolgáltatások világa [The World of Services]*, ed. E. Hetesi, Z. Majó, and M. Lukovics, 157–167. Szeged: JATEPress.
Farkas, F., and M. Molnár. 2005. "A nonprofit szervezetek elszámoltathatósága" ["The Accountability of Non-Profit Organizations"]. *Civil Szemle* 2 (2): 5–12.
Glaser, B. G., and A. L. Strauss. 1967. *The Discovery of Grounded Theory: Strategies for Qualitative Research*. Chicago: Aldine.
Groves, R. M., R. B. Cialdini, and M. P. Couper. 1992. "Understanding the Decision to Participate in a Survey." *Public Opinion Quarterly* 56 (4): 475–495.
Groves, R. M., and M. P. Couper. 1998. *Nonresponse in Household Interview Surveys*. New York: Wiley and Sons.
Kelemen, E., I. Kovách, and L. Kristóf. 2006. "Demographics and Civil Society in Hungary." In *Civil Society and Demography in Rural Central Europe (the Czech, Hungarian and Polish Cases)*, ed. I. Kovách and V. Majerová, 43–64. Budapest: Hungarian Academy of Sciences.
Miles, M. B., and A. M. Huberman. 1994. *Qualitative Data Analysis*. London: Sage.
Molnár, M. 2008. "The Accountability Paradigm: Standards of Excellence. Theory and Research Evidence from Hungary." *Public Management Review* 10 (1): 127–137.
———. 2010. "Civil Society Organizations and the Accountability Movement in Hungary: From Theory to Practice." In *A Panacea for all Seasons? Civil Society and Governance in Europe*, ed. M. Freise, M. Pyykkönen, and E. Vaidelyte, 143–162. European Civil Society Series, Baden-Baden: Nomos Publishing.
Newell, P., and S. Bellour. 2002. "Mapping Accountability: Origins, Contexts and Implications for Development." IDS Working Paper, Brighton, Institute of Development Studies.
Osborne, S., G. Jenei, G. Fabian, and E. Kuti. 2005. "Government/Non-Profit Partnerships, Public Services Delivery, and Civil Society in the Transitional Nations of Eastern Europe: Lessons from the Hungarian Experience." *International Journal of Public Administration* 28 (9/10): 767–778.
Salamon, L. M., H. K. Anheier, R. List, S. Toepler, and S. W. Sokolowski, eds. 1999. *Global Civil Society: Dimensions of the Non-Profit Sector*. Baltimore: The Johns Hopkins University Press.

10 Reporting for Public Sector Agencies
A Stakeholder Model

Daphne Rixon and Sheila Ellwood

INTRODUCTION

The increasing trend of governments delegating responsibility for public services to agencies raises the issue of how such agencies can be held sufficiently accountable to their stakeholders. The semi-autonomous nature of certain government agencies leads to difficulties in holding these agencies sufficiently accountable, since they often operate in an arm's length manner from government. The accountability issue is compounded when agencies are self-funding. Such agencies do not require government funding and, consequently, they are not subject to the same level of budgetary scrutiny and monitoring as a funded agency.

This chapter examines stakeholder accountability issues of a Canadian workers' compensation board, a self-funded agency that provides workplace insurance coverage to employers and benefits to workers who are injured during the course of their employment. Workers' compensation is a mandatory, collective liability system that is compulsory for employers and workers, is funded solely through employer premiums, and does not receive any government funding. Accountability is particularly important since stakeholders have relinquished significant legal rights under this system as they are not permitted to pursue litigation to establish fault for an injury. The study explores how well this agency meets stakeholders' accountability expectations and identifies how multidimensional reporting comprised of financial results and performance outcomes combined with stakeholder consultation may enhance the agency's accountability.

Following this introduction is a review of the literature regarding stakeholder accountability; the third section outlines the research method; research findings, discussion, and analysis are presented in the fourth section; and the fifth section provides conclusions.

STAKEHOLDER ACCOUNTABILITY AND ENGAGEMENT

Accountability in the public sector is significantly broader in scope than accountability in the private sector. While the private sector focuses on financial results and creation of shareholder value, the public sector encompasses a diverse group of stakeholders which often includes most citizens and taxpayers, along with a myriad of accountability expectations (Brignall and Modell 2000; Kloot and Martin 2000; Mayston 1985). The concept of accountability has expanded well beyond its core definition of being called to account for one's actions to include internal responsibility of public servants to professional standards, external responsiveness to the needs of clients, and public dialogue (Mulgan 2000). This broadening of the definition of accountability leads to various complexities due to the multidimensional nature of the public sector environment.

Accountability is defined by Stewart (1984) as several steps which he describes as a Ladder of Accountability (see Table 10.1).

For the account to be beneficial, Stewart (1984) contends it must be given in a manner that is easy to understand and inclusive of several languages other than financial, such as a legal account and a policy account. Information in the account should enable stakeholders to evaluate and identify appropriate actions or responses. At the performance step, outcome data must be added to financial data, and at the program level, the account (stakeholder report) must provide information on objectives and how well they are met. Information requirements for financial, legal, and process accountability can be defined with a high degree of precision, while it is more difficult to define standards for program accountability since this requires greater judgement (Stewart 1984).

When examining public sector accountability, it is beneficial to clearly identify and classify the stakeholders to whom the organisation is held accountable by narrowly defining stakeholders to a manageable size since government and their agencies cannot "be all things to all people". Clarkson (1995, 106) defines stakeholders as:

Table 10.1 Ladder of Accountability

Bases of Accountability	Description
1. Probity and legality	Probity—ensures funds are used properly and spending is authorized. Legality—ensures powers given by law are not exceeded.
2. Process	Encompasses whether procedures are adequate and efficiently use time, effort, and resources.
3. Performance	Considers whether performance meets required standards—output data must be added to financial data.
4. Program	Concerns whether work carried out meets the agency's objectives.
5. Policy	There are no set standards for the formulation of policy; government is ultimately accountable to the electorate for its policies.

Source: Adapted from Stewart (1984, 17–18).

Persons or groups that have, or claim, ownership, rights, or interests in a corporation and its activities, past, present, or future. Such claimed rights or interests are the result of transactions with, or actions taken by, the corporation, and may be legal or moral, individual or collective.

Although information is critical in forming the raw material for the stakeholder report, it does not constitute the whole of accountability (Stewart 1984). Indeed, the importance of facilitating stakeholder involvement and engagement rather than determining their needs based on subjective managerial perceptions cannot be overstated (Daake and Anthony 2000). Friedman and Miles's (2006, 162) Ladder of Stakeholder Management and Engagement sets out twelve steps ranging from the highest level, stakeholder control (step 12) to the lowest levels, manipulation and therapy (steps 1 and 2, respectively). As the ladders are mounted, stakeholder engagement moves from non-participatory to wielding stakeholder power; stakeholders at the lowest rung have merely knowledge of decisions, but at the higher levels help form or agree to decisions.

METHODOLOGY

The methodology employed in this case study of the workers' compensation agency in the province of Newfoundland and Labrador, Canada, is

Table 10.2   Management Approach and Stakeholder Engagement and Influence

Stakeholder Engagement	Management Approach	Stakeholder Influence
Power	12 Stakeholder control	Forming or agreeing to decisions
	11 Delegated power	
	10 Partnership	
Involvement	9 Collaboration	
	8 Involvement	Having influence on decisions
	7 Negotiation	
Tokenism	6 Consultation	Being heard before a decision
	5 Placation	
	4 Explaining	
Non-participation	3 Informing	Knowledge about decisions
	2 Therapy	
	1 Manipulation	

Source: Adapted from Friedman and Miles (2006) and Arnstein (1969).

comprised of a documentary review of the Workers' Compensation Board (WCB)[1] annual report, Balanced Scorecard (BSC), key performance indicators (KPIs), and face-to-face semi-structured interviews. The advantages of the case study methodology have been well established. Case studies are defined as multifaceted research strategies which typically involve an in-depth examination of one organisation, situation, or community and can deal with documentary reviews and interviews (Yin 1994). According to Singleton and Straits (2002), face-to-face surveys are useful when examining complex issues; they allow for maximum degree of probing, yield a better response rate, provide flexibility over question content, and facilitate clarification of questions and terminology. Case studies result in richer and more in-depth information than could be derived solely from a survey of a statistical sample of the population at large.

Respondents were selected by classifying individual stakeholders into groups, using Clarkson's (1995) primary/secondary typology. This typology defines primary stakeholder groups as shareholders, employees, customers, or suppliers who, if they become dissatisfied and withdraw from the organisation, will impair its continued viability. Secondary stakeholder groups are those such as media and special interest groups, who are not engaged in transactions with the organisation and are not essential for its continued operation. WCB stakeholders are classified into the following two groups: (a) primary stakeholders comprised of employers, insured workers, government, health care providers, and WCB staff; and (b) secondary stakeholders, consisting of general public and environmental groups.

Although a total of twenty-one representatives from all primary stakeholder groups were interviewed, this chapter concentrates on employer groups to illustrate stakeholder accountability issues for the WCB agency. In particular, chief executives of six employer associations representing various industries as well as large and small organisations in urban and rural areas were selected for this study from the seventeen employer associations that participate in the WCBs semi-annual round-table stakeholder meetings. Employer associations are considered to be representatives of the underlying population and are viewed as experts since they regularly lobby government and the board of directors on behalf of their constituents. This approach is supported by Creswell (1994), who suggests that qualitative researchers should purposefully select those informants who will best answer the research questions. In addition, three WCB executives were interviewed to gain an understanding of the agency's perspective. Responses of employer group interviewees are coded as ER and WCB agency executives are displayed as EX.

Semi-structured interviews were of one to two hours duration and were held at respondents' worksites. Interviews consisted of a series of open-ended questions, followed by self-completion of a questionnaire comprised of checklists and Likert scale questions. Responses to the open-ended questions were audiotaped and the transcripts were coded using NVivo software.

This software enabled the researchers to code passages under key headings, thus facilitating grouping and sorting of responses and production of reports by topic. Checklist and Likert scale questions were summarised and tabulated using spreadsheets. Results are analysed and discussed using the frames provided by Stewart's Ladder of Accountability and Friedman and Miles's Ladder of Stakeholder Involvement and Engagement.

RESEARCH FINDINGS: DISCUSSION AND ANALYSIS

Reporting

The WCB annual report contains reports from the CEO and board chairperson, BSC, financial statements, organisational chart, five-year financial results, and KPIs. As depicted in Table 10.3, respondents did not place significant reliance on annual reports. This may be attributed to their participation in semi-annual round tables where the CEO and senior executives provide interpretation of year-to-date operational results, the status on achievement of strategic plan targets, along with future proposed plans. Consequently, round-table participants have more frequent and timely information than that obtained solely from relying on annual reports. Further, annual reports are not a timely information source as they are usually not available until at least five to six months after year-end.

In comparison, WCB executives believe the annual report is a main source of information. It seems that not only are executives' views biased since they prepare the annual report, but they are also not attuned to information sources preferred by employers. Alternatively, WCB executives may be satisfied that employer informational needs are met through round-table meetings.

Table 10.3 Employer and Agency Perceptions of Annual Report and Strategic Plan

	Annual Report Source of Information		Annual Report Information Quality		Annual Report Understanding		Strategic Plan		Strategic Plan Targets	
	ER	EX	ER	EX	ER	EX	ER	EX	ER	EX
Strongly Disagree	6	0	0	0	0	0	0	0	1	0
Disagree	0	0	0	0	0	1	2	1	1	1
Neither Agree/ Disagree	0	0	2	0	1	1	0	0	1	0
Agree	0	2	4	2	5	1	4	1	2	2
Strongly Agree	0	1	0	1	0	0	0	1	1	0

Although annual reports are not their main source of information, four employer groups agreed they are meaningful (Table 10.3). Not surprisingly, WCB executives also view annual reports as providing meaningful (quality) information, with two agreeing and one strongly agreeing.

Coy and Pratt (1998) suggest that annual reports are not widely read due to the level of expertise and effort needed to understand them. However, interviewees did not totally support this claim with five of the six employer associations agreeing annual report information is easy to understand (Table 10.3). When saying this, respondents are likely referring to the BSC and non-financial performance information rather than financial statements since they later indicate that financial statements are difficult to understand. Ironically, WCB executives are divided on this issue, with one agreeing the report is easy to understand, one disagreeing, and one neither agreeing nor disagreeing.

Financial statements form a critical component of annual reports and are viewed as essential to accountability (ER6). For some employers, the act of providing financial statements is, in itself, a form of accountability, even if users do not have a good understanding of it. Respondents indicate that while financial statements provide comfort, few people other than accountants understand them since they require interpretation and explanations (ER4, ER3, and ER1).

Comparisons to other jurisdictions were viewed as important in improving the usefulness of financial statements (ER6). Interjurisdictional comparisons provide employer groups with a broader context than year-over-year comparisons and enhance their understanding of the agency's performance relative to the industry. Six employers preferred regional (Atlantic Provinces) comparative referents while five expressed interest in national comparisons. Currently, the agency does not provide national comparisons, publishes only two regional referents, and presents only year-over-year comparisons, thereby limiting the ability of stakeholders to fully evaluate performance.

The BSC is comprised of six goals which are supported by twenty-eight measurable strategies. Three of these goals correspond with the customer aspect of Kaplan and Norton's (1992) BSC, while the three remaining goals are aligned with the financial, internal business process and learning, and growth perspectives of the BSC. The BSC contains a comparison of actual to targeted results for the twenty-eight strategies, along with a narrative explanation of the agency's progress towards achievement of its strategic plan. In addition to its inclusion in the annual report, the BSC is also provided on a semi-annual basis to round-table participants.

While there was a fair degree of support for the strategic plan, respondents believed the BSC targets were not set high enough, particularly since many of the five-year targets were achieved in the first two years (Table 10.3). There was only moderate employer support (two agreeing and one strongly agreeing) for the targets, and of the remaining three employers, one neither agreed/disagreed, one disagreed, and one strongly disagreed. In response, one WCB executive concurred with employers' views that the targets were not ambitious enough, while two believed the targets were appropriate (Table 10.3). Artificially low targets may cause constituents to lose faith in the strategic planning and BSC reporting process. If after the first year or two it appears that five-year targets have been achieved, employers expect the agency to adjust them accordingly (ER1). This view was shared by the WCB, as noted by an executive:

> We need to go back and revisit the measures, the goals, and make sure the goals are the ones that reflect our reason for being. The stakeholders would have to be involved in this process. There should some provision . . . that we can modify the goals at some predetermined interval, that you go back and revisit your goals. The current strategic plan right now is so far ahead in certain goals that the original goals are really meaningless, we should go back and revisit those and if we have to, revise the targets. (EX1)

This research identified, through checklist questions and Likert scale questions, KPIs desired by employers. As illustrated in Table 10.4, the twenty-one KPIs desired by employer groups have been classified along the rungs of Stewart's Ladder of Accountability. The majority of KPIs are considered to fit the criteria of the lower levels of Stewart's (1984) Ladder of Accountability (probity, process, and performance) and none of the KPIs desired by employer associations reflect the highest step (policy). Indeed, five (24 percent) can be classified as probity; eight (38 percent) can be viewed as process; four (19 percent) can be categorised as performance; and four (19 percent) can be considered as program. As one moves up the WCB Ladder of Accountability, there are fewer performance and program indicators. Although KPIs are needed on lower levels (probity, process, and performance), it can be argued that accountability is enhanced when emphasis is placed on higher levels (program) since this rung focuses on whether the agency meets its goals and objectives. Policy indicators are possibly not provided since this is the responsibility of government rather than the agency.

As illustrated in Table 10.4, the research identifies several gaps between performance information desired by employers and that provided by the WCB. For example, the agency's failure to provide performance indicators on its return-to-work programs is a significant gap since ensuring that injured workers return to work is the agency's main function.

Overall, three employer groups agreed the agency is effective in demonstrating accountability compared, with one strongly disagreeing and two neither agreeing nor disagreeing. In response, WCB executives believed they are effectively demonstrating accountability, with two strongly agreeing and one agreeing. These responses show the disconnection between the

Table 10.4 Comparison of Desired and Reported Key Performance Indicators

Key Performance Indicators	Employer Interest	Reported by WCB	Accountability Step
Injury frequency	4	Yes	Program
Types of injuries	5	Yes	Process
Time to first payment	4	Yes	Process
Return-to-work success rate	5	No	Program
Outcomes for Early & Safe Return-to-Work program	4	Yes	Program
Outcomes for Duty to Accommodate program	3	Yes	Program
Number of claims denied	5	No	Probity
Number of claims accepted	5	Yes	Probity
Number of claims paid directly by employer	4	No	Process
Percentage of claims appealed	5	Yes	Probity
Administration costs	6	Yes	Process
Funded positions	5	Yes	Performance
Total costs (employer paid and WCB paid)	6	No	Process
Investigation results	4	No	Probity
Average assessment rate	6	Yes	Performance
Percentage of claims in receipt of LTD	4	Yes	Performance
Cost per claim (WCB portion)	6	No	Process
Percentage of claims successfully appealed	0	No	Probity
Duration of claims by category of length	1	No	Performance
Period of time from claim acceptance to case manager	1	No	Process
Cost per claims by injury type	1	No	Process

Source: Semi-structured interviews and accountability steps based on Stewart (1984).

perceptions of the agency and its stakeholders. Ultimately, the accountability relationship between the agency and its employer stakeholder groups can be strengthened through mutual understanding of the issues and concerns for each group.

Stakeholder Engagement

Consultation and communication is conducted primarily through semi-annual round-table meetings with employer and worker stakeholder groups. During these meetings, WCB executives provide BSC and financial and operational reports along with future planned initiatives. Throughout the interviews, respondents frequently commented on how the agency could improve its consultation process.

> At the last round-table meeting most people were disappointed. They just couldn't believe that they were given the annual report and the balanced scorecard, and then the WCB made a presentation on it. It should be provided a week before so you can analyse it. The WCB controls the consultation too much. I went to one of the round-table meetings where we were provided with the agendas and documentation. It was very scripted. Nothing unexpected was said or done; there was some opportunity for questions, but relatively few. There is defensiveness in the culture of the WCB. There is not a real culture of consultation; it is more of a culture of presentation . . . check the list and say the consultation is done. No questions. (ER4)

Use of round-table meetings reflects steps 3 and 4 (informing and explaining), and to a degree, step 5 (placation) of Friedman and Miles's (2006) Ladder of Stakeholder Management. These meetings are largely comprised of one-way communication, with WCB executives giving presentations about its strategic and operational plans. While most respondents indicate round-table meetings are a step in the right direction, some believe they are too controlled and too tightly scripted to be anything more than placation of stakeholders. According to Freidman and Miles, round-table meetings are a form of involvement where participants have a degree of influence in decision-making. In contrast, the WCB tends to portray round-table sessions as a form of consultation where employers are involved (step 8); whereas employers regard the process as informing, explaining, and placation (steps 3, 4 and 5) as it consists mostly of one-way communication and dissemination of information.

Clearly, with only one of six employers agreeing there is an adequate level of two-way communication, this represents a major gap in the WCBs ability to meet employer accountability expectations. Respondents stressed the importance of having two-way communication and suggested the onus is on the agency to report information that stakeholders can understand (EX1 and ER6). In addition, an employer respondent suggested the process should also encompass feedback:

> I think it [accountability] would have to include providing information as well as a measure of feedback . . . for example, if the WCB comes to

employers and provides certain information—annual report or quarterly or monthly updates. It can't just be the provision of that data. It has to be the feedback that we would give, and then being flexible and being responsible in what we say in terms of our concerns. It is to be a two-way street, such that our concerns would be represented. (ER4)

While some WCB executives believed round-table meetings provide a forum to engage in two-way communication with employers, one respondent recognised an opportunity for improvement:

Yes, we can be more accountable . . . be more transparent by providing more information. I think it is important that we improve the communication between the WCB and the stakeholders, especially in providing them the information they feel they need to assess whether or not we are accountable. (EX1)

The fault does not necessarily lie with round-table meetings as a forum, but rather with the way these meetings are conducted. Employers are not convinced they are being fully engaged in meaningful consultation, whereby they have a say in the decision-making process. The agency does not appear to recognise that round-table meetings do not constitute genuine consultation and feedback. It could be argued the WCB is trying to placate stakeholders through round-table meetings rather than providing them with a real opportunity for involvement (step 8 on Friedman and Miles's Ladder of Stakeholder Management and Engagement).

Multidimensional Stakeholder Reporting

From this research, it appears that a greater level of accountability could be attained through provision of information (financial and non-financial) which reflects higher levels of Stewart's Ladder of Accountability (performance and program). As one progresses up the rungs of the ladder, the forms of accountability become wider and include more dimensions. At the lower levels of Stewart's ladder, accountability involves one-way communication in the form of audited financial statements. At higher levels, financial statements are supplemented with the annual report narrative, statistics, BSC, performance outcomes, and comparisons to budgets, targets, and other jurisdictions; ultimately, at the program level, stakeholder consultation is required in the form of involvement and collaboration.

A multidimensional stakeholder reporting model for public sector agencies is presented in Table 10.5. This model juxtaposes Stewart's Ladder of Accountability with Friedman and Miles's Ladder of Stakeholder Management and Engagement to provide an approach to demonstrate stakeholder accountability through multidimensional reporting. Demonstration of accountability at each level of Stewart's Ladder of Accountability requires

varying types of stakeholder management. To demonstrate accountability for the first level, probity/legality, minimal stakeholder management is
needed. At this level, one-way provision of information is sufficient. The
next level of accountability, process, requires an increased level of stakeholder management, including a basic level of two-way dialogue with
stakeholders. Provision of non-financial performance information fits with
the informing rung of Friedman and Miles's stakeholder management ladder, while WCB executives' discussions at round-table meetings reflect the
explaining rung.

The third rung on Stewart's Ladder of Accountability, performance,
requires more interaction with stakeholders in order to demonstrate
accountability for outcomes and expected standards. Friedman and Miles's
Ladder of Stakeholder Management includes advisory panels and task
forces as ways to solicit stakeholder feedback regarding their performance
outcome expectations. The WCBs use of round-table meetings, which are
largely comprised of one-way presentations of plans and objectives, is more
reflective of Friedman and Miles's placation style of stakeholder management than consultation.

Stewart's program rung includes the highest level of stakeholder management techniques. To determine if the agency has fulfilled its accountability obligations for program delivery, a number of stakeholder management
techniques may be employed: consultation, involvement, negotiation, collaboration, and partnership. An effective multidimensional model would
employ consultation and involvement (steps 6 and 8 on Friedman and Miles's
Ladder of Stakeholder Management). Consultation, defined as surveys by
Friedman and Miles, enables the agency to ascertain stakeholders' views,
while involvement invites stakeholders to advance proposals regarding strategic direction. According to the interviewees, stakeholders want to be more
involved and have a greater control over the direction of the organisation.
They want to submit proposals rather than just provide feedback on the
agency's plans. The fifth rung, policy on Stewart's Ladder of Accountability and steps 11 and 12 (delegated power and stakeholder control) on Friedman and Miles's Ladder of Stakeholder Management and Engagement, are
excluded from this model since responsibility for policy and delegation of
power is the responsibility of government, not the agency.

CONCLUSIONS

A key contribution of this research is the linking of Stewart's Ladder of
Accountability with Friedman and Miles's Ladder of Stakeholder Management and Engagement into an analytical frame. This linkage recognises that at the performance and program accountability rungs agencies
need to more fully involve stakeholder groups in order to adequately
achieve accountability. The analysis has illustrated how the employer

Table 10.5   Employer Stakeholder Reporting Model

Accountability Ladder	Stakeholder Management Ladder	Form of Accountability to Employers
1. Probity and Legality	1. Manipulation 2. Therapy	Financial reportingCompliance with legislation
2. Process	3. Informing 4. Explaining	Financial reporting, statistics, annual report
3. Performance	5. Placation	Financial reporting, statistics, annual report, BSC, round-table meetings
4. Program	6. Consultation 7. Negotiation 8. Involvement 9. Collaboration 10. Partnership	Financial statements, statistics, annual report, BSC, and outcome-based performance information, expanded narrative explanation, comparisons to budgets/ other jurisdictions, employer involvement in decision-making regarding the agency's strategic plan and targets

Source: Developed from Stewart (1984); Friedman and Miles (2006); and Rixon (2007).

stakeholder group is engaged with the public sector agency (a Canadian workers' compensation agency) and how the stakeholder power and influence of this group can be improved. The involvement of other stakeholder groups and the balancing of their needs are considered in the full study (Rixon 2007).

This case study illustrates that while the WCB gives the appearance of being accountable to the employer stakeholder group in various ways, such as through producing financial statements, BSC, KPIs, and stakeholder consultation, this does not automatically meet stakeholders' accountability expectations. Indeed these mechanisms may be used to achieve organisational legitimacy rather than meet the substantive needs of stakeholders. This study revealed that employer stakeholder groups are not satisfied with a superficial approach to consultation. These groups want to move further up the ladder of engagement and influence decisions, for example, to help determine appropriate KPIs. At present their involvement is largely "tokenism" (Arnstein 1969; Friedman and Miles 2006). Instead, they want to have a deeper level of involvement (and perhaps even a degree of stakeholder power), including making proposals to the agency rather than just providing advice and feedback on the agency's plans.

This research has used the frames developed by Stewart (1984) and Friedman and Miles (2006) to show that a comprehensive multidimensional reporting model can be developed for a public sector agency that moves beyond the mere provision of information to embrace a deeper level of stakeholder involvement. This is achieved through the inclusion of financial and wider non-financial performance information that is designed for their needs, along with an increased focus on (employer) communication and engagement.

A fruitful area for future research would include the examination of the role of institutional theory in influencing the accountability tools employed by agencies as well as research into the oversight role of government in ensuring its agencies are sufficiently accountable. Such research would be beneficial for the public management and social accounting disciplines.

NOTE

1. Most provinces in Canada refer to their workers' compensation agencies as WCBs. Others such as New Brunswick and Newfoundland use the term "Workplace Health Safety and Compensation Commission". However, for simplicity, WCB will be used to refer to all workers' compensation agencies in Canada.

REFERENCES

Arnstein, S. R. 1969. "A Ladder of Citizen Participation." *Journal of the American Planning Association* 35 (July): 216–224.

Brignall, S., and S. Modell. 2000. "An Institutional Perspective on Performance Measurement and Management in the New Public Sector." *Management Accounting Research* 11:281–306.

Clarkson, M. 1995. "A Stakeholder Framework for Analyzing and Evaluating Corporate Social Performance." *Academy of Management Review* 20 (1): 92–117.

Coy, D., and M. Pratt. 1998. "An Insight into Accountability and Politics in Universities: A Case Study." *Accounting, Auditing and Accountability Journal* 11 (5): 540–561.

Creswell, J. 1994. *Research Design: Qualitative and Quantitative Approaches.* Thousand Oaks, CA: Sage.

Daake, D., and W. Anthony. 2000. "Understanding Stakeholder Power and Influence Gaps in a Health Care Organization: An Empirical Study." *Health Care Management Review* 25 (3): 94–107.

Friedman, A., and S. Miles. 2006. *Stakeholders: Theory and Practice.* Oxford: Oxford University Press.

Kaplan, R. S., and D. P. Norton. 1992. "The Balanced Scorecard: Measures that Drive Performance." *Harvard Business Review* (January/February): 71–79.

Kloot, L., and J. Martin. 2000. "Strategic Performance Management: A Balanced Approach to Performance Management Issues in Local Government." *Management Accounting Research* 11:231–251.

Mayston, D. 1985. "Non-Profit Performance Indicators in the Public Sector." *Financial Accountability and Management* 1 (1): 51–74.

Mulgan, R. 2000. "Accountability: An Ever-Expanding Concept?" *Public Administration* 78 (3): 555–573.

Rixon, D. 2007. "A Stakeholder Reporting Model for Semi-Autonomous Public Sector Agencies: The Case of the Workers' Compensation Agency in Newfoundland, Canada." PhD diss., University of Warwick.

Singleton, R., and B. Straits. 2002. "Survey Interviewing." In *The Handbook of Interview Research*, ed. J. Gubrium and J. Holstein, 59–82. Thousand Oaks, CA: Sage.

Stewart, J. 1984. "The Role of Information in Public Accountability." In *Issues in Public Sector Accounting*, ed. A. Hopwood and C. Tomkins, 13–34. Oxford: Philip Allan Publishers Limited.

Yin, R. K. 1994. *Case Study Research: Design and Methods, 2nd Edition, Applied Social Research Methods 5*. London: Sage.

11 Agencies as Instruments of New Public Management

Models of Accountability in Italy

Sandro Brunelli, Alessandro Giosi, and Silvia Testarmata

INTRODUCTION

Under the New Public Management (NPM), the role of political leadership has encompassed strategic planning and economic policy target setting, while the administrative structure has had responsibility for public services management (Osborne and Gaebler 1992). In addition, this separation between politics and administration has increased due to processes of downsizing and decentralisation in central administration (Gains 1999; Talbot 2004). This chapter argues that this split necessitates the adoption of models of accountability that respond to the information needs of both citizens and political leaders.

More specifically, our concern is with an effective approach to accountability for public agencies. As the Organisation for Economic Co-operation and Development (OECD) has recognised, public agencies have managerial autonomy which needs to be offset by planning and control mechanisms, both ex ante (such as budget process), and ex post (such as reporting mechanisms and audit; see OECD 2002). Building on the findings of the OECD, this chapter develops a model for comparative studies of public agency accountabilities. Our model highlights the factors that make the public agency "accountable" using concepts of internal control, political leadership, and citizen satisfaction. We exemplify our model using case study data from Italian public agencies.

The second and third sections of this chapter discuss definitions of public agency and key aspects of public sector accountability mechanisms in extant literature. The fourth section proposes a conceptual model of the public agency accountability cycle, which is then applied to case studies of several Italian public agencies. The fifth outlines our research methods. The sixth section presents our case study results, and the seventh sets out a comparative discussion of these empirical findings. The final section draws conclusions in the context of our proposed model.

A DEFINITION OF PUBLIC AGENCY

The creation of public agencies—bodies that specialise in specific operating tasks—is advocated as a means of outsourcing from the hierarchy in order to increase efficiency in public services provision (OECD 2002; Rolland and Aagotnes 2003; Pollitt, Talbot, and Caulfield 2004; Christensen and Yesilkagit 2005; Pollitt 2006; Ongaro et al. 2006). An important consequence is that public policy and operating functions are subjected to a sharp differentiation. Given the delegation of public services provision, it is arguably necessary to define a priori co-ordination and control mechanisms, which can also be formalised in contracts (contracting-in; Harlow 1999).

The definition of a public agency and its boundaries has been the focus of recent research. In the international arena, the public agency model emerged as part of the functional decentralisation of central administration. Scholars have (Pollitt, Talbot, and Caulfield 2004) identified three parameters that outline the public agencies phenomenon (*tripod model*) as follows:

1. The public agency arises from ministry disaggregation; however, it maintains intense but differently structured relations with the parent ministry (arm's length principle).
2. The public agency holds operational functional autonomy for the management of resources to achieve agreed objectives.
3. The public agency regulates its relationship with parent ministry through a contract.

The tripod model constitutes a definition of public agency as executive agency. However, in every country there are public organisations performing operating tasks that do not fully possess the characteristics outlined by the tripod model (OECD 2002).

To accommodate for this, the OECD advocates a broader definition of public agency, recognising that an organisation aims to manage the function of public services provision in a close relationship with the parent ministry, but not necessarily regulated by contract. In addition, public agencies must be understood in the context of national culture (Hofstede 2001; Lynn, Heinrich, and Hill 2001) and/or the national institutional patterns (Christensen and Laegreid 2006; Kickert 2000; Pollitt and Bouckaert 2004). Different institutional contexts and administrative systems, with more or less developed welfare schemes, are characterised by differences in public agencies' governance systems which, in turn, shape accountability mechanisms (Pollitt 2006).

OECD research examined the situations in Canada, France, Germany, the Netherlands, New Zealand, Spain, Sweden, the UK, and the US and outlines a basic classification of public agencies based on an analysis of the legal framework. The OECD analysis offers three classifications: departmental agencies, public law, and private law bodies (OECD 2002). Typically, departmental agencies are divisions of the ministry characterised by a high level of autonomy but with no legal separation. Although legal separation is more of a formal than substantive criterion for being a public agency, in this chapter we assume legal separation between the ministry and the public agency as a necessary condition in order to delimit the field of investigation. Indeed, according to the OECD approach, the legal framework determines the intensity of the public agency's relationship with the political body, in turn affecting matters of governance and accountability.

Accordingly, in the Italian context, executives agencies and functional public bodies both constitute public law bodies. Conversely, private law bodies in the Italian context include all public agencies which function predominantly under private law, whether or not they operate in a competitive environment. The case study organisations chosen for this research exemplify these distinctions within the Italian legal framework, and thus provide the basis for a comparative analysis of accountability mechanisms. The following public agencies are considered in this analysis: the Revenue Agency as an executive agency, the National Institute of Social Security (INPS) as a functional public body, and National Procurement Agency (CONSIP) as a private law body.

ACCOUNTABILITY PROFILES

Some key features of accountability addressed in the literature include: transparency, responsibility, and attitudes to being accountable. We argue that there is wide agreement about the concept of accountability shifting from a concern with procedures and respect for rules to a marked emphasis on processes and, in turn, performance results. Moreover, at the stakeholder level the focus has been shifted from a generic responsibility to parliament (political accountability) to a more specific commitment to the market, customers, and the community (external accountability; see Guthrie 1993; Cochrane 1993; Ogden 1995; Sinclair 1995; Jones and Pendlebury 1996; Rubin 1996; Broadbent, Jacobs, and Laughlin 1999; Parker and Gould 1999).

Although there is no or single shared definition of accountability in the literature, we argue that some fundamental features qualifying the concept of accountability in the public sector can be identified. A review of the major authors' positions (Stewart 1984; Guthrie 1993; Gray and Jenkins 1993; Sinclair 1995; Stone 1995; Roberts 1996; Rubin 1996; Barberis 1998; Johnston and Romzek 1999; Caperchione and Pezzani 2000; Taylor and Rosair 2000; Mulgan 2000; and Kearns 2003) indicates that the concept of accountability involves a relationship between a principal (accountee) and an agent (accountor), in which the former has some expectations of the latter, who is held to account as the principal demands (Mulgan 2000).

According to Steccolini (2003), a useful concept in public administration is the "cycle" of accountability. This cycle starts from an ex ante definition of the accounting objective (programming moment), leads to the agent activity of information production and communication (account moment), which, in turn, is the basis of the principal evaluation (judgement moment) that feeds the planning process, redefining the accounting objective.

However, this accountability cycle assumes greater complexity in the context of public agencies. We argue that the principal–agent relationship (accountee–accountor) in public agencies operates at three levels: political, administrative, and citizen. Accordingly, the principal–agent relationships are as follows:

1. The public administration is accountor to both the political leadership and the citizens. Simultaneously, the public administration plays the role of accountor and accountee to itself.
2. The political leadership is accountor to the citizens and accountee to the public administration.
3. The citizens are accountee to both the political leadership and the public administration.

Consequently, we contend that four different profiles of accountability are apparent (illustrated in Figure 11.1):

1. The political profile: The public administration provides an account to the political leadership for the operating activities it undertakes in response to guidelines.
2. The social profile: The political leadership provides an account to the citizens for its actions concerning the expressed needs of the community.
3. The internal profile: The public administration plays both the principal and agent roles. This profile summarises how the management control system for activities undertaken assists in redefining priorities and realigning administrative action.
4. The external profile: The public administration is in contact with the citizens concurrently with service providers. This enables citizens to assess and evaluate services based on the available evidence, and to provide feedback to assist in redefining both political and administrative strategies.

An important caveat here is that, conventionally, political accountability is nearly exclusively conceived in terms of a relationship between political leadership and citizens—without taking sufficiently into account the importance of the continuous processes of negotiation (that exist or should exist) between political leadership and public administration. In addition, the literature has failed to provide an in-depth examination of the accountability cycle for public agencies in the context of administrative decentralisation and downsizing phenomena (such as in the Italian case). Finally, there is a need to take into consideration the mutual influence between

Figure 11.1   Public agency accountability profiles.

accountability mechanisms and planning and control processes. For these reasons, this chapter proposes an interpretive model for the accountability cycle in public agencies, which we then apply to the Italian case. Our aim is to describe models of accountability, enquire into the relationships among the four profiles of accountability, and to identify the factors that make a public agency accountable.

A CONCEPTUAL MODEL OF ACCOUNTABILITY

The development of a public agency accountability cycle that satisfies the accountability needs of both the community and political leaders is a complex process involving diverse actors. An initial definition of the phases of the accountability cycle should identify existing links between these actors, including evaluation mechanisms, whereby measurement and communication facilitate the accountability process. In this context, because of the separation between politics and administration in public agencies, extant planning and control systems would seem to have a crucial role in both achieving political targets and responding to citizens' needs (see Figure 11.2).

The relationship between community and political leadership exists at both a general level, which could be termed "social", where the community (citizens) present their needs (social problems) that should be satisfied by public policies; and at an "individual" level, characterised by the public services required by a single citizen.

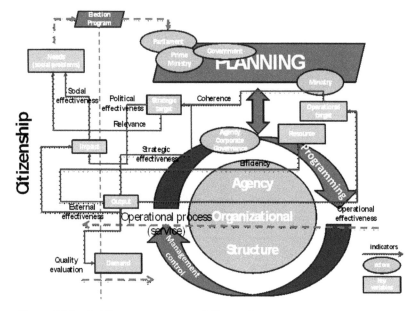

Figure 11.2   Public agency accountability cycle.

The public policy planning stage involves (mainly) political leaders at different levels (parliament, government, prime ministry, ministry) whose output is a strategic plan setting out priorities and political targets. The strategic targets of public policy should be relevant to the needs expressed by the community and should be connected to political programs approved by citizens through an elective mechanism. As a result, the strategic plan and the targets outlined are the basis for the preparation of the financial documents that establish and fund the public policies that, in turn, should be implemented through the administrative action and its operating programs.

The operational targets, expressed in terms of services to be provided in the public agency budget, come after a bargaining phase involving the public agency's whole governance system.

Once the service levels expected by political leaders are defined, the political leadership becomes simply an indirect customer of the public agency. In fact, via contact with the citizen demanding the public service, the citizen becomes the main customer for the public agency, to whom it should answer directly. The measurement of the degree of response to the citizen demand and the evaluation of the provided service level are monitored by the direct and immediate effects of provided output respectively. Hence the output of operating processes constitutes a key variable that allows us to measure the performance of the whole public administration in terms of the various accountability profiles shown in Figure 11.1.

Public agency evaluation may be investigated with reference to an evaluation model proposed by the European Commission (1999), drawing out the distinction between inputs, outputs, immediate effects (results), and long-term effects (impacts). In addition, the Commission defined relationships between these variables, which represent the key aspects that should be taken into account in a final evaluation of public agency operations. These aspects are:

- relevance: the relationship between needs and goals
- efficiency: the relationship between resources and, respectively, outputs and results
- effectiveness: the relationship between targets and impacts
- sustainability and utility: the maintenance of benefits over time

We adapt the logic of this model of evaluation outlined by the European Commission to the specific context of public agencies, taking into account planning and control systems in order to define the public agency accountability cycle, as shown in Figure 11.2. This figure illustrates the main variables and their relationships, which are the key aspects of evaluation in the case of public agency as follows:

- efficiency
- operational effectiveness
- coherence
- strategic effectiveness
- political effectiveness
- quality evaluation
- external effectiveness
- social effectiveness
- relevance

We propose a matrix (see Figure 11.3) that summarises the relationships between accountability profiles (as shown in Figure 11.1) and the key aspects of evaluation (as shown in Figure 11.2). From one point of view, social and external accountability concerns the relationship between the public administration as a whole (political leadership and public agency) and the environment, whereas political and external accountability deal with the relationship between the political leadership and the public agency. On the other hand, the competence of political leadership is reflected in political and social accountability, whereas the competence of public agency is reflected in the internal and external accountability profiles. This framework may be used for assessing whether the public agency achieves its goals or not, and, in turn, whether the public agency responds to demands from the political leadership and citizens.

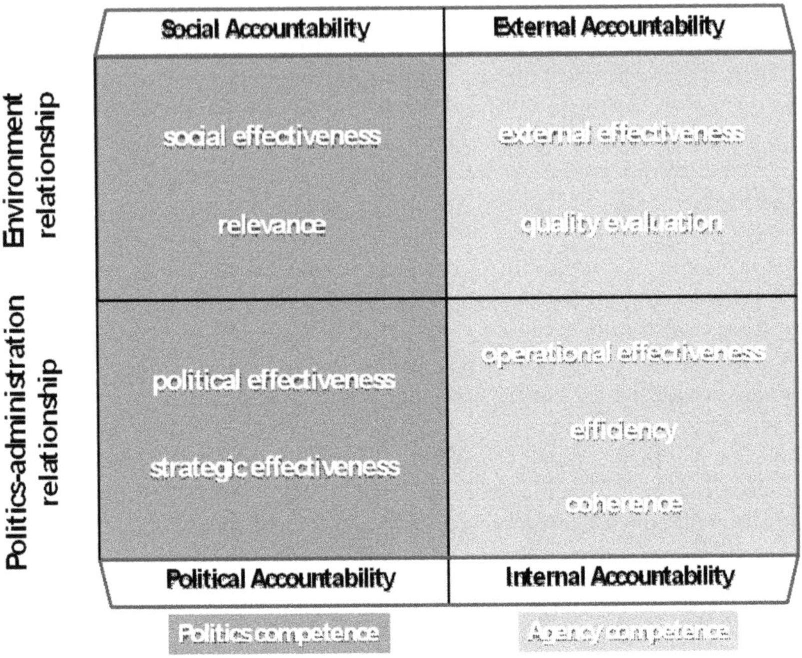

Figure 11.3   Public agency accountability matrix.

Internal accountability requires disclosure of the relationships between output and resources (efficiency) and between output and operational targets defined ex ante (operational effectiveness). In addition to this, it requires disclosure of the relationship between operational targets and strategic targets (coherence), which highlights the public agency's ability to provide the predetermined level of service.

Political accountability reflects the problem of alignment between administrative action and political targets. Firstly, the reporting system should enable analysis of the extent to which the achievement of results by the public agency allows the political leadership to achieve its strategic targets (strategic effectiveness). Secondly, political accountability requires measurement of long-term effectiveness, via reporting of the relationship between achievement of strategic targets and their impact on citizens (political effectiveness).

External accountability entails analysis of how the provision of service impacts citizens' satisfaction (quality evaluation). Indeed, quality evaluation comprises perceived quality (the relation between demand and output) and the quality of process (the relation between demand, operational processes, and resources). A positive feeling perceived by citizens does not necessarily entail that political action has answered community needs. In addition, we need to measure the level of effectiveness through the relationship between outputs and impacts (external effectiveness).

Social accountability is the final process. It aims to define the level of social effectiveness achieved and the degree of the public policy implementation. The former is measured by verifying correlations between impacts on the community and expressed needs (social effectiveness). The latter is measured by the degree of alignment between strategic targets set out by the political leadership and social problems (relevance).

RESEARCH METHODS

The research method consisted of a multiple case study analysis (Yin 1989) concerning three Italian public agencies: Revenue Agency, INPS, and CONSIP.

The selection of public agencies was carried out according to purposeful sampling logic. In particular, we consider an exemplar case for each legal framework according to OECD definitions. These public agencies have an essential role in the state activity; in fact, saving public expenditure and tax evasion reduction are two of the main strategic targets of political leadership. Moreover, the amount of financial resources assigned to these public agencies is strictly related to the national budget. In addition, the CONSIP case is relevant because it reflects the opposite of the downsizing process—that is, the centralisation of operational functions.

Semi-structured interviews and documentary analysis were carried out in order to explore the public agencies phenomenon. Each public agency was investigated according to case study research protocol developed with well-defined steps that take account of peculiarities and particular features that emerged during the previous analysis. The steps are as follows:

1. selection of case studies
2. semi-structured interviews with public agency managers
3. analytical systematisation of documents
4. processing and interpretation of data
5. extrapolation of the research results
6. discussion of the results of each case
7. discussion of the results in comparative terms

For cases we analysed the following documents: specific regulation; statute and other legal documents regulating the organisation; legal and internal documents concerning the planning and control process; financial statements; and all audit documentation. By applying our interpretive model of accountability cycle in the context of Italian public agency practice, we verify empirically the development of the accountability cycle and the legal framework incidence.

EMPIRICAL RESULTS

Revenue Agency

The Revenue Agency is one of the four central executive agencies born as a result of a Ministry of Finance reorganisation. Its operative task is to carry out all functions concerning the management of taxes, and assisting and informing taxpayers in order to achieve the highest fulfilment of tax obligations, combating tax evasion, and managing tax disputes.

The Revenue Agency is subject to the supervision of the Ministry of Finance, which maintains control over policy guidelines. However, the Revenue Agency takes full managerial and operating charge of its affairs even if its internal general directives must be submitted to the ministry for approval, in terms of both legitimacy and merits. In addition, the relationship between the Revenue Agency and the ministry is regulated by a "performance contracting" arrangement, which allows the ministry to determine both the strategic targets and resource allocation. The Minister of Finance defines the political targets concerning tax management through a three-year strategic act, which is accompanied by a three-year contract (updated every financial year) outlining the services to be provided, the programming objectives to be reached, and the assignment of related financial resources.

The governance structure seems sufficiently articulated, but most power is concentrated in the hands of a general manager, a direct appointment of the Ministry of Finance, who has responsibility for the strategic orientation of the public agency's operations. The board of directors, chaired by the general manager, has approval and advisory functions in respect to general manager proposals. In practice, the board of directors does not seem to be a decision-making body.

The Revenue Agency has a well-developed planning and control system guaranteeing coherence with political targets fixed by the parent ministry through the approval of strategic plans and consequent operating contract bargaining with the same agency. We found that structured tools, such as a balance scorecard for strategic control and a "tableau de bord" for monitoring operational activities, allow the agency to answer to the requirements of efficiency and operational effectiveness. In this case, strategic effectiveness is also a feature of the Revenue Agency as a result of the high level of autonomy granted. In terms of external accountability, the Revenue Agency produces a range of documents linked to customer satisfaction: a service charter, customer satisfaction survey, and social report. These documents enable accountability to the citizens in terms of quality evaluation and external effectiveness. As an example of an executive agency, the political effectiveness, the social effectiveness, and the relevance are exclusively features of political leadership.

INPS

The INPS was established in 1933 as a functional public body with legal personality and managerial autonomy. Their main function consists of liquidation and payment of both social security and welfare pensions.

The corporate governance model was found to be extremely complex. There are three governing bodies: a board of directors, a general manager, and the CIV (a strategic and supervision committee appointed by the ministry). The board has propositional and advisory functions, whereas the CIV approves and deliberates the various plans submitted by the other governing bodies. The autonomy of the governing bodies is also high. Indeed, the CIV is composed by a majority of independent members and the general manager is confirmed when there is a change in political majority. However, the coherence of administrative action seems ensured by the presence of parent ministry representatives within the board of directors and through a periodic evaluation of the general manager's contract, which is subject to parent ministry approval.

As a result of the absence of strategic guidelines defined by the parent ministry and the lack of strategic plan approval directly by the ministry, political accountability assumes less relevance in this case and converges towards the internal accountability, which is well developed. In fact, the planning phase ends up with CIV approval of the programmatic relationship proposed by the board of directors. The budget is defined as the consequence of an internal negotiation and involves the labour unions. On the other hand, we found that the internal audit system was not fully developed—instead it was perceived as control over the management control function, rather than a tool for monitoring processes. This situation might cause potential conflicts between planning and control direction and security and audit direction.

Conversely, the external accountability and the social accountability seemed to be quite weak. An external audit function is absent, apart from the National Audit Court activity, and strategic outcome disclosures and customer satisfaction documents are also absent. These weaknesses could create a deep disharmony in the relationship between the agency and the parent ministry, that is, the Treasury Ministry.

CONSIP

The CONSIP S.p.A. is a state-owned enterprise founded with a double purpose: firstly, improving the level of information and communication technology (ICT); secondly, rationalising the procurement processes through the use of ICT. Although the CONSIP is a private law body, it controls specific operating processes coming from the Ministry of Finance—hence the reasons for its creation are contrary to the tripod model, which is based on disaggregation.

The governance model adopted by this agency is similar to that of a private corporation. The board of directors has the highest decision power and could delegate its power to a CEO. There is no general manager, but instead a supervising body (supervision committee) made up of independent members, appointed by the board of directors. The aim of this body is monitoring the organisational model at each level of the structure and its alignment with the operational process. However, the level of the governing body's autonomy in terms of political power is noteworthy. This is mainly due to the presence of independent directors and the confirmation of a CEO when there is a change in political majority. Moreover, the absence of directors appointed by other entities apart from the ministry, plus the presence of parent ministry managers on the board of directors, creates a stronger link between management and political targets.

Both the core activities are regulated by contracts stipulated with the parent ministry which funds the functional expenses and investment. The constitutional acts assert that CONSIP "work according to the strategic targets defined by ministry". Thus the agency's strategic planning for IT investment, as well as procurement targets, is defined by ministry departments in accordance with the national budget. Hence the ministry exclusively delegates operational processes management to CONSIP. The CONSIP operational budget is set after the approval of the national budget and becomes an exclusive commitment of the operational planning. This low level of freedom in the budgeting process, even if limiting the agency autonomy, allows it to be coherent with the political targets fixed in the annual financial act.

Moreover, the ministry evaluates the work-in-progress of projects approved via contracts in order to control forecast public expenditure. This fact explains the development of operational control and the monitoring of efficiency, operational effectiveness, and strategic effectiveness through the reporting system. In addition, CONSIP is sensitive to institutional customer requirements—that is, from the parent ministry and the other public administrations. Since 2004, the agency has annually arranged a program aimed to ensure the "continuous improvement" based on the European Foundation for Quality Management (EFQM) guidelines. Although these documents are crucial for the transparency of the agency activity, they do not highlight the external effectiveness measure. Finally, as in the other agencies, there is an absence of political and social effectiveness.

ACCOUNTABILITY MECHANISMS IN PUBLIC AGENCIES

The empirical results of the case study analyses are showed in the Figure 11.4, which highlights our research findings in comparative terms.

Our analysis demonstrates that, in all cases, external and internal accountability are held by the public agency, independently of the legal framework.

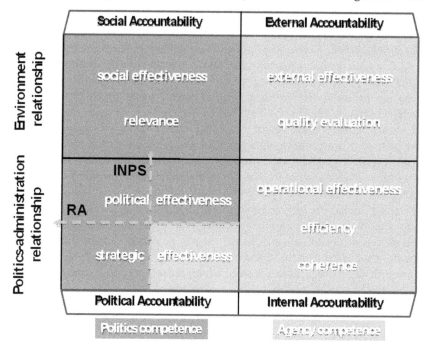

Figure 11.4 Public agency accountability matrix in the Italian case.

This is due to the development of planning and control systems that are able to counterbalance the autonomy granted to each public agency. However, the external effectiveness seems to be developed by means of a social report or other documents showing both the medium- and long-term effects on the community and the public agency's mission achievement. In addition, the planning and control systems seem to be more structured in contexts characterised by an individual service provision, a greater level of autonomy, and a more complex organisational structure (in the case of the Revenue Agency and INPS). On the other hand, CONSIP tends to ensure the diffusion of information about its activity merely to fulfil transparency obligations. This behaviour may be due to the fact that the planning and operating control system is a part of the parent ministry operating process. The evaluation of impacts is thus a competence of the parent ministry.

The accountability matrix shows that, in the Italian case, there is an appropriation of political competences by the public agencies. Indeed, strategic effectiveness tends to be more developed in CONSIP and the Revenue Agency, in which the relationship with the parent ministry is regulated through a contract and the governance model is more streamlined. In addition, the Revenue Agency's strategic effectiveness is internalised by the public agency because this agency is derived from a decentralisation of parent ministry expertise and is linked to the ministry director through a trust relationship. This situation entails obvious risks due to public agencies' self-referential nature. Conversely, political effectiveness showing the achievement of public policy targets is essential to reactivate the entire planning and control process and update the government's strategic plans. Generally speaking, political effectiveness is an exclusive competence of the parent ministry; thus, it could not be evaluated through the analysis of the public agencies' documents. However, in the INPS case, the public agency tends to take part of this evaluation as a result of its higher level of autonomy.

With respect to social accountability, we argue that periodic diffusion of the results achieved in public policies in different sectors would be desirable to increase the transparency of public administration to the community. In fact, the publication of government strategic plans does not appear satisfactory as their contents are often general. In addition, the impacts generated by the achievement of political targets should underpin the mandate report—that is, the main document regulating the relationship between community and political leadership, which reflects the skills and abilities of politicians in satisfying community expectations.

CONCLUSIONS

The aim of this chapter has been to analyse the effect of administrative decentralisation on the accountability cycle. Following the OECD, we adopted a classification of public agencies based on the legal framework that reflects the Italian context. We proposed an interpretive model for comparative studies of public agency accountability. Moreover, we defined the accountability cycle and its distinctive aspects, which were used to evaluate the Italian situation.

Our analysis showed that specific aspects of political accountability tend to become a feature of public agency in the presence of strong delegation and high autonomy. Inevitably, this fact leads to risk associated with accountability cycle implementation and produces friction between political leadership and administration (public agency).

The proposed model could be replicated in different contexts and applied in comparative studies of public agencies. However, we recognise that the model is based on a descriptive approach of the accountability process. Future research might usefully define a quantitative measurement system of the evaluation aspects aiming to provide an ordinal scale of the cases studied.

REFERENCES

Barberis, P. 1998. "The New Public Management and a New Accountability." *Public Administration* 76 (3): 451–470.

Broadbent, J., K. Jacobs, and R. Laughlin. 1999. "Comparing Schools in the UK and New Zealand: Individualising and Socialising Accountabilities and Some Implications for Management Control." *Management Accounting Research* 10 (4): 339–362.

Caperchione, E., Pezzani, F. 2000. *Responsibilità e Transparenza nella Gestione dell'Ente Locale*. Milano: Egea.

Christensen, J. G., and K. Yesilkagit. 2005. "Delegation and Specialization in Regulatory Administration: A Comparative Analysis of Denmark, Sweden and the Netherlands." Paper presented on the SOG and Scancor Workshop on "Autonomization of the State: From Integrated Administrative Models to Single Purpose Organizations." Stanford University, Scancor.

Christensen, T., and P. Laegreid. 2006. *Autonomy and Regulation, Coping with Agencies in the Modern State*. Cheteham, UK: Elgar Publications.

Cochrane, A. 1993. "From Financial Control to Strategic Management: The Changing Faces of Accountability in British Local Government." *Accounting, Auditing and Accountability Journal* 6 (2): 30–51.

European Commission. 1999. *Indicators for Monitoring and Evaluation: An Indicative Methodology. Working Paper Number 3*. Brussels: Commission Staff Working Paper.

Gains, F. 1999. "Implementing Privatization Policies in 'Next Steps' Agencies." *Public Administration* 77 (4): 713–730.

Gray, A., Jenkins, W. 1993. Codes of Accountability in the New Public Sector, *Accounting Auditing and Accountability Journal* 6 (3): 52–67.

Guthrie, J. 1993. "Australian Public Business Enterprises: Analysis of Changing Accounting, Auditing and Accountability Regimes." *Financial Accountability and Management* 9 (2): 101–114.

Harlow, C. 1999. "Accountability, New Public Management, and the Problems of the Child Support Agency." *Journal of Law and Society* 26 (2): 150–174.

Hofstede, G. 2001. *Culture's Consequences: Comparing Values, Behaviors, Institutions and Organizations across Nations*. 2nd ed. London: Sage Publications.

Johnston, J. M., and B. Romzek. 1999. "Contracting and Accountability in State Medicaid Reform: Rhetoric, Theories and Reality." *Public Administration Review* 59 (5): 383–399.

Jones, R., and M. Pendlebury. 1996. *Public Sector Accounting*. London: Pitman Publishing.

Kearns, K. P. 2003. "Accountability in a Seamless Economy," In *Handbook of Public Administration*, ed. G. Peters and J. Pierre, 581–589. London: Sage Publications.

Kickert, W. 2000. "Public Governance in Europe: An International Perspective." In *Governance in Modern Society*, ed. O. Heffen, W. Kickert, and J. J. A. Thomassen, 223–255. Deventer, NH: Kluwer Academic.

Lynn, L., C. Heinrich, and C. Hill. 2001. *Improving Governance: A New Logic for Empirical Research*. Washington, DC: Georgetown University Press.

Mulgan, R. 2000. "Accountability: An Ever Expanding Concept." *Public Administration* 78 (3): 555–573.

Ogden, S. G. 1995. "Transforming Frameworks of Accountability: The Case of Water Privatization." *Accounting, Organizations, and Society* 20 (2/3): 193–218.

Ongaro, E., P. Fedele, D. Galli, and G. Valotti. 2006. *Le Agenzie Pubbliche. Modelli istituzionali e organizzativi*. Soveria Mannelli: Rubettino.

Organisation for Economic Co-operation and Development. 2002. *Distributed Public Governance. Agencies, Authorities and other Government Bodies*. Paris: OECD.

Osborne, D., and T. Gaebler. 1992. *Reinventing Government: How the Entrepreneurial Spirit is Transforming the Public Sector.* New York: Addison-Wesley.

Parker, L., and G. Gould. 1999. "Changing Public Sector Accountability: Critiquing New Directions." *Accounting Forum* 23 (2): 109–135.

Pollitt, C. 2006. "Performance Management in Practice: A Comparative Study of Executive Agencies." *Journal of Public Administration Research and Theory* 16 (1): 25–44.

Pollitt, C., and G. Bouckaert. 2004. *Public Management Reform.* Oxford: Oxford University Press.

Pollitt, C., C. Talbot, and J. Caulfield. 2004. *Agencies: How Governments Do Things Through Semi-Autonomous Organizations.* Basingstoke: Palgrave Macmillan.

Roberts, J. 1996. From Discipline to Dialogue: Individualizing and Socialising forms of Accountability. In *Accountability: Power Ethos and the Technologies of Managing*, ed. R. Munro and J. Mouritsen. London: International Thompson Business Press.

Rolland, V. W., and J. E. Aagotnes. 2003. *A Database on the Organization of the Norwegian State Administration (NSA) 1947–2003.* Belgium: COBRA, Comparative public administration data base for research and analysis. http://www.publicmanagement-cobra.org.

Rubin, I. 1996. "Budgeting for Accountability: Municipal Budgeting for the 1990s." *Public Budgeting and Finance* 16 (2):112–132.

Sinclair, A. 1995. "The Cameleon of Accountability: Forms and Discourses." *Accounting, Organizations, and Society* 20 (2/3): 219–237.

Steccolini, I. 2003. "L'Accountability delle Pubbliche Amministrazioni: Definizione, Profili di Classificazione, Evoluzione." In *L'Accountability delle Amministrazioni Pubbliche*, ed. E. Guarini, E. Ongaro, F. Pezzani, C. Raimondi, and I. Steccolini, 17–33. Milan: Egea.

Stewart, J. D. 1984. "The Role of Information in Public Accountability." In *Issues in Public Sector Accounting*, ed. A. Hopwood and C. Tomkins, 13–34. London: Phillip Allan Publishers Limited.

Stone, B. 1995. "Administrative Accountability in the Westminster Democracies: Towards a New Conceptual Framework." *Governance* 8 (4): 505–526.

Talbot, C. 2004. "Executive Agencies: Have They Improved Management in Government?" *Public Management and Money* 24 (2):104–112.

Taylor, D. W., and Rosair, M. 2000. The Effects of Participating Parties, the Public and Size on Government Departments' Accountability Disclosures in Annual Reports. *Accounting, Accountability and Performance* 6(1):77–97.

Yin, R. K. 1989. *Case Study Research. Design and Methods.* London: Sage Publications.

12 Evolving Accountabilities
Experience and Prospects from Scottish Public Services

Tony Kinder

INTRODUCTION

Accountability systems are contested, provisional, and imperfect because people have different values, resources are uneven, and opportunities differ. The argument pursued here is that accountability by the managers of public service professionals is best situated in local community contexts, and is helpfully understood in dynamic settings by referencing psychic distances between providers, users, and stakeholders.

This chapter focuses on the accountability of middle managers of innovative services, since, as Bardach (1998) argues, they are at the pinch-point of service change: in this case, in locally provided care services and perhaps undergoing radical modernisation, integration, and adapting advanced technologies, subject to close scrutiny by the citizenry as a whole (Ostrom 1973; Behn 2001). Middle managers are important in performance management and interpreting social accounting and accountability. Managing professional staff, in a context of rapid change (including changing inter-professionals relations), poses particular accountability issues for middle managers, including changes in their own professional identity and esteem (Raelin 1985). From a stakeholder analysis perspective, managing service user expectations and experiences in a context characterised by a widening scale and scope of professional accountability necessitates situating accountability; whilst also referencing general financial, professional body, and regulatory standards. Situated accountability is analysed here referencing a widening scale and scope of accountability, the localised heritage and habitus, and a particular set of accountability relations using the idea of psychic distance between middle managers and their staff and stakeholders.

NATURE OF ACCOUNTABILITY

In the old joke when the businessperson asks the accountant what profits are likely to be, the accountant replies, "What do you want them to be?" Increasingly, stakeholders seek justification of decisions, intentions, acts, and omissions in what is an interpretative art (Crowther 2002; Crane and Matten 2004).

Accountability is the measuring, recording, reporting, justifying, and responding to performance metrics of judgements, actions, and outcomes. It presumes the acceptance of responsibility by agents as the cause of effects (Kennett 2001); though often the relationship between accountability and responsibility spans time and may be indirect. Agents may benefit from moral luck (Athanassoulis 2005), moral hazard, or luck in time, place, or character (personality), developmental luck, situational luck, and resultant luck (see Nagel 1993). Managerial responsibility may entail direct punishment when obligations are unmet, without direct power to alter outcomes: Strawson's (1966) idea of responsibility ascription. A wider moral (adjective) sense of responsibility (subjective blame) may be taken in Ricoeur's (1995) sense, on behalf of a collective, without direct individual guilt causation or blameworthy guilt accepted as vicarious or role responsibility (Hart 1973). The migration of accountancy metrics and method from simple numbers towards a pluralistic discipline featuring qualitative methods (Lee 2006) may result in multiple accountability disorder (Koppell 2005), disconnecting accountability and responsibility.

Accountability and Middle Managers

Neat Weberian separation of powers seem irrelevant as the diversity of organisational forms increases, though authors such as Thompson (2005) emphasise Weber's view that ethically the senior manager's role is to take responsibility with junior managers carrying out instructions (without patronage and within ethical boundaries), confining power delegation within standard operating procedures and structures (Moore 1993). Arendt (1963, 2003) argues that rules and structures cannot ensure integrity: Individuals have responsibility to reference moral codes wider than those imbedded in organisational rules. Crimes of obedience, Kelman (1973) argues, result in dual irresponsibility by those creating such structures and those accepting them. Adams and Balfour (1998) argue that organisations perpetrate (non-religious) evil where they deprive individuals of their humanity. Romzek and Dubnick (1987) suggest that evil may be masked (unintended as in the *Challenger* disaster) or unmasked (intended but without breaking rules). Masked evil, in the form of inadequate autonomy to middle managers, privileges upward over downward accountability; for example, if care packages privilege financial targets above client needs. Provided managers of professionals situate their accountability, performance metrics do not necessarily result in abrogation of professional accountability (Dillard and Ruchala 2005). assuming, as Bezzina et al. (2001) argue, that middle managers are able to align competing accountabilities.

SITUATED ACCOUNTABILITY

For Habermas (1991) practical rationality is socially situated in the communications practices of communities. Social learning theories (Vygotsky 1987) and situated ethics (Held 2006) also emphasise situatedness as arising from the interplay between agents, situation, and context; privileging relations between people in a community above universal or abstract norms (Rohlfing, Rehm, and Goecke 2003). Traditional accountancy privileges universally comparability in monetary values. Situated accountability, whilst often using generalisable values—an example being Beauchamp and Childress's (2001) ethical principles—presumes that culture, heritage, and social structures nuance or alter standards and accountabilities. A danger in best practice transfer strategies is failure to recontextualise practice (Kinder 2002); three aspects of situatedness seem most important for local care service professionals: roundedness, space, and risk.

Roundedness

Accountability is 360 degrees (Behn 2001), that is, upward, downward, and horizontal. For example, the social work manager's upward accountability may feature financial out-turns, service take-up rates, compliance with regulatory standards, and accountability to politicians. Sideways, inter-organisational accountabilities will include negotiations, monitoring and joint delivery of services with technology partners, voluntary organisations, and suppliers. Intra-organisational sideways accountability is with other sets of professionals (for example, local doctors, housing officials, hospital doctors, community health) and may include measures of integratedness with (previously fragmented) housing and health services, such as (hospital) discharge efficiency (that is, delays in return to independent living after treatment). Downward accountability to service users is broadly service satisfaction and access, and is shaped by the degree to which services are statutory (for example, mental health, children at risk) and useable. Weightings attached to accountability direction are likely to vary by case and space.

Space and Heritage

Upward and sideways inter-organisational accountability regimes are polycentric—crossing national, regional, or governance boundaries (Black 2008). Care services can face the additional issue of investment by one set of partners (for example, local government) resulting in savings for others, for example, health providers (see Dobalian and Rivers 1998). The case considered here exceptionally features co-terminus boundaries between health, housing, and social care providers. Heritage in care decisions combines some mix of commodification and co-production inherent in Esping-Andersen's

(1990) typology of welfare regimes (social democratic, conservative, and liberal). For both service providers and users, this heritage prescribes some of the boundaries of risk (Powell and Barrientos 2004).

Risk

Care, especially of vulnerable people, comes with risks such as wrong diagnosis, prognosis, or timing. Beck (1992), who discusses risk-taking by people who do not bear the consequences of the risk (for example, professionals), highlights the importance of mitigating risk by deeply rooting reflexivity in practice: a theme in Sennett's (2003) work. Lean public service models invariably reduce costs by integrating assessments across professional boundaries and (on the basis of typical customer journeys or life events) articulating referrals or actions: colloquially criticised as tick-boxing. Power (2007) views tick-boxing as mere process compliance; the aim of which is to avoid blame rather than enhance service quality. In this he harks back to Moore's (1995) argument that local service mangers, especially of professionals, are not neutral providers; they operate best with a professional commitment to clients. Risk reduction from the client perspective involves the exercise of professional judgement (including risk analysis) based upon the holistic needs of the individual and not the average needs of individual types. I now turn to the environment in which such services flourish—those in which care professionals and service users enjoy close psychic distance.

SERVICE USABILITY AND PSYCHIC DISTANCE

Situated accountability references service effectiveness and efficiency; the challenge in new service models is often not technological, rather it is in aligning the technology with service usability from the perspective of formal and informal carers and users (Kinder 2004).

Rhodes (1988) argues that new network organisational forms require new indeterminate forms of accountability suiting a diversity of local habituses featuring new (often) informal political processes emerging with new accountability organisational forms. For Yang and Callahan (2005), downward accountability is under-researched—neglected in Weberian rational behaviour models. These arguments align closely with Storper's (1997) idea of untraded interdependencies, Amin and Thrift's (1995) notion of institutional thickness, and Putnam's (2000) social capital argument. To understand how accountability to the citizenry as a whole operates in the particular situated context analysed in this chapter, I use the idea of psychic distance.

The term *psychic distance* is borrowed from international trade studies (Beckerman 1956) and comparative social capital studies (Brewer 2007) to mean the degree of interaction and understanding between service users and providers. Trust and interdependency lowers risk (Brouthers and Brouthers 2001). Psychic distance describes the proximity of service providers to service users, emphasising non-market habitus. Low psychic distance promotes trust (openness to misunderstanding and vulnerability) in an innovative environment of managed risk. It can make transformative innovations (such as independent living replacing institutional care) easier to implement. The idea of psychic distance aligns with Sennett's (2008) craftsmanship argument, Raelin's (1985) emphasis on empathetic reflexivity, and Freidson's (1988) notion of professions as dynamic. In summary, psychic distance is shared destiny, exploiting social capital based upon mutual trust, and service values, users are rewarded by effective (and efficient) services and providers earn professional integrity.

As Goffman (1959) indicates, we construct identities for others and ourselves. Sennett (2003) focuses upon the ability of professionals to define themselves through their work, arguing that many professionals become rootless and negative about their professional status when positioned as mere operatives in service delivery processes. Banks (2004), for example, argues that some professionals are defined by their accountabilities rather than their knowledge, judgement, and professional integrity to do well. Understandably, as professions evolve (Torstendahl 1990) accountability arrangements alter, and the pecking order between professions changes. Psychic distance is one way in which craftsmanship and professionalism can be articulated in local care service design and delivery.

Professionals' identities can alter where there is a broadening of knowledge domains (a feature of integrated and technologically assisted care) and as relations between sets of professionals change. In a context where professional accountabilities and identities are reshaping, close psychic distance disrupts existing power relations—between sets of professionals, professionals and their managers, and professionals and the client group.

Publicly organised social work services choose which services to offer and, given levels of demand (especially for good quality services), rationing or distribution. How have/are the changing accountabilities (and identities) of social work managers altering their power relations? As Schattschneider (1975, 71) states:

All forms of political organisation have a bias in favour of the exploitation of some kinds of conflict and the suppression of others, because organisation is the mobilisation of bias.

Is it possible that—in Lukes's (1974) terms—close psychic distance shifts more service decisions from the realm of conflict towards areas of no conflict? If so, we would expect the (latent or overt) exercise of force, coercion, and manipulation to be replaced by influence in the form of inducement, encouragement, and persuasion. In short, the managers of social work professionals able to exercise accountability with less overt downward exercise

of power (bad faith in Sartre's sense of being objects in beyond-control structures). Close psychic distance would enable social work managers to become
more ethical not less so, in Adams and Balfour's terms (1998, 165). The situated accountability arising from integrated and technological-enabled care
services, from this perspective, will show social work managers displaying
rising self-esteem, greater reflexivity, and a widening span of control (Perri
et al. 2002). The alternative perspective, of managers of tick-boxing, will
show that social work managers are becoming evil in Adams and Balfour's
terms (1998), displaying the opposite tendencies, suffering from what Munro
(1995) suggests is a shift of responsibility downwards, without power.

METHOD

This exploratory study builds upon two decades of engagement by the
author with social work services in West Lothian (WL), Scotland, bringing a great deal of pre-understanding of practice to the study. Data gathering from previous research has included longitudinal study, structured
and semi-structured interviews, and cognitive conversations with senior
council and health service officials and professional doctors, nurses, teachers, IT professionals, social workers, and local government officials. Data
presented in the following arises in particular from interviews conducted
jointly with Susan Hunter from the University of Edinburgh with fourteen
social workers' managers including the head of social services and chief
executive at the West Lothian Community Health and Care Partnership
(WLCHCP). Employing the conventions of enhanced cognitive conversation
method, we used open-ended, broad questions that enabled interviewees to
choose their own language, context, reference points, and framework in a
process guided gently as a conversation to interrogate focus research questions, often reiterating stories to explore depth (see Geiselman et al. 1985).
Encouraging thinking aloud, we sought to maximise interviewees' interpretations of events and trajectories by relating stories, sequenced by their
own sense-making, until the final phase, during which direct questioning
elicited detailed data. Our data analysis triangulated between general theory, data, and grounded theory, and featured quantitative and qualitative
statistics, supporting rigorous reflection upon initial results.

CASE STUDY: ACCOUNTABILITY IN
TRANSFORMED SERVICES TO THE ELDERLY

Background

Following a brief introduction to WL, this section situates social work
managers in WL, referencing previous research into independent living,
performance management, and health and social care integration.

WL is a small county in central Scotland comprising 160,000 people. Its unitary local council directly provides education, social services, and housing with some twenty-five thousand staff. Service quality is high. In 2006, the UK *Local Government Chronicle* awarded WL Council (WLC) the accolade of Council of the Year, and in 2007 it became the first UK council to achieve Charter Mark status across all of its services.

Social work services (staff and budget), along with housing and primary health care (a National Health Service function) are delivered in WL by the CHCP. Social work is highly regulated. The CHCP board, via its chief executive, is to Lothian Health Board and WLC. A CHCP subcommittee reports to a strategy-making integration care group that includes service users, voluntary organisations, partners, and stakeholders. Its executive management, the CHCP board, is composed of four nominees from the council and four from the primary care trust, plus a chair: It oversees strategic direction, implementation, and accountability. Ultimate fiscal accountability for the CHCP's £120 million budget remains with the Lothian Health and WLC to the chief executives to which the CHCP chief executive reports.

Independent Living

WL is home to the largest technologically assisted independent living cluster in Europe: sixty-five hundred homes. Citizens over seventy enjoy independent living in their own homes with free alert, alarm, and assistive technologies limiting the use of institutionalised care and speeding up hospital discharge. Some 83 percent of applicants receive the core package, with 8 percent getting a fuller package. Most smart housing involves kitting-out peoples' own homes. The ambient care network features integrated formal care services, for example, social workers, community nursing, home care, meals, housing, and medical services. Alerts and alarms signal to a central call centre and/or formal and informal carers. The technology includes fall, movement, security and fire alert, and assistive technologies: customised from the over ten thousand devices available. The smartness of independent living is not in the technology but in the ambient care and service networks (Kinder 2002). Smart housing is popular with elderly people. At an average cost of under €1,000 per unit, it enables the council to provide higher quality care at a lower cost than institutional care: dramatically expanding access to care services, with twenty people per week converting to smart housing. Social workers contribute smart housing to care packages with their managers redirecting budgets from institutional care.

Performance Measurement and Management

Local authorities in Scotland comply with fourteen hundred performance indicators (PIs) and face twenty-seven separate inspections. WLC provides five hundred services using innovations such as digital joined-up government (in 1997) and interoperable services. A quality development team was charged with training and establishing innovation circles in each service unit: All innovation circles include wider stakeholders and service users. Launched in 2002, the West Lothian Assessment Model (WLAM) integrates previously used quality standards drawn from the EFQM Excellence Model, the Investors in People and Charter Marks; additionally, it integrates principles taken from service standards such as ISO 9001:2000 and ISO 14000. Using a scoring system to plan and monitor continuous improvement, WLAM has enabled WLC to become the first UK council to get Charter Mark status for all of its services—the entire organisation (see Kinder 2007). The process relies upon the active participation of service users. Each social work service has an innovation circle, as does the service as a whole. Social work managers actively use WLAM to cross-reference their own rates of improvement with other council services.

Integrated Health and Social Care

Like all councils in Scotland, WLC engages in joint community planning between health, social work, housing, police, fire, and community education services. In 2002, WL established the first CHCP to manage and deliver primary care, social services, and housing services, with a €150 million budget devolved from the council and the health board. The CHCP has no bed-blocking to zero and enjoys joint teams, joint training, and an integrated IT system. Increasing numbers of staff are co-located. Shared (online) assessments typically feature input from hospital doctors, GPs, social workers, (smart) housing officials, and community nurses. Care plans are rapidly drawn up and implemented to the great satisfaction of clients. The CHCP is a service integration vehicle, not organisational integration (Kinder 2009). Social workers find that integrated assessments and databases give them more time for client visits and making judgements. Social work managers are able to track case loads and client progression. Co-location improves interaction with other sets of professionals.

In summary, WL is atypical: It has transformed its social services model over ten years and continues to innovate. Changing the social service model, structures, and care technologies are associated with no less radical changes in accountability systems, governances, learning processes, and power distribution.

Middle Managers

From the cognitive conversations conducted with fourteen social work managers in WL, this section extracts comments and direct quotations relating to care of the elderly, relevant to accountability issues.

Upward Accountability

No interviewee spoke of cuts, shortages, or deteriorating services. Several spoke of financial accountability being "imbedded into practice". Four, mentioning "upward accountability", spoke of the fairness resulting from the practice of social workers knowing the cost of services; another said that costs are always referenced in shaping care packages, without it being a limitation. Six managers referred to financial and performance measurement as areas featuring prominently in social workers' practice. Two suggested that external scrutiny "shifted power to the individual client away from the local council". One manager commented that "there are no financial constraints and therefore no dilemmas around gatekeeping". Several referred to access equity ("we have a clear evidence base") and its inclusion as a best-value performance measure. Three mentioned gendering of the social work hierarchy and absence of career structure in flattened organisations. They balanced the performance culture against "opportunities for personal and professional development, financial rewards, and innovative services to keep clients in their own homes, being forward thinking". All were optimistic for the profession: They felt that more people were getting more and better services and argued that social work continues to "make a difference" and social workers take pride in this, though they bemoaned the negative media portrayal of the profession.

Other Professionals and Colleagues and Voluntary Organisations

A manager with twenty years of experience said that "rising expectations in quality of care from other professionals and clients" is the principal change in social work practice. Most cited relations with the police as much improved. Two managers said that the main change in practice was less time spent gathering information and more spent "exercising professional judgement".

Managers in mental health and criminal justice emphasised that they had always had close relations with other professionals. Several managers said that diversity in joint teams means social workers now access a wider knowledge base, citing epidemiology, community health planning, CitiStat socio-demographic data, and the C-Me children at risk register.

Several managers commented that relations with the voluntary sector have improved because of the "less hierarchic nature of social work"; all agreed that relations with the voluntary sector are now more formalised and subject to performance measurement.

One manager suggested that social workers are more attuned to the independent care model than housing officers or GPs, who "increasing[ly] defer to social work judgement"; another that "GPs can give low priority to requests from other professionals, claiming lack of time". One manager said that "despite the expertise of social workers in these wider risk assessments, some GPs continue to regard them as of a lower status". Another commented that social workers "find themselves continually reminding other professionals of the organisationally shared vision and policies". Another manager explained that "quicker referrals increase GP workload" or require them to be up to date with initiatives such as the memory clinic. The majority agreed that GPs interact ("answering letters") more with social work. Overall, social work managers believe health professionals have more of a "silo mentality"; however, all applauded this as a creative tension, one commenting, "long may medical and social work practices clash".

Technology and Professional Standards

The core package of alert, alarm, and assistive technologies, linked by Bluetooth and Internet signal to (in)formal carers via the call centre is supplemented by some eight thousand devices that may be installed in particular smart homes. The CARENAP database of potential assistive technologies is accessible from social workers' desktops and gives prompts and suggested packages. Additionally, online and physical one-stop shops are access points. Another innovative system is the cross-service C-Me database of children at risk, which features joint assessment and recording. The managers greatly respect these partnerships. Social workers lead the training of GPs and community nurses on using these technologies in joint training.

A manager summed up the drivers of practice change in WL as "legislation, accountability, accessibility, visibility, evidence-based practice, and inter-agency working (especially health, education, and voluntary organisations)". Many expressed the view that "inter-agency working is more important in changing practice than the new technology". Managers from statutory services placed most emphasis on legislation. Four managers referred to quality systems and accountability, though one suggested these were too often used to "protect the organisation's back".

Downward Accountability: Staff

Managers argue that allowing community care assistants to conduct simple risk assessments frees social workers for more complex cases involving professional judgement. Several referred to accountability systems (for example, the random pulling of client files by managers to check quality). Joint assessment was continually referred to as an achievement by the CHCP—benefiting both clients and service efficiency. One suggested that efficiency was now less of a challenge than effectiveness. Several commented that the new model enabled social workers to do more of what they are trained for. Their main concern is that inexperienced social workers avoid a "tick-box mentality" or "social work by numbers", using the online joint assessments, and see their new role as promoting team-level discourse and ensuring that social workers get to know clients and not over-focus on performance indicators and care plans.

Downward Accountability: Users

Several managers mentioned that the core home care package being free stimulates demand. One manager commented that "in principle ethical dilemmas should abound but don't". Most agreed that "technology and joint working has assisted risk-taking and risk management, enabling people to maintain their independence longer". Every manager interviewed expressed the view that integration and smart housing had improved services and enhanced social worker commitment to the elderly clients.

The managers explained the commitment to clients and services variously. One described WL as "like an Apache village—we look after our own". Some referenced high retention rates amongst qualified social workers (half of the senior managers have worked for twenty years in WL). They noted that retention figures applied in children and family teams. Several mentioned the involvement of users in continuous improvement groups, consultative committees, and public participation forums. Others mentioned the fact that social workers live, work, exercise, shop, and educate their children in the same places as clients, using the phrase "we meet our user on a daily basis". Two managers referred to the local newspaper monitoring and commenting upon the detail of service quality.

DISCUSSION

These middle managers were mainly qualified social workers comfortably living with Lee's (2006) quantitative *and* qualitative accountabilities and avoiding multiple accountability disorder (Koppell 2005). Having learned performance culture from the WLAM, these social work managers operate with broadly scoped financial and non-financial accountability systems and metrics in a highly regulated service area prone to media attention. None felt masked evil or moral luck relevant to their situation. The managers, along with senior professionals, scan the regulatory environment for change and, coupled with service process changes, lead the workplace learning of junior staff collegiately—a managed community of practice. An environment driven by cost-downs and budgetary pressure, whilst making (upward) accountabilities perhaps simpler, can make widening the scale and scope of 360-degree accountability more difficult. However, in this case, the environment is one of technologically enabled independent living, integrated health and care services, and a modernising performance culture, which is releasing funds from labour-intensive institutions (often pre-IT) to provide improved quality of care at a lower cost (see Kinder 2002). These middle managers are renegotiating accountabilities in the propitious circumstance of an improving and popular service enjoying the increasing esteem of fellow professionals.

Having joined the WLCHCP, social work managers have carried their WLAM heritage into the wider space of WLCHCP's integrated care organisation. The learning has been multidirectional. Managers spoke of accountability systems encouraging equity of service access and referred to tools used by housing (CitiStat) and medical practitioners (epidemiological studies). For social work, equity of access and rationing are important issues. One manager recalled how in a previous era, social workers targeted "nice" families. Others recounted balancing the demand for a housing extension from one client against the (same cost) of twenty-five wheelchair ramps. These social work managers have broadened the accountability scale and scope of the professionals they now work more closely with, whilst at the same time, their own accountabilities have been enriched by these other professional groups.

In some areas the CHCP effectively uses balanced scorecards (for example, IT quality and integratedness) to record progress; in other areas strategic objectives merge knowledge domains and evolve new transdisciplinary knowledge that is less subject to social accounting tools. The social work managers proudly recount the widening scale and scope of their social accountability, reflecting the professional's heritage in community development, for example, in less hierarchic relations with the voluntary sector. Social work middle managers via the CHCP structure aim to operationalise the joint strategy and planning framework into a shared delivery model within a highly regulated environment that includes detailed KPIs and an established complaints procedure. Social work managers express less satisfaction with some informal social accountability arrangements. For example, they fear becoming too dependent on the technology provider (Tunstall) and bemoan some GPs' low level of engagement with themselves and service users, whilst recognising that other GPs enthusiastically embrace the new arrangements, for example, fully engaging with social workers and clients in service planning, scrutiny, and delivery. GPs heritage is as small businesses, with national contracts to deliver services with social accountability mediated via health trusts.

What then characterises the situatedness of social work middle managers in WL? It is 360 degrees and in part strong and meaningful even in the outer concentric circles (Tunstall, NHS, other professionals, voluntary organisations, and informal carers). Whilst tick-boxing by junior colleagues is seen as a risk, especially given the joint and online assessments, social work middle managers are able to scrutinise activity and insist on client interviews and have restored case conferencing. Risk is further mitigated by the involvement of clients in the range of formal and informal arrangements designing and monitoring services. Social work in WL enjoys rising self-esteem and inter-professional esteem, resulting from their ability to deliver independent living (smart housing) in the integrated care setting.

In this sense, the social space social workers occupy has shifted towards territory more suited to their styles of accountability. In this new situation, social workers are taking leading roles in promoting service integration and successfully portraying new identities to fellow professionals and clients.

CONCLUSIONS

New (combined) service structures, technologies, and performance management systems serve to explain social work managers' accountabilities only in the situated context of WL, provided the relations between the people (social work professionals and clients) are fully understood. Here, the concept of psychic distance appears useful. Social work services appear to be operating with increased authority arising from shared values and understanding. However, the close psychic distance is uneven: close upward to top management, downward (staff and clients), and some horizontal relations (some GPs and voluntary organisations); less close in some horizontal relations (some GPs, some hospital doctors, and the technology provider). High levels of engagement and the richness of social discourse between social work managers and clients seems to have created an unusual degree of communicative action (Habermas 1991) and psychic distance. It is the close psychic distance typical of a village, where responsibility arises from actions of individuals being known and easily commented upon from the perspective of a shared set of values. This perspective supports Banks's (2004) argument that some professionals are defined more by their accountability than by their knowledge base or professional association membership.

The typicality of the WL case rests in the three trends identified in the fourth section of this chapter: independent living, performance management, and integrated care, which appear to be general trends in the care of the elderly in the mixed economy and Nordic welfare settings. However, WL's size and heritage, resulting in close psychic distance between social work managers around the 360 degrees, make the case untypical. Detailed research in other areas innovating new care models for the elderly will be needed before generalised conclusions can be drawn from this research. The research does reveal the usefulness of a situated approach to accountability and the potential importance of psychic distance for an understanding of social accountability.

My analysis reveals that complex accountabilities are best understood in a specific situated social context. As these social work managers have broadened and renegotiated their identities as professionals (joint assessments, care integration, and broader ethical judgements), they are shown to have rising self- and peer-esteem, resulting from their ability to successfully deliver a rising standard of service relevant to both users and fellow professionals. Adopting 360-degree accountability is only possible because the social space in which the social work managers are operating is richly understood and the service model and associated risks are contrived with short psychic distance between service providers and users.

REFERENCES

Adams, G. B., and D. L. Balfour. 1998. *Unmasking Administrative Evil.* London: Sage.

Amin, A., and N. Thrift. 1995. "Institutional Issues for the European Regions: From Markets and Plans to Socioeconomics and Powers of Association." *Economy and Society* 24 (1): 41–66.

Arendt, H. 1963. *On Violence.* London: Harcourt.

———. 2003. *Responsibility and Judgement.* New York: Schocken.

Athanassoulis, N. 2005. "Common-Sense Virtue Ethics and Moral Luck." *Ethical Theory and Moral Practice* 8 (3): 265–276.

Banks, S. 2004. *Ethics, Accountability and the Social Professions.* Basingstoke: Palgrave.

Bardach, E. 1998. *Getting Agencies to Work Together—The Theory and Practice of Managerial Craftsmanship.* Washington, DC: Brookings Institution Press.

Beauchamp, T. L., and J. F. Childress. 2001. *Principles of Biomedical Ethics.* Oxford: Oxford University Press.

Beck, U. 1992. *The Risk Society.* London: Sage.

Beckerman, W. 1956. "Distance and the Pattern of Intra-European Trade." *The Review of Economics and Statistics* 38 (1): 31–40.

Behn, R. D. 2001. *Re-Thinking Democratic Accountability.* Washington, DC: Brookings Institution.

Bezzina, M. B., L. B. Fischer, L. Harden, K. Perkin, and D. Walker. 2001. "Leadership in Uncharted Territory: Developing the Role of Professional Practice Leader." *International Journal of Health Care Quality Assurance* (June): vi–xi.

Black, J. 2008. "Constructing and Contesting Legitimacy and Accountability in Polycentric Regulatory Regimes." *Regulation and Governance* 2 (2): 1–28.

Brewer, P. 2007. "Operationalising Psychic Distance: A Revised Approach." *Journal of International Marketing* 15 (1): 44–66.

Brouthers, K. D., and L. E. Brouthers. 2001. "Explaining the National Cultural Distance Paradox." *Journal of International Business Studies* 32 (1): 177–189.

Crane, A., and D. Matten. 2004. *Business Ethics: A European Perspective.* Oxford: Oxford University Press.

Crowther, D. 2002. *A Social Critique of Corporate Reporting.* Aldershot: Ashgate Publishing.

Dillard, J. F., and L. Ruchala. 2005. "The Rules Are No Game." *Accounting, Auditing and Accountability Journal* 18 (5): 608–630.

Dobalian, A., and P. A. Rivers. 1998. "Accountability and Quality in Managed Care: Implications for Health Care Practitioners." *International Journal of Health Care Quality Assurance* 11 (4): 137–142.

Esping-Andersen, G. 1990. *The Three Worlds of Welfare Capitalism.* New York: Polity Press.

Freidson, E. 1988. *Profession of Medicine: A Study of the Sociology of Applied Knowledge.* Chicago: University of Chicago Press.

Geiselman, R. E., R. P. Fisher, D. P. MacKinnon, and H. L. Holland. 1985. "Eyewitness Memory Enhancement in the Police Interview: Cognitive Retrieval Mnemonics versus Hypnosis." *Journal of Applied Psychology* 70 (2) 385–401.

Goffman, E. 1959. *The Presentation of Self in Everyday Life.* New York: Doubleday.

Habermas, J. 1991. *The Theory of Communicative Action (Volume 1).* Cambridge: Polity Press.

Hart, H. L. A. 1973. *Punishment and Responsibility.* Oxford: Oxford University Press.

Held, V. 2006. *The Ethics of Care.* Oxford: Oxford University Press.

Kelman, H. 1973. "Violence without Moral Restraint." *Journal of Social Issues* 29:29–61.

Kennett, J. 2001. *Agency and Responsibility.* Oxford: Clarendon Press.

Kinder, T. 2002. "Good Practice in Best Practice." *Science and Public Policy* 29 (3): 1–14.

———. 2004. "Usable Networked Technologies Supporting Complex Services for Non-Networked People." *Problems and Perspectives in Management* 1 (1): 22–54.

———. 2007. "An Iconoclastic View of Performance Measurement Based upon the Experience of West Lothian Council, UK Council of the Year 2006." University of Edinburgh Working Paper.

———. 2010. "Social Innovation in Services: technologically assisted new care models for people with dementia and their usability." *International Journal of Technology Management* 51(1): 106–120.

Koppell, J. C. S. 2005. "Pathologies of Accountability: ICANN and the Challenge of Multiple Accountabilities Disorder." *Public Administration Review* 65 (1): 94–108.

Lee, B. 2006. "More than a Numbers Game: Qualitative Research in Accounting." *Management Decision* 44 (2): 180–197.

Lukes, S. 1974. *Power: A Radical View.* London: Macmillan.

Moore, M. H. 1993. *Accounting for Change: Reconciling the Demands for Accountability and Innovation in the Public Sector.* Washington, DC: Council for Excellence in Government.

———. 1995. *Creating Public Value.* Cambridge, MA: Harvard University Press.

Munro, R. 1995. "Governing the New Province of Quality: Autonomy, Accounting and the Dissemination of Accountability." In *Making Quality Critical: New Perspectives on Organizational Change*, ed. A. Wilkinson and H. Willmott, 127–155. London: Routledge.

Nagel, R. 1993. "Experimental Results on Interactive, Competitive Guessing." University of Bonn Working Paper.

Ostrom, V. 1973. *The Intellectual Crisis in American Public Administration.* Tuscaloosa: Alabama University Press.

Perri 6, D. Leat, K. Seltzer, and G. Stoker. 2002. *Towards Holistic Governance.* London: Palgrave.

Powell, M., and A. Barrientos. 2004. "Welfare Regimes and the Welfare Mix." *European Journal of Political Research* 43:83–105.

Power, M. 2007. *Organised Uncertainty.* Oxford: Oxford University Press.

Putnam, R. 2000. *Bowling Alone: The Collapse and Revival of American Community.* London: Simon and Schuster.

Raelin, J. A. 1985. *The Clash of Cultures: Managers and Professionals.* Boston: Harvard Business School Press.

Rhodes, R. 1988. "The New Governance: Governing without Government." *Political Studies* 44 (4): 652–667.

Ricoeur, P. 1995. *Oneself as Another.* Chicago: University of Chicago Press.

Rohlfing, K. J., M. Rehm, and K. U. Goecke. 2003. "Situatedness: The Interplay between Context(s) and Situation." *Journal of Cognition and Culture* 3 (2): 132–156.

Romzek, B. B. A., and M. J. Dubnick. 1987. "Accountability in the Public Sector: Lessons from the *Challenger* Tragedy." *Public Administration Review* 47 (3): 227–238.

Schattschneider, E. E. 1975. *The Semisovereign People: A Realist's View of Democracy in America*. Hinsdale, IL: Dryden.

Sennett, R. 2003. *Respect—The Formation of Character in a World of Inequality*. London: Penguin.

———. 2008. *The Craftsman*. London: Allen Lane.

Storper, M. 1997. *The Regional World: Territorial Development in a Global Economy*. New York: Guilford Press.

Strawson, P. 1966. *The Bounds of Sense: An Essay on Kant's Critique of Pure Reason*. London: Methuen.

Thompson, D. 2005. *Restoring Responsibility*. Cambridge: Cambridge University Press.

Torstendahl, R. 1990. "Essential Properties, Strategic Aims and Historical Development: Three Approaches to Theories of Professionalism." In *The Formation of Professions: Knowledge, State and Strategy*, ed. M. Burrage and R. Torstendahl, 1–10. London: Sage.

Vygotsky, L. S. 1987. "The Problem of Consciousness." In *Problems of the Theory and History of Psychology, Collected Works*, ed. W. Rieber and J. Wollock, 129–138. New York: Plenum.

Yang, K., and K. Callahan. 2005. "Assessing Citizen Involvement Efforts by Local Governments." *Public Performance and Management Review* 29 (2): 191–216.

Part III
Social Accounting and Sustainability

13 The Carbon Neutral Public Sector
Governmental Accounting and Action on Climate Change

Amanda Ball, Ian Mason, Suzana Grubnic, Phil Hughes, and S. Jeff Birchall

INTRODUCTION

This chapter considers whether New Zealand, Australian, and UK government strategies for a "carbon neutral public sector" constitute meaningful action on climate change. Drawing from the significant early lessons, we set out the core questions for future research into climate change strategy for public services.

Climate change moved to centre stage on the political agenda of many western countries in concert with a number of landmark publications (Gore 2006; Gore et al. 2006; Stern 2006; Intergovernmental Panel on Climate Change [IPCC] 2007), and the award of the 2007 Nobel Peace Prize to Al Gore and the IPCC. The international scientific consensus, articulated in the IPCC report, is that "[w]arming of the climate system is unequivocal" and that "[m]ost of the global average warming over the past 50 years is *very likely* [IPCC emphasis] due to anthropogenic greenhouse gas (GHG) increases" (IPCC 2007, 72). We proceed on the basis that this science can be accepted. However, we believe along with others (for example, Metz and van Vuuren 2006) that the nature of the climate change problem will require more than economic or technical solutions; and that the academic community must work in a multidisciplinary fashion in order to integrate social, technical, engineering, and economic perspectives to contribute solutions. In this spirit, this chapter is co-written by academics, an environmental engineer, and a practitioner with substantial policy and practical experience of "greening" public sector organisations.

The backdrop to the chapter is the response by several governments to the climate change agenda. This chapter is motivated by evidence that core public sector organisations are either taking up carbon neutrality or being asked to become carbon neutral. According to widely adopted protocols (World Business Council for Sustainable Development/World Resources Institute [WBCSD/WRI] 2004; International Standards Organisation [ISO] 2006), the process for achieving carbon neutral status includes an organisation measuring greenhouse gas (GHG) emissions associated with its activities, reducing emissions where possible, and offsetting remaining emissions to have a zero carbon impact. We adopt the UK Sustainable Development Commission (SDC) definition of a carbon neutral organisation, as follows:

> one that causes no net accumulation of CO_2 emissions to the atmosphere. Therefore carbon neutrality allows emissions to be netted off in some other location, a process which is called "offsetting". However the SDC would caution against a carbon neutrality policy which is focused solely on carbon offsetting. As the aim should be to reduce overall emissions over time, simply offsetting emissions without a carbon management strategy in place is at best misconceived, and at worst counter-productive. (SDC 2005)

At the same time, there is little evidence of academic debate or research that provides a detailed analysis of the outworking of a carbon neutral approach to climate change policy for different public sector functions. This situation needs to be redressed, given the huge political, media, and public concern with international policy goals for stabilising global temperature and the possibility that "carbon neutrality" will become a widespread policy goal.

In order to contribute an agenda for research, the remainder of this chapter is structured into three sections. The second section looks in more detail at how policies and approaches to carbon neutrality are being implemented in New Zealand, Australia, and the UK. Building on insights from the theory and practice of carbon neutrality in the public sector, the third section provides an analysis and agenda for research on carbon neutrality. Our concluding remarks are set out in the final section.

DEVELOPMENTS IN PRACTICE

Introduction

The selection of countries in this section was based on the authors' experience of living, working, and researching in their respective home countries.

New Zealand

In February 2007, New Zealand Prime Minister Helen Clark announced to parliament: "I believe that New Zealand can aim to be the first nation to be truly sustainable—across the four pillars of the economy, the society, the environment, and nationhood. I believe that we can aspire to be carbon neutral in our economy and way of life" (Clark 2007, 7237). The New Zealand government proposed relatively detailed plans and guidelines for the achievement of carbon neutrality following on from the 2007 announcement by Prime Minister Helen Clark (Clark 2007). This mandate was passed to the Ministry for the Environment (MfE), which assumed a leadership and co-ordination role, but also to individual departments, each of which has a responsibility to deliver contracted services to a minister of the crown. Six "lead" departments out of a total of thirty-four core agencies were selected to become carbon neutral by 2012 on the basis of their data collection performance in a sustainability initiative known as "*Govt*³", which focused on waste reduction, buildings, transport, office consumables, and equipment (MfE 2008). This program produced energy data, which would be crucial in assessing carbon emissions and sustainable procurement information. Significant features of the carbon neutrality guidelines include: (a) an emphasis on mitigation prior to offsetting, (b) a clear statement that some offsetting will nonetheless be required, and (c) that offsetting projects will be located within New Zealand and managed by a single agency.

The "leading by example" ethic was clearly invoked as the primary rationale for the initiative (MfE 2007b), whilst recognising at the same time that the direct impact of core public sector carbon neutrality on national CO_2 emissions will be small at approximately 2 percent of New Zealand's total emissions (MfE 2007c). The emphasis on mitigation prior to offsetting is explicitly stated and justified in terms of maintaining credibility. Offsetting emissions without having made plausible efforts to reduce emissions first would compromise the credibility of a carbon neutrality initiative and could possibly prevent external verification of departments' carbon neutral status (MfE 2007c).

The subsequent use of offsetting was justified on the basis that 100 percent emissions reduction solely by mitigation measures was not considered a practical possibility, largely on account of transport issues (MfE 2007a). The issue of achieving authentic permanent carbon sequestration (permanence) from offsetting projects was included, and in fact made a legal requirement (MfE 2007d). The potential for conflict between carbon neutrality aspirations and conventional economic goals was recognised and the need to identify the threshold at which offsets become the preferred option has been highlighted as a matter for further investigation (MfE 2007c). The threshold issue is one which we believe to be of particular relevance for future research.

Various provisions clearly spelt out the management structures to be set in place. The potential role of carbon markets and the price of carbon were identified, signalling an expectation the public sector would be involved in some aspects of carbon trading (MfE 2007c). Credits would be managed through a New Zealand Emissions Units Register.

Predating Helen Clark's commitment to a carbon neutral public sector, the government funded the Communities for Climate Protection-New Zealand (CCP-NZ) Program, launched in July 2004. This was a voluntary initiative in association with the International Council for Local Environmental Initiatives (ICLEI) Oceania[1] to support local, regional, and territorial councils wishing to reduce GHG emissions in both the residential community and in their own corporate spheres. CCP-NZ operated within ICLEI's five-step program involving inventory measurement, emissions reduction, and monitoring. Six out of nineteen councils had set a range of targets by 2006, which would result in a collective reduction in corporate emissions over base year levels of 3 percent by 2010, and for five councils, a collective reduction of 1.4 percent by 2010.[2] By the end of June 2009, thirty-four councils, representing more than 83 percent of New Zealand's national population, were involved in the program (ICLEI 2009).[3] Although not a full carbon neutrality initiative, this program has nonetheless resulted in awareness raising, action, and has highlighted targeted GHG reductions in relation to business as usual projections as well as the base year.

Overall we believe that a relatively robust approach to implementing a carbon neutral strategy in the public sector was in New Zealand, particularly for the first six central government departments involved in the CNPS initiative. Following the national election in November 2008, John Key (National) replaced Helen Clark (Labour) as prime minister, and Labour's climate change policies were reviewed. In March 2009, Climate Change Minister Nick Smith deleted the CNPS and *Govt*[3] programs and ended funding to the CCP-NZ program. Nonetheless, we argue that the early experience, the barriers and opportunities revealed in the early stages of the CNPS, and the rationales for policy termination were informative, and provide considerable opportunities for research. This we will elaborate on in the discussion and analysis to follow.

Australia

In Australia, there has been a range of carbon neutral public sector responses at commonwealth, state, and territory levels, with differing levels of commitment. Most Australian governments have emphasised the role of government in "leading by example" to reduce GHG emissions in key policy documents. For example, on 18 February 2008, South Australian Premier Mike Rann declared that "the State Government must set a clear example by reducing its carbon footprint" given it was one of the largest GHG emitters in South Australia (Rann 2008). The state government would work towards becoming carbon neutral for its own operations by accelerated purchases of accredited Green Power and other carbon offsets (Rann 2008):

- By 2010, offsetting 30 percent of GHG emissions by purchasing Green Power and the balance through the purchase of other carbon offsets.
- By 2014, offsetting 50 percent of GHG emissions from its operations, achieved by purchasing of 50 percent of its electricity requirements from Green Power and the balance by purchasing other carbon offsets.

• By 2020, offsetting all of its emissions to achieve carbon neutrality by purchasing an equal amount of Green Power and other carbon offsets.

Earlier, in January 2008, South Australia's cabinet ministers became the first in Australia to offset the GHGs used in the course of their duties, including all air travel. In other jurisdictions, not all government ministers or members of parliament have been as ready to commit to carbon neutrality, often leaving it to the core public sector.

Environment Protection Authority (EPA) Victoria is an example of an independent agency that has gone carbon neutral. EPA Victoria's primary approach to carbon management is to implement cost-effective, direct emission-reduction projects in its operations. EPA is committed to improving its carbon management plan each year in line with its own draft Carbon Management Principles (EPA Victoria 2007a), and the plan will be externally assured each year. Two key lessons learned by EPA Victoria were the "concept of 'carbon neutrality' is not yet well defined" and "the market for green power and offset products is evolving" (EPA Victoria 2007b, 4).

Australian governments have seemingly recognised their significant purchasing power to influence the supply of renewable energy (Green Power) and the supply of low emission goods and services. In Victoria, the government has stated it will use its significant purchasing power when buying everything from cars to chapter, to send strong market signals for sustainable products and services. The Queensland government also recognises its notable levels of spending on goods, services, and construction.

At its peak, the ICLEI Oceania Cities for Climate Protection (CCP) Australia campaign involved 230 local governments representing some 84 percent of the population. CCP Australia was a performance-oriented campaign that offered a framework for local governments to reduce GHG emissions and improve liveability within their municipalities. CCP Australia may or may not have involved a local council adopting a carbon neutral approach, but some local councils, such as the city of Sydney or the shire of Yarra Ranges, were aiming to be carbon neutral by 2008. Commonwealth government funding for the CCP Australia program ended in June 2009.

Australia is still determining how it will respond to climate change at the commonwealth (national) level. Although there was a commitment to a national emission trading system (ETS) by 2010 (Wong 2008), following the global financial crisis, the Carbon Pollution Reduction Scheme (that is, the ETS) has been delayed until July 2011 with an initial carbon pollution permit price fixed at AU\$10 for one year (Rudd 2009). The future outlook for a carbon neutral public sector may in part be unclear pending the full implementation of an ETS, and decisions on what other climate change programs are required that are "efficient, effective and complementary to the emissions trading scheme" (Tanner and Wong 2008).

United Kingdom

Former Prime Minister Tony Blair pledged that the public sector would lead by example to combat climate change (SDC 2005), and this was reaffirmed by then Secretary of State for the Environment David Miliband (Defra 2006). Government has committed to making its office space carbon neutral by 2010/11–2012 with the wider public sector following by 2015; and there is an aspirational target of cutting GHG emissions from government offices by 30 percent by 2020. Furthermore, government has established that departments will be carbon neutral throughout the entire lifetime of ICT by 2020. Following consultation, the government has defined "carbon neutrality"[4] and, within guidance, promotes the reduction of emissions prior to the acquisition of carbon credits for offsetting purposes. The guidance is clear that purchase of 100 percent offsets does not count as carbon neutrality.

The government's intent may be inferred from the Climate Change Act, a framework on the management of carbon emissions (Defra 2007) that became law on 26 November 2008. The act binds the UK to at least an 80 percent reduction in carbon dioxide emissions by 2050 against a 1990 baseline, a target reduction of at least 34 percent[5] by 2020, and a system of carbon budgets that will constrain the total amount of emissions in a given time period. In a change to provisions in the draft Climate Change Bill, international aviation and shipping emissions are (potentially) included in the 80 percent target and must be taken into account in making decisions on carbon budgets. The Department of Energy and Climate Change (DECC) was created in October 2008 to bring about the transition towards a low carbon economy.

Following commitments of a carbon neutral estate, the government developed the Sustainable Operations on the Government Estate (SOGE) framework for assessing the sustainability of its activities.

Twenty-one core departments, together with executive agencies and self-selected non-departmental public bodies, report data to the SDC, an independent adviser to the UK government, who analyse the data and illustrate performance against each of the SOGE targets in a traffic light system. For the period 2008–2009, it is expected that data will be collected by the newly formed Centre of Expertise in Sustainable Procurement (CESP) using an existing central government property database, thereby reducing the reporting burden on departments. Data used for different purposes will be collected once rather than multiple times.

Overall results reported by the SDC for the 2007–2008 time period show signs of improvement, although they are not encouraging. Despite a decrease of 6.3 percent in carbon emissions from offices since 1999–2000, government is not on track to meet the 2010–2011 target of a 12.5 percent decrease (SDC 2008). On the SOGE targets, excellent progress is reported against waste reduction and water consumption targets, good progress against procurement of renewable electricity, carbon emissions from road vehicles, recycling and biodiversity targets, and some progress against the sourcing of electricity from combined heat and power target. Furthermore, the SDC have reported concerns on data quality and have emphasised the need for external verification of departmental data prior to sign-off and, additionally, centralised verification once in receipt of the entire data set. More positively, the SDC in their latest report recognise that progress has been made at the pan-governmental level and report on improvements to data quality following issue of guidance on re-baselining in cases where departmental boundaries change. CESP has been tasked with ensuring accelerated progress in future years and targets are now included in the personal objectives of permanent secretaries of government departments, implying greater attention (2007).

In direct contrast to New Zealand, UK offsetting projects are required to take place "outside" the physical boundaries of the nation. Guidance issued by DECC in 2009 recognise that funding for domestic projects "could" help the UK to meet its emission reduction targets, but justify their decision on the basis that, due to the introduction of policies and national measures, the emissions savings may have happened anyway. Government ministers and officials can purchase carbon credits from the Government Carbon Offsetting Fund (GCOF, now GCOF II) to offset emissions from air travel. This fund includes projects located in, for example, Brazil and Vietnam.

The local government sector accounts for approximately 1.4 percent of the total UK building energy consumption,[1] and emits in the region of 0.95 million tonnes of CO_2 per annum (Anon. 2008). More than seventy local authorities participated voluntarily in the Carbon Trust's[2] Carbon Management Programme in 2008–2009 (Dudman 2009) in order to identify and reduce carbon emissions. However, all local authorities are expected to collect data and report progress on three national indicators (NI) relating to climate change. Specifically, the Audit Commission now monitors local authorities on CO_2 reductions from operations (NI 185) and per capita reduction in CO_2 emissions in local authority areas (NI 186) as part of the new assessment regime (Department for Communities and Local Government 2007). Further, all local authorities are required to comply with the Carbon Reduction Commitment and Energy Performance in Buildings Directive recently introduced by government.

In summary, central government in the UK has focused upon legally enforcing the need to reduce carbon emissions as a nation and on establishing accountability frameworks to ensure progress within government departments. Work is required within departments and the broader public sector to develop and maintain effective systems to monitor, measure, and assess environmental impacts of operations. Present systems are orientated toward housekeeping and "quick wins", and the most current results by SDC suggest the need to reverse the trend in amounts of carbon emitted. Local government has a longer history in environmental practices compared to other parts of the public sector, although additional regulation is providing greater impetus to reducing carbon emissions.

ANALYSIS: DETERMINING THE RESEARCH AGENDA

Introduction

In this section we draw on the description and discussion in the preceding section to formulate a research agenda. Ultimately, it is only the global set of carbon accounts that really matters. Here we seek to examine whether "public sector carbon neutrality" contributes to reduction of GHG concentrations in the global atmosphere. In the following we set out a research agenda in component parts, each potentially contributing to the "bottom line". The topics identified are likely to be interlinked and are not exhaustive.

Implementing Carbon Neutrality: Processes and Systems

A useful research exercise will be to survey and summarise practice in implementing carbon neutrality, with the aim of widely disseminating examples of best (and worst) practice to the research and practice communities. The role of, and approach taken with, carbon accounting and third-party verification and assurance, including standards (for example, WBCSD/WRI 2004; ISO 2006), will be an important focus here. We expect other (financial) accounts to be robust and audited. The same should apply to carbon accounting (or any form of environmental accounting) and to disclosures via annual reports, stand-alone reports, and web sites, for example.

The UK experience with the SOGE framework indicates a need for research into the ease with which organisations establish data systems and establish baselines for setting targets; and whether concern with production of data per se serves to postpone or divert attention from framing how services could be delivered in low-carbon ways. Moreover, further research is warranted into the regulation of data sets submitted to government or government "watchdogs" for purposes of analysing progress towards targets. It seems, for example, that self-regulation is expected at the departmental level in the UK and that a lack of external verification is impacting upon results reported.

The "Offset Threshold"

A recurrent theme in this chapter has been the determination of the critical "offset threshold"—that is, the point at which public sector organisations "hit the wall" for whatever reason, are unable to reduce carbon emissions beyond a certain level, and go for offsetting. An important area for research will be to identify where this critical point of balance is being struck in different organisations and jurisdictions; and what sort of paradigm shift is required to move to a situation where carbon neutral strategies become "mitigation intensive"—that is, where offsetting is the minor part of the strategy and activities become decoupled from fossil fuel consumption.

We anticipate thorny issues arising in the use of offsetting, given that offsetting is known to sometimes bring perverse environmental outcomes, for example, the planting of single species plantations negatively affecting biodiversity and stream flow. An important collaborative research exercise with the scientific and engineering community will be to continually monitor the quality and permanence of carbon offset programs, including evaluation of the range of standards for offsetting (for example, The Gold Standard 2008).

Leading by Example?

The New Zealand, Australian, and UK governments all stressed that the core public sector would lead by example on carbon neutrality. A challenging topic for research will be to examine whether any leading actually takes place, what its character is, and what its outcomes are.

An interesting experiment would be to track the number of enquiries about how to go carbon neutral received by lead agencies, and to track developments in organisations seeking advice from public sector organisations. Our discussion of developments in Australia demonstrated that the public sector's use of its purchasing power will be an important focus for research. A useful research exercise would be to track the changes public sector organisations actually make over time, and in what areas of expenditure, in order to try to influence the supply chain through the purchase of goods and services that are sustainable, ethical, and demonstrate value for money. A further question is how far agencies would be prepared to go in changing purchasing or contracting behaviour. As Kerr (2006) argues, the political economy of structural reform in natural resource use is fraught with understandably resistant responses from parties who lose out. Thus we concur with O'Riordan (2004) that an important aspect of this research will be to investigate partnership arrangements between government, private capital, and civil associations.

Given that public services are often determined by basic, personal social needs, research into the public sector's response to the use of offsets in particular should reveal important insights about people's behaviour. Could it be that going carbon neutral simply seems too full of contradictions and difficulties for people to handle? Herein lays a fascinating research topic.

International Comparative Research

In writing this chapter and focusing briefly on only three OECD countries, we have been struck by the differences between governments' approaches to committing their public sector to become carbon neutral as part of a wider program of policies on climate change. Our brief country case studies reveal possibilities including a direct mandate from the prime minister (NZ); the Australian experience appears to be somewhat laissez-faire; and the UK model has evolved out of government's attempts to increase accountability for the sustainability of the government estate. A worthwhile topic for international collaborative research will critically evaluate the differences in approaches over a range of governmental systems. It would be of particular value to hear from researchers in less economically developed (as opposed to western industrialised) countries, where governments seem to have no voice in debates about a carbon neutral public sector.

Will Carbon Neutrality Come to Dominate at the Expense of a Fuller Understanding of Sustainability Issues?

We anticipate that carbon neutrality will become an important focus and a key performance indicator for core public sector organisations and agencies. Here we are mindful that accounting, including "carbon accounting", whilst hugely useful, can also turn the world into a series of quantifications; questions of how many? how much? at what level? and so forth. Further dangers lie in the enduring performance measurement focus in the public sector (Lapsley 2008). Our concern here, per the lessons of critical accounting research, is that to privilege the calculative eye of carbon accounting may render social and economic ideals less visible. The alternative is to keep to the fore the wider picture, inspired by the central problematic, as Orr (2007) puts it: "So, what does a carbon-neutral society and increasingly sustainable society look like?" A key concern for future research is whether and how government agencies can stay focused on building community capacity to mitigate emissions and adapt to climate change. The notion of accounting and accountability for a carbon neutral public sector is arguably, at best, a necessary but insufficient step in this direction.

Here we are also mindful of the wider mentality of business-case, win-win arguments for eco-efficiency, or going carbon neutral in the private sector; which privilege easy wins but do not address underlying problems of what gets produced and consumed and why (Milne, Kearins, and Walton 2006; Milne, Ball, and Gray 2007; Milne, Tregidga, and Walton 2007; Orr 2007).

Unit of Analysis

In carbon neutral public sector strategies in New Zealand, Australia, and the UK, the unit of analysis is the core government department, agency, or other organisation. An important area for research is to examine whether this is the appropriate unit of analysis in the context of the national and global carbon account. At a first level, there is the question of whether a department-by-department approach is the appropriate way to manage the emissions of government agencies. Thinking of the six lead departments in the New Zealand carbon neutral public sector program, it is fairly straightforward to identify the "big hitters" in the emissions stakes. The carbon impacts of the policy-based treasury are far less significant in absolute terms in comparison to the much larger, operations-based Department of Conservation. Should, then, these departments be managed differently? And should they receive funding for carbon reductions measures in proportion to possible absolute reductions?

At a second and more profound level, there is the question of what can be achieved through a focus on the core public sector, as opposed to considering the more significant domain of the public services. As Broadbent and Guthrie (2008) argue, so significant now is the involvement of for-profit companies and third sector organisations in the provision of public services, that the traditional concept of the state-owned and state-operated "public sector" is superseded. An important question for research, then, is whether and how accounting and accountability for the carbon impacts of public service providers can be achieved. And, importantly, what are the accounting and accountability requirements where public service providers are engaged in major climate change–causing activities? An example here is the New Zealand coal industry, which operates as a state-owned enterprise.

Time Frame and Rate of Contraction of Emissions

We argue that at the heart of any concern with climate change strategies must be a connection with the ineluctable reality of climate change science. All the available evidence points to a need for a rapid rate of emissions reduction in order to improve our chances of living comfortably on the planet (Meyer 2000), with targets commonly set to be met by 2030–2050 (that is, soon). Perhaps out of all possible roles for academics is the need to design research which continually engages politicians, policymakers, and decision-makers about the essential concern with achieving a stabilisation of GHG concentrations in the atmosphere, and about their professional and personal motives for actions they take which increase or reduce GHG emissions.

CONCLUSIONS

Public sector carbon neutrality has been mandated or voluntarily adopted in three OECD countries where climate change issues are high on the political agenda. In all jurisdictions reviewed in this chapter, government agencies have consistently stressed the rationale of "leading by example" for adoption of carbon neutral strategies. Our introductory look at developments internationally suggests that there are at least three different paths to public sector carbon neutrality. These are "direct mandate" by the prime minister (New Zealand); "organic development" from wider central government sustainability initiatives (UK); and a more "laissez-faire" attitude as in the Australian commonwealth government situation. The UK government has legally enforced reductions in carbon dioxide emissions as a nation, and has established the Committee on Climate Change to further strengthen accountability mechanisms.

The public management literature is notable in that it contains virtually no academic analysis or debate regarding public sector carbon neutrality or climate change strategies. We believe that there is an urgent need to redress this situation, and have therefore identified an agenda of pressing issues for research. These are, to summarise: understanding the implementation process; identifying and debating the offset threshold; critically evaluating the "leading by example" rationale; initiating country comparisons across various governmental systems; understanding the relationship with economic and social aspects of sustainability; and investigating the appropriate unit of analysis. An overriding goal is to evaluate and engage debate about the efficacy of carbon neutrality in the context of the time frame and scale of reductions of GHG emissions which are so urgently required.

Given the current predominance of carbon neutrality as a national, public sector, and business response to climate change, we urge academics from a range of disciplines to consider addressing these issues both from the perspective of their own disciplines and with a view to contributing to the interdisciplinary solutions which we believe are required.

NOTES

1. ICLEI Oceania is the regional secretariat for ICLEI. ICLEI was founded in 1990. ICLEI–Local Governments for Sustainability is an international association of local governments and national and regional local government organisations that have made a commitment to sustainable development (see http://www.iclei.org/index.php?id=global-about-iclei).
2. See http://www.iclei.org/index.php?id=3922, accessed 19 September 2008.
3. According to ICLEI (2009), "the total reported and quantifiable emission reductions from CCP-NZ council activities, since councils' inventory base-year (2004) to 30 June 2009, has been conservatively calculated to be more than 400,000 tonnes CO2e."
4. The Department of Energy and Climate Change (DECC) state, "Carbon neutral means that—through a transparent process of calculating emissions, reducing those emissions and offsetting residual emissions—net carbon emissions equal zero" (DECC 2009, 7).
5. Scottish parliament in June 2009 voted to cut the nation's CO_2 emissions by a tougher 42 percent target by 2020.
6. The statistic encompasses administrative offices, housing and local estate offices, community centres, and sports centres. Energy is consumed in

heating and lighting of buildings as well as in use of office equipment and air conditioning, for example.
7. The Carbon Trust is an independent organisation established by government to help meet its climate change obligations. It is funded by grants from the Department for Environment, Food and Rural Affairs, the Scottish Executive, the Welsh Assembly, and Invest Northern Ireland.

REFERENCES

Anon. 2008. *Local Government.* http://www.carbontrust.co.uk/energy/startsaving/sectorselector/localgovernment_13.htm (accessed 4 March 2008).
Broadbent, J., and J. Guthrie. 2008. "Public Sector to Public Services: 20 Years of 'Contextual' Accounting Research." *Accounting, Auditing and Accountability Journal* 21 (2): 129–169.
Clark, H. 2007. "Prime Minister's Statement." *Hansard* 637:7237.
Defra. 2006. *Sustainable Operations on the Government Estate.* London: Department for Environment, Food and Rural Affairs. http://www.sustainable-development.gov.uk/government/estates/index.htm.
———. 2007. *Draft Climate Change Bill CM 7040.* London: Department for Environment, Food and Rural Affairs.
Department for Communities and Local Government. 2007. *The New Performance Framework for Local Authorities and Local Partnerships—Single Set of National Indicators.* Wetherby, UK: Department for Communities and Local Government.
Department of Energy and Climate Change. 2009. *Guidance on Carbon Neutrality.* London: Department of Energy and Climate Change.
Dudman, J. 2009. "Greening by Example." *The Guardian,* 9 September.
Environment Protection Authority Victoria. 2007a. *Draft Carbon Management Principles Discussion Chapter.* Melbourne: Environment Protection Authority Victoria.
———. 2007b. *EPA Goes Carbon Neutral.* Melbourne: Environment Protection Authority Victoria.
Gore, A. 2006. *An Inconvenient Truth: The Planetary Emergency of Global Warming and What We Can Do about It.* Emmaus, PA: Rodale Press; London: Bloomsbury.
Gore, A., et al. 2006. *An Inconvenient Truth.* Hollywood, CA: Paramount Pictures Corporation.
Intergovernmental Panel on Climate Change. 2007. *Climate Change 2007: Synthesis Report.* Geneva: Intergovernmental Panel on Climate Change.
International Council for Local Environmental Initiatives. 2009. *Communities for Climate Protection—New Zealand: Action Profile 2009.* Melbourne: ICLEI Oceania and New Zealand Ministry for the Environment.
International Standards Organisation. 2006. "Greenhouse Gases—Part 1: Specification with Guidance at the Organization Level for Quantification and Reporting of Greenhouse Gas Emissions and Removals." ISO 14064–1, Geneva, Switzerland, International Standards Organisation.
Kerr, S. 2006. "The Political Economy of Structural Reform in Natural Resource Use: Observations from New Zealand." Chapter prepared on behalf of Motu, Wellington, NZ, for the National Economic Research Organisations Meeting, Paris, June.
Lapsley, I. 2008. "The NPM Agenda: Back to the Future." *Financial Accountability and Management* 24 (1): 77–95.

178 Amanda Ball, et al.

Metz, B., and D. van Vuuren. 2006. "How and at What Cost Can Low-Level Stabilization Be Achieved?" In *Avoiding Dangerous Climate Change*, ed. H. J. Schellnhuber, 337–146. Cambridge: Cambridge University Press.

Meyer, A., 2000. *Contraction and Convergence: The Global Solution to Climate Change*. Devon, UK: Green Books for the Schumacher Society.

Milne, M. J., A. Ball, and R. Gray. 2007. "From Soothing Palliatives and towards Ecological Literacy: A Critique of the Triple Bottom Line." Proceedings of the 5th Asia-Pacific Interdisciplinary Research in Accounting Conference, Auckland, New Zealand, 8–10 July.

Milne, M. J., K. N. Kearins, and S. Walton. 2006. "Creating Adventures in Wonderland? The Journey Metaphor and Environmental Sustainability." *Organization* 13 (6): 801–839.

Milne, M. J., H. Tregidga, and S. Walton. 2007. "Words of Action: The Centrist and Pragmatic Discourse of Sustainable Development Reporting." Working Chapter, University of Canterbury, Christchurch, New Zealand.

Ministry for the Environment. 2007a. *CAB(07)15: Towards a Sustainable New Zealand: Next Steps*. Wellington: New Zealand Government.

———. 2007b. *POL(07)84: Towards a Sustainable New Zealand: Overview.* Wellington: New Zealand Ministry for the Environment.

———. 2007c. *POL(07)131: Towards a Sustainable New Zealand: Carbon Neutral Public Service*. Wellington: New Zealand Ministry for the Environment.

———. 2007d. *POL(07)215: Towards a Sustainable New Zealand: Carbon Neutral Public Service—Offset Portfolio*. Wellington: New Zealand Ministry for the Environment.

———. 2008. *About Govt³*. Wellington: New Zealand Government. http://www.mfe.govt.nz/issues/sustainable-industry/govt3/about.php.

O'Riordan, T. 2004. "Environmental Science, Sustainability and Politics." *Transactions of the Institute of British Geographers* 29 (2): 234–247.

Orr, D. 2007. "Optimism and Hope in a Hotter Time." *Conservation Biology* 21 (6): 1392–1395.

Rann, M. 2008. "Opening of the 3rd International Solar Cities Congress." Presented at the 3rd International Solar Cities Congress, Adelaide, Australia, 18 February. http://www.ministers.sa.gov.au/news.php?id=2789.

Rudd, K. 2009. "Carbon Pollution Reduction Scheme: Support in Managing the Impact of the Global Recession." Media Release, Canberra, Australia, 4 May.

Stern, N. 2006. The Economics of Climate Change. Cambridge: Cambridge University Press.

Sustainable Development Commission. 2005. Climate Change Programme Review: The Submission of the Sustainable Development Commission to HM Government. London: Sustainable Development Commission.

———. 2007. Sustainable Development in Government: Annual Report 2007. London: Sustainable Development Commission.

———. 2008. Sustainable Development in Government: Challenges for Government. London: Sustainable Development Commission.

Tanner, L., and P. Wong. 2008. "Strategic Review of Climate Change Policies." Joint Media Release, PW 26/08, Canberra, Australia, 27 February.

The Gold Standard. 2008. The Gold Standard: Premium Quality Carbon Credits. http://www.cdmgoldstandard.org.

Wong, P. 2008. "Government Announces Detailed Timetable on Emissions Trading." Media Release PW 35/08, Canberra, Australia, 17 March.

World Business Council for Sustainable Development/World Resources Institute. 2004. *The Greenhouse Gas Protocol: A Corporate Accounting and Reporting Standard; Revised Edition*. Geneva: World Business Council for Sustainable Development; Washington, DC: World Resources Institute.

14 Choosing a Smart Set of Sustainable Development Indicators for "Governments at All Levels"

Dick Osborn

[T]he potential to change development paths is predominantly a regional, national or even local privilege. For this reason, it remains imperative to measure whether sub-global entities—particularly nations, but also sub-national jurisdictions and supra-national groupings like the European Union—are developing sustainably. (United Nations Economic Commission for Europe 2009, 25)

INTRODUCTION

Meeting the information needs of decision-makers at all levels so that they too "think global, act local" is a key element in the United Nations' (UN) action plans for dealing with unsustainable development (UN Environment Programme 1972; UN Department of Economic and Social Affairs 1992, 2002). How to communicate knowledge effectively through multiple levels of decision-making has thus been part of the sustainable development challenge facing the scientific and technological communities for over three decades. Examples of previous work on this task include: the Social and Environmental Accounting project, originating in 1971 and ongoing (Mathews 1997; Owen 2008); the Linking Knowledge with Action for Sustainable Development project (Clark and Holliday 2006); and the UN's Decade of Education for Sustainable Development 2005–2014.

A project managed by the Bureau of the Conference of European Statisticians (hereafter the CES project) on sustainable development indicators (SDIs) takes learning how to "think global, act local" into difficult terrain. Its central thesis is that there can be no meaning or real purpose attached to a situation where government entities differ over space and time on how they measure sustainable development, since sustainable development only makes sense for the planet as a whole. Yet political actions at regional, national, and local scales at least influence, and may even determine, the extent and nature of change along development paths. So, the thesis goes, measuring whether the planet as a whole is on a sustainable development path means combining the sustainable development measures of all government entities. Thus, the CES project's twin aim in designing a common and scientifically sound SDI set for governments at all levels is "to show whether or not nations and their associated supra- and sub-national entities are managing their own territories in a sustainable manner and whether or not they contribute to global sustainability" (United Nations Economic Commission for Europe [UNECE] 2009, 25).

An SDI set consistent with the aims of the CES project is, by definition, an innovation: "an idea, object, or practice that is perceived as new by the individual or other unit of adoption" (Rogers 2003, 12). The prospects for its universal adoption will depend in part on its performance as a knowledge transfer instrument in a wide range of contexts, and also on the number of adoption units in the social system within which it is to be diffused. A conservative estimate by the author places the number of national and sub-national governments at all levels throughout the world at some 661,000 entities (see Table 14.1).

Data is compiled from three sources: *The World Factbook* (Central Intelligence Agency 2009); the Institutional Tables of the 2008 *Government Finance Statistics Yearbook* (International Monetary Fund 2008); and the 2007 yearbook on local governments in the world (United Cities and Local Governments 2008).

The estimate does not include some five hundred thousand villages distributed through Cambodia, China, and other countries where data sources disagree on their status as local self-governments. Even so, some 661,000 national and sub-national administrative divisions can be identified from the public record with little effort. Recognising the result should temper the international community's acceptance of abstract terms when seeking to engage governments at all levels in addressing unsustainable development or other global issues.

Table 14.1   Estimated National and Sub-National Governments *circa* 2008

World Bank Income Category for Nations	National Governments	Federated States & Other 1st-Order Administrative Divisions	Local Self-Governments	Row Total
High Income	53	457	185,281	185,791
Upper Middle	44	584	54,013	54,641
Lower Middle	52	585	375,220	375,857
Low	43	441	44,079	44,563
Column Total	192	2,067	658,593	660,852

Many different SDI sets are already in use within the public sector. Some sixty-four hundred municipalities throughout the world are formally committed to implementing Local Agenda 21 (World Resources Institute n.d.), and create SDIs relevant to their own community's vision in doing so. The International Institute for Sustainable Development (IISD) maintains a compendium containing more than six hundred entries on sustainability indicator initiatives, many at scales of decision-making beyond local communities (IISD n.d.). The options in choosing a smart SDI set for governments at all levels thus lie along an axis from a point where effectively there is no choice to a point where many thousands of possibilities already exist.

This chapter considers a research question in sustainability communication design: What makes an SDI set smart enough to achieve widespread adoption among governments at all levels? It assumes that adopting a common and scientifically sound SDI set through the world's governments at all levels cannot be through authority-led innovation since no authority with such power exists, and proceeds as follows. The following section provides the context and background necessary for addressing the question. The third section then describes two blueprints for SDI sets designed to be smart: one co-ordinated by key agencies in the international community, and drawing on the resources of some fifty countries; the other undertaken pro bono by a small group of scholar-practitioners with two Australian local authorities. The final section compares the two designs against criteria for being smart and, in doing so, identifies which of the two alternatives could probably achieve widespread adoption among governments at all levels, concluding with some observations on future research.

CONTEXT AND BACKGROUND

In her performance review on governance for sustainable development within the European Union, Baker (2009) argues that its policymakers have yet to make smart choices from the knowledge-transfer and other instruments available to them. What then characterises a knowledge-transfer instrument as smart enough to guide sustainability decision-making through a network linking governments at all levels?

According to Boulanger (2005), a smart instrument facilitates knowledge transfer for sustainable development in four ways: by connecting policies horizontally and vertically; by aligning innovations with existing institutions and practices; by presenting relevant facts, data, problems, and concerns; and by providing opportunities for sharing views, standpoints, and perspectives. Other designers identify two complementary tasks: first, creating real or virtual communicational spaces robust enough to accommodate change in political and other actors over many decades (Galligan and Fletcher 1993; Frascara 2006; Fischer-Kowalski and Rotmans 2009);

second, translating available knowledge into messages that engage actors within the spaces created, that is, translating knowledge into messages that actors understand, are affected by, and which provide opportunities for response (Lorenzoni, Nicholson-Cole, and Whitmarsh 2007).

Here, a set of SDIs is considered smart if it meets at least six of the following nine criteria drawn from the literature cited in the preceding:

- connects policies horizontally
- connects policies vertically
- its innovation aligns with existing institutions and practice
- presents relevant facts, data, problems, and concerns
- provides opportunities for dialogue
- is robust enough to accommodate political and policy changes over decades
- translates knowledge into messages that actors understand
- translates knowledge into messages that affect actors' emotions
- translates knowledge into messages that elicit a response from actors

Measuring progress towards sustainable development through a capitals framework has been considered smart for some time, in many contexts, and across a range of decision-making scales. Daly (1973: 8), Chambers and Conway (1991), Ekins (1992), Kretzmann and McKnight (1993), and Meadows (1998) are prominent among scholars arguing that the advantages in doing so outweigh any disadvantages. More recent studies link a capitals framework to SDIs sourced from statistical collections used to construct national accounts and satellite accounts (United Nations et al. 2003; Pinter, Hardi, and Bartelmus 2005; World Bank 2006).

The satellite account—System for integrated Environmental and Economic Accounting (SEEA 2003)—comprises four categories of accounts: flow accounts on materials and energy; expenditure accounts on environment protection and natural resources management; asset accounts; and those dealing with a national economy's impact on the environment. One of its key developers acknowledges that SEEA 2003 is so large and complex that no country has yet implemented it fully, nor is ever likely to do so (Smith 2007). Providers and users of SEEA 2003 data therefore face considerable uncertainty and risk using SEEA 2003 as an SDI source, particularly through a knowledge-transfer process that has to be continuous over many decades into the future.

Many hundreds of Australia's local governments experienced the uncertainty and risk associated with discontinuities in SEEA 2003 accounting. They acted as data providers and users of SEEA's Environment Protection Expenditure Account and Natural Resource Management Account during 1996–2003.[1] The Australian Bureau of Statistics then shifted its SEEA 2003 resources to energy and water accounting, thereby moving from closing a knowledge gap for sustainability decision-makers at a local level to reopening it. Some Australian local governments and interested scholar-practitioners responded by agreeing to test more robust statistical collections as sources for SDI designs built on a capitals framework. They did so by implementing the "Towards Accountable and Sustainable Communities" (TASC) project in 2004 (Osborn 2005).

The CES project on linking SEEA 2003 and other statistical collections to measuring sustainable development through a capitals framework began a year later (UNECE 2009). It draws on resources from member states in the European Union and the OECD; connects to the World Bank, the UN, and other key agencies in the international community; and anticipates reporting further progress in 2011.

DESIGN BLUEPRINTS FOR THE CES AND TASC PROJECTS

The SEEA 2003 handbook lists three approaches to measuring sustainable development. They are:

- The three pillars approach, which emphasises interdependencies between humanity's environmental, social, and economic needs.
- The ecological approach, where sustainability of humanity's social and economic systems is accepted as subordinate to sustainability of the earth's environment.
- The capital approach, whereby "[s]ustainable development is development that ensures non-declining per capita wealth by replacing the source of that wealth; that is, stocks of produced, human, social and natural capital" (United Nations et al. 2003, 2–5).

SDI Design for the CES Project Using the Capital Approach

The CES project's choice of the capital approach applies theoretical reasoning described elsewhere (see, for example, World Bank 2006, 2009; Dasgupta and Seo 2008; UNECE 2009). The method rests on periodic assessments of a country's portfolio of capital stocks, weighting the result by an appropriate price, and summing the values for all capital stocks. The CES project's Terms of Reference stipulate work on a portfolio with four types or domains of capital: economic, natural, human, and social (UNECE 2009, 2).

Progress in the CES project through 2006–2008 is documented in a draft report submitted to the Conference of European Statisticians in March 2008 (UNECE 2008) and in a final report on the project's first phase (UNECE 2009). The project's blueprint appears in the draft report, decomposing real per capita economic wealth into four domains: real per capita produced, human, natural, and social capital. The blueprint is reflected in the first column of Table 14.2. Major design changes from draft to final report appear in the second column of Table 14.2.

A number of points can be noted. First, big ambitions in the CES project are recognised by its workers, at least for the time being, as impractical. The changes in the first and last data rows of Table 14.2 provide evidence for this. Second, capital frameworks are plagued by different opinions on how many types or domains should be recognised in a portfolio. For example, the body of statistical experts working on the CES project apparently do not see financial capital as a form of produced capital. Tensions within a SDI set designed to support both international comparisons and decision-making by sub-national governments are evident. For example, the physical indicators important to ecosystem services and agricultural production at sub-national scales have been withdrawn from the draft report and replaced by indicators drawn from SEEA 2003's asset accounts. Fourth, arguments that limiting SDIs to stock indicators so that decision-makers can see the forest rather than the trees have been lost, with the number of indicators in a small set doubling through the introduction of flow indicators.

SDI Design for the TASC Project Using Mixed Methods

The design blueprint for SDIs in the TASC project draws together elements from a range of studies and analytical methods.

The Portfolio

A key design decision taken in conducting the TASC project through 2005–2008 was to replicate the portfolio of five capital stocks used in the World Bank (2006) study. The decision was taken in response to the study's results that estimate the sources of wealth for the world as a whole. Natural capital is estimated to contribute 4 percent to the world's total wealth, produced capital some 18 percent, with an intangible residual contributing 78 percent (World Bank 2006, 4). The results should push stakeholders and interested scholars into giving meaningful recognition to the quantities and qualities of the intangible residual's three main components:

* human capital
* social capital (trust held by actors through contacts within networks of informal institutions; World Bank 2006, 87; Rothstein 2007)
* governance capital (trust held by actors through contacts within networks of formal institutions; World Bank 2006, 87)

The Assessment Methods

The integrated assessment model—SoCial, ENvironmental, and Economic (SCENE)—is designed to support decision-making by governments

Table 14.2   Changes in the CES Project's Design

Blueprint Indicator in 2008 Draft Report	Major Changes in 2009 Final Report
Real per capita economic wealth:	Omitted.
Real per capita produced capital:	Financial capital introduced as an additional domain, with emphasis on foreign holdings. Introduction is contrary to the project's Terms of Reference, where four types of capital—economic, natural, human, and social—are specified.
Real per capita human capital:	
Physical indicator of educational attainment:	
Physical indicator of health status:	
Real per capita natural capital:	Indicators for energy, mineral, timber, and marine resource stocks added.
Physical indicator of climate:	
Physical indicator of air quality:	
Physical indicator of water quantity/ quality:	
Physical indicator of ecological integrity:	
Physical indicator of biological diversity:	Omitted.
Physical indicator of soil productivity:	Omitted.
Real per capita social capital (place holder):	
Physical indicator of social capital (place holder):	
An indicator reflecting a nation's impact on global wealth:	Omitted.
Set with fifteen stock elements	Set with fifteen stock and fifteen flow elements

Source: UNECE (2008, 2009).

at all levels (Grosskurth 2003; Grosskurth and Rotmans 2006). SCENE mixes the "three pillars" and "capital" approaches to measuring sustainable development, using Qualitative Systems Analysis in dialogue to capture the interdependencies between social, environmental, and economic needs recognised by stakeholders. Elements in the SDI sets used in SCENE applications are assigned quantitative, qualitative, functional, and locational characteristics. A social network analysis tool—Actor, Process, Event, Scheme (APES)—is similarly designed to assign quantitative and qualitative characteristics to contacts between actors in policy and other social networks (Serdult et al. 2005). Elements from the SCENE model and from the APES tool were incorporated into the TASC project.

The International Standards and Collections

Given the consequences to decision-making among Australian local governments when the Australian Bureau of Statistics first closed and then reopened the knowledge gap through its occasional SEEA 2003 collections, the TASC project reverted to more stable and enduring statistical collections for sourcing SDIs. Stakeholders and scholar-practitioners collaborated in identifying potentially useful indicators, with stakeholders making a final selection according to relevance. Cross-referencing from the World Bank/TASC portfolio of five capital stocks to international standards (UN Statistics Division n.d.; United Nations et al. 2003, 5) occurred as follows:

- *Population and Housing Censuses* for selecting indicators of change in human capital, together with opportunities for selecting produced capital indicators through income and housing variables
- *System of National Accounts* for selecting indicators of change in produced assets
- *Standard Classification of Land Use* for selecting indicators of change in natural capital
- *Classification of the Functions of Government* for selecting and categorising the formal institutions of governance capital relative to either human, produced, or natural capital stocks
- *International Standard Industrial Classification (ISIC) of All Economic Activities* for selecting and categorising the informal institutions of social capital relative to either human, produced, or natural capital stocks
- *System for integrated Environmental and Economic Accounting (SEEA 2003)* for definitions and examples of "resource", "sink", "survival", and "amenity" functions

Field-testing the blueprint of mixed-methods design in the TASC project took place in two phases and in two locations. First, changes in the produced, human, and natural capital stocks of a local authority's jurisdiction were assessed over a five-year interval[2] using the SCENE model. Second, changes in the governance capital and social capital stocks of a local authority's jurisdiction were assessed over the same five-year interval (Osborn and Mcfarlane 2006; Osborn 2008).

COMPARING DESIGN BLUEPRINTS AND CONCLUSIONS

The designs of SDI sets identified in this chapter are experimental, involving discussion and testing of ideas under conditions far removed from those necessary to meet the imperative of engaging governments at all levels in tracking progress along their sustainable development paths. This is especially so given journeys lasting many decades when the planning horizons of many governments and their agencies may be measured in months.

Any judgement now on whether the designs are yet smart enough for the task ahead therefore signals where further changes may be beneficial. Table 14.3 compares the two designs against the nine criteria identified at the beginning of this chapter. The preliminary design in the CES Project presents, in the author's opinion, a SDI set that fails to meet criterion numbered 2, 3, 4, 5, 6, 7, 8, 9; and is thus not smart enough for adoption by national and sub-national governments at all levels.

Table 14.3   Comparing SDI Designs in the CES and TASC Projects

Criteria for a smart SDI set	*Preliminary design in the CES project*	*Design tested in the TASC project*
1. Connect policies horizontally.	Centralised statistical collection could avoid comparability issues where portfolio departments in central governments otherwise have autonomy and choose their own SDIs.	Horizontal co-ordination easier in the smaller organisations of local governments.
2. Connect policies vertically.	Assumes top-down penetration, probably without understanding depth necessary to diffuse among a very large population of sub-national governments.	Assumes aggregation upward through well-established statistical geography, thus assuring penetration through multiple levels within any adopting nation(s).
3. Align innovations with existing institutions and practices.	Radical innovation, primarily through monetising measures of human and social capital. Uncertainties in method will slow down adoption rates. More years of research and experimentation required.	Incremental innovation. Quantifiable indicators for human, produced, and built stocks drawn primarily from long-standing census collections. Feasibility of non-monetised measures for social and governance capital demonstrated.
4. Present relevant facts, data, problems, and concerns.	Weighting a national, real per capita indicator by jurisdictional population is assumed in penetrating to sub-national levels. Relevance questionable, and yet relevance is essential for any good indicator.	Stakeholder dialogue necessary input to design. The spatial place of assessment is where quantitative data originates.

continued

Table 14.3   Continued

Criteria for a smart SDI set	Preliminary design in the CES project	Design tested in the TASC project
5. Provide opportunities for sharing views, standpoints, and perspectives.	Opportunities for contributing to design choices seems limited to a relatively small group of experts from few disciplines. No evidence in public domain on the mechanisms or instruments for its diffusion and promotion.	Design recognises extent to which sub-national governments already use census collections in decision-making and their engagement in existing institutional arrangements for planning collections.
6. Absorb change in political and other actors over many decades.	Not yet tested.	Tested. Censuses of, say, Population/Housing, Agriculture, and Manufacturing collected for many decades.
7. Translate knowledge into messages that actors understand.	Extension of real per capita from produced capital to intangibles may be difficult to understand.	Messages created through stakeholder dialogue.
8. Translate knowledge into messages that affect actors' emotions.	Emotional affect of a national average weighted by a jurisdictional population of, say, a few hundred persons is likely to limited.	Emotional affect of using own quantitative data, plus own qualitative scoring, likely to high.
9. Translate knowledge into messages that elicit a response from actors.	Difficulty in understanding, compounded by limited emotional affect, not likely to elicit response.	Ease in understanding, compounded by emotional affect, likely to elicit response.

The design decisions taken so far in the CES project may, if they remain, facilitate international comparisons on the sustainable development of national governments. However, applying the criteria adopted for this chapter shows the CES project's design to date is not smart enough to contribute to its stated aim: "to show whether or not nations and their associated supra- and sub-national entities are managing their own territories in a sustainable manner and whether or not they contribute to global sustainability" (UNECE 2009, 25).

Results in Table 14.3 favour a mixed-methods approach over attempts to design a "one-size-fits-all" SDI set for governments at all levels. The outcome is consistent with a significant body of work recognising that no single solution or panacea will be sufficient to guide decision-makers through the wicked and complex situations of sustainable development. Recent examples firming those beliefs include those by the Australian Public Service Commission (2007) and by Ostrom (2007).

Those conducting the CES project are to be applauded for recognising that sub-national governments influence the development paths taken in their jurisdictions, and thus, alongside national governments, are likely to influence the prospects for global sustainable development. That recognition, however, takes the harmonising process for SDI sets well outside the comfort zone. It may be feasible (but unlikely) to create sufficient political influence within a social system of some two hundred sovereign national governments to diffuse a radical innovation from the CES project. But attempting the same process in a social system with some 661,000 potential adopting units is neither feasible nor likely. What to do next?

Asking and answering the question "are the contributions of sub-national governments to global sustainable development immaterial relative to those by national governments?" would seem to be very useful. If the answer is in the affirmative, then the CES project can avoid the harmonising issues it has created for itself. If the answer is in the negative, then the design blueprint from the TASC project, as reported in this chapter, demonstrates a way forward. It is offered in the strong belief that sub-national governments can and do make significant contributions to global sustainable development.

NOTES

1. See ABS Catalogue Numbers 4603.0 and 4611.0, http://www.abs.gov.au.
2. Australian Population and Housing Censuses occur every five years. This interval, or even one spanning ten years, seems necessary for assessing past change in capital stocks; for social learning sufficient to understand fully results and agree on responses; and for the responses made to become evident in the next round.

REFERENCES

Australian Public Service Commission. 2007. *Tackling Wicked Problems: A Public Policy Perspective.* Canberra: Commonwealth of Australia.
Baker, S. 2009. "In Pursuit of Sustainable Development: A Governance Perspective." Keynote Address 8th International Conference of the European Society for Ecological Economics, University of Ljubljana, Slovenia, 29 June–2 July. http://www.esee2009.si/ESEE2009.html.
Boulanger, P. M. 2005. "Integration in Sustainability Impact Assessment: Meanings, Patterns and Tools." Working Paper Methodology and Feasibility of Sustainability Impact Assessment, Belgium, Institut pour un Development Durable. http://users.skynet.be/idd/documents/EIDDD/WP02.pdf.
Central Intelligence Agency. 2009. *The World Factbook.* https://www.cia.gov/library/publications/the-world-factbook/.
Chambers, R., and G. Conway. 1991. *Sustainable Rural Livelihoods: Practical Concepts for the 21st Century.* Brighton: Institute of Development Studies.
Clark, W. C., and L. Holliday. 2006. *Linking Knowledge with Action for Sustainable Development: The Role of Program Management.* Washington, DC: The National Academies Press.

190   *Dick Osborn*

Daly, H. E. 1973. *Towards a Steady-State Economy.* San Francisco: W. H. Freeman and Co.
Dasgupta, P., and S. N. Seo. 2008. "Natural Capital and Economic Growth." In *Encyclopedia of Earth*, ed. C. J. Cleveland. Washington, DC: Environmental Information Coalition, National Council for Science and the Environment. http://www.eoearth.org/article/Natural_capital_and_economic_growth.
Ekins, P. 1992. "A Four-Capital Model of Wealth Creation." In *Real-Life Economics: Understanding Wealth Creation*, ed. P. Ekins and M. Max-Neef, 147–155. London: Routledge.
Fischer-Kowalski, M., and J. Rotmans. 2009. "Conceptualizing, Observing, and Influencing Socio-Ecological Transitions." *Ecology and Society* 14 (2): 3. http://www.ecologyandsociety.org/vol14/iss2/art3/.
Frascara, J. 2006. "Creating Communicational Spaces." In *Designing Effective Communications: Creating Contexts for Clarity and Meaning*, ed. J. Frascara, xiii–xxi. New York: Allworth Press.
Galligan, B., and C. Fletcher. 1993. "New Federalism, Intergovernmental Relations and Environmental Policy." In *Coastal Zone Inquiry: Consultancy Report.* Canberra: Resources Assessment Commission.
Grosskurth, J. 2003. "Sustainable Development: Understanding the System with SCENE and QSA." In *More Puzzle Solving for Policy: Integrated Assessment from Theory to Practice*, ed. P. Valkering, B. Amelung, R. van der Brugge, and J. Rotmans, 50–55. Maastricht: International Centre for Integrated Assessment and Sustainable Development.
Grosskurth, J., and J. Rotmans. 2006. "The SCENE Model: Getting a Grip on Sustainable Development in Policy-Making." *Environment, Development and Sustainability* 7 (1):133–149.
International Institute for Sustainable Development. n.d. *Compendium: A Global Directory to Indicator Initiatives.* http://www.iisd.org/measure/compendium/.
International Monetary Fund. 2008. *Government Finance Statistics Yearbook 2008.* Washington, DC: International Monetary Fund.
Kretzmann, J. P., and J. L. McKnight. 1993. *Building Communities from the Inside Out: A Path towards Finding and Mobilizing a Community's Assets.* Evanston: Asset-Based Community Development Institute, Northwestern University.
Lorenzoni, I., S. A. Nicholson-Cole, and L. Whitmarsh. 2007. "Barriers Perceived to Engaging with Climate Change among the UK Public and Their Policy Implications." *Global Environmental Change* 17:445–459.
Mathews, M. R. 1997. "Twenty-Five Years of Social and Environmental Accounting Research: Is There a Silver Jubilee to Celebrate?" *Accounting, Auditing and Accountability Journal* 10 (4): 481–531.
Meadows, D. 1998. *Indicators and Information Systems for Sustainable Development: A Report to the Balaton Group.* Hartland: The Sustainability Institute.
Osborn, D. 2005. "Packaging Innovations to Sustain River Murray Communities." Proceedings of the Asia-Pacific Extension Network's Symposium on Natural Resources Management. http://www.regional.org.au/au/apen/2005/2/2767_osbornrc.htm.
———. 2008. "Comparing Accounting Designs for Sustainability Governance." Work-in-progress presented at the International Workshop on Social Audit, Social Accounting and Accountability, Charles University Prague, 15–16 May. http://cpas.anu.edu.au/people/pdfs/Osborn_CESES-125-version1.pdf.
Osborn, D., and M. Mcfarlane. 2006. "Sustaining Communities by Learning from Integrated Assessments of Place." Presented at the In Practice Change for Sustainable Communities: Exploring Footprints, Pathways and Possibilities: APEN 2006 International Conference, La Trobe University, Beechworth, Victoria, Australia, 6–8 March. http://www.regional.org.au/au/apen/2006/refereed/3/2911_osbornrc.htm.

Ostrom, E. 2007. "A Diagnostic Approach for Going beyond Panaceas." *Proceedings of the US National Academy of Sciences* 104 (39): 15181–15187. http://www.pnas.org/content/104/39/15181.full.

Owen, D. 2008. "Chronicles of Wasted Time?: A Personal Reflection on the Current State of, and Future Prospects for, Social and Environmental Accounting Research." *Accounting, Auditing and Accountability Journal* 21 (2): 240–267.

Pinter, L., P. Hardi, and P. Bartelmus. 2005. *Sustainable Development Indicators: Proposals for the Way Forward: Prepared for the United Nations Division for Sustainable Development.* Winnipeg: International Institute for Sustainable Development. http://www.iisd.org/pdf/2005/measure_indicators_sd_way_forward.pdf.

Rogers, E. M. 2003. *The Diffusion of Innovations.* New York: Free Press.

Rothstein, B. 2007. *When All Is Said and Done. . . . What Is This Thing Called Social Capital.* Gothenburg, Sweden: Department of Political Science, University of Gothenburg. https://www.jyu.fi/en/congress/soca07/presentations/borothstein.

Serdult, U., C. Vogeli, C. Hirschi, and T. Widmer. 2005. *APES—The Actor-Process-Event Scheme.* Zurich: IPZ, University of Zurich. http://www.apes-tool.ch/.

Smith, R. 2007. "Development of the SEEA 2003 and Its Implementation." *Ecological Economics* 61 (4): 592–599.

United Cities and Local Governments. 2008. *Local Governments in the World: Basic Facts on 82 Selected Countries.* Madrid: United Cities and Local Governments.

United Nations, Commission of the European Communities, International Monetary Fund, Organisation for Economic Cooperation and Development, World Bank. 2003. *Handbook for Integrated Environmental and Economic Accounting.* New York: United Nations. http://unstats.un.org/unsd/envaccounting/seea.asp.

United Nations Department of Economic and Social Affairs. 1992. *Agenda 21: The United Programme of Action from Rio.* http://www.un.org/esa/dsd/agenda21/.

———. 2002. *World Summit on Sustainable Development: Johannesburg Plan of Implementation.* http://www.un.org/esa/sustdev/documents/WSSD_POI-/English/PO1Toc.htm.

United Nations Economic Commission for Europe. 2008. *Report on Measuring Sustainable Development: Statistics for Sustainable Development: Commonalities between Current Practice and Theory: Note by the Joint UNECE/OECD/Eurostat Working Group on Statistics for Sustainable Development.* http://www.unece.org/stats/documents/2008.06.ces.htm.

———. 2009. *Measuring Sustainable Development: Prepared in Cooperation with the Organisation for Economic Co-operation and Development and the Statistical Office of the European Communities (Eurostat).* http://www.unece.org/stats/archive/03.03f.e.htm.

United Nations Environment Programme. 1972. *Action Plan: Stockholm 1972.* http://www.unep.org/.

United Nations Statistics Division. n.d. http://unstats.un.org/unsd/methods.htm.

World Bank. 2006. *Where Is the Wealth of Nations? Measuring Capital in the 21st Century.* Washington, DC: World Bank.

———. 2009. "Measuring Sustainable Development: Wealth and Adjusted Net Savings." Working Paper 5, Joint UNECE/OECD/Eurostat Task Force for Measuring Sustainable Development, First Meeting, Geneva, 23–24 September. http://www.unece.org/stats/documents/2009.09.sust-dev.htm.

World Resources Institute. n.d. *Earth Trends.* http://earthtrends.wri.org.

15 Social and Sustainability Reporting in Italian Local Governments
What Is Not Reported?

Federica Farneti, James Guthrie, and Benedetta Siboni

INTRODUCTION

The World Commission on Environment and Development (WCED 1987) has argued for the importance of "sustainable development". However, to date various studies have focused on corporate sustainability (Gray and Bebbington 1993; Elkington 1997; Bebbington 2007), rather than the public or not-for-profit sectors (Ball and Grubnic 2007).

This lack of sustainability research is significant because public sector organisations should play a part in sustainability (Ball and Bebbington 2008). The public sector accounts for approximately 40 percent of all economic activity in western economies, and consequently has a "huge operational impact on the environment, society and economy" (Ball and Grubnic 2007, 243). Because of this impact, the public sector can make a significant contribution to sustainability by adopting "green" policies and activities. Also, as a purchaser of private sector services and products, the public sector can use this influence to contribute to sustainability (for example, green public procurement, energy use, recycling rates). With an overarching mission to deliver public policies in the interest of society generally, the public sector has a responsibility to create policies that support sustainability (Ball and Grubnic 2007).

In recognising these responsibilities of the public sector, the European Commission has issued a variety of policies to encourage central and local governments to voluntarily adopt sustainability strategies.[1] It is therefore crucial for the public sector to account for its performance in relation to sustainability (Dumay, Farneti, and Guthrie 2009; Farneti, Guthrie, and Siboni 2009) and to report on these activities, including social, environmental, and economic policies, strategies, actions, and results (Ball and Grubnic 2007).

Internationally, social and sustainability reporting has been widely debated (Adams and McNicholas 2007), both within the academic literature and at a political and practical level. For instance, Adams and Narayanan (2007, 71) state that "the reporting of sustainability issues by organisations is an important part of the sustainability agenda". Within this debate, the accounting and reporting techniques used are also central to discussions about sustainability (Unerman, Guthrie, and Striukova 2007). The various Global Reporting Initiative (GRI) guidelines (GRI 2006) are of particular interest because of their attempts to provide an international framework of reporting for all types of organisations. In Italy, a recent study demonstrated that there is a trend for Italian local governments to produce social reports, with 14 percent of municipalities and 38 percent of provinces producing social reports in 2005 (Siboni 2007).

This study aims to explore the social reporting practices in a selection of "better practice" Italian local government organisations and, in particular, to observe what has and has not been reported in comparison to the GRI guidelines. It uses an analytical framework developed in a prior study, in which the voluntary sustainability practices of a sample of Australian public sector organisations were examined (Guthrie and Farneti 2008). The specific research questions considered are:

1. What has been reported in Italian local government social reports?
2. What has or has not been reported in terms of the GRI guidelines?

This examination of Italian local government organisations establishes that their stand-alone social reports are actually "social reports" in name only. There were relatively few environmental, social, labour, product, or wider societal disclosures when compared to the GRI guidelines.

The chapter has been structured as follows: the following section provides a brief insight into the meaning of legitimacy theory, its use in the sustainability reporting literature, and how it is applied to this chapter. The third section discusses the research method applied and describes the group of organisations that have been studied. The fourth section provides the results of the analysis and the main findings of the study. The final section summarises and provides conclusions and outlines the limitations of the study.

THEORETICAL PERSPECTIVE OF THE STUDY

This chapter examines social reporting in Italian local governments using legitimacy theory. This particular theoretical perspective was chosen as it offers an explanation as to how accounting disclosures are used to influence an organisation's relationships with different parties. Guthrie and Parker (1990, 166) state that "disclosures have the capacity to transmit social, political, and economic meanings for a pluralistic set of report recipients". They also state that although reporting can be considered a strategic tool, disclosures cannot be considered neutral. Deegan and Rankin (1996, 50–51) argue that "in the general absence of specific environmental reporting requirements companies may elect to present only that information which is favourable to themselves. That is, they may elect to use environmental disclosures in a self-laudatory manner".

Legitimacy theory considers the way in which an organisation seeks to "legitimise" its activities and therefore meet society's expectations. For this reason, legitimacy theory is based on the notion of the social contract, which implies that organisations gain their right to operate through seeking and gaining social approval (Deegan and Unerman 2006).

Public expectations go further than the expectations of stakeholder groups. A failure to consider the concerns of society can result in a loss of trust in the organisation. One means by which organisations can answer community concerns is through social disclosures in their annual report or other media. In this way, Italian local governments can use the social report as a means to communicate with various stakeholders about management, environmental, labour, policy, and social responsibility matters.

The purpose of this chapter is to extend discussion on social reporting practice by focusing on "better practice" organisations and identifying what is actually reported. Hence, this chapter sets out to explore the presence or otherwise of voluntary disclosures relating to certain management, environmental, labour, and social responsibility matters within a group of social reports.

RESEARCH METHOD

In a previous study, Siboni (2007) investigated Italian provinces and municipalities by submitting a questionnaire to determine "which" local governments adopted social reports and "how" social reporting was carried out in practice. Siboni determined that 120 municipalities and forty-five provinces produced a social report. Her study investigated the stakeholder engagement practices of those organisations in terms of social reporting. She found that of the 165 local governments, just seventeen of them had developed stakeholder engagement.[2] This sample of seventeen local government's "better practice" social reports is analysed in the present study.

The current study uses content analysis to determine the type of disclosure in the stand-alone social reports produced by this group of seventeen local governments. Content analysis was chosen as it is the "dominant research method for collecting empirical evidence" in social and environmental reporting (Guthrie and Abeysekera 2006, 115; Parker 2005). Content analysis is "a technique for gathering data, involves codifying qualitative and quantitative information into pre-defined categories in order to derive patterns in the presentation and reporting of information" and "is a method of codifying the text of writing into various groups or categories based on a selected criteria" (Guthrie and Abeysekera 2006, 120).

There is considerable debate in the literature on the choice of the most appropriate "unit of analysis" that should be used in content analysis (Gray,

Kouhy, and Lavers 1995). For instance, Unerman (2000) indicates that the unit of analysis could take the form of words, pictures, phrases, characters, lines, sentences, and page proportions devoted to categories of social disclosure. In this study, a pilot test was undertaken and, because of the nature of the disclosures within the Italian social reports, it was decided to focus only on the use or otherwise of an individual element. Therefore, the results only indicate if an element was used or not used. The Guthrie and Farneti framework, developed for a previous study (2008), was applied. This framework was based on the International GRI guidelines (GRI 2006) and their public agencies supplement (GRI 2005). These guidelines are the most commonly used within the private and public sectors (Farneti, Guthrie, and Siboni 2009). The framework consists of eighty-one elements, grouped into six categories[3] (see Guthrie and Farneti 2008). An index was constructed of total possible disclosures (that is, elements = 81 x 17 organisations = 1,377 possibilities). Also, type of disclosure (that is, declarative, monetary, non-monetary, and monetary and non-monetary) was observed. This form of classification is common in the literature (Guthrie et al. 2004). Using the index, one coder analysed the social reports. A reliability check was undertaken whilst the coding was at an early stage, which found that no major issues of difference were reported, showing that the coding was reliable.

This study analysed both provincial and municipal Italian local governments. Farneti, Guthrie, and Siboni (2009) analysed three frameworks (A, B, and C) developed by different Italian institutional bodies to provide guidelines for social reports for Italian public sector organisations. However, social reporting is not mandatory for Italian public sector organisations, nor has any indication been given as to what guidelines should apply. While the coding instrument used was based on the GRI, none of the Italian organisations in this study referred to the GRI framework, nor consistently to any of the Italian frameworks in their social reports (Farneti, Guthrie, and Siboni 2009). As indicated earlier, the key characteristic for selecting "better practice" Italian local government organisations had been the inclusion of stakeholder engagement in the stand-alone social reports. The characteristics of the social reports and the frameworks adopted for each of the organisations are listed in Table 15.1.

The next section reports on the results of the analysis developed, as well as the main findings.

RESULTS OF THE ANALYSIS

The following analysis examines "what" has been disclosed in the social reports.

Table 15.2 highlights "what" has been disclosed in terms of categories.

The first column of Table 15.2 shows the categories (n = 6). The second column gives the sum of the elements within the GRI coding instrument

Table 15.1   Length and Framework Followed for Social Report

Organisation	Number of pages in the social reports	Frameworks of social report followed
A	84	None (model of social report developed internally)
B	106	None (model of social report developed internally)
C	71	None (model of social report developed internally)
D	281	Italian Directive for social report issued by Department of Public Affairs
E	173	None (model of social report developed internally)
F	72	None (model of social report developed internally)
G	108	Italian Directive for social report issued by Department of Public Affairs
H	101	None (model of social report developed internally, only partially following the Italian Directive)
I	76	None (model of social report developed internally)
L	91	None (model of social report developed internally)
M	166	None (model of social report developed by external consultancy)
N	31	Italian Directive for social report issued by Department of Public Affairs
O	160	None (model of social report developed internally with the help of academic consultant)
P	147	None (model of social report developed internally)
Q	78	None (model of social report developed internally with the help of academic consultant)
R	491	None (model of social report developed internally with the help of external consultant)
S	415	None (model of social report developed internally with the help of academic consultant)

Table 15.2   Total Disclosures by Categories

Category	Number of elements in the coding instrument	Total used
1. Environmental	30	7.1%
2. Human Rights	9	0.0%
3. Labour Practices and Decent Work	14	18.5%
4. Product Responsibility	9	0.0%
5. Society	8	0.7%
6. Public Agencies	11	52.4%
Total	81	13.0%

(n = 81). The third column provides the percentage of the GRI elements disclosed, divided into the six categories. The analysis undertaken shows that of a possible total of 1,377, only 179 disclosures have been reported, which is 13 percent of the possible elements that could have been reported by the seventeen organisations.

Furthermore, Table 15.2 shows that the category of "Public Agencies" accounts for the highest number of disclosures within the data set analysed, with 52.4 percent, followed by "Labour Practices and Decent Work" with 18.5 percent, and "Environment" only accounting for 7.1 percent of total possible disclosures. Moreover, of the total elements, only 0.7 percent of disclosure elements were for "Society", while "Human Rights" and "Product Responsibility" both had no disclosures. This highlights that in Italy the reporting practice commonly referred to as social reporting does not include social aspects (based on the GRI categories "Human Rights", "Labour Practices and Decent Work", "Product Responsibility", and "Society"), nor does it incorporate environmental elements.

Table 15.3 Number of Incidents for Each Element

Elements	*Total*	*Elements*	*Total*
1. Environment		**4. Product Responsibility**	
EN6	2	No disclosure	
EN7	2	**5. Society**	
EN11	1	SO8	1
EN14	1	**6. Public Agencies**	
EN16	1	PA2	11
EN17	1	PA3	10
EN18	12	PA4	9
EN22	1	PA5	9
EN30	15	PA6	17
2. Human Rights		PA7	9
No disclosure		PA12	17
3. Labour Practice		PA15	16
LA1	14		
LA2	5		
LA7	1		
LA8	3		
LA10	7		
LA11	1		
LA13	11		
LA14	2		

While there were specific disclosures relating to the environment among the reported elements as shown in Table 15.3 such as: "initiatives to reduce greenhouse gas emissions and reductions achieved" (EN18) and "total environmental protection expenditures and investments by type" (EN30), the other thirteen elements were not used or only used once. Therefore, most of the environmental elements were not used by this group of Italian local governments.

Table 15.3 illustrates that there was no reporting of Human Rights as per the eight GRI elements. A review of the elements indicates that most of these are applicable to Public Agencies. The most reported labour practices category concerns workers, in particular: "total workforce by employment type, employment contract, and region" (LA1). Also, the "composition of governance bodies and breakdown of employees per category according to gender, age group, minority group membership, and other indicators of diversity" (LA13) was reported.

A significant observation in relation to Table 15.3 concerns the number of elements which were not used. As Table 15.3 shows, out of the eighty-one elements, fifty-four were not used at all. Many elements and entire categories such as "Product Responsibility" and "Human Rights" were not used, whereas "Society" was reported only once.

Concerning what is not reported, it is observed that from the environmental category (based on thirty possible elements) only nine were actually used. Table 15.3 indicates that important elements such as "direct energy consumption by primary energy source" (EN3) or "energy saved due to conservation and efficiency improvements" (EN5) were not reported at all. This leads to a general observation that there was little disclosure of environmental matters in the "better practice" social reports of the local government organisations analysed.

Furthermore, for "Labour Practices", which has fourteen elements, few disclosures were observed. Of the fourteen elements, eight were reported, but only LA1—"Total workforce by employment type, employment contract, and region"—was used by the organisation.

For the category "Society" only one element was found. All other elements such as nature, scope, and effectiveness of any programs and practices that assess and manage the impacts of operations on communities were not reported.

Finally, the category "Public Agency" was by far the most commonly reported, not only as a percentage of total disclosures, but also by the most number of elements taken up. Also the analysis reveals a focus on reporting on goals (PA6) and financial aspects (PA12), as well as administrative efficiency (PA15).

A general finding is that of the social reports examined the organisations used these voluntary stand-alone reports primarily to report on administrative and managerial matters. What was missing from these social reports was the reporting of environmental, social, labour, product, or societal information.

The analysis of the type of information disclosed, as shown in Table 15.4, indicates that of the 179 elements recorded, most were "non-monetary" (32.4 percent), followed by "monetary and non-monetary" (31.8 percent).

Finally, analysis of the specific category "Public Agencies" (refer to coding instrument) indicates that from the total group of eleven elements analysed, only eight were actually used in the reports. This finding is unexpected because the public agencies' indicators have been developed specifically for public sector organisations. Three elements were the main focus of the social reports examined. The first is PA6, the reporting of activities undertaken during the year, the second is PA12, the reporting of allocation of activities, and the last is PA15, administrative efficiency. Reporting on these aspects is further divided into two types of information: (a) non-monetary and (b) monetary and non-monetary.

CONCLUSIONS

This study explores social reports in a group of "better practice" Italian local governments, providing data to identify what has been disclosed and what has not been disclosed. The findings highlight that in Italy, social reports are still in their infancy and that in practice they do not include all the elements outlined by the GRI framework. Examination of this group of Italian local governments indicates that social reports focus on administrative and managerial matters. Similar findings emerge from a study on Italian university social reports (Del Sordo et al. 2009).

Furthermore, the study finds that the disclosure practices analysed do not conform to the expected content of GRI reports. This may be related to the fact that social reporting in Italy is voluntary and there is no commonly accepted framework to guide practice.

In addition, only 13 percent of possible elements from our disclosure instrument was reported by the seventeen "better practice" organisations. This level of disclosure is lower than that found in Guthrie and Farneti's (2008) study of Australian public sector "better practice" organisations, which found that

Table 15.4   Type of Information Disclosed

Summary	Number	Percentage
1. Declarative	45	25.1%
2. Monetary	19	10.6%
3. Non-Monetary	58	32.4%
4. Monetary and Non-Monetary	57	31.8%
Total	179	Total 100%

the GRI framework was used but that its use was fragmented. That the Public Agencies category was the most reported (at 52.4 percent) suggests that in Italy the focus of social reports is administrative policies and programs. The finding that the type of information disclosed, in terms of quality, was either "non-monetary" or both "monetary and non-monetary" contrasts with findings by Steccolini (2004) and Monfardini (2004), who demonstrated that the social reports analysed in their research were mainly declarative.

By examining the social reports via legitimacy theory, the study finds that the Italian local governments have used their social reports as a means to communicate with a variety of stakeholders in an attempt to legitimise their activities. Since the disclosure practices of these local governments are not primarily environmental or social in nature, the term "social report" can be considered a misnomer. Boedker, Mouritsen, and Guthrie (2008) argued that in order for social and environmental reports to be genuinely considered extended performance reports, global guidelines are needed, which could be useful for harmonisation.

NOTES

1. COM(2001) 264 final; COM(2002) 82 final; COM(2005) 658 final; COM(2005) 37 final; and local governments COM(2006) 385 final.
2. This study goes further than Siboni (2007) by checking the veracity of organisations' claims of stakeholder engagement. Specifically, stakeholder engagement practices were established analysing the content of social reports, including: (a) declaration, within the social reports, of stakeholder engagement developed by the local governments and the verification of the stated stakeholder engagement in the report by one of the authors; (b) stakeholder evaluation about the effectiveness of public activity (e.g., customer satisfaction survey); (c) stakeholder evaluation concerning the social report, in terms of completeness, transparency, clarity, and, on the other hand, the lack of data; and (d) a stakeholder survey (at the end of the social report) that explored the embedding of social reporting practices in local governments policies.
3. The disclosure instrument was framed via six categories:
   1. Environmental (EN)
   2. Social–Human Rights (HR)
   3. Social–Labour Practices and Decent Work Social Performance: Labour Practices and Decent Work (LA)
   4. Social–Product Responsibility (PR)
   5. Social–Society (SO)
   6. Public Agencies
   The content codes were further specified into aspects (n = 33) and then into elements (n = 81; see Guthrie and Farneti 2008).

REFERENCES

Adams, C. A., and P. McNicholas. 2007. "Making a Difference: Sustainability Reporting, Accountability and Organisational Change." *Accounting, Auditing and Accountability Journal* 20 (3): 382–402.

Adams, C., and V. Narayanan. 2007. "The 'Standardization' of Sustainability Reporting." In *Sustainability Accounting and Accountability*, ed. J. Unerman, J. Bebbington, and B. O'Dwyer, 71–85. Oxon and New York: Routledge.

Ball, A., and J. Bebbington. 2008. "Accounting and Reporting for Sustainable Development in Public Service Organizations." *Public Money and Management* 28 (6): 323–326.

Ball, A., and S. Grubnic. 2007. "Sustainability Accounting and Accountability in the Public Sector." In *Sustainability Accounting and Accountability*, ed. J. Unerman, J. Bebbington, and B. O'Dwyer, 243–265. Oxon and New York: Routledge.

Bebbington, J. 2007. *Accounting for Sustainable Development Performance.* Oxford: CIMA publishing, Elsevier.

Boedker, C., J. Mouritsen, and J. Guthrie. 2008. "Enhanced Business Reporting: International Trends and Possible Policy Directions." *Journal of Human Resource Costing and Accounting* 12 (1): 14–25.

Deegan, C., and M. Rankin. 1996. "Do Australian Companies Report Environmental News Objectively? An Analysis of Environmental Disclosures by Firms Prosecuted Successfully by the Environmental Protection Authority." *Accounting, Auditing and Accountability Journal* 9 (2): 50–67.

Deegan, C., and J. Unerman. 2006. *Financial Accounting Theory.* European ed. Berkshire: McGraw-Hill.

Del Sordo, C., F. Farneti, S. Pazzi, and B. Siboni. 2009. "Voluntary Reporting in Italian Universities: What Do They Report?" Paper presented to the 1st International Conference on Sustainable Management of Public and Not for Profit Organisations, University of Bologna, Italy, 1–3 July.

Dumay, J., F. Farneti, and J. Guthrie. 2009. "Critical Analysis of International Guidelines for Sustainability Reporting in Public and Not for Profit Sector Organisations." To be presented to the XXXII Convegno AIDEA, Le Risorse Immateriali dell'Economia Aziendale, Ancona, 24–25 September.

Elkington, J. 1997. *Cannibals with Forks. The Triple Bottom Line of 21ˢᵗ Century Business.* Oxford: Cupstone Paperbook.

Farneti, F., J. Guthrie, and B. Siboni. 2009. "Social Reporting in Italian Local Governments: What They Do Not Report." Presented at the 9th Interdisciplinary Perspectives on Accounting Conference, Innsbruck, Austria, 9–11 July.

Global Reporting Initiative. 2005. *Global Reporting Initiative: Sector Supplement for Public Agencies.* http://www.globalreporting.org/SSPA (accessed 5 December 2006).

———. 2006. *RG. Sustainability Reporting Guidelines.* http://www.globalreporting.org/Home/BottomBlock3/G3C.htm (accessed 5 December 2006).

Gray, R., and J. Bebbington. 1993. *Accounting for the Environment.* London: Sage Publications.

Gray, R. H., R. Kouhy, and S. Lavers. 1995. "Corporate Social and Environmental Reporting: A Review of the Literature and a Longitudinal Study of UK Disclosure." *Accounting, Auditing and Accountability Journal* 8 (2): 47–77.

Guthrie, J., and I. Abeysekera. 2006. "Using Content Analysis as a Research Method to Inquire into Social and Environmental Disclosure: What Is New?" *Journal of Human Resource Costing and Accounting* 10 (2): 114–126.

Guthrie, J., and F. Farneti. 2008. "GRI Sustainability Reporting by Australian Public Sector Organizations." *Public Money and Management* 28 (6): 361–366.

Guthrie, J., and L. Parker. 1990. "Corporate Social Disclosure Practice: A Comparative International Analysis." *Advances in Public Interest Accounting* 3:159–175.

Guthrie, J., R. Petty, K. Yongvanich, and F. Ricceri. 2004. "Using Content Analysis as a Research Method to Inquire into Intellectual Capital Reporting." *Journal of Intellectual Capital* 5 (2): 282–293.

202 *Federica Farneti, James Guthrie, and Benedetta Siboni*

Monfardini, P. 2004. "An Ethical Model for Social Reporting: The Case of Italian Local Public Administrations." Paper presented at the annual Conference of the European Group of Public Administrations, Ljubljana.

Parker, L. 2005. "Social and Environmental Accountability Research: A View from the Commentary Box." *Accounting, Auditing and Accountability Journal* 18 (6): 842–860.

Siboni, B. 2007. *La rendicontazione sociale negli enti locali. Analisi dello stato dell'arte.* Milan: Franco Angeli.

Steccolini, I. 2004. *Accountability e sistemi informativi negli enti locali. Dal rendiconto al bilancio sociale.* Turin: Giappichelli.

Unerman, J. 2000. "Methodological Issues: Reflections on Quantification in Corporate Social Reporting Content Analysis." *Accounting, Auditing and Accountability Journal* 13 (5): 667–680.

Unerman, J., J. Guthrie, and L. Striukova. 2007. *United Kingdom Reporting of Intellectual Capital.* London: Research Monograph for ICAEW Intellectual Capital Reporting Project, ICAEW.

World Commission on Environment and Development. 1987. "From One Earth to One World: An Overview." Oxford: Oxford University Press. http://www.wsu.edu/~susdev/WCED87.html (accessed 25 November 2009).

16 Stakeholder Responses to a Social and Environmental Reporting Model for the Credit Union Sector

Dianne McGrath

INTRODUCTION

This chapter describes a reporting model for the credit union sector in Australia. Credit unions are financial institutions within in the banking sector offering community-based competitive financial service. Credit unions can be distinguished from banks by virtue of a focus imbedded in the credit union principles (World Council of Credit Unions [WOCCU] 2007). Being mutual organisations, credit union customers are both members and owners, resulting in a focus on members and benefits to those members, and not on generating profit for external shareholders. The sector is growing with 149 credit unions currently operating throughout Australia, which together hold more than AU$35 billion in assets, providing services to more than 3.5 million Australians (Association of Building Societies and Credit Unions [ABACUS] 2006).

Like organisations in other industry sectors, credit unions are faced with the challenge of managing social and environmental impacts. The efforts of credit unions to provide financial services, while at the same time adding to the welfare of their community, means credit unions have adopted various mechanisms to report on their activities. These mechanisms have included the generation of stand-alone sustainability reports, integrated triple-bottom-line reports, reports in accordance with the Global Reporting Initiative (GRI), and the in-house developed Sustainability Toolkit (Credit Union Foundation Australia 2006). Reporting in the credit union sector has mirrored the broader business environment with no single preferred method or format for reporting (Mathews 1997a, 1997b, 2003).

Changes in the provision of Australian banking services and the uniqueness of this sector have motivated the exploration and development of a reporting model for the credit union sector. There has been a significant shift in the way deposit services are provided within the banking sector. The major deposit taking institutions, commercial banks, have adopted strategies to reduce bank branches, encourage the use of electronic facilities, and reduce employee numbers. At the same time, there has been an increase in the services being offered in regional communities by the credit union sector. This has included a greater physical presence and broadening the products available to clients.

The proposed model seeks to improve the accountability of organisations by establishing, under a conceptual framework, a reporting mechanism for social and environmental accounting. The model retains the qualitative attributes of financial accounting information in accordance with the Australian Accounting Standards Board (AASB) Framework, namely understandability, relevance, reliability, and comparability (CPA Australia 2007). While acknowledging the limitations of the model, given that it is based on a single case study organisation with data limited by a small response rate, the extended model of the financial reporting framework presented and discussed in this chapter has the potential to improve the transparency of decision-making systems and provide integrity to the reporting processes of organisations in the sector.

BACKGROUND

Increasingly, traditional financial reporting is failing to satisfy the needs of firms and stakeholders. Focusing exclusively on financial measures is no longer practical, particularly where a firm has multiple objectives and multiple stakeholders and faces dynamic forces such as the global movement toward the disclosure of social and environmental impacts.

Motivations for social and environmental reporting include: reducing adverse effects of certain events (Deegan, Rankin, and Voight 2000); maximising competitive advantage (Nash 2001); and managing pressures to administer social and environmental responsibilities, public image, and legitimacy (O'Donovan 2002).

Studies (Adams, Hill, and Roberts 1998; Hackston and Milne 1996) have examined the influences of size, industry grouping, country of origin, and risk on corporate social reporting. Certain industry sectors may be perceived to carry greater risks, often environmental. The banking sector, as a service industry, has low environmental risk but may have higher incentives to disclose social aspects to support the notion of a good corporate citizen (McGrath 2003).

Despite increasing interest in social and environmental accounting, major corporate reporters have retained the traditional accounting reporting model, disclosing social and environmental information on a fragmentary and ad hoc basis (Adams, Hill, and Roberts 1998). While a number of reporting mechanisms have been proposed, such as the GRI (2006), Social Accountability 8000 (SA 8000; CEPPA 2001), and the Institute of Social and Ethical Accountability's AA1000 (AccountAbility 1999), there is yet to be agreement on one consistent format.

Critics have questioned whether social and environmental reports are intended to provide an independent and "objective" picture of performance or are instead intended to counteract existing or anticipated negative perceptions of the organisation (Laufer 2003; Ramus and Montiel 2005). Overcoming definitional inconsistencies and improving the quality of the disclosures via enhanced content, independence, and reliability will result in increased integrity in the reporting process—avoiding willing or unwilling deception.

As more companies make social and environmental disclosures, there has been a call for such impacts and their consequences on society and the environment to be included as a primary part of the decision-making process of organisations (Dando and Swift 2003). In order to achieve this, social and environmental impacts must be recognised as elements of organisational performance management and control systems. The well-entrenched and significant role played by accountants in a firms' decision-making processes (Hoskin and Macve 1994), however, potentially limits the information provided to management because of their strong focus on traditional financial reporting. This focus often ignores non-economic costs on the basis that they are not directly quantifiable in money terms. When such costs are identified, they are often left as "bracketed" items and considered as secondary qualitative issues (Robson 1991). Financial decision-making is limited in providing only a single dimension to the organisation, implying profit as the only determinant of success. Profit maximisation as the only goal of the firm has come under severe criticism from many quarters (Adams, Hill, and Roberts 1998; Deegan 1999; Nash 2001).

Report Formats and Purpose

The term *social accounting* includes "all forms of accounts that go beyond the economic and for all the different labels under which it appears" (Gray 2002, 687).

Two distinctly different reporting approaches to corporate social reporting (CSR) have emerged from the literature. Firstly, the reporting format can treat disclosures as an addendum to conventional accounting activity. This assumes that the principle users are in the financial community. This limits the perception of CSR to that which can be articulated within the current confines of conventional accounting, that is, linked to and articulated as a financial event. Not all organisational impacts are able to be reliably quantified in monetary terms and thus restrict the dimensions that can be reported.

An alternative approach is to adopt a report separate from the financial report. Formally prepared reports fall into two types: Corporate Social Reports (also referred to as Corporate Social Disclosure) or Sustainability Reports. Corporate Social Reports/Corporate Social Disclosure (CSR/CSD) are content specific, reporting on the social dimensions and excluding the financial aspects. Sustainability Reports incorporate all three (social, environmental, and economic) aspects of the "triple-bottom-line" (Elkington

1997) but continue to report the financial aspects as a discrete section and do not integrate the financial aspects with the social and environmental issues.

The model presented in this chapter adopts a framework that seeks to integrate social, environmental, and financial dimensions. Gray, Kouhy, and Lavers (1995) have noted that full integration requires a re-examination of the traditional role of reported organisation information. The model presented is based on a notion of reporting on the comprehensive goals of the organisation, which include both financial and non-financial goals, rather than the traditional profit-oriented focus. It is argued that this change in reporting expectations presents a more robust reporting regime that will meet the decision needs of internal and external stakeholders.

Reporting Mechanisms

Three commonly adopted mechanisms evident in the reporting practices of organisations are the GRI (2006), SA 8000 (CEPPA 2001), and AA1000 (AccountAbility 1999). The GRI (2006) reports are based on core indicators—those of interest to most stakeholders—with an assumption of "materiality", and additional indicators which consist of emerging practices or issues specific to an industry or context but not material for the majority of stakeholders. Problems arise concerning selectivity in what is to be included in respect to both the core and the additional indicators, and those which are not overcome by the reporting principles and qualitative characteristics provided in the GRI guidelines. These characteristics have similarities to the qualitative characteristics of financial reporting. While claiming to be prepared in accordance with the GRI guidelines, the ability to selectively include items in the report calls into question the veracity of the reports.

The Council for Economic Priorities SA 8000 (CEPPA 2001) limits its reporting requirements to matters concerned with human rights and the rights of children, benchmarking performance in these areas against the UN Declaration of Human Rights, the International Labour Organisation conventions, and the UN Convention on the Rights of the Child.

The third commonly cited reporting standard, AA1000 (AccountAbility 1999), presents guidelines for a system of reporting rather than specifying benchmarks or reporting indicators. In addition, a Sustainability Toolkit has been developed for the use of credit unions; largely a guide to preparing a report under the GRI guidelines, but to date there has been very little adoption.

A 2005 research report commissioned by CPA Australia, *Sustainability Reporting Practices, Performances and Potential*, identifies current reporting practices in Australia (Jones et al. 2005). The report found no overwhelming adoption of any particular reporting mechanism.

In summary, the literature reveals two broad categories of focus—studies examining what drives the organisation to report and studies of the reporting outputs and their form and content. The model described in this chapter responds to a call by Loftus and Purcell (2006) to explore how to extend traditional financial reporting to make transparent the decision-making processes and performance criteria for the social and environmental dimensions of organisational operations. The model presents an integrated framework that requires financial reporting to extend beyond matters only of financial concern in order to integrate the impacts of the organisations' activities on the society and the environment. The model does not simply add the financial costs and benefits of corporate social responsibility into the existing accounting regimes, but adopts an approach whereby the social and environmental dimensions are integrated into reporting and the congruence between the social, environmental, and financial dimensions is recognised. It is the element of congruence that creates the transparency in decision-making that is missing under current approaches. The model seeks to integrate the financial and social/environmental reports, not necessarily requiring a single report, but rather it attempts via the congruence element to ensure consistency in the principles adopted across the financial and non-financial aspects of operations.

DEVELOPING THE MODEL

This chapter presents a model developed as part of a larger project which explored and ranked the reporting needs of internal and external credit union stakeholders. The model assumes a political economy perspective, acknowledging that the final reports are social, political, and economic documents. The model also adopts a legitimacy perspective strongly relying on the notion of a social contract between the organisation and the society in which it operates. This mirrors the suggestions of Tinker and Neimark (1987) and Mathews (1997b), who advocate a move away from profit as the key measure of performance and industry practice, as seen in the increased number of organisations providing social and environmental reports (Hackston and Milne 1996).

The proposed conceptual framework for a reporting model was developed based on data previously reported (McGrath 2006). This earlier study found that credit union stakeholders desired information beyond the traditional financial measures of performance. There was a strong preference for other measures rather than the traditional financial measures. However, there was also a clear message that the style of traditional reports was favoured. The question posed was how to satisfy the demand for information and yet retain the qualities of traditional financial reports. This resulted in a closer look at the existing conceptual framework for financial reporting and the characteristics of the information reported, as well as currently available social and environmental reporting guidelines.

CHALLENGES AND ASSUMPTIONS OF THE PROPOSED MODEL

The first challenge encountered in designing the model was the need to keep the model flexible. By its very nature, legitimacy theory requires an understanding of society's expectations and these expectations are dynamic. Failure to accommodate the dynamic nature of society's expectation would inevitably lead to the legitimacy gap identified by Sethi (1978).

The model also seeks to overcome criticism of conceptions of social and environmental reporting as merely being an exercise in greenwashing the public (Laufer 2003; Ramus and Montiel 2005). The establishment of a framework for reporting, bearing common characteristics between financial and social dimensions, will achieve a transparency lacking in the current ad hoc approach.

The inclusion of corporate governance performance, in addition to social and environmental performance, stemmed from the need for the model to ensure that the philosophy of social responsibility is imbedded into the organisation's goals and decision-making processes. This fourth dimension to the accepted social, environment, and economic dimensions was noted by Woodward, Woodward, and Rovira Val (2004, 8) as being the "umbrella" over the other three dimensions.

The model does not disregard the indicators and standards developed under GRI (2006), SA 8000 (CEPPA 2001), or AA1000 (AccountAbility 1999). The model accepts the value of these indicators where there is a holistic approach resulting from consistency in the application of the required information characteristics.

The model attempts to take into account the findings of the previous study in acknowledging the importance placed on the current format of financial reports and thus the framework in which they are prepared. Further, the model seeks to reflect the level of importance attributable to the social and environmental issues that were revealed in the preference rankings of research subjects (McGrath 2006). As the model has been based on research conducted within the narrow confines of the credit union sector, its application is proposed only for that sector.

COMPONENTS OF THE MODEL

The current conceptual framework utilised by Australian and international accounting standard setters (CPA Australia 2007) and the International Accounting Standards Board (IASB 2006) provided the basis for the development of the model (Figure 16.1).

The primary objective of the model reflects the objectives as set out in paragraph one of SAC1 of the Australian Accounting Standards and supported by the IASB (2006). In order to support this primary objective, information generated should be of sufficient range to enable users

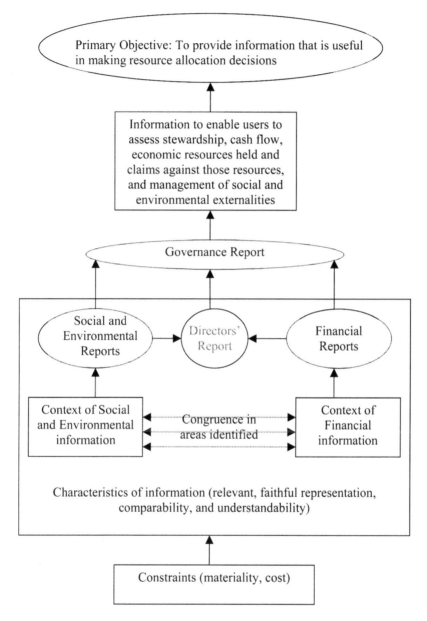

Figure 16.1 Conceptual reporting framework for credit unions.

to judge the performance of the organisation from a holistic perspective. This suggests the information should encompass all dimensions of performance, including social and environmental impacts and not just profitability.

The Governance Report is informed by the Australian Stock Exchange (ASX) *Principles of Good Corporate Governance and Best Practice Recommendations* (Australian Stock Exchange 2007). The Governance Report highlights the structures in place which encourage organisations to create value, to be accountable, and to have control systems commensurate with the risks involved. The report will also include some degree of reliance on, and reference to, AA1000 (AccountAbility 1999) and the guidance it provides in setting goals, targets, and measurement of performance against those targets, incorporating the key component of consultation with stakeholders. This reflects stakeholders' concerns that the stated objectives to provide a balance of social, environmental, and financial aspects to the management of the entity are reflected in the operations of the enterprise with information on policy ranked higher than operational issues.

Social and Environmental Reports (see Figure 16.1) would be prepared as a combination of the GRI (2006) and SA 8000 (CEPPA2001) reflecting both reporting categories and processes. The report will provide a mix of qualitative and quantitative information and is the subject of further research. The Directors' Report and Financial Reports continue to be prepared in accordance with International Accounting Standards (and relevant legislative requirements).

The characteristics of the information are defined by the Accounting Conceptual Framework (IASB 2006). The framework builds on the existing financial accounting frameworks and the characteristics are conceptually consistent with the GRI (2006) reporting principles. In adopting the IASB and FASB characteristics, the model embraces the fundamental characteristics of the traditional financial reporting categories as preferred by the respondents to the study. The model acknowledges the similarities between characteristics developed for social and environmental information and financial information and seeks to have a set of fundamental characteristics common to all three dimensions of reporting.

A fundamental component of the model is the congruence between the social and environmental information and the financial information to be included in the respective reports. When considering the characteristics of information to include, if an activity is sufficiently relevant to be reported under either the financial or social and environmental branches, then its impact on all aspects should be reflected. For example, if philanthropic activity is of such a level or of such importance to the community, then the activity should be reported as both a social element and a financial element. Similarly, if environmental damage has occurred and is to be remedied, then both the damage must be reported as well as the cost of remedial action. Where externalities are identified in the social and environmental activities, current and future impacts on assets and liabilities should be noted. It is not required that such impacts be necessarily reflected in the bottom-line profit; however, guided by the accounting standards, they might appear as a note to the financials.

Ultimately, the benefit from providing the information must justify the costs to obtain and prepare it. The justification lies in how material the information is to the users and is a matter to be considered by the preparers of the reports, taking into account both the nature of the item and the amount. Referring to the previous example of philanthropic activity, its materiality and thus subsequent reporting would not be dependant solely on the amount; indeed, based on the value of the support alone few of these activities would be deemed material. However, if the nature of the activity has a significant impact on community, relations with community, happiness of the workforce, or like factors, then the activity is "material" (it matters) and it should be specified in both the financial and social and environmental reports. Currently this is often not the case, with activities of this nature well documented within the social report, but receiving little, if any, mention in the financial reports. In discussion with participants in the study it was noted that financial and non-financial data for reporting is already collected by many organisations. It is mooted that adjustments to traditional data output formats can be enacted to efficiently extract the information, as opposed to imposing new cost burdens with separate data collection systems for collecting additional information.

EVALUATION OF THE MODEL

The proposed conceptual framework model was taken to three credit union stakeholder groups; directors, management, and a representative of the regulatory bodies. For consistency, credit unions of a similar size and characteristics, and which were geographically based and regional, were also selected to provide feedback on the model. Credit unions satisfying the criteria and located in the three major states on the Australian east coast were identified. Of the total of 131 credit unions in Queensland, New South Wales, and Victoria, thirty-five qualified to be approached for interviews. Telephone and e-mail were used to seek participation in a two-hour interview. Four organisations were able to provide access to management and directors for the interviews. Two of the organisations had a social and environment agenda, although neither had published a report in the past year. The remaining two had not reported at any time. A member of one of the supporting bodies of the credit union sector also agreed to be interviewed. This elite sampling was founded on the belief that the views of the group that would be most closely involved in using the model to prepare the reports would have the most to offer in critically evaluating the proposed model.

The interviews were semi-structured and, while focused on the model, allowed for exploration of issues raised. Respondents were offered flexibility in how they evaluated the model—some opted for a top-down approach, others focused on particular aspects of the model. The interviews were taped and transcript content analysed to identify themes. The unit of analysis was a phrase, rather than a single word, as phrases better captured meaning in the responses.

Three important issues were identified:

1. The model was static.
2. Congruence between the social and environmental information and the financial information was critical.
3. The model would assist transparency and thus mitigate risk.

It was commented that the model should be more strategic, including: "model implies static reporting, but governance is dynamic" and the "model needs to be dynamic, possibly a strategic planning link into the model." Two participants suggested that the goals and mission of the organisation should feed into the primary objective to ensure that all dimensions of performance were reflected in resource allocation decisions. It was further suggested that goals be linked to report preparation, reinforcing the purpose of reporting.

All respondents identified the congruence issue as a concern for them as it allowed for the linkage between the financial, social, and environmental dimensions:

> Congruence is essential as pure focus on financial says greatest purpose is profit, which is not the only measure. For example buy local requires 30 percent of our spending cost of office expenses may be more, i.e., greater than 10 percent but by focusing local we may lose profit but are giving local support.

This organisation was prepared to lose profit and felt that this was an important message to send to the community. This was lost in reporting models that did not link community actions with the financial reports. The congruence aspect of the model also prompted one respondent to reflect on current practice, stating that the "question is, do we tell our members how much it is actually costing us to be green?" Another respondent stated: "[We] currently have congruence required by [the] governance model, but not explicit". It seems that this aspect of the model has resonance with current practice.

Respondents raised two aspects of transparency. The most common concerned the importance of showing that what you say is in fact what you are doing:

> I think if it is important it is transparent . . . saying you're ethical, doing all your social accounting and environmental accounting, then surely the underlying thing is transparency as well to your membership.

The other aspect revolved around directors' responsibilities for decision-making and the transparency of the decision-making process when integrating social and environmental impacts:

> Directors need to have some liability . . . responsibilities [can be] dumbed-down as a result of compliance risk and can thus avoid this perspective and this [is] not helpful if [you are] going to let social and environmental blossom and become meaningful.

Overall there was support for the model and only one change was introduced, in respect to goals and missions (see Figure 16.2).

Respondents also reflected on the process of reporting that was or was not taking place. Their comments provide further insight into challenges faced by these organisations in moving forward with social and environmental reporting and highlight areas for future research.

- The recognition that training and education is required: "[S]kill set really needs to change to the culture of today to adopt a broader issues approach".
- The need for resources and focus: "[Our organisation was] at the forefront when it all started, but it probably hasn't kept up to speed and it hasn't kept up with all the changes and best practice".
- The need for systems change: "[S]ocial and environmental bookkeeping system needs better development and [should] allow better data collection".

CONCLUSIONS

This chapter proposes a conceptual framework for reporting to integrate social and environmental information with financial information. The model built on prior research which documented the requirements for social and environmental accounting information by members and management associated with an organisation in the credit union sector and, as such, limits itself to that sector.

The credit union sector is founded on the goals of operating for the benefit of members and acting with social responsibility. Credit unions are unique within the deposit and loan sector of the industry; unlike banks, there is a clearly articulated social goal. While credit unions function to make a surplus, any surplus is applied to the benefit of members and so management is not focused on generating profit and wealth for shareholders. Credit unions are well placed to focus attention on CSR strategies and reporting. The strength in market position, based on assets of over AU$35 billion, and their strong presence in communities create the potential for

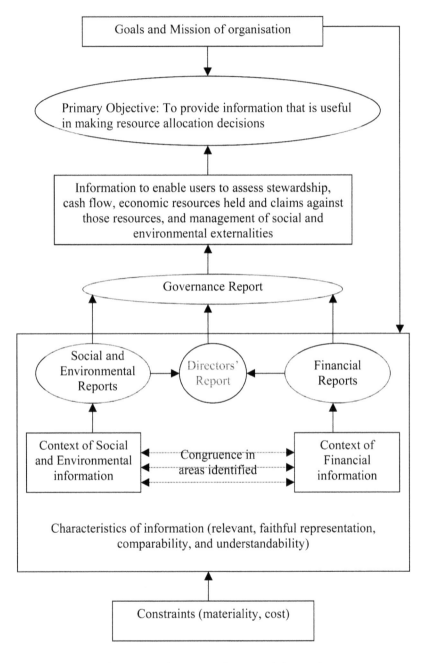

Figure 16.2   Revised conceptual reporting framework for credit unions.

credit unions to take a leadership role in the establishment of a reporting regime that would be relevant to the broader banking and finance sector. The development of a model for reporting is timely in the wake of the recent international credit crisis. Arguably, a lack of attention to ethical decision-making and a focus on profit at all costs contributed to the credit crisis. Arguably the same approach contributed to the spate of high-profile corporate collapses prior to the credit crisis. Greater attention to the concept of corporate responsibility by the banking sector in terms of both daily operations and lending and product policies could reduce the incidence of corporate failures in the future.

The opportunity exists to further explore the adoption and reporting of social and environmental reporting across international borders. The model has potential to be adopted internationally. The flexibility of the model would be able to be tested in the context of national concerns and for applicability in countries of varying economic development.

REFERENCES

AccountAbility. 1999. *AA1000 Assurance Standard: Institute of Social and Ethical Accountability.* http://www.accountability.org.uk/intro5.htm (accessed 15 September 2003).

Adams, C. A., W. Y. Hill, and C. B. Roberts. 1998. "Corporate Social Reporting Practices in Western Europe: Legitimating Corporate Behaviour?" *British Accounting Review* 30:1–21.

Association of Building Societies and Credit Unions. 2006. *Association of Building Societies and Credit Unions.* http://www.abacus.org.au/credit_unions/creditunion.htm.

Australian Stock Exchange. 2007. *Principles of Good Corporate Governance and Best Practice Recommendations.* http://asx.ice4.interactiveinvestor.com.au/ASX0701/Corporate%20Governance%20Principles/EN/body.aspx?z=1&p=-1&v=1&uid= (accessed 24 November 2007).

CEPPA. 2001. *SA8000. The Council for Economic Priorities.* http://www.sa-intl.org/index.cfm?fuseaction=document.show DocumentByID&nodeID=1&DocumentID=136 (accessed 5 December 2005).

CPA Australia. 2007. *Australian Accounting Handbook.* Pearson Australia.

Credit Union Foundation Australia. 2006. *CUFU Information.* http://www.cufa.com.au/introduction/Overview/index.jsp (accessed 5 December 2008).

Dando, N., and T. Swift. 2003. "Transparency and Assurance: Minding the Credibility Gap." *Journal of Business Ethics* 44 (2/3): 195–200.

Deegan, C. 1999. "Triple Bottom Line Reporting: A New Reporting Approach for the Sustainable Organisation." *Charter* 70 (3): 38–40.

Deegan, C., M. Rankin, and P. Voight. 2000. "Firm's Disclosure Reaction to Major Social Incidents: Australian Evidence." *Accounting Forum* 24:101–130.

Elkington, J. 1997. *Cannibals with Forks: The Triple Bottom Line of 21st Century Business.* Oxford: Capstone Publishing.

Global Reporting Initiative. 2006. *G3 Sustainability Reporting Guidelines.* http://www.globalreporting.org/ReportingFramework/ReportingFrameworkDownloads/ (accessed 1 January 2007).

Gray, R. 2002. "The Social Accounting Project and Accounting, Organizations and Society: Privileging Engagement, Imaginings, New Accounting and Pragmatism Over Critique?" *Accounting Organizations and Society* 27(7): 687–707.

216   Dianne McGrath

Gray, R., R. Kouhy, and S. Lavers. 1995. "Corporate social and environmental reporting: A review of the literature and a longitudinal study of UK disclosure." *Accounting, Auditing and Accountability Journal* 8(2): 47.

Hackston, D., and M. J. Milne. 1996. "Some Determinants of Social and Environmental Disclosures in New Zealand Companies." *Accounting, Auditing and Accountability Journal* 9 (1): 77–108.

Hoskin, K., and R. Macve. 1994. "Writing, Examining, Disciplining: The Genesis of Accounting's Modern Power." In *Accounting as Social and Institutional Practice*, ed. A. G. Hopwood and P. Miller, 92. Cambridge: Cambridge University Press.

International Accounting Standards Board. 2006. *Preliminary Views on an Improved Conceptual Framework for Financial Reporting: The Objective of Financial Reporting and Qualitative Characteristics of Decision-Useful Financial Reporting Information.* International Accounting Standards Board. From http://www.iasb.org/NR/rdonlyres/4651ADFC-AB83-4619-A75A-4-F279C175006/0/DP_ConceptualFramework.pdf (accessed 15 November 2006).

Jones, S., G. Frost, J. Loftus, and S. Van Der Laan. 2005. *Sustainability Reporting Practices, Performances and Potential.* Melbourne: CPA Australia.

Laufer, W. S. 2003. "Social Accountability and Corporate Greenwashing." *Journal of Business Ethics* 43:253.

Loftus, J. A., and J. A. Purcell. 2006. "Corporate Social Responsibility—Concepts, Approaches to Regulation and Public Sector Application of the GRI." *Financial Reporting, Regulation and Governance* 5 (1): 1–36.

Mathews, M. R. 1997a. "Towards a Mega-Theory of Accounting." *Asia-Pacific Journal of Accounting* 4 (2): 273–289.

———. 1997b. "Twenty-Five Years of Social and Environmental Accounting Research: Is There a Silver Jubilee to Celebrate?" *Accounting, Auditing and Accountability Journal* 10 (4): 481–531.

———. 2003. "A Brief Description and Preliminary Analysis of Recent Social and Environmental Accounting Research Literature." *Indonesian Management and Accounting Research* 2 (2): 197–264.

McGrath, D. 2003. "Aspects of Social Accounting: Bank Disclosures." Charles Sturt University Working Papers, No.12/03.

———. 2006. "Stakeholder Demand for Social and Environmental Reporting: Its Importance and Influence on Decision-Making." Paper presented at the 3rd International Conference on Contemporary Business, Leura, Australia.

Nash, I. 2001. "Sustaining the Test of Time." *Australian CPA* 71 (2): 33–34.

O'Donovan, G. 2002. "Environmental Disclosures in the Annual Report: Extending the Applicability and Predictive Power of Legitimacy Theory." *Accounting, Auditing and Accountability Journal* 15:344–371.

Ramus, C. A., and I. Montiel. 2005. "When Are Corporate Environmental Policies a Form of Greenwashing?" *Business and Society* 44 (4): 377–414.

Robson, K. 1991. "On the Arenas of Accounting Change: The Process of Translation." *Accounting, Organizations, and Society* 16 (5/6): 547–570.

Sethi, S. P. 1978. "Advocacy Advertising—The American Experience." *California Management Review* (Fall): 58–64.

Tinker, T., and M. Neimark. 1987. "The Role of Annual Reports in Gender and Class Contradictions at General Motors: 1917–1976." *Accounting, Organizations, and Society* 12:71–88.

Woodward, D., T. Woodward, and M. R. Rovira Val. 2004. "Quadruple Bottom Line Reporting amongst a Sample of Spanish Water Industry Businesses." *Social and Environmental Accounting Journal* 24 (2): 8–14.

World Council of Credit Unions. 2007. *World Council of Credit Unions Inc.* http://www.woccu.org/ (accessed 10 January 2007).

17 Prolegomena to Sustainability Reporting

Preventing Premature Closure of Debate Surrounding the Meaning of Sustainability

Marie-Andrée Caron, Alain Lapointe, and Corinne Gendron

Accounting [nature] is the main obstacle which has always impeded the development of the public voice. (Latour 1999, 21)

INTRODUCTION

Corporate social and environmental responsibility (CSR), along with the concept of sustainable development largely associated with it since the Brundtland Commission Report (1987), has prompted a broadening of the notion of corporate forms of governance and underlines the importance of dialogue in a corporate setting. The stakes posed by the CSR are no longer sufficiently recognised by the tripartite framework made up of financial markets, boards of directors, and top management.

We will discuss how the *seemingly* objective nature of social accounting has the effect of preventing debate concerning the sustainable nature of a company, and also inhibits the emergence of a dialogue. Suggesting an engagement research perspective (Adams and Larrinaga-Gonzalez 2007; Bebbington et al. 2007), we intend to show how social actors who hold divergent representations of CSR (notably CSR experts, CSR managers, and civil society) could use a dialogic space to debate uncertainties and compromises inherent in the production of societal performance reports and make better use of social accounting. By considering social accounting as a collective creation that can be built through dialogue, we can prevent democratic debate about corporate social performance from prematurely closing.

Pasquero (2005) defines governance as the entirety of mechanisms that frame the decision-making freedom of economic actors, taking into account the broader regulatory context which imposes itself on businesses from three main poles, namely: the market, social control, and compliance with social values. The growing social concerns in regards to CSR affect these three poles, even though companies still have a lot of latitude in dominating the power relations of these mechanisms. Companies can benefit from the fact that this concept, still very vague and malleable (Acquier and Gond 2006), allows them to consolidate and expand their positions in the discursive space of reporting with the production of their societal performance report (Everett 2004).

However, even if stakeholders continue to occupy a central place in this broadened concept of governance, a constructivist approach (Calton and Kurland 1996) facilitates a better understanding of the learning processes that are underway, both in terms of compiling scientific knowledge about CSR and its concrete practice. In this chapter we propose an analytical framework to study the conditions that support the potential of social accounting to sustain collective and democratic learning.

This chapter is divided as follows: The following section presents the controversy that exists between the role of social accounting and sustainability reporting. The third section then identifies the object at the centre of that controversy (according to Latour 1987), the societal performance or sustainability report. From there, we introduce in the fourth section the human and non-human actors of CSR, acknowledging that they hold different and sometimes diverging expectations about sustainability reporting. We then discuss in the fifth section the conditions under which a dialogic action space could be offered to them in the form of a hybrid forum, exploring how the concept of hospitable translation can be used for the study of meaning given to social accounting on the basis of these interactions. The final section concludes by recalling the main objective and hopefully the contributions of this chapter: Although social accounting has the potential to sustain collective and democratic learning, it may also contribute to prematurely closing the debate around the meaning of CSR and sustainability.

SOCIAL REPORTING: THE NATURE OF THE CONTROVERSY

In order to promote dialogic learning about the new concept of CSR for businesses, a central role is attributed to social accounting (Dillard 2007; Bebbington et al. 2007; Unerman 2007). All accounting constituents are involved, including the accounting discipline, researchers, and accounting practitioners. According to Dillard (2007, 46):

> The social accounting project presumes that the academic accounting community has a responsibility to facilitate, and engage in, dialogue among members of the community regarding accounting's (the profession, the professionals, the systems) and organizational management's public interest responsibilities. Accountants, the business community,

members of the academy, and representatives of the civil community have a responsibility to engage in and sustain this discourse.

In contrast, Milne and Gray (2007, 199) have shown the counter-productive effect of social accounting as a discipline, arguing that it "help[s] businesses mask their socially and ecologically unsustainable practices to legitimate ongoing exploitation of people and the environment". Given that CSR reporting is voluntary and that CSR is akin to a self-service of good practice standards and certificates, any company can proclaim itself to be responsible, especially when assisted by social accounting, the main accomplice able to provide it with an aura of truth.

In this sense, the inevitable "objectivity" of social accounting prevents the establishment of public debate concerning activities within a company, thereby keeping democracy from evolving because it hinders the process of creation of a collective (as suggested by Latour 1999). In other words, the objective nature of social accounting closes the possibility of debate before it has time to evolve, instead inciting the social actors (the parties concerned) to have a priori confidence in the sustainable character of a company's practices.

In such a context, what happens to the dynamic of learning, dialogue, and democracy that social accounting is supposed to generate? Or, to put it differently, to what extent does social accounting actually contribute to shutting down debate concerning the sustainable nature of a company? Not only does the objective nature of social accounting have the effect of preventing this debate, but this feature also inhibits the emergence of a dialogue. Thus, in order to revive the debate, we advocate discussing the controversies it engenders, revealing the compromises and assumptions on which it rests.

Social accounting bears many controversies within itself, in addition to being subjected to attacks from traditional accounting. The lack of homogeneity of its intentions, issues, interests, approaches, and methodologies creates a field in constant state of flux (Gray 2002). At best, accountability takes the triple bottom line metaphorically (Elkington 1997), incapable of ensuring a meaningful integration of the three dimensions—economic, social, environmental—of sustainable development.

Some see this confusion as fertile ground for enriching the multiple meanings given to social accounting, from the narrow-minded utilitarianism of those who regard CSR as a profit strategy to the extravagant humanism claimed by others (Pasquero 2005). In contrast, we see meanings created by unequal forces. From this inequality arises a risk of "locking in" the meaning given to social accounting, because if it seems like a compromise, it is always a compromise between parties constrained by multiple contingencies (De la Broise 2006). Social accounting, when it seeks to project an aura of objectivity by means of traditional authoritative accounting pronouncements, risks shutting down the debate to the advantage of the company, allowing practicing accountants to proclaim to be CSR experts.

THE SOCIETAL PERFORMANCE REPORT OF THE COMPANY: THE OBJECT OF THE CONTROVERSY

Researchers have shown that despite the fact that the production of societal performance reports is not purely "free", and is subject to a certain regulation, their content is largely anchored in the company's structures of meaning (Caron and Turcotte 2009). De la Broise (2006, 44) identifies this as the emergence of complicity between the company and civil society, "with which this mutual recognition potentially supposes complicity and indulgence" (author translation). These studies thus expose the domination of the company in the "game of reporting", a "playful space" where they have all the resources required for transferring any meaning of CSR onto their own meaning structures to assimilate them with their traditional activities, and even to intervene in a standard setting. This explains why the societal performance report makes more mention of a "sustainable company" than of sustainable development.

It also seems increasingly evident that if dialogue between the company and its stakeholders is slow to come about, the production of the societal performance report takes place largely internally, by taking into account the perceptions of the actors inside the organisation and their influence in any process of evaluation and improvement of practices (Bodet and Lamarche 2006). In this context, the framework for societal performance reports provided by the Global Reporting Initiative (GRI) constitutes a management tool that is more dynamic than normative (Quairel 2004).

Problems of quantification, measurement, evaluation, and delimitation weaken the content of societal performance reports, whether they are unidimensional indicators or multidimensional indicators, or input only or input/output indicators (Berthoin-Antal et al. 2002). The report is therefore conceptualised as an artefact (Caron and Turcotte 2009), a "new genre" of company report (D'Almeida 2006), an improbable co-statement (De la Broise 2006), or a complex and costly exercise (Capron and Quairel-Lanoizelée 2007). In fact, the report is expected to play a structuring role in building new compromises, to the extent that it is used to reflect on CSR practices, on what should be done, on what is feasible, and the way of implementing it (Bodet and Lamarche 2006).

We thus could benefit from the controversy present in the field of social accounting to question the objectivity of the information produced in societal performance reports and to open the debate on their pertinence. Actor network theory (ANT), with the concepts of human and non-human actors, allows us to shed light on this controversy (Callon 1986; Latour 1987).

HUMAN AND NON-HUMAN ACTORS OF CSR

An agreement seems to have taken place between the different actors of governance, namely, the state, civil society, and companies (Capron and Quairel-Lanoizelée 2007), to try to redefine the social conventions that underlie the current socio-economic system by taking into consideration the fragility of ecosystems (Gendron 2007). However, for Gendron (2007) the compromise can only be temporary, because it involves dominated actors who will try to escape the authority of the dominant actors. These dynamics are evident in the light of the increasing presence of new social economic movements (NSEM).

New Social Economic Movements

NSEM are defined by Gendron (2004) as a new era of collective action that moved from the field of politics to economics in order to reinvest socio-political content and meaning in the "economic transaction". NSEM thereby preside over the implementation of new spaces for dialogue and social regulation at the margins of traditional institutional spaces, and even at the periphery of the central powers. Responsible investments, an example of NSEM, can be analysed as an appropriation of economics by civil society (subpolitics; Beck 2001). These social actors participate in a social and political structuring of the market on the basis of which businesses are evaluated according to new parameters (GRI, certifications, rating firms, and so forth). The production of a societal performance report thus cannot be entirely voluntary given that it reveals practices that are part of a framework of social dialogue and thereby respond to a certain "necessity".

However, these new institutions result from a certain social dialogue and seal, temporarily, a compromise between the different actors concerning the content of corporate social responsibility and the expectations in regards to accountability (and social accounting).

The Market of CSR Expertise

Concurrent with NSEM actions, a market of CSR expertise is emerging to help companies measure CSR in the absence of reliable accounting tools. Taking advantage of the flexible and malleable nature of CSR and sustainable development, the commodification of CSR is gaining ground (Acquier and Gond 2006), promoted by social actors proclaiming themselves CSR experts. Although the CSR expertise market is being developed largely at the periphery of scientific knowledge production concerning social accounting and CSR, its proponents come from multiple disciplines including law, communications, and accounting. This market sheds light on the innovative and experimental character of CSR management and reporting practices and, in particular, on the lucrative character of these practices.

If these self-proclaimed experts come to be perceived as the source of objective information, there is a risk that the CSR concept will become "locked in" instead of resulting from the testing of information produced by the actors involved with sustainable development. The Big Four Firms are already settling down in this emerging market but, as Gray, Dillard, and Spence state (2008, 8), even if accountants do possess the competencies to contribute to social accounting, their "largely deserved reputation for conservatism and avoidance of risk and innovation . . . [bears] little evidence to suggest that, as a group, they would be your first choice to embrace a public interest which privileged civil society and the disfranchised over capital and the powerful."

The CSR Reporting Manager: Producer of the Societal Performance Report

Traditional accounting, anchored in an individualist methodological perspective (Colasse, Saboly, and Turrillo 2001), regards societal performance reports as an optimum, that is, the one best way (Synnestwedt 2001) resulting from a cost-benefit analysis. These researchers showed the crucial role of the manager in building the corporate communication strategy (Cormier, Gordon, and Magnan 2004; Henriques and Sadorsky 1999). However, their actions are restricted by stakeholder management, which is mainly done in an isolated manner and without considering what other business managers do, whether they are competitors or simply producers of the same type of information. With this perspective, the CSR report manager is preoccupied with confidential information theft and keen to control exclusive costs.

On the other hand, from an interpretative and critical perspective, the production of the societal performance report falls under a holistic methodological perspective (Colasse, Saboly, and Turrillo 2001). This perspective places the choices of the manager in their political, social, and institutional context. Igalens (2006) explains the wave of societal performance report publishing of the last few years essentially in terms of organisational mimetism typical of neo-institutional theory (DiMaggio and Powell 1983). Organisations imitate each other; they adopt managerial practices because others do.

This leads us to view the CSR report manager as a socially situated actor who interacts through a network of constraints (of the type *homo ludens*) and not, as suggested by the paradigm of information economics, a homogenous market subject (of the type *homo economicus*). The existence of such constraints mould their logic of action (Gendron 2006), which cannot be reduced to a rationale as simple as the one serving as the basis for the paradigm of accounting information economics. Among those constraints (and resources) are the CSR tools which also come into play in the reformulation of the poles of governance.

The Global Reporting Initiative Reporting Framework

Five frameworks for CSR tools are largely recognised in the literature and in practice:

1. GRI
2. International Standards Organisation (ISO) 14000 series of standards
3. World Business Council for Sustainable Development (WBCSD)
4. Institute of Social and Ethical AccoutAbility (AA1000) standards
5. Sustainability Integrated Guidelines for Management (SIGMA) project

The GRI reporting framework, by far the most popular measure, is a good example of pragmatism (Tinker and Gray 2003). It successfully penetrated the corporate world in less than five years, while social accounting, after more than forty years of existence, still has gained very little legitimacy in that sector (Everett 2004).

The GRI guidelines constitute an intermediary object (Latour 1999), creating a link between the largely diverging social actors of the movements of meaning creation (for example, NSEM, the CSR expertise market, and the CSR manager) and the ecological modernisation of the poles of governance. These guidelines facilitate concrete experimentation with social accounting, and are capable of offering flexibility (so as to create a win-win situation for everyone) and credibility (so that many want to adhere to them and have confidence in their capacity to bring together and constitute a common world). The power of the GRI guidelines derives from the potential for managers to be reassured by the implementation of universal criteria, while at the same time allowing them to respond to the uniqueness of the situations confronting them (Berry 1983).

This reporting framework thus constitutes a boundary object, defined by Star and Griesemer (1989, 393) as: "an analytic concept of those scientific objects which both inhabit several intersecting worlds [. . .] and satisfy the informational requirements of each of them. Boundary objects are objects which are plastic enough to adapt to local needs and the constraints of the several parties employing them, yet robust enough to maintain a common identity across sites". An essential characteristic of these objects is to be able to serve many different interests; those of the CSR managers, whose goal is to exhibit in a credible manner the specificity of their company to the users of the report; and those of the users of the report, whose goal is to evaluate accurately the company's ecological footprint (Wackernagel and Rees 1996) and/or sustainability impacts.

Adams and Narayanan (2007, 83) showed that the objectivity of this framework is formed in a dialogue: "[W]ithout a robust stakeholder dialogue and reporting process [. . .] reporting guidelines may be used as a legitimating exercise by organizations that report the minimum required in such guidelines but omit material impacts not specifically covered by them".

A "hybrid forum" is an effective way to generate such a dialogue; it is a privileged realm of action where issues that are still vague and controversial can be discussed and innovative solutions developed, concerning the conception of sustainability reporting and the role of social accounting.

THE HYBRID FORUM AS A PRINCIPLE OF ACTION: SPACE OF INTERACTION

The concept of "hybrid forum" (Callon, Lascoumes, and Barthe 2001) refers to open spaces where social actors (for example, NSME, CSR experts, CSR managers) mobilise to debate the technical choices concerning the collective. A controversy emerges from the divergence of the perspectives developed by experts, those defended by involved or ordinary citizens, and the choices produced by government representatives and CSR managers. Much more than a procedure of public consultation, it is the formation and conception of a common world that constitutes the strength of these dialogic procedures.

A hybrid forum is thus a privileged place to the test the meaning given to CSR and to construct an intersubjective space (Schütz 1987) concerning the information to be produced by social accounting. A hybrid forum allows not only interdisciplinary crossovers, but also cross-overs between researchers and practitioners, and experts and laymen. These cross-overs aim to break the dichotomy that divides studies on social accounting and to allow interested parties to participate in the conception of this critical emerging disciplinary field.

A hybrid forum opens two complementary opportunities:

1. De/confine the research on social accounting in a dialogic and research-action perspective and bring it out of the laboratories.
2. Allow experts and lay social actors to meet and provide the laymen with a legitimate space for expression and action.

As suggested by Cooper and Owen (2007, 653), we explore "the conditions of an ideal speech situation and for dialogue". A hybrid forum thus offers actors a space of dialogue to discuss the content of the controversial object (the societal performance report).

However, this forum puts together a great diversity of representations of CSR and raises a translation problem. While translation has been amply studied by ANT, we propose to view it here more from a perspective of philosophy of law, on the basis of works by Ost (2003).

Ost (2008) highlights the difference between hospitable translation, capable of taking into account the perspective of the other (users of social accounting in our case), and hegemonial translation, resulting from the overbearing objectivity of social accounting. A hospitable translation implies a true relation to the other and allows conception of social accounting as something to build within a dialogue. To avoid the pitfalls of a hegemonial translation, universalising and inhospitable, a "mise sous tension" is required, that is, a democratic debate that does not exclude opposing views, precisely like the one operated in hybrid forums.

In order for the interactions between social actors involved in reformulating governance to be able to formulate and conceive of a common intersubjective world beyond a simple public consultation procedure, the hybrid forum must be a space where the actors form a public collective. This is defined by Dewey (1927), who tries to define, organise, and build strategies for political competencies going beyond sensory awareness and changing a specific reporting weakness and its consequences posing the problem into a veritable *public problem*. For that purpose, the forum must mobilise the actors in collaborative and co-operative research to culminate in a problem provided with a sharable meaning and true social representation as described by Dewey (1927). That is, the expanded dimensions of which take into account the societal stakes of all parties concerned. A hybrid forum thus constitutes a place capable of curbing the plurality of the representations on the meaning to be given to reporting practices and the content of the societal performance report. The forum can thus serve to increase the regulatory potential of CSR reporting practices to arrive at a true accountability, encompassing the diverse points of view according to Caron et Gendron (2007).

CONCLUSIONS

This chapter is essentially conceptual and limits itself to discussing the prolegomena of sustainability reporting. We maintained that the open space provided by a hybrid forum does help expose and partially reconcile the divergent perspectives emerging from different actors (CSR managers, experts, citizens, and political representatives). Tensions between hospitable and hegemonic translation could be palpable, some actors considering CSR as something that should be defined by "those who know" and imposed to "laymen", while others favour a collective and democratic understanding of CSR. However, the dialogic space could help escape the "locking in" of the meaning of CSR by experts, as discussed here.

Coming back to our larger discussion about social accounting, this would suggest that social accounting might indeed inhibit the democratic formulation and evaluation of sustainability reports when considered and used as a source of objective and non-debatable information. Prioritising verifiability at the expense of pertinence tends to prematurely close the debate around the meaning of CSR and sustainability, but it is not necessarily so; social accounting also has the potential to sustain collective and democratic learning.

This is akin to Gray, Dillard, and Spence (2008), who emphasise the potential of social accounting, despite its difficulties in being acknowledged. The discussion that took place during the Prague workshop about social accounting and public policy showed the importance of social accounting for the emergence of a structured and systematic dialogue with the stakeholders, particularly considering the diversity of interests and objectives of the different stakeholders in the public arena (Osborn 2008; Ellwood 2008). The concepts of hospitable translation and hybrid forums, applied to social accounting, allow the concrete acknowledgement of the diversity of engagement typical of forums and learning groups such as those proposed in this book.

REFERENCES

Acquier, A., and J. P. Gond. 2006. "Les enjeux théoriques de la marchandisation de la responsabilité sociale de l'entreprise." *Revue Internationale de Gestion* 31 (2): 83–91.

Adams, C. A., and C. Larrinaga-Gonzalez. 2007. "Engaging with Organisations in Pursuit of Improved Sustainability Accounting and Performance." *Accounting, Auditing and Accountability Journal* 20 (3): 334–355.

Adams, C., and V. Narayanan. 2007. "The 'Standardization' of Sustainability Reporting." In *Sustainability Accounting and Accountability*, ed. J. Unerman, J. Bebbington, and B. O'Dwyer, 70–85. London: Routledge.

Beck, U. 2001. *La société du risque: Sur la voie d'une autre modernité*. Paris: Flammarion/Aubier.

Bebbington, J., J. Brown, B. Frame, and I. Thomson. 2007. "Theorizing Engagement: The Potential of a Critical Dialogic Approach." *Accounting, Auditing and Accountability Journal* 20 (3): 356–381.

Berry, M. 1983. *Une technologie invisible: l'impact des instruments de gestion sur l'évolution des systèmes humains*. Paris: Centre de Recherche en Gestion (CRG) de l'École Polytechnique.

Berthoin-Antal, A., M. Dierkes, K. Macmillan, and L. Marz. 2002. "Corporate Social Reporting Revisited." *Journal of General Management* 28 (2): 22–42.

Bodet, C., and T. Lamarche. 2006. "Le bilan sociétal: un processus praticipatif multi-parties prenantes pour la responsabilité sociale de l'entreprise." In *Responsabilité sociale: vers une nouvelle communication des entreprises?*, ed. P. De la Broise and T. Lamarche, 135–150. Villeneuve d'Ascq: Presses Universitaires du Septentrion.

Callon, M. 1986. "Some Elements of a Sociology of Translation: Domestication of the Scallops and the Fisherman of St. Brieux Bay." In *Power, Action and Belief: A New Sociology of Knowledge?*, ed. J. Law, 196–229. London: Routledge and Kegan Paul.

Callon, M., P. Lascoumes, and Y. Barthe. 2001. *Agir dans un monde incertain*. Paris: Seuil.

Calton, J. M., and N. B. Kurland. 1996. "A Theory of Stakeholder Enabling: Giving Voice to an Emerging Postmodern Praxis of Organizational Discourse." In *Postmodern Management and Organization Theory*, ed. D. M. Boje, R. P. Gephart Jr., and T. J. Thatchenkery, 154–177. Thousand Oaks, CA: Sage.

Capron, M., and F. Quairel-Lanoizelée. 2007. *La responsabilité sociale d'entreprise*. Paris: La Découverte.

Caron, M.-A., and C. Gendron. 2007. "Séminaire sur la production de rapports de développement durable et les lignes directrices de la Global Reporting Initiative—Compte rendu des travaux." *Cahier de la Chaire de responsabilité sociale et de développement durable*, Montréal, ESG, UQAM, No. 03–2007, 36.

Caron, M.-A., and M. F. Turcotte. 2009. "Path Dependence and Path Creation: Framing the Non-Financial Information Market for a Sustainable Trajectory." *Accounting, Auditing and Accountability Journal* 22 (2): 272–297.

Colasse, B., M. Saboly, and B. Turrillo. 2001. "De la scientificité des théories issues de la recherche en comptabilité financière." In *Faire de la recherche en comptabilité financière*, ed. R. Teller and P. Dumontier, 3–18. Paris: Vuibert.

Cooper, S. M., and D. L. Owen. 2007. "Corporate Social Reporting and Stakeholder: The Missing Link." *Accounting, Organizations, and Society* 32:649–667.

Cormier, D., I. M. Gordon, and M. Magnan. 2004. "Corporate Environmental Disclosure: Contrasting Management's Perceptions with Reality." *Journal of Business Ethics* 49 (2): 143–165.

D'Almeida, N. 2006. "La perspective narratologique en organisation." In *Responsabilité sociale: vers une nouvelle communication des entreprises?*, ed. P. De La Broise and T. Lamarche, 27–38. Villeneuve d'Ascq: Presses Universitaires du Septentrion.

De la Broise, P. 2006. "Entre reddition et légitimation: le rapport annuel d'entreprise." In *Responsabilité sociale: vers une nouvelle communication des entreprises?*, ed. P. De la Broise and T. Lamarche, 39–51. Villeneuve d'Ascq: Presses Universitaires du Septentrion.

Dewey, J. 1927. *Le Public et ses problèmes*. Trans. J. Zask. Pau, France: Editions Farago/Université de Pau.

Dillard, J. F. 2007. "Legitimating the Social and Accounting Project: An Ethic of Accountability." In *Sustainability Accounting and Accountability*, ed. J. Unerman, J. Bebbington, and B. O'Dwyer, 37–53. London: Routledge.

DiMaggio, P., and W. Powell. 1983. "The Iron Cage Revisited: Institutional Isomorphism and Collective Rationality in Organizational Fields." *American Sociological Review* 48:147–160.

Elkington, J. 1997. *Cannibals with Forks: The Triple Bottom Line of 21st Century Business*. Oxford: Capstone Publishing.

Ellwood, S. 2008. "Stakeholder Accountability for Public Sector Bodies: A Theoretical Reporting Model." Paper presented at the IRSPM/EGPA International Workshop on Social Audit, Social Accounting and Accountability, Prague, 15–16 May.

Everett, J. 2004. "Exploring (False) Dualisms for Environmental Accounting Praxis." *Critical Perspectives on Accounting* 15:1061–1084.

Gendron, C. 2004. "Le commerce équitable: un nouveau mouvement social économique au cœur d'une autre mondialisation." In *Altermondialisation, économie et coopération internationale*, ed. L. Favreau, G. Larose and S. A. Fall, 158–183. France (co-editor) amd Québec (editor): Karthala (co-editor) and Presses de L'Université du Québec (editor).

———. 2006. *Le développement durable comme compromis: la modernisation écologique de l'économie à l'ère de la mondialisation*. Quebec: PUQ.

228 Marie-Andrée Caron, Alain Lapointe, and Corinne Gendron

————. 2007. *Vous avez dit développement durable?* Montreal: Presses Internationales Polytechniques.

Gray, R. H. 2002. "The Social Accounting Project and Accounting, Organizations and Society: Privileging Engagement, Imaginings, New Accountings and Pragmatism over Critique?" *Accounting, Organizations, and Society* 27:687–709.

Gray, R. H., J. Dillard, and C. Spence. 2008. "Social Accounting Research as if the World Matters. Postalgia and a New Absurdism." Paper presented at the IRSPM/EGPA International Workshop on Social Audit, Social Accounting and Accountability, Prague, 15–16 May.

Henriques, I., and P. Sadorsky. 1999. "The Relationship between Environmental Commitment and Managerial Perceptions of Stakeholder Importance." *Academy of Management Journal* 42 (1): 87–99.

Igalens, J. 2006. "L'aporie du discours sur la responsabilité sociale de l'entreprise." In *Responsabilité sociale: vers une nouvelle communication des entreprises?*, ed. P. De La Broise and T. Lamarche, 203–212. Villeneuve d'Ascq: Presses Universitaires du Septentrion.

Latour, B. 1987. *Science in Action: How to Follow Scientists and Engineers through Society*. Milton Keynes: Open University Press.

————. 1999. *Politiques de la nature: comment faire entrer les sciences en démocratie*. Paris: La Découverte.

Milne, M. J., and R. H. Gray. 2007. "Future Prospects for Corporate Sustainability Reporting." In *Sustainability Accounting and Accountability*, ed. J. Unerman, J. Bebbington, and B. O'Dwyer, 184–207. London: Routledge.

Osborn, S. 2008. "Comparing Accounting Designs for Sustainability Governance." Paper presented at the IRSPM/EGPA International Workshop on Social Audit, Social Accounting and Accountability, Prague, 15–16 May.

Ost, F. 2003. *La nature hors la loi, l'écologie à l'épreuve du droit*. Paris: La Découverte.

————. 2008. "La septième cité: la traduction." In *Traduire nos responsabilités planétaires. Recomposer nos paysages juridiques*, ed. C. Eberhard, 87–110. Brussels: Bruylant.

Pasquero, J. 2005. "La responsabilité sociale de l'entreprise comme objet des sciences de gestion. Le concept et sa portée." In *Responsabilité sociale et environnementale de l'entreprise*, ed. M. F. Turcotte and A. Salmon, 112–143. Quebec: PUQ.

Quairel, F. 2004. "Responsable mais pas comptable: analyse de la normalisation des rapports environnementaux et sociaux." *Comptabilité, Contrôle, Audit* 10 (1): 7–36.

Schütz, A. 1987. *Le chercheur et le quotidian*. Paris: Méridiens Klincksieck.

Star, S. L., and J. R. Griesemer. 1989. "Institutional Ecology, 'Translations' and Boundary Objects: Amateurs and Professionals in Berkeley's Museum of Vertebrate Zoology, 1907–39." *Social Studies of Science* 19:387–420.

Synnestvedt, T. 2001. "Debates over environmental information to stakeholders as a policy instrument." *Eco-Management and Auditing* 8(3):165–178.

Tinker, T., and R. H. Gray. 2003. "Beyond a Critique of Reason Pure. From Policy to Politics to Praxis in Environmental and Social Research." *Accounting, Auditing and Accountability Journal* 16 (5): 727–761.

Unerman, J. 2007. "Stakeholder Engagement and Dialogue." In *Sustainability Accounting and Accountability*, ed. J. Unerman, J. Bebbington, and B. O'Dwyer, 86–103. London: Routledge.

Wackernagel, M., and W. E. Rees. 1996. *Our Ecological Footprint: Reducing Human Impact on the Earth*. Philadelphia: New Society Publishers.

Part IV

Social Accounting, Social Capital, and the Social Economy

18 Social Accounting and Auditing
Assessing the Contribution of Social Capital to Social Enterprise and the Social Economy

Guenther Lorenz and Alan Kay

INTRODUCTION

Across Europe there is a belief that "social capital" should be nurtured to enable inclusive forms of economic development. It has been suggested that what drives social capital within communities are people and not-for-profit organisations. Their initiatives create employment and strengthen social cohesion—using social capital as a key resource (Kay 2006).

There are a number of unresolved problems related to this notion of social capital, including:

- reaching agreement on what social capital actually is
- how to measure its growth or decline as a resource for development
- understanding how it can be created in areas where it is lacking

The CONSCISE Project (The Contribution of Social Capital in the Social Economy to Local Economic Development in Western Europe) had a threefold focus. It asked, firstly, how local social capital contributes to the growth of social enterprises; secondly, how local social enterprises generate social capital; and finally, how social enterprises working together can generate social capital and develop the local social economy.

THE CONSCISE PROJECT

The CONSCISE[1] Project (2000–2003) was funded under European Framework V Key Action "Improving the Socio-Economic Knowledge Base". Five partners carried out research in eight European fieldwork localities. Each examined the extent to which social enterprises produce and reproduce social capital and facilitate local economic development, social cohesion, and inclusion.

Firstly, the project undertook an extensive literature review to define the concepts of social capital, social enterprise, and social economy.

Secondly, the concepts and appropriate indicators were incorporated into methodologies: (a) to prepare a socio-economic profile of each location focusing on the level of social capital prevalent; and (b) to prepare social accounts for a social enterprise in each locality, adapting existing social accounting methods to include exploring how social capital is used and created in the development of a social enterprise. Fieldwork locations and a social enterprise willing to participate in action-research in each location were identified. "Action-research" meant that findings were recorded while carrying out the work. A socio-economic profile was compiled for each locality and social enterprises were supported for over one year to prepare social accounts for audit. Local people were involved in the action-research. Socio-economic profiles paid particular attention to the presence and growth of social capital, the extent of social enterprise development, and the scope of the local social economy. The social accounts assisted the social enterprise in measuring its performance against its social objectives and impact on local development. They also explored how enterprises used and generated social capital.

Thirdly, the results from the eight socio-economic profiles and the eight social accounts were summarised in two separate compilation reports (Lorenz and Schillat 2002).

Fourthly, a final report distilled and presented the main findings from all stages of the action-research and findings were presented at an international conference.

CONSCISE PROJECT DEFINITIONS

The Social Economy

The social economy can be understood as a dynamic economic system that emerges from the third sector and consists of formally structured organisations. The third sector is distinct from the private, profit-oriented, and the public or governmental sectors. It reflects shared values of reciprocity and shared aims in which production for need and not for private profit is pursued.

Social Enterprise

The characteristics common to all social enterprises are as follows:

• They tackle specific social aims by engaging in economic and trading activities.
• They are not-for-profit-organisations. All surplus profits are reinvested in economic activities or are otherwise used to tackle the social aims of the enterprise.

- Their assets and accumulated wealth do not belong to any individual(s) but are held in trust to be used for the benefit of persons or areas that are intended beneficiaries of the enterprise's social aims.
- Full participation of all members is encouraged on a co-operative basis with equal rights accorded to all members.

In addition, the social enterprise sector encourages mutual co-operation between social enterprises and with other organisations in the wider social and local economy.

This working definition accords with those emerging from work by the Centre for International Research of the public and social economy (CIRIEC 2000) and the EMES Network (a European Network researching "Emergence of Social Enterprises"). It also borrows aspects from Johns Hopkins Comparative Research (European Network for Economic Self-Help and Local Development 2001; Evers, Rauch, and Stitz 2002; Borzaga and Defourny 2001; Anheier 2002).

Social Capital

A vast literature demonstrates the struggle involved in defining the social capital concept and in extracting useful and practical ideas.

The term was first used explicitly by Jane Jacobs in 1961, although the concept has been recognised by writers since the nineteenth century. The work of James Coleman (1990/1994), Robert Putnam (2000), and to a lesser extent Bourdieu (1986) and Hirschman (1984), has also been influential.

Putnam recognised that good governance was closely related to civic engagement and that social cohesion in communities depends on social networks and recognised norms of behaviour and trust. Coleman's social theory stated that the "closure" of social networks can produce closer connections between people, which generate obligations and sanctions on the community. Bourdieu showed how social capital exists alongside economic and cultural capital, and that individuals and groups may strategise to reproduce more social capital and/or convert it into other forms of capital. Hirschman uses the term "social energy" and suggests that it is made up of three components—friendship, emphasising the personal impact of social capital; "ideals", which may lead to a shared vision based on values; and "ideas", which enable groups and individuals to present new solutions to their problems.

The general consensus is that social capital is "something" that exists *between* individuals and organisations. This "something" emerges from connections (relationships) and is further developed through growing trust, mutual understanding, and reciprocal actions based on shared norms and values.

Social capital comprises those connections and trusting contacts that people make while going about their daily business. These contacts may lead to mutual and reciprocal actions which further the development of a community. Social capital is productive and exists as a "stock" that can be used. It differs from other forms of capital in that the more it is used, the more social capital is generated.

Other "dimensions" to social capital are: "bonding", "bridging", and possibly "linking" social capital (Beugelsdijk and Smulders 2003).

Bonding social capital can strengthen the sense of identity and purpose of a community or of an interest group—it is the "glue" which binds a community together. Bridging social capital reflects the relationships that build links with other people and bodies external to the immediate community or interest group—it is the "grease" which helps to access resources and get things done. Some have sought to identify a third dimension: linking social capital, which forms connections between different levels of power or social status. The CONSCISE Project felt that such links may be developed as part of bridging social capital.

The CONSCISE Project adopted the following working definition for social capital:

> Social capital consists of resources within communities which are created through the presence of high levels of . . . trust, reciprocity and mutuality, shared norms of behaviour, shared commitment and belonging, both formal and informal social networks, and effective information channels . . . which may be used productively by individuals and groups to facilitate actions to benefit individuals, groups and community more generally. (CONSCISE Project 2000)

By way of further explanation:

- *Trust* expresses a confidence about the reliability of other people and is often the unintended outcome of exchanges and transactions. It is both a medium and an outcome of a relationship. "Institutional-based trust" recognises that trust is not always based on personal relationships (and does not demand personal familiarity) but is imbedded in a level above the individual.
- *Reciprocity* in social relationships is when one actor acts with regard to another in the same way as another acts in regard to the first. At one level, reciprocity is simply instrumental in that both parties are aware of an "exchange" of equivalent value, acting out of self-interest. Putnam refers to this reciprocity as "balanced" (a favour for a favour). Another important type of reciprocity is identified by Putnam. This is "generalised" reciprocity, which is unbalanced; favours may be given without any certainty of when they will be "repaid", at least not in the short term.
- *Shared norms of behaviour* create the value context for the growth of social capital. "Norms" highlight the informality, the shared perspective, and the everyday "taken-for-granted" view that is important for the sustainability of trust, reciprocity, and mutuality within a group.

- *Shared commitment and belonging* is about the belonging to a society where civic engagement (such as neighbourhood associations, choral societies, and co-operatives) is seen as essential in the creation and maintenance of social capital.
- *Formal and informal social networks* are an essential part of social capital. Co-operation for mutual benefit is likely to be high in dense networks.
- *Effective information channels* indicate the presence of free-flowing information and depend on trust—time is not needed to check the accuracy of the information. Co-ordinated actions are more likely and transaction costs reduced.

The research group operationalised the definition for social capital in a rather eclectic but pragmatic way. The six components of social capital were used within questionnaires, interviews, and so forth, as indicators of levels of social capital. This approach was similar to studies in Britain, Germany, Spain, and Sweden as well as the approach of Onyx and Bullen (1999). Using the components of social capital rather than "social capital" has proved to be useful in the development of research tools.

DESCRIBING THE SOCIO-ECONOMIC PROFILE METHODOLOGY

The five CONSCISE Project partners followed a similar methodology across the eight locations to prepare socio-economic profiles of each locality.

A data profile for each locality was constructed about: its geography, history, population, housing, local employment, economic activity, consumer services, education and training, qualifications and skills, entertainment, sports and leisure facilities, health care, transport, community and voluntary organisations, crime, religion, politics and civic engagement, and information channels.

A social capital survey was carried out using a questionnaire which employed proxy indicators for the identified characteristics of social capital. The same questionnaire was distributed to a sample of residents in the eight localities and provided a rough-and-ready general index of local social capital.

The proxy indicators used in the CONSCISE Project were in the form of statements, and local people were asked to decide how much they agreed with the statements.

Some of the examples of the statements on trust:

"When everything is taken into account, this locality is a safe place to live."

"If I were looking after a child and in an emergency I needed to go out for a while, I would trust my neighbours to look after the child."

Some of the examples of the statements on reciprocity and mutuality:

"By helping other people you help yourself in the long run."

"If I see litter in the neighbourhood, I normally pick it up even if I have not dropped it there."

In addition, a survey of the social enterprises in each locality was carried out in order to indicate the size, nature and extent of the local social economy. The survey questionnaire was the same in all the eight localities but was administered differently in different locations (sometimes through a postal survey and sometimes by face-to-face interviews).

An important element of the method was the use of a "soundings group". Soundings groups are key stakeholders within a neighbourhood who act as gateways to information and also as monitors of the research. This group both "drove" the fieldwork and generated data. The soundings group had four purposes: The people recruited to the group acted as discussants on the data and on the draft reports prepared; as informants by providing information about the area and insights on local social capital, the impact of social enterprise, and the relationship between social capital and social enterprise; as gatekeepers who identified sources of local data; and, finally, as advisors to the action-researchers regarding the direction of the local socio-economic profiling exercise.

LEARNING FROM THE SOCIAL-ECONOMIC PROFILE METHODOLOGY

The CONSCISE Project drew on both secondary and primary data which was discussed in the soundings group meetings. This interpretative discussion itself generated further qualitative data, which aided understanding of social capital in the area and how it's used.

The examination of social capital had to be placed in context, which the soundings groups in particular emphasised. For example, history can provide an understanding of past social capital and how it has been used and, maybe, lost. It was felt that context cannot be captured by applying survey research or using secondary data as proxy indicators.

Data is not neutral and is open to interpretation. Despite this, members of the soundings group reported the benefit of having local data gathered into a profile which could then be used for various purposes. Also, the socio-economic profiles were based on interpretations as much as facts and gave a sense of local "ownership" of both the process and the profile itself. Interpretation allowed the project researchers to make connections between different data while the local socio-economic profile brought alive the use and the purpose of the methodology.

The research and the discussion in the soundings group strengthened and actually built new local social capital as the researchers and local people learned on the job just what social capital is. This raised awareness of social capital, using existing networks and instigating new ones. Research and action were not separate. In some cases, the soundings group meetings led to new developments, which in turn built social capital and generated new actions.

The level of social capital revealed by the survey using proxy indicators corresponded well to other social capital indicators—such as the density of voluntary organisations in the area and the level of turn-out in local and national elections. However, this should not be seen as a substitute for the exploration of social capital using other, more qualitative and discursive methods. It has to be said that although the proxy indicators quantified the level of local social capital, they should be treated cautiously.

THE SOCIAL ACCOUNTING AND AUDIT METHODOLOGY

The CONSCISE Project adopted the Five Stage Social Accounting process as described in the *Social Audit and Accounting Manual* (2001; CBS Network with Merseyside Social Enterprise Network).

Five Stages of Social Accounting

Stage 1: Introducing Social Accounting and Audit

Collect information about social accounting and audit and look at the reasons why the organisation should keep social accounts. Investigate what they already do and the information they have already collected. Consider how the process will be managed.

Stage 2: The Foundations

Clarify the organisation's objectives and write them down, listing all the activities that they do to achieve these objectives. State their values. Also prepare a stakeholder map of the organisation, identify key stakeholders, and determine the scope of the social accounts. Stakeholders are people or groups who are affected by or who can affect the activities of the organisation.

Stage 3: Social Bookkeeping

For each objective there will be a number of activities. Agree on what indicators might be used to check on the performance of these activities. Some will be quantitative; some will be qualitative. Make sure the indicators are practical and that the information can be collected. Set up a social bookkeeping system to make sure the organisation collects the facts and figures they need on a regular basis. Decide the most appropriate way to consult stakeholders. Produce a Social Accounting Plan and Timetable and implement it.

Stage 4: Preparing and Using the Social Accounts

At the end of the year, collect together all the information and interpret it to prepare the social accounts. Identify key issues for action, review the objectives and activities, set targets, discuss them with the stakeholders, and review the social accounting and audit process.

Stage 5: The Social Audit

The organisation will arrange for a social auditor or panel to verify that the information in the social accounts is accurately reported and has been properly gathered. The panel may interview some of the stakeholders; they will trace some data to source. They will rigorously review the social accounts together with the organisation and make recommendations for the next social audit. When the revised social accounts are prepared the social auditor will issue the Social Audit Statement. The organisation can then circulate the report, or a summary, to all stakeholders.

Each of the eight social enterprises prepared social accounts based on their own values, objectives, and activities. They also adopted two Social Capital Objectives formulated by the CONSCISE Project and included in their social accounting plans a range of methods to gather information and consult stakeholders about social capital, involving interviews and focus groups. The Social Capital Objectives are as follows:

Social Capital Objective 1: To use social capital in sustaining our social enterprise by:

- using relations of trust with the social economy, other organisations, and relevant individuals
- engaging with social enterprises and other local organisations in order to receive help on a reciprocal and mutual basis
- receiving support from a strong local network of support
- using a sense of shared commitment and belonging to the local area

- using shared values and norms of behaviour in the local social economy
- using extensive information channels

Social Capital Objective 2: building relations of trust within the social economy, other organisations, and relevant individuals

- engaging with social enterprises and other local organisations in order to offer help on a reciprocal and mutual basis
- contributing to and supporting local networks
- contributing to a sense of shared commitment and belonging to the local area
- strengthening the shared values and norms of behaviour in the local social economy
- building information channels and sharing information

LEARNING FROM THE SOCIAL ACCOUNTING METHODOLOGY

Our findings indicate that quantitative indicators for social capital were rather elusive. This was despite the fact that some research partners attempted to chart the range of a social enterprise's contacts (that is, social networks) and the frequency, nature, and extent of the social enterprise's dealings with other bodies (relationships). Partners found the proposed methods of gathering information were too demanding of time and also came to believe that quantitative indicators were not as directly relevant as qualitative ones.

Once the concept of social capital had been separated into its component elements, partners found that people were able to relate to them. In face-to-face situations questions were answered and examples given as respondents began to discuss the concept and see how they both used *and* created social capital. This gave the richest qualitative information, while self-completed questionnaires were not very successful.

During the course of the research, the distinction between the two social capital objectives (distinguished in terms of using and building social capital) was found to be difficult to maintain and it would have been better to have treated it as one social capital objective.

With hindsight, the CONSCISE Project believes that it was mistaken to separate the exploration of social capital from the main social accounts of the social enterprises. The research demonstrated that social capital is so very closely entwined with the values, objectives, and activities of the social enterprises that attempting to look at social capital as an abstract entity was difficult. Future projects might better take the route of exploring social capital as imbedded in the day-to-day work of the social enterprise, and as something which underpins the way the enterprise behaves toward other stakeholders.

Nonetheless, the research did demonstrate that the social accounting process is capable of looking at certain issues in a uniform way across a number of social enterprises, allowing enterprises to explore and report on their own values, objectives, and activities. This has important implications for the way social accounting might be used to explore the collective impact of a group of social enterprises in relation to societal goals.

We would like to draw attention to one experience with a large social enterprise which asked to be supported in carrying out social accounting and audit when it was going through severe difficulties to achieve sustainability. This enterprise carried out large intermediate labour market (ILM) schemes, but had severe problems in generating and using trust.

The problems started with complaints from employees about how they were treated. The employees found a local magazine which published their grievances widely, and due to this bad publicity, the job centre did not provide more ILM schemes for the enterprise. This meant a decrease in income.

There was also a problem concerning trust within the organisation. Managers did not appear to care about co-operating with other organisations—even with their key stakeholders.

These facts led to the involvement of another agency—the local authority responsible for the economic activities that the enterprise was carrying out. They implemented a monitoring exercise around the enterprise's activities and found some irregularities which led to the demise of more contracts.

The social accounting procedure began to reveal some of the things that were happening and only weeks after carrying out social accounting, the enterprise went into final bankruptcy.

This example demonstrates the huge importance of local social capital for economic success. The enterprise was, in monetary terms, highly effective. It had a huge turnover, many employees, and many contracts but all this success was to no avail due to their lack of generating or using trust from the local community and from other stakeholder groups.

FINDINGS: SOCIAL CAPITAL

Through the socio-economic profiling and the social accounting procedures used, the research project detected some interesting findings concerning social capital and social enterprises, as well as the whole social economy and its impact on local development.

General Findings

The findings suggest that social capital does exist and is a "graspable" and understandable concept. Certainly, it is not easily definable or measurable and is perhaps most useable as a heuristic device. It is interesting to note that through using heuristic indicators and measures, the researchers identified differences of social capital building and use between rural and urban areas whereby the rural regions were much better at building and using social capital.

When the concept of social capital is fully understood by social economy practitioners, it has a significant effect on the way that they plan their work. They see social capital as a valuable resource to use alongside other forms of capital. When the researchers started interviewing people in the localities, the term "social capital" was neither known nor understood. However, when the concept was broken down into component parts and examples used, the persons interviewed not only understood the term, but also the relevance of social capital for their organisation's survival.

Processes of social accounting can be used to explore objectives common to a group of social enterprises in addition to their own specific objectives. Social accounting could be used to measure performance across a group of social enterprises and in relation to objectives set down by wider society.

Re-examining Social Capital

Social capital can best be understood by disaggregating it into the six key elements, which paradoxically then allows people to understand how they fit together as an integrated concept. Furthermore, the relationship between the elements of social capital can be expressed in different ways. Trust, social networks, and reciprocity/mutuality are about relations between people and organisations (a "structural" analysis); while shared norms/ values and commitment/belonging are about what people or organisations believe and feel (a "cognitive" analysis).

Making a distinction between "bonding" and "bridging" social capital is useful for analysis and understanding of the overall concept. However, the researchers concluded that "linking" social capital is really a form of "bridging" social capital—although it was accepted that "linking" did draw attention to hierarchical relationships of power and powerlessness, and this on occasion can be useful. Having a *balance* between "bonding" and "bridging" social capital is important. The consequences of too much of either can be negative. Too much "bonding" creates communities that are suspicious of outsiders; too much bridging undermines the strength of the immediate organisation or group. It was also noticeable that "bonding" social capital in urban settings is mostly associated with ethnic groups and special interest organisations. Smaller, more isolated, and often rural communities demonstrate higher levels of social capital—although this tends to be more "bonding" than "bridging".

Context and history are very important for understanding how social capital operates in communities. History can show how the use of different resources of social capital has developed, and this can indicate how social capital can best be built within a community.

Shared values, and the extent to which key stakeholders adhere to them, are critically important to the development of social enterprises. They are also central to building social capital within the social enterprise and between the social enterprise and the local community. Trust is a key ingredient of social capital, but it is interesting to note that trust between organisations really depends on the relations of trust between individual people.

Social capital is a "neutral" resource and it can have positive or negative consequences. It can be used to either exclude or include other individuals and groups. This confirmed Bourdieu's thinking, which showed diamond dealers or even the mafia use social capital—but for antisocial reasons.

Finally, in the re-examination of social capital it was accepted as an intangible concept, but arguably more useful as a heuristic devise than as a measurable yardstick.

Links Between Social Capital and Social Enterprises

Local social capital influences the development of social enterprises in rural and more isolated communities especially. Social capital, in general, as used by specific interest groups, can also influence the establishment of social enterprises in more urban areas. Isolation, social homogeneity, and small population numbers appear to impact positively on the level of local social capital—particularly "bonding" social capital.

Social capital cannot be a direct substitute for other forms of capital; although it may, in disadvantaged communities, compensate to some extent for low levels of human capital. Social capital, especially bridging social capital, can provide access to other forms of capital essential to development and to the growth of the social economy. Using social capital to form links with the public sector is important in the development of social enterprises.

Social enterprises tend to use more "bonding" social capital during their initial formation phase but need to use more "bridging" social capital when they become more established and wish to expand.

Finally, key individuals within communities can initiate the use of social capital to make things happen—but not in isolation. Effective community action requires a sense of collective endeavour and ownership.

Links Between Social Capital and the Social Economy

Social enterprises are often required to compete with each other for limited resources and contracts. This competition acts in opposition to the growth of social capital between social economy organisations. However, it was noted that the establishment of a social enterprise in a particular area can lead to other social enterprises being created. In this way, social capital generated by the development of an initial social enterprise can be used to develop other social enterprises.

The reputation and trustworthiness of social enterprises are important, especially for how private and public sector institutions perceive the social economy. Trust has to be built up between social enterprises and public and private sector institutions.

Social capital in the social economy can reduce transaction costs between organisations. "Good" social capital (that is, for the common good) between organisations enables them to trust that they will work for each other for mutual benefit. In addition, network relationships between social enterprises in the social economy can usefully be formalised through membership of collective associations.

Modelling Social Capital, the Social Economy, and Local Development

High levels of local social capital do not always give rise to social enterprises. In other words, local social capital itself is not always the stimulus for the creation of social enterprise. Other forms of capital, like human and physical capital, are important for the founding and sustainability of social enterprises.

Social enterprises often emerge from the social capital of groups responding to socio-economic problems, such as industrial decline, youth unemployment, and rural isolation. Social capital is therefore a crucial resource where a social enterprise is formed to tackle such problems, and hitherto often the starting point of the setting up of social enterprises. Responding to a crisis may be the stimulus for a community to begin to work together and, by doing so, to begin to create the social capital they need to help tackle the crisis.

CONCLUSIONS

The experience of the CONSCISE Project suggests that the levels of social capital generated and used by a social enterprise can be assessed using social accounting and audit. Social enterprises should be encouraged to take stock of their social capital as part of the management process. In applying social accounting and audit, they can measure their performance in meeting social capital objectives as well as individual objectives.

Finally, social capital is not the exclusive preserve of social enterprises. On the contrary, public and private sector organisations have been using social capital for years in different ways and for different ends. This chapter argues that social enterprises and similar organisations should become more aware of using and generating social capital—and then use it as a valuable resource to help their sustainability and expansion.

244 Guenther Lorenz and Alan Kay

NOTES

1. See www.conscise.info.

REFERENCES

Anheier, H. 2002. "Dritter Sektor. Ehrenamt und Zivilgesellschaft in Deutschland. Thesen zum Stand der Forschung aus internationaler Sicht." In *Perspektiven gesellschaftlichen Zusammenhalts 2*, ed. E. Kistler, H.-H Noll, and E. Priller, 145–170. Berlin.
Beugelsdijk, S., and S. Smulders. 2003. *Bridging and Bonding Social Capital: Which Type Is Good for Economic Growth?* http://www.eea-esem.com/papers/eea-esem/2003/119/EEA2003.PDF.
Borzaga, C., and J. Defourny. 2001. *The Emergence of Social Enterprise*. Andover: Routledge.
Bourdieu, P. 1986. "Forms of Capital." In *Handbook of Theory and Research for the Sociology of Education*, ed. J. Richardson, 241–258. Westport, CT: Greenwood Press.
Centre International de Recherches et d'Information sur l'Économie Publique, Sociale et Coopérative (CIRIEC). 2000. *The Enterprises and Organizations of the Third System: A Strategic Challenge for Employment*. Liège: University of Liège.
Coleman, J. C. 1990, 1994. *Foundations of Social Theory*. Cambridge, Mass.: Harvard University Press.
CONCISE Project. 2000. *The Contribution of Social Capital in the Social Economy to Local Economic Development in Western Europe. Report of Workpackage 1: Key Concepts, Measures and Indicators*. www.conscise.info.
European Network for Economic Self-Help and Local Development. 2001. *Community Economic Development and Social Enterprises: Experiences, Tools and Recommendations*. Berlin: Technology Network.
Evers, A., U. Rauch, and U. Stitz. 2002. *Von öffentlichen Einrichtungen zu sozialen Unternehmen: Hybride Organisationsformen im Bereich sozialer Dienstleistungen*. Berlin: Sigma Verlag.
Hirschmann, A. 1984. "Against Parsimony: Three East Ways of Complicating Economic Analysis." *American Economic Review* 74:88–96.
Jacobs, J. 1961. *The Death and Life of Great American Cities*. New York: Random House.
Kay, A. 2006. "Social Capital, the Social Economy and Community Development." *Community Development Journal* 41 (2): 160–173.
Lorenz, G., and M. Schillat. 2002. *Lokale sozio-ökonomische Profile. Soldiner Kiez und Wrangelkiez (Berlin)*. Berlin: Veröffentlichungsreihe des Technologie-Netzwerkes Berlin e.V., (B36).
Onyx, J., and P. Bullen. 1999. *Measuring Social Capital in Five Communities in NSW: An Analysis*. Sydney: CACOM University of Technology.
Pearce, J. 2001. "Social Audit and Accounting Manual." CBS Network and Merseyside Social Enterprise.
Putnam, R. 2000. *Bowling Alone—The Collapse and Revival of American Community*. New York: Simon and Schuster.

19 Social and Public Value Measurement and Social Audit

The Czech Experience

Magdalena Hunčová

INTRODUCTION

The ideas of social enterprise, social audit, and social accounting have recently come to attention in the Czech Republic, linked to new conditions and challenges following entry into the European Union (EU) and, in particular, implementation of EU funds.

More specifically, the new EU program (2007–2013)—the Lisbon Program—introduces a new approach to funding social economic development based on social capital improvement. This is tested by social and public added value via support of public money or investment. Social and public added-value measurement is a method of social audit intended to ensure "better accountability and increased transparency . . . to ensure that EU funds, which are public money, are used properly at all levels" (Office for Official Publications of the European Communities 2008, 4). Any increase or decrease in social and public value added may be used to assess the social accountability of a public or private authority, as well as the effectiveness of finance and governance quality.

This chapter is motivated by, and explores, the poor perception and understanding of the social enterprise, social accounting, and social audit phenomena in the Czech Republic. Czech public authorities and civil society are making efforts to follow the newly introduced financial rules for transparency and accountability in order to be eligible for funding under the Lisbon Program. This chapter identifies, however, fundamental differences in understanding of the concepts of social economy and social enterprise, as well as social accountability, between western and eastern countries of EU. It explores how the Czech experience contrasts with that of the original fifteen EU countries because of cultural specifics derived from Czech's institutional heritage.

Despite this, the situation improves every year as Czechs learn more about the values, function, and role of social enterprises and social audit. The modernisation of the welfare state has been ongoing in the Czech Republic in recent years, as in other European countries. The institutional framework and responsibilities of sectoral actors (Laville et al. 1995), as well as approaches and processes in public service delivery, are all chang-ing in response to implementation of the new EU program (2007–2013). In addition, social enterprises operating on non-profit (not established and operated for profit) and not-for-profit (operating in the market for profit, but not distributing profit) bases are a natural target group eligible for a significant portion of EU funding because they are involved in many areas covered by EU policies—a precondition for EU funding.

Given that the EU is driving a normative agenda for social enterprise, this chapter argues that in order for the Czech Republic to respond, it is critical to develop a proper understanding and adequate application of the concepts of social economy and social enterprise (or social entrepreneurship), social accounting and social audit, as well as social and public added value.

The following section of this chapter discusses the concept of social enterprise as a producer of social and public value added. The third section discusses the challenges of the EU program (2007–2013) and the new EU financial rules in the Czech context. The fourth section develops the argu-ment that western and eastern concepts of social economy are fundamen-tally different, and explores the implications this has for the implementation of EU rules. The final section provides conclusions and recommendations for how the Czech Republic should proceed.

SOCIAL ENTERPRISE AS A PRODUCER OF PUBLIC (VIA SOCIAL) ADDED VALUE

Broadly, a social economy is one that produces positive social externalities. The social economy meets social needs using monetary and non-monetary resources, at the local and/or regional levels. Social economic bodies are characterised by a tendency to create co-operative networks which foster social and regional capital. In other words, the social economy produces social and public value through the development of social potential at both local and regional levels, and promotes both social and territorial potential into social and territorial capital (Zich 2008, 31).

As a starting point for thinking about the concept of social economy in the Czech context, we can think of the social economy as a civil, self-governed sector (Pestoff 1995) that plays an important role as a partner to the social state. It comprises predominantly non-governmental, non-profit, and not-for-profit organisations.

To understand the disparities in recent perceptions of the social economy and social enterprise phenomenon in the Czech Republic in comparison to more common conceptions, the following observations of Chavés and Monzon (2006, 18) are helpful:

> The most recent conceptual delimitation of the SE [social enterprise], by its own organisations, is that of the Charter of Principles of the

Social Economy promoted by the European Standing Conference of Co-operatives, Mutual Societies, Associations and Foundations (CEP-CMAF). The principles in question are:

- The primacy of the individual and the social objective over capital
- Voluntary and open membership
- Democratic control by the membership (does not concern foundations as they have no members)
- The combination of the interests of members/users and/or the general interest
- The defence and application of the principle of solidarity and responsibility
- Autonomous management and independence from public authorities
- Most of the surpluses are used in pursuit of sustainable development objectives, services of interest to members or the general interest.

This chapter contends that weaker characteristics in the Czech social economy are membership and democratic control, which are explained by the prevalence of non-member social enterprises (notwithstanding that the number of civic associations exceeds any other forms of Czech non-profit legal bodies—a point which is taken up later in the chapter).

Lorenz and Kay (Chapter 18, this volume) outline characteristics of social enterprise as follows:

1. Social enterprises seek to tackle specific social aims by engaging in economic and trading activities.
2. Social enterprises are not-for-profit organisations, in sense that all surplus profits generated are either reinvested in the economic activities or are used in other ways to tackle the stated social aims of the enterprise.
3. Social enterprises' legal structures are such that all the assets and accumulated wealth of the enterprise don't belong to any individuals but are held in trust to be used for the benefit of those persons or areas that are intended beneficiaries of the enterprises' social aim.
4. Social enterprises' organisational structures are such that the full participation of all members is encouraged on a co-operative basis with equal right accorded to all members.

It is further characteristic of the social enterprise sector that it encourages mutual co-operation between social enterprises and with other organisation in the wider social and local economy.

Again the value of mutuality and self-help are emphasised, as well as the heterogeneity of acts and actors and the multi-financing of activities of social enterprises by multi-stakeholdership.[1] Whilst this statement is not contended, it remains the fact that in order to demonstrate the distinctiveness of Czech social enterprise (both in theory and practice) in the context of EU funding, there is a need to demonstrate these characteristics. In the author's experience, it is mainly the dual nature of "social enterprise"—as a body with *both* economic and social values (or the idea of a group of people undertaking enterprise, as in a co-operative)—which creates difficulties in Czechs' understanding of the concept.

Indeed, this chapter argues that Czechs have lost their civil society experience because of their historical heritage. Czech co-operatives lost the majority of their autonomy and spontaneity within the central planned economy of the totalitarian period and their mutuality and democracy after 1990 as a result of processes of privatisation. In addition, co-operatives grew in concentration during the totalitarian period (operating as housing co-operatives with five thousand or more flats, for example), but many changed their legal status after 1990. Between 1948 and 1990, Czech civic associations developed in the first instance in the field of free-time activity; after 1990 they reflected social purposes again, but with some legal problems. Mutual funds were nationalised by the state after 1948, the majority continuing in state ownership after 1990, where they were not commercialised.

Against this backdrop, it is difficult to demarcate "the group of people" (as an association or common interest exteriorised) on the one hand, and "the enterprise" (as an economic activity or "assets and liabilities") on the other. In the author's experience, the interrelationship between society and its enterprises can be usefully summarised in three ways: (a) an enterprise hidden in an association, (b) an enterprise established "on the property" owned by an association, or (c) an enterprise that has founded its own property but is under constant control of an association.

Social enterprise does not necessarily have to be a legal body or a specific form of legal body. It often takes the form and value of a co-operative, of a mutual society and/or fund, or an association of interests, meaning associated people and/or property, in contrast to an association of capital (Pestoff 1995). Additionally, social enterprise is usually understood to be a petty or small enterprise (in a town or the countryside) within a network or in partnership with a municipality, providing subsistence to people and the local community. These socio-economic bodies play an important role in the implementation of the European and national public policies for employment, social cohesion, regional development, sustainability, and in relation to the competitiveness of SMEs. The size and structure of Czech civil society and its social economy is apparent within these considerations.

More specifically, Work Integration Social Enterprises (WISE; Borzaga and Defourny 2001) brings economically active NGOs together with social, productive, and workers' co-operatives. This concept (echoing the idea of "social entrepreneurship" from the United Kingdom) provides the foundation of the "Czech social enterprise definition", which has recently been formulated under the direction of the Czech Ministry of Employment and Social Affairs.[2]

THE NEW FINANCIAL RULES OF THE NEW EU PROGRAMMES FOR 2007–2013: ADDED VALUE, BETTER ACCOUNTING, AND ACCOUNTABILITY

At the beginning of 2007, the EU launched a new set of financial rules to enable effective use of funds representing EU programs worth €975 billion over a seven-year period. Broadly, the new rules simplify access to funding and reduce administrative procedures to a strict minimum (EUROPA 2007). In the new EU programming period (2007–2013), to enable the Lisbon strategy, there are three funds—the European Regional Development Fund, the European Social Fund, and the Cohesion Fund—and four goals—convergence, regional competitiveness, employment, and European territorial co-operation.

Important values and principles related to funding goals and access to funds set out the general conditions of the European funds 2007–2013, and national implementation of the new financial rules, including the principle that public money should create social and public added value (Commission of the European Communities COM 2004). Lacina (2007) presents seven fundamental principles for the implementation of these new financial rules in the Czech context:

1. *The Principle of Concentration*: European funds are to be more strategic, oriented towards the priorities of the Union, and goals which are all European. Specific or national goals are to be financed by national and sub-national sources.
2. *The Principle of Partnership*: Network creation at the local level is mostly supported within the concept of public–private partnership and multi-stakeholdership. This principle corresponds to the demand for sustainability of processes started by the European funds co-financing.
3. *The Principle of Programming*: This obliges national authorities to prepare their own scheme of programming documents, with goals that correspond to both national and European purposes.
4. *The Principle of Additionality*: The EU funds are not to substitute national money, but to start sustainable socio-economical processes and activities which will be self-financed after the start period and bring sustainable (multi-)effects. Funds are used in a regime of co-financing where any supported body bears the majority of its own financing and economic risks.

5. *The Principle of Monitoring and Evaluation*: Those who physically as well as legally implement the projects are responsible to the national authorities for spending public money and achieving goals. The national authorities are likewise accountable to the European authorities.[3]

6. *The Principle of Subsidiarity*[4] (and proportional intervention): This states that "implementation of operational programmes shall be the responsibility of Member States at the appropriate territorial level, in accordance with the institutional system specific for each Member State" (Commission of the European Communities COM 2004).

7. *The Principle of Solidarity*: This is the basic principle of economic and social cohesion policies. Under the pressure of the increasingly globalised market, rich countries help weaker countries through the EU funds and programs. We can also understand this principle as the EU funds serving to improve and modernise systems of solidarity organised previously by the welfare state in the EU, empowering citizens again and fostering citizens' horizontal solidarity.

It would seem uncontentious that the principles of subsidiarity and solidarity, as well as the principle of sustainability, marry well with the concept of social enterprise, as discussed in the previous section. In this context, sustainability is a special value which lies primarily in self-government and self-financing social enterprises like socio-economic private bodies. These bodies would be supported by public money only carefully and partially, so as not to lose their own values. To maintain sustainability as a value, public authorities would provide support for social economic enterprises (in the name of public interest) mostly in indirect ways: through tax benefits, government contracts, special targeted endowments, free loans, and friendly legal conditions; and sometimes in direct ways in special cases, but through "start-ups only".[5] More specifically, sustainability is a particular value, reflected in such factors as duration of economic activity, environmental richness, variability of diversity, cross-generation solidarity, citizens remaining in the countryside, and fostering regional and social capital. As public money is usually spent by public authorities, the onus is on them to evaluate its effectiveness. This suggests that social and public added value will increase if sustainability is a requirement. It is contended that the phenomenon of the democratic, social economy and its social enterprises can play a big role in this context. When the author was involved in working on the aforementioned definition of the "Czech social enterprise", in order to operationalise EU program financing, the values of sustainability and internal values of social enterprises were to be kept in mind. This was achieved only partially.

The EU's new financial rules for 2007–2013 also introduce measures to ensure maximum transparency and tighter control of the distribution and spending of EU funding. The new rules make EU grants easier to access, especially for beneficiaries with limited resources, such as small NGOs and small companies (social enterprises) at the local and regional level. The financial rules emphasise better, simpler, and more practical provision of solutions, while ensuring effective control over public spending.

A particular innovation is that the financial rules introduce a requirement for publication of lists of beneficiaries who receive EU money through governments in the Member States, governments in the countries outside the EU, or through international organisations, and the exchange of information on proven fraud cases. Member States are also expected to improve reporting on how they spend EU funds managed directly by them.

Transparent procedures also mean equal access to information. Calls for proposals are published on the Commission web sites. The same principle applies to EU funds managed at the national or regional level. Calls for the Commission tenders can be found online.

Stricter accountability and control is another aspect of the new EU regulations. National governments must take their share of responsibility as to how EU funding is managed at the national level and improve Member States' reporting. National governments have committed themselves to putting in place effective and efficient internal control systems and making the necessary checks on EU funds. Each Member State is now obliged to provide an annual summary of the audits available on these funds. Under the new rules, the Commission will also have better tools to prevent fraud and corruption via a central database of organisations excluded from EU funding.

Since 2005, the EU accounting has been based on so-called accrual accounting, which reflects commercial accounting standards traditionally used by the private sector. The new accounting is based on the International Public Sector Accounting Standards (IPSAS), the relevant International Accounting Standards (IAS), and International Financial Report Standards (IFRS) (European Commission 2008; Grybauskaité 2006). Until recently, Czech public authorities have used cash accounting for budgeting purposes but have used accrual accounting for additional economic sources observation. This means it is now possible to extend accrual accounting toward EU funds monitoring.

Finally, Czech governmental authorities responsible for EU funding have endorsed these financial and accounting rules and introduced them into national documents. The specific criteria by which an organisation is considered eligible for EU funding is explained in detail in individual calls for proposals. Applicants are asked to demonstrate the purpose, benefits, and the group of people targeted by public support of their project—as well as indicate some of the aims and sustainability of a co-financed project proposal.

To summarise, the only question remaining is whether the Czech public authorities can actually implement EU funds effectively for the purpose of increasing social and public value and its sustainability when they do not fully understand the role and functions of the social economy. Given that the related procedures are very formal, as in the case of public contracts, matters of formalities may predominate when the law is observed. Certainly there are some indications that the ensuing years will bring some improvement, which is what we hope.

THE WEST DOESN'T UNDERSTAND THAT THE EAST DOESN'T UNDERSTAND THE CONCEPT OF SOCIAL ECONOMY

Concepts of social economy and social enterprise were developed in the "old" EU countries (the original fifteen) based on their particular historical experience of civil society, membership, and mutuality. The social economy has worked alongside the social state, as well as the market, since the foundation of the welfare state after the Second World War. By contrast, in the Central and Eastern European countries the tradition of democratic economy and civil society were interrupted twice: after 1938 (or 1948) and again after 1990. Historically, the central planned economy taught us how to manage large socio-economic systems in a strategic and paternalistic way (from the top to the bottom). Nowadays, teaching us to use strategic planning would resemble adding salt to already salt water! On the other hand, we have forgotten or rejected formal membership and mutuality, as well as civil democracy, given that representative democracy was only reliably reinstated after 1990.

However, some problems of misunderstanding could also be a result of the "jungle" of political ideas and the promotion of a strong neoliberal dogma during the period of transformation—resulting in the present-day legal and institutional framework—or thanks to the English to Czech translation of books only from the United States on economics from the 1990s. For example, in the Czech language "social" is not understood as "societal", but much more narrowly as a concern with handicapped people and their employment, about people at the bottom of society, or personal care. Another example: "Enterprise" (and "entrepreneurship") is usually not distinguished from "business" (and "doing business") because there is one Czech word for both these terms (*podnik* and *podnikání*). People can further confuse "enterprise" and "firm" as well. (In the case of "social enterprise", we may better explain it as a not-for-profit organised economic activity that corresponds to a group of people or their initiative.)

The distance between Anglo-American traditions versus Continental European ones are well known. When we study the experience of the social economy in practice and in terms of the legal network in Western and Eastern Europe, we observe that only some western countries have a similar problem in understanding the social economy phenomenon. Countries such as Germany and Austria, for example, also experienced central economic planning during the Second World War.

So, what is the current situation in the Czech Republic? Although some state roles and functions were decentralised to lower levels of territorial public self-governed entities in 2000, the major part of social responsibility (and related public finance redistribution) remains in the hands of the Czech central political and administrative authorities even today. The role of municipalities as a centre of social responsibility has been a tradition in the Czech Republic since the end of the eighteenth century, and it has worked well. Nonetheless, Czech municipalities are now widely dependent on tax sources distributed by the state—and less so on their own taxes, property, and economy. Additionally, public property has been privatised, and the empowerment of social responsibility is mainly the responsibility of individual citizens. Beyond this, and on a positive note, the Czech state systematically cares for the employment of people threatened by labour market exclusion through the Employment Code.

Czech social economic practice, as well as the development of civil society, is still weak in terms of relevant law and policy and the necessary conditions for democratic decision-making and multi-financing. Nevertheless, we can identify many types of social enterprise practiced across the Central and Eastern European countries in large numbers when the "bright" (Pestoff 1995) definition of socio-economical entities is applied (that is, the social economy as an economy that produces positive social externalities based on citizens' initiative and responsibility). From this perspective, in the Czech Republic we can identify a number of co-operatives (housing, production, agricultural, workers', and cultural), as well as civic associations producing services for the common good, foundations, common beneficiary organisations, associations of municipalities, some facilities of religious bodies, and a high number of SMEs—traders. Additionally, the structure of Czech civil society and the social economy is endowed with a high number of public facilities (created by municipalities on municipal property for the purpose of producing social goods). These facilities could be included in the number of social enterprises in situations where citizens/clients (and other stakeholders) participate in decision-making processes and multi-financing, which is the case. In general though, Czech public authorities, as well as those of other Central and Eastern European countries, only seldom properly understand the phenomenon of the social economy in this wider sense and in the context of the EU new financial rules and its financing program for 2007–2013.

Following entry into EU structures in 2004, and under new EU financial rules after 2006, it became necessary to formulate consensual criteria to define the social economy. For this reason, Czech public authorities have started to call for the identification, definition, and regulation of social economic actors. The Czech Ministry of Employment and Social Affairs have contracted work to identify "the Czech social enterprise definition", as noted earlier in this chapter. Subsequently the "National network of experts—Part C (social economy)" was established within the CIP EQUAL project, as well as its informal platform named the NESEA. A starting point for the definition was the principles used by the United Kingdom's social entrepreneurship strategy.

The network of experts and its informal platform worked up a draft definition of Czech social enterprise, but discussions were conflict-laden with distinct points of views and experiences amongst practicing experts and those from the academic field. The final definition brings together the social firm phenomenon, WISE of EMES, some aspects of co-operative strategy in practice, and Schumpeter's (social) enterprise definition (Borzaga and Defourny 2001). In the end, a draft of the definition was created, but it remained stigmatised by a confusion of terms: social economy, social enterprise, social entrepreneurship, and social firm. There was also misunderstanding of some deeply rooted values in the concept of social economy. The main factors causing this situation were: the administrative toolbar required by the ministry, the specific institutional heritage of the Czech Republic, and current legal environment. The definition is to be improved within a new EU project. In the end, social economic actors will be recognised according to their legal form and not according to the substance of their activities and nature. This mirrors the existing approach used by the Czech contractors—which is very formal, regardless of their own concepts of responsibility and accountability.

Generally, the "non-profit" nature of social enterprises is specified in terms of economic activities that benefit not only profit for profit's sake, but also profit for the common or public good; while the not-for-profit nature of social enterprises is based on market activity producing "non-distributed profit". In the Czech Republic there appears to be legal problems related to these social enterprise values and concerning their interpretation. There is no special co-operative law, for example. An additional problem is that Czech law does not make the terms clear ("public" and "common interest", "not-for-profit", "non-distributed profit", "multi-financing", *inter alia*), when the law is primarily interpreted to the letter.

It is contended that many of the problems that arose during the process of defining "the Czech social enterprise" were connected to the interpretation and implementation of terms and ideas in the social economy. These included: autonomy, self-governance, self-financing, economical risk bearing, stakeholder, mutuality, membership, 1-member-1-voice, not-for profit, non-distribution of profit, community, group of people, common good, citizens' democracy, social and/versus entrepreneurship, accountability. The explanation lies not only in the weak knowledge of concepts, but also significantly in Czech institutional conditions—their legal networks, politics, dogmas, approaches to privatisation, the non-critical uptake of US and UK concepts, and a "strategy" of legal positivism. This case shows that the implementation of any vision out of context is problematic; it concerns not only the Czech Republic but also the rest of Central and Eastern Europe, and even the expectations and information provision of the rest of the EU. Yet surely we can learn to understand each other?

CONCLUSIONS

Social enterprise produces positive social externalities and promotes local social potential to become local social capital—as well as the social capital of a larger territory. It is suggested that we can measure the added value produced in this way in terms of social and public added values. EU funding arrangements and financial rules are oriented towards investing in the start-up of economical and social developments that will remain sustainable. Social enterprise is a natural target group. Those receiving support are required to document their accountability and the outcomes of spending public money to the national authorities and to the EU.

The implementation of EU funding arrangements has met with difficulties in the Czech Republic as well as in other Central and Eastern European countries. Problems arise when we test the understanding of the concepts of social economy and social enterprise in these countries. This happens because of specific historical, institutional—and even cultural heritage—experiences. The problem on the one hand seems to be one of weak mutuality and citizen's experiences of democracy over the last fifty years, and on the other hand can be traced back to the market economy after 1990.

In general, Czech social enterprises, as in any other EU countries, contribute to the delivery of non-market services or other types of social cohesion, create innovative jobs, or seek accountability for money to finance non-individual benefits. These enterprises are co-operatives (although they have lost some value due to their transformation and being subject to the Commerce Code), civic associations, and foundations, as well as some other non-member organisations and facilities. Until recently in the Czech Republic, some of these functions were covered systematically by governmental activity via specific codes, public funds, and budgets, and via public facilities, enterprise, and agency, or via the market. Yet, the Czech state redistributive system of solidarity is now undergoing significant changes. Some governmental institutions have been privatised and their legal status changed.[6]

Czech civil society and its social economy are developing with increasing social economic activities and memberships with mutuality. Changes in the law and due to regulation of public authorities have been positive as well as negative.

Central and Eastern European countries need to learn much more about the concepts and values of the social economy. These ideas are explained differently to those in Western Europe. For instance, social enterprise is usually understood as small; yet we can expect a large variety in size of social enterprises (as well as in the scope of their activities). As social enterprise is usually understood as a democratic economy, we can expect many non-member organisations and firms, sometimes in some way subordinated to public authorities. As a result of their historical heritage, social enterprises in the Czech Republic currently tend to be non-personal and non-member. In order to support the employment of handicapped or regional development via public co-financing, for example, at present the Czech public authorities prefer mostly social firms, as well as non-personal and non-member legal bodies, and favour quasi-public bodies or entrepreneurs. The reason for this is the expectation for effectiveness of public money and higher public "accountability", with higher transparency of responsibilities and of public finance in bookkeeping.

Czechs need to relearn values which correspond to the social economy (based on personal membership and citizens' democracy) in order to understand them and to spend EU funds much more effectively. Czech people need to recognise the socio-economical and democratic dimension of the social economy, and these values need to be introduced into the legal system. They need to understand their taxpayers' requirement for public authority accountability.

The development of new methods of social values accumulation measurement would be an important contribution to improve the Czech situation. We can learn through good accounting practices abroad or through our own experience at present and in the past. However, legal and political willingness and public bureaucracy practices present basic limitations. Within the social economy concept and European funding implementation, it seems that Western Europe seeks systems and strategies within its social policy and modernising systems of solidarity (and maybe something from Central and Eastern European countries can be learnt), but first Central and Eastern Europe needs to consolidate citizens' economical democracy (and they need to learn this from Western European countries).

NOTES

1. The necessity of multi-financing by multi-stakeholdership is because of the specificity of public and common goods. They are produced with higher total costs contrary to clients' direct payments.
2. For this definition, see http://www.scmvd.cz/download/standardy_se.pdf (in Czech language only).
3. Lacina (2007) emphasises the upwards accountability within the mechanism of European funds implementation, not the accountability of governments to taxpayers.
4. The principle of subsidiarity: The initiatives are developed from the bottom to the top; problems are to be solved at the basic (national, regional, local) level of effectiveness; the higher level will act only if the lower level fails. In other words, we can understand this principle of subsidiarity as the responsibility of bodies on the lowest level of activity, which are supervised and guaranteed by authorities on upper levels within public policies.

5. Public money can destroy co-operative values and increase corruption levels in related regions. See Paez (2000).
6. For example: (a) Some hospitals (the responsibility of regional governments) changed their legal bodies from public facilities into shareholders' companies, hoping to become active in not-for-profit regimes; (b) homeless people are no longer given personal care in public asylums, which was directly paid for by the state budget, but are now given the choice between family care or a public/private asylum (and only a portion of public money is assigned directly to asylums within budgets or grants depending on their legal status); and (c) retirement funds are now held by the state, but people are encouraged to save individually through the market with additionally secured funds.

REFERENCES

Borzaga, C., and J. Defourny. 2001. *The Emergence of Social Enterprise*. London: Routledge.
Chavés, R., and J. L. Monzon. 2006. "The Social Economy in the European Union." Report No. CESE/CoMM/05/2005 EESC. http://eesc.europa.eu/groups/3/categories/soceco/booklets/EN_Web.pdf.
Commission of the European Communities COM. 2004. *Communication from the Commission to the Council and the European Parliament: Financial Perspectives 2007–2013*. http://eur-lex.europa.eu/LexUriServ/site/en/com/2004/com2004_0487en01.pdf.
EUROPA. 2007. "New Financial Rules Facilitate Use of EU Funds." Europe Press released RAPID—IP/07/424. http://europa.eu/rapid/pressReleasesAction.do?reference=IP/07/424&format=HTML&aged=0&language=EN&guiLanguage=en.
European Commission. 2008. *Modernising the EU Accounts*. Brussels: Publications Office. http://ec.europa.eu/budget/library/publications/fin_manag_account/modernising_EU_accounts_en.pdf.
Grybauskaité, D. 2006. "Modernising Accounting in the Public Sector." Presented at the European Commission, European Parliament, Brussels, 28 September. http://www.fee.be/fileupload/upload/Grybauskaite%20speech4102006321849.pdf. Lacina, L. 2007. *Projektový manažer [Project Manager]*. Brno: Eurion. http://usti.elearningove kurzy.cz.
Laville, J. L., C. Borzaga, J. Defourny, A. Evers, J. Lewis, M. Nyssens, and V. Pestoff. 1995. *Third System: A European Definition (Paper of the Research Project)*. http://www.istr.org/networks/europe/laville.evers.etal.pdf.
Office for Official Publications of the European Communities. 2008. *New Funds, Better Rules: Overview of New Financial Rules and Funding Opportunities 2007–2013*. Luxembourg. http://ec.europa.eu/budget/library/publications/financial_pub/pack_rules_funds_en.pdf.
Paez, C. C. 2000. *Within the Limits of Legislative Rhetoric and over the Limits: Co-Operative Law, the Problems of Asia and Pacific Region (Conference Paper). International Legislative Conference*. Prague: Cooperative Association of the Czech Republic.
Pestoff, V. 1995. *Reforming Social Services in Central Eastern Europe and Eleven National Overview*. Krakow: GRYF (Poland).
Zich, F. 2008. "Konceptuální východiska—diskuse" ["Conceptual Base—Discussion"]. In: *Sociální potenciál průmyslových regionů a možnosti jeho zjišťování [Social Potential of Industrial Regions and Possibilities of Its Identification. Book of Proceedings]*. Usti nad Labem: Faculty of Social and Economic Studies, University J.E.P. in Ústí nad Labem, Czech Republic.

20 The Contribution of Religious Congregations to the Local Social Economy

Ram A. Cnaan

INTRODUCTION

Non-profit organisations in general and congregations in particular contribute to the quality of life of local people. Numerous qualitative testimonies attest to the positive transformation these organisations support. Yet
these many externalities[1] are often presented in qualitative ways that do
not show the total contribution of these organisations. The non-profit field
has struggled with how to quantify its positive externalities and much good
work goes unaccounted for.

Valuation is an economic field that attempts to assess value where the market does not reach. In such cases as environmental protection and cultural
goods, scholars have attempted to ask the public if they would be willing to
pay for these services and how much, which is known as contingent valuation
(Moon et al. 2002; Quiggin 1998). When applicable, they made comparisons
to market goods (Boehm 1996) and they asked experts to carry out cost-
benefit or risk analysis (Efroymson et al. 2004; Gregory 2000).

Yet valuation is thought to be unequipped to quantify the externalities
of non-profit organisations. This chapter therefore provides the first ever
systematic valuation of one group of non-profit organisations—urban religious congregations—to the local social economy. It employs a replacement
value approach (Van den Berg, Brouwer, and Koopmanschap 2004).

The focus is local religious congregations because their major impact
is local and not regional or national. For example, staff members often
reside in the proximity of the congregation (Cnaan et al. 2006; Farnsley
2003) and maintenance is often carried out by locals. Some activities are
impressive and praiseworthy, but are distinctively not local—for example,
helping victims of disasters (Airriess et al. 2008). These are excluded from
the assessment of congregational externalities.

WHAT EXTERNALITIES CAN BE ESTIMATED?

Some dilemmas involved in estimating the contribution of urban religious
congregations[2] are imbedded in the following example: How does one

measure and assess a congregation's contribution to reducing the suicide rate in its community? While congregations serve as buffers against suicide, no one is able to measure how many suicides are saved as a result (Lizardi et al. 2008). Can we distinguish the contribution of a religious congregation as distinct from that of the family or other groups? What is the value of one life saved?

These questions are just one example of the complexity involved in assessing the contributions of local religious congregations to their local social economy. While valuing suicide prevention, (or health promotion and teen pregnancy prevention) are beyond the scope of this chapter, other positive externalities are possible to assess.

A simplistic assessment approach takes the congregational annual budget as the congregation's contribution to the local economy, without paying any attention to externalities. I discuss this approach in the third section of this chapter. In the fourth through the eleventh sections I use a more sophisticated approach, detailing the positive externalities emanating from the local congregations in order to provide a more holistic valuation. A final section of the chapter draws conclusions.

OPERATING BUDGETS

Chaves and Miller (1999) found that congregations save very little of the income they receive; hence the budget can be viewed as the economic contribution to the community. Notably, congregations are not required to report their budgets; many congregations do not see the need for an overall budget and can have a host of independent mini budgets for each of its programs or ministries.

Examining over two thousand Lutheran churches, Stonebraker (2003) reported a median budget of around $150,000.[3] This includes all expenditures from clergy and staff salary to rebuilding the church's property. Pressley and Collier (1999) reported estimates of between $42,900 and $200,000 for Black churches. Cnaan and colleagues (2006), in a congregational census of Philadelphia, included a higher proportion of storefront churches and found a median operating budget (exclusive of capital campaign and schools) of $90,000. Finally, the Barna Group (2001), in a national survey of Protestant churches, estimated the average operating budget of a Protestant church to be $115,000.

Multiplying the number of congregations in a given area by one of the aforementioned estimates provides a conservative estimate of the average contribution of an urban religious congregation to the local social economy. Accordingly, the mean contribution to the local social economy is assessed as a minimum of $115,000 per congregation (as measured in 2000, not adjusted for inflation). This includes the costs of clergy salary, building repairs, property maintenance, and the costs of social and spiritual ministries.

Salaries, most social services, maintenance, and upkeep are all spent locally and enhance the local social economy. A small portion finds its way outside the community in the form of dues to denomination, international mission, and disaster relief. To be on the safe side, I deduct 10 percent of the $115,000, giving a value of $103,500. Attempts to use congregations' budgetary contributions to their local social economy as a measure of their impact are still considered cutting edge (Stritt 2008). Yet, this easily arrived at estimate disregards many aspects of congregational contributions to the local economy detailed in a rich literature on religion and congregations. These include: social and human services, contributions to crime reduction and property value, contributions to the local economy through religious tourism and reunions, saving public schools boards the cost of educating thousands of students who study in congregational-based schools, and the economic value of bringing people and resources from the suburbs to the city. Finally, a few congregations are actively involved in operating community development corporations and housing initiatives that revitalise local neighbourhoods.

HUMAN AND SOCIAL SERVICES

A large literature documents the social, community, economic, and political contributions of local religious congregations (Ammerman 2005; Ammerman and Farnsley 1997; Chaves 2004; Cnaan et al. 2006). Some contributions to the local social economy are easily detected, such as donating money/goods to the poor. The majority of contributions however are not easily detected—for example, the contribution of congregations in enhancing moral values and reducing levels of risk behaviours (Sinha, Cnaan, and Gelles 2006). Yet whilst the monetary cost of services may be modest, their impact can be impressive. Congregations use resources such as in-kind support, member volunteers, and congregational space in social programs.

Cnaan and colleagues (2006, 99) culminated replacement value as a method for the fiscal contribution of congregational social and human services:

> replacement value is the amount it would cost others to provide the same services or programs at the level stipulated, if they did not have the congregational property and member volunteers at hand. To illustrate . . . the value of the space is a congregational contribution, which in real terms, has a cost and a financial value. Similarly, if a clergy member invests time in a social program; his or her salary should be recognised as money paid by the congregation, which then allows him or her to spend time providing community-oriented services.

Table 20.1 details the results of Cnaan et al. (2006). They asked for the fiscal value of the seven components shown in Table 20.1 in order to account for the replacement value of services.

Table 20.1 Monthly Replacement Value of an Average Program and Congregational Social and Community Programs in Philadelphia (N = 4,287)

Source	Percent of congregations reporting cost	Average cost per program	Average cost per congregation[1]
Financial support by the congregation	59.5%	$417.86SD = 970.99	$1,287.01
Value of in-kind support	67.0%%	$167.22SD = 493.7	$515.04
Value of utilities for programs	64.8%	$166.73SD = 446.4	$513.53
Estimated value of space used for the program	75.5%	$613.33SD = 1057.7	$1,889.06
Number of clergy hours (@ $20.00 per hour)	69.9%	$258.40SD = 32.2	$795.87
Number of staff hours (@ $10.00 per hours)	34.8%	$187.93SD = 54.6	$578.82
Number of volunteer hours (@ $17.19 per hour)	83.9%	$1,517.88SD = 2341.8	$4,675.07
Total		$3,329.35	$10,254.40
Total outside of the congregation's operating budget (only bolded items)			$7,079.17

Note: 1. Since each congregation studied provides on average 3.08 programs, I multiplied 3.08 programs by the value obtained in the "average cost per program" column to receive the estimate for the "average cost per congregation" column.

The unit of analysis in this method is a single program offered by a congregation. For each program, they determined estimated cost per month, which proved to be convenient for respondents to provide accurate information. When respondents were unable to provide an assessment of any of the program components' cost, they assigned the value of zero cost. Only three items are not already counted in the congregational budget: in-kind support, value of space, and value of volunteer work.[4]

The monthly replacement value of congregational social programs that is not accounted for in the congregation's operating budget is $7,079.17. The annual replacement value (multiplying by twelve months) is $84,950.04.

Cnaan and colleagues (2006) contended that this method is conservative. For example, only five programs per congregation were included in their analysis. The value of additional programs where congregations had more than five programs was not fully represented. Second, informal services performed by congregations such as one-time rent assistance were excluded from the analysis. They truncated the reported values to avoid the inclusion of what may have been outliers. Finally, this calculation did not count spin-off services that started as congregational programs and grew into major social services that serve the city.

CRIME REDUCTION

Few studies have focused on the effect of congregations on urban crime rates (Lee 2006; Lee and Ousey 2005). The linkage may be explained using the "moral communities thesis" (Lee and Bartkowski 2004; Stark 1996; Stark, Kent, and Doyle 1982). The basic premise of "moral communities" is that religious groups, especially congregations, promote a strong moral community that is based on shared values and ideas of what is right and wrong. Studies show that congregational members are less likely to be involved in crime or risky behaviour (see, for example, Sinha, Cnaan, and Gelles 2006; Smith 2003).

Religious congregations create community via group dynamics processes (Cnaan et al. 2002). They can affect crime through the formation of strong social networks that increase social capital (Lee and Ousey 2005). Individuals choosing to join a congregation will strive to meet the moral and behavioural expectations of existing members. Through this process, they meet like-minded others and friendships develop; they develop networks and interact and gain support from others. Religious congregations also facilitate community action and develop leadership and pro-social skills (Ammerman and Farnsley 1997; Cnaan et al. 2002; Warner 1994). As such, congregations send clear messages and offer a variety of programs that are designed to reduce crime and risky behaviour. Neighbourhoods with more civically engaged churches have lower rates of vehicle theft, commercial burglary, and larceny; however, civically engaged churches have no effect on homicide, robbery, aggravated assault, assault, and residential burglary (Lee and Bartkowski 2004).

The involvement of congregations in crime reduction far exceeds the impact they have on members of the congregation. Cnaan and Boddie (2001) found that 20 percent of all Philadelphia congregations offer programs for gang members, 2.5 percent provide organised programs for youth offenders, 7 percent work with prisoners' families, 1.4 percent offer half-way houses for persons released from prison, and 13.9 percent provide prison ministries. Other congregations assist the work of other organisations in these areas and many more help with other services that may reduce crime from co-operation with police (9.1 percent) to midnight basketball (1.5 percent).

Methodological drawbacks to these findings include the problem that the causality of the findings is not clear-cut. For example, is it the relationship with the congregation that impacts teens to behave in a manner more socially accepted or are those teens less likely to commit crimes attracted to join congregations? Do more "geeks" come to pray while the "cool teens" are busy taking risks? Arguably more involved families influence teens to attend congregations. Further, influences may not be long-term. Many religious teens arriving at college binge drink (Holt et al. 2006). Also, it is difficult to assess the economic value of people not engaged in risk behaviours.

It is close to impossible to assess how many people avoided a criminal path or ended criminal careers due to congregational involvement, yet their impact is indisputable (Hercik et al. 2004). I assume that each congregation, annually, prevents at least one person from being incarcerated at any given time. This is a conservative estimate as congregations are often housed in areas where social problems are rampant and actively promote crime prevention (Cnaan et al. 2006).

Based on 1996 data and calculated in 2001 value, the average cost of housing an inmate in prison is estimated at $23,000 (Stephan 2004), excluding building costs. In the UK, the cost including building costs has been estimated at £37,500 (Nuttall 1998). I use the US estimate.

Each person that is not incarcerated is likely to be employed and pay taxes. I assume that the person pays at a minimum $5,000 in taxes,[5] not to mention paying rent, buying food, and consuming goods locally. At a minimum, I assessed contribution of an average congregation to the safety of its local social economy at $28,000.

CONTRIBUTION TO THE VALUE OF PRIVATE PROPERTIES

Often, the pride of a faith group is embodied in the edifice it possesses and maintains (Ammerman and Farnsley 1997). Places of worship are known to attract stability and reverence in their neighbourhoods (Cnaan et al. 2006; Farnsley 2003). In America, with the move to the suburbs, the gentrification of some centre cities, the loss of industry, and the decline of the "mom-and-pop" stores, urban façades are continually changing; the most stable social institutions and physical structures are local religious congregations. Amongst Philadelphia congregations, Cnaan et al. (2006) found that only some 18 percent of congregations reported an inclination to relocate—most of them due to growth. Most congregations (82.5 percent) own their property and, as such, are invested in the quality of the property and in the community. Congregations usually withstand the impact of economic recession, community disintegration, loss of industrial base, and rise in crime and drug use and serve as a temporary buffer against decline.

It is difficult to estimate the average contribution of a congregation to its local housing market and the dollar value of this assessment. In Cleveland, the nearby presence of a parish building or a Catholic school increases housing value between 3.2 percent and 11.6 percent, increases rent 2.2 percent to 7.2 percent, and reduces vacancy rates 6.9 percent to 15.5

percent (Ottensmann 2000). Do, Wilbur, and Short (1994) found that the presence of congregations had a small negative effect on housing prices; however, Carroll, Clauretie, and Jensen (1996) reported that the presence of congregations had a positive effect on housing prices. Finally, Kinney and Winter (2006, 335) found that in poor neighbourhoods in St. Louis "storefront churches . . . may be overlooked contributors to the sort of stable urban space where residential population is preserved and investment maintained".

In order to provide a conservative estimate, I use the lowest estimate from Ottensmann's (2000) study. I assume that congregations add 3.2 percent to the value of the properties around them. In the first quarter of 2006, average housing prices in the United States fell from $225,300 to $217,900 (Christie 2006). Assuming that houses around congregations are on average 3.2 percent more expensive, congregations add $6,972.80. At the least, a congregation is surrounded by four properties (assuming four directions). As such, I multiply by four to obtain a total conservative estimate of $27,891.20.

TOURISM AND REUNIONS

Two types of congregational activities promote tourism and enhance the local social economy. First, some congregations attract visitors due to their historical or religious significance—religious tourism. The second type of activity is reunions—an attraction for many Black tourists (Grant 2005). Sites and churches that attract travellers add to the local economy via admission, meals at restaurants, hotel nights, buying books and pamphlets, and donations for restoration.

In Philadelphia 5.8 percent of the city congregations reported that they are regularly involved in "architectural and historical tours". The most attractive site is most likely the museum of Mother Bethel AME Church, which attracts between fifteen to twenty thousand visitors annually.[6] Other congregations attract fewer tourists. I assume that the average number of tourists that visit one of these churches engaged in "architectural and historical tours" is not less than one thousand annually. I assume that an average visitor leaves at least fifty dollars value of support for the local economy. I therefore assess the contribution of participating congregations to local tourism at $5,000. Given that 5.6 percent of congregations are engaged in tourism, the average congregation's contribution from religious tourism to the local social economy is approximately $280.

Many African-Caribbean's who live abroad routinely attend family reunions that centre on churches (Sutton 2004). In Wilmington, Delaware, I found that 17.6 percent of congregations are involved in reunions. On average, a reunion involves thirty persons who, in addition to travel cost (not directly contributing to the local social economy), spent an average of $300 per person. This includes food, lodging, and space rented for the event. A church that holds a family reunion may add to the local social economy the total sum of $9,000. Given that that only 17.6 percent of the congregations offered in the past year such service, the average annual local contribution coming from reunions is estimated at $1,584.

CONGREGATIONAL-BASED SCHOOLING

Schools are often budgeted for and incorporated separately from the congregation, and have their own boards. Yet, these schools are congregationally based, with the congregation providing theological support and teaching. Funds come from tuition, denominational funds, and donations. The congregation may also fundraise and provide volunteers.

In Philadelphia it was found that 14.5 percent of the congregations operate a school. Parents of children who attend a congregational-based school still pay local public education taxes, saving the cost to the public of educating the child. Schools vary between forty and more than a thousand students. The average number of enrolments is 120.

The cost of a student per year in the public education system is estimated at $9,866 (WikiAnswers 2008)—the cost reported by most boards of education in most major American cities.

Using these figures ($9,866 yearly and 120 students per school), I assess that those congregations that maintain a school (elementary, middle, or high school) save the taxpayer, on average, annually $1,183,920. Given that only 14.5 percent of the congregations maintain schools, the average contribution of one urban congregation to its local social economy is assessed at $171,668.40. This estimate excludes the taxes that parents pay to sustain the public education system.

BRINGING THE AFFLUENCE OF THE SUBURBS TO THE CITY

Congregations bring suburban resources to the city. First, many well-to-do people leave the city and move to the suburbs, but continue to worship in the "old neighbourhood" on weekends. They consume meals, parking, and (often) attend theatre or shop. Second, as reported both in Philadelphia and Wilmington, many affluent suburban congregations provide fiscal and technical grants to inner-city congregations to support social activities.

In Philadelphia, Cnaan and colleagues (2006) found that the average congregation is composed of 322 members including children, with 13.6 percent living outside the city limits (see also Farnsley 2003; Dudley and Roozen 2001). That implies that forty-four individuals, per congregation, enter the city to attend services. Assuming that some actually live nearby and some do not attend every weekend, it follows that on a weekly basis, twenty-five individuals, per congregation, cross over and use some service in the inner-city. I modestly assume that an average visitor spends ten dollars per visit. Assuming that twenty-five different people visit the city four times a month (one hundred separate visits) and each visit brings ten dollars of business, the monthly contribution of an urban congregation on average stands at $1,000 and the annual contribution at $12,000.

Further support from urban congregations to their social economies is retaining resources from rich suburban organisations. Cnaan and colleagues (2002) reported the case of St. Gabriel Episcopal Church in Philadelphia. This church, located in a declining neighbourhood, retained the expertise and financial support of the richer Gradwyn Episcopal Church, as well as volunteers from four colleges outside the city. Altogether, the value of such collaboration reached $200,000 a year. In Wilmington, I found a suburban church that has an outreach budget of $400,000 for work with inner-city congregations.

The suburban support for an average collaborating congregation is assessed at $3,200 annually per participating congregation. Given that only 25.3 percent of the local congregations are engaged in such activity, per urban congregation the annual estimated contribution is $809.60.

COMMUNITY DEVELOPMENT CORPORATION AND HOUSING INITIATIVES

Not many congregations are involved in the area of Community Development Corporation (CDC) or economic and housing initiatives. Table 20.2 draws on the Philadelphia census of congregations (Cnaan at al. 2006) to assess the percentage of congregations involved in activities of soliciting external funds to enhance the local economic and housing conditions. One congregation, in West Philadelphia, purchased the land next to its worship hall and built sixty housing units for the elderly. The congregation was instrumental in leveraging state and federal government funding and in the neighbourhood development. Without the congregation, this housing would not have been constructed.

Table 20.2 shows nine similar activities, reports the percentage of congregations (ranging from 4.6 percent to .08 percent) involved, and provides estimates of the contribution to the local economy as found in the literature. It should be noted that the data from Philadelphia is quite conservative in comparison to other studies (for example, Jackson et al. 1997). The total annual contribution assessed in Table 20.2 is $45,980 per average urban congregation.

OVERALL VALUATION

The total estimated value of the contribution of a typical urban congregation is estimated at $476,663.24. Although this suggests a rather astronomical valuation, it forces us to reflect on the value of institutions that for a long time have been taken for granted as serving only religious needs.

Table 20.2 Calculation for CDC and Other Economic and Housing Initiatives

Activity	% of congregations involved	Average local contribution for engaged congregation	Source	Averaged contribution per urban congregation
Co-ops	3.0	30,000	Philadelphia Census	900
Credit unions	2.2	1,000,000	Frame, Karels, and McClatchey (2003)	22,000
Job training	4.3	10,000	Philadelphia Census	430
Recruitment of new businesses	4.6	30,000	Philadelphia Census	1,380
Commercial venture	1.1	30,000	Philadelphia Census	330
Investment club	1.6	15,000	Cox and Goff (1996); National Association of Investors Corporation (ND)	240
New building initiatives	2.5	600,000	Walker (1993); Reese and Shields (1999); Mares (1994)	15,000
Housing rehabilitation	4.1	1000,000[1]	Walker (1993); Vidal (2001)	4,100
CDC[2]— (Community Development Corporation)	0.8	200,000	Rolland (2004); Vidal (2001)	1,600
Total				$45,980

Notes: 1. Based on an average of ten units at $10,000 each. 2. Non-housing CDC (those involved in youth development, crime prevention, social and cultural enhancement, and more). See also Reese (2004).

SUMMARY AND CONCLUSIONS

In this chapter I have necessarily made a number of assumptions in order to advance understanding of the value of the contribution of a typical urban congregation. I always elected to choose the most conservative number and thereby may have underreported these contributions.

Table 20.3   Summary of the Assessed Value of an Average Urban Congregation to Its Local Social Economy

Source	Amount
Operating budget	$103,500.00
Replacement value for social services	$84,950.04
Crime prevention and reduction	$28,000.00
Contribution to property value	$27,891.20
Religious tourism	$280.00
Family and church reunions	$1,584.00
Congregational-based schools	$171,668.40
Contribution from commuter members	$12,000.00
Support from suburban congregations and organisations	$809.60
Housing and economic development	$45,980.00
Total	$476,663.24

A challenge for future scholars will be to consider the possible negative externalities of local religious congregations (Do, Wilbur, and Short 1994) as a deduction from the final estimate. One can conceive, for example, that religious hate crimes or religious-based harassment are congregationally based and are costly.

Religious congregations, by federal law, are tax exempt organisations. They also benefit from preferred status when it comes to local property taxes. While this can be interpreted to mean that congregations are not contributing to the local social economy, I argue that the estimated value of an urban religious congregation's contribution to the local social economy exceeds potential taxes collected. Further, by exempting these organisations, more money may be available for other social programs.

Future work will fine-tune the measures used in this chapter, will add additional externalities, focus on other non-profits, and be based on data gathered specifically to assess valuation. This chapter has been a first step in a new direction.

NOTES

1. The by-products of activities that enhance (positive externalities) or damage (negative externalities) the well-being of people or the environment, where those impacts are not reflected in market prices. There can be positive and negative externalities to any intervention.
2. The term *congregation* in this chapter refers to all houses of worship regardless of religion or denomination.

3. All monetary figures are in American dollars.
4. To determine the value of volunteer hours, they used the standard of $17.19 per hour established by the Independent Sector in 2003.
5. Based on the assessment of the supervisor in the Philadelphia city tax office.
6. Based on information provided by the museum staff on 15 April 2008.

REFERENCES

Airriess, C. A., W. Li, K. J. Leong, A. C. Chen, and V. M. Keith. 2008. "Church-Based Social Capital, Networks and Geographical Scale: Katrina Evacuation, Relocation, and Recovery in a New Orleans Vietnamese American Community." *Geoforum* 39:1333–1346.
Ammerman, N. T. 2005. *Pillars of Faith: American Congregations and Their Partners.* Berkeley: University of California Press.
Ammerman, N. T., and A. Farnsley. 1997. *Congregation and Community.* New Brunswick, NJ: Rutgers University Press.
Barna Group. 2001. *Pastors Paid Better, but Attendance Unchanged.* http://www.barna.org/FlexPage.aspx?Page=BarnaUpdate&BarnaUpdateID=85.
Boehm, A. 1996. "Forces Driving Competition in Human Service Organizations and Positional Competitive Responses." *Administration in Social Work* 20 (4): 61–78.
Carroll, T. M., T. M. Clauretie, and J. Jensen. 1996. "Living Next to Godliness: Residential Property Values and Churches." *Journal of Real Estate Finance and Economics* 12 (3): 319–330.
Chaves, M. 2004. *Congregations in America.* Cambridge, MA: Harvard University Press.
Chaves, M., and S. L. Miller. 1999. *Financing American Religion.* Walnut Creek, CA: AltaMira.
Christie, L. 2006. "Real Estate Cools Down." *CNNMoney,* 16 May. http://money.cnn.com/2006/05/15/real_estate/NAR_firstQ2005_home_prices/index.htm.
Cnaan, R. A., and S. C. Boddie. 2001. "Philadelphia Census of Congregations and Their Involvement in Social Service Delivery." *Social Service Review* 75 (4): 559–580.
Cnaan, R. A., with S. C. Boddie, F. Handy, G. Yancey, and R. Schneider. 2002. *The Invisible Caring Hand: American Congregations and the Provision of Welfare.* New York: New York University Press.
Cnaan, R. A., with S. C. Boddie, C. C. McGrew, and J. Kang. 2006. *The Other Philadelphia Story: How Local Congregations Support Quality of Life in Urban America.* Philadelphia: University of Pennsylvania Press.
Cox, D. R., and D. C. Goff. 1996. "Starting and Operating a Student Investment Club." *Financial Practice and Education* 6 (2): 78–85.
Do, A. Q., R. W. Wilbur, and J. L. Short. 1994. "An Empirical Examination of the Externalities of Neighborhood Churches on Housing Values." *Journal of Real Estate Finance and Economics* 9 (2): 127–136.
Dudley, C. S., and D. Roozen. 2001. *Faith Communities Today: A Report on Religion in the United States Today.* Hartford, CT: Hartford Seminary. http://fact.hartsem.edu/Final%20FACTrpt.pdf.
Efroymson, R. A., F. W. Whicker, T. J. Hinton, M. M. MacDonell, J. E. Pinder III, and L. J. Habegger. 2004. "New Environmental Benefits Analysis." *Science* 306 (5698): 976–977.
Farnsley, III. A. E. 2003. *Rising Expectations: Urban Congregations, Welfare Reform, and Civic Life.* Bloomington: Indiana University Press.

Frame, W. S., G. V. Karels, and C. A. McClatchey. 2003. "Do Credit Unions Use Their Tax Advantage to Benefit Members? Evidence from a Cost Function." *Review of Financial Economics* 12 (1): 35–47.

Grant, E. 2005. "Race and Tourism in America's First City." *Journal of Urban History* 31 (6): 850–871.

Gregory, R. S. 2000. "Valuing Environmental Policy Options: A Case Study Comparison of Multiattribute and Contingent Valuation Survey Methods." *Land Economics* 76:151–173.

Hercik, J., R. L. Lewis, B. Myles, C. Gouvis, J. Zweig, A. Whitby, G. Rico, and E. Mcbride. 2004. *Development of a Guide to Resources on Faith-Based Organizations in Criminal Justice: Final Report.* Washington, DC: The Urban Institute.

Holt, J. B., J. W. Miller, T. S. Naimi, and D. Z. Sui. 2006. "Religious Affiliation and Alcohol Consumption in the United States." *The Geographical Review* 96 (4): 523–542.

Jackson, M. C., J. H. Schweitzer, M. T. Cato, and R. N. Blake. 1997. *Faith-Based Institutions: Community and Economic Development Programs Serving Black Communities in Michigan.* East Lansing: Urban Affairs Program, Michigan State University.

Kinney, N. T., and W. E. Winter. 2006. "Places of Worship and Neighborhood Stability." *Journal of Urban Affairs* 28 (4): 335–352.

Lee, M. R. 2006. "The Religious Institutional Base and Violent Crime in Rural Areas." *Journal for the Scientific Study of Religion* 45 (3): 309–324.

Lee, M. R., and J. P. Bartkowski. 2004. "Love thy Neighbor? Moral Communities, Civic Engagement, and Juvenile Homicide in Non-Metro Communities." *Social Forces* 82 (4): 1001–1035.

Lee, M. R., and G. C. Ousey. 2005. "Institutional Access, Residential Segregation, and Urban Black Homicide." *Sociological Inquiry* 75 (1): 31–54.

Lizardi, D., K. Dervic, M. F. Grunebaum, A. K. Burke, J. J. Mann, and M. A. Oquendo. 2008. "The Role of Moral Objections to Suicide in the Assessment of Suicidal Patients." *Journal of Psychiatric Research* 42 (10): 815–821.

Mares, A. S. 1994. "Housing and the Church." *Nonprofit and Voluntary Sector Quarterly* 23 (2): 139–157.

Moon, W., W. J. Florkowski, B. Brückner, and I. Schonhof. 2002. "Willingness to Pay for Environmental Practices: Implications for Eco-Labeling." *Land Economics* 78:88–102.

Nuttall, C. 1998. *Reducing Offending: An Assessment of Research Evidence on Ways of Dealing with Offending Behaviour. Home Office Research Study 187.* London: Home Office. http://www.homeoffice.gov.uk/rds/pdfs/hors187.pdf.

Ottensmann, J. R. 2000. *Catholic Diocese of Cleveland: Economic Value of Selected Activities.* Indianapolis: Indiana University–Purdue University Indianapolis, School of Public and Environmental Affairs, Center for Urban Policy and the Environment.

Pressley, C. O., and W. V. Collier. 1999. "Financing Historic Black Churches." In *Financing American Religion,* ed. M. Chaves and S. L. Miller, 21–28. Walnut Creek, CA: AltaMira.

Quiggin, J. 1998. "Individual and Household Willingness to Pay for Public Goods." *American Journal of Agricultural Economics* 80 (1): 58–63.

Reese, L. A. 2004. "A Matter of Faith: Urban Congregations and Economic Development." *Economic Development Quarterly* 18 (1): 50–66.

Reese, L. A., and G. Shields. 1999. "Economic Development Activities of Urban Religious Institutions." *International Journal of Economic Development* 2 (2): 165–199.

Rolland, K. A. 2004. "Church-Based CDC Helps Build Assets and Skills in Delaware." http://www.philadelphiafed.org/cca/fall04_2.html.

Smith, C. 2003. "Theorizing Religious Effects among American Adolescents." *Journal for the Scientific Study of Religion* 42 (1): 17–30.

Stark, R. 1996. "Religion as Context: Hellfire and Delinquency One More Time." *Sociology of Religion* 57 (1): 163–173.

Stark, R., L. Kent, D. P. Doyle. 1982. "Religion and Delinquency: The Ecology of a 'Lost' Relationship." *Journal of Research in Crime and Delinquency* 19 (1): 4–24.

Stephan, J. J. 2004. *State Prison Expenditure, 2001.* Washington, DC: National Institute of Justice, Bureau of Justice Statistics. http://www.ojp.usdoj.gov/bjs/pub/pdf/spe01.pdf.

Stonebraker, R. J. 2003. "Allocating Local Church Funds to Benevolence: The Impact of Congregation Size." *Review of Religious Research* 45 (1): 48–58.

Stritt, S. B. 2008. "Estimating the Value of the Social Services Provided by Faith-Based Organizations in the United States." *Nonprofit and Voluntary Sector Quarterly.* http://nvs.sagepub.com/cgi/rapidpdf/0899764008321802v1.

Sutton, R. 2004. "Celebrating Ourselves: The Family Reunion Rituals of African Caribbean Transnational Families." *Global Networks* 4 (3): 243–258.

Tisdell, C. 2007. "Knowledge and the Valuation of Public Goods and Experiential Commodities: Information Provision and Acquisition." *Global Business and Economics Review* 9 (2/3): 170–182.

Van den Berg, B., W. B. F. Brouwer, and M. A. Koopmanschap. 2004. "Economic Valuation of Informal Care." *The European Journal of Health Economics* 5 (1): 36–45.

Vidal, A. C. 2001. *Faith-Based Organizations in Community Development: A Report Prepared for the U.S. Department of Housing and Community Development, Office of Development and Research.* Washington, DC: The Urban Institute.

Walker, C. 1993. "Nonprofit Housing Development: Status, Trends, and Prospects." *Housing Policy Debate* 4 (3): 369–414.

Warner, S. R. 1994. "The Place of Congregations in the Contemporary Religious Context." In *American Congregations,* ed. J. Wind and J. Lewis, 159–221. Chicago: University of Chicago Press.

WikiAnswers. 2008. "National Average Cost per Student in Public School?" http://wiki.answers.com/Q/National_average_cost_per_student_in_public_school (accessed 25 April 2008).

Part V

Social Accounting, Accountability, and Ethics

21 A Social Accountability Framework for Public Sector Conflict of Interest

Private Interests, Public Duties, and Ethical Cultures

Gordon Boyce and Cindy Davids

INTRODUCTION

The problem of conflict of interest arises when private or sectional interests are (or may be) pursued ahead of the public interest. Conflict of interest represents a failure of public sector accountability because it undercuts the duty of impartiality that is incumbent on all public officers[1] and counteracts the pursuit of the public interest. Acting in the public interest encompasses obligations in regard to administration, ethics, and performance, in accordance with recognised public sector principles and values that include the need for public officials and public institutions to consistently demonstrate integrity and trustworthiness. Across the world, conflict of interest is recognised to have contributed to a general decline in perceived standards of conduct in public office, undermining public trust in government and the integrity of democratic systems more broadly (Pope 2000; Stark 2000; Organisation for Economic Co-Operation and Development 2003, 2006; Cepeda Ulloa 2004; Raile 2004; Asian Development Bank and Organisation for Economic Co-Operation and Development 2006; Young 2006; The Ombudsman 2008).

This chapter draws on two empirical studies of conflict of interest in the public sector in the Australian state of Victoria. The first project studied conflict of interest complaints against police officers over a ten-year period, and was conducted with the co-operation of Victoria Police.[2] The second study involved an in-depth examination of a sample of conflict of interest complaints against employees in all government departments and agencies, and was undertaken in collaboration with the Victorian Ombudsman.[3] In both studies, original case files were examined in their entirety and in their original state and the primary analytical aim was to develop an empirically driven and theoretically informed explanation of conflict of interest and its components in a way that provided a comprehensive and operationally relevant understanding of the problem.[4]

The aim of this chapter is to delineate the dimensions of conflict of interest in the public sector and to outline an appropriate framework for regulation, management, and accountability, drawing mainly from the research we undertook in the government departments and agencies study, supported by the findings from the Victoria Police study. The next section defines and delineates the problem of conflict of interest in terms of three components: interests, conflicts, and perceptions. The third section outlines essential elements of a regulatory and management strategy to deal with the problem, namely, restricting the holding of some private interests and the appropriate structuring and administration of official work duties in the public sector. The final section outlines the social accountability framework that was developed out of both studies as a means for understanding and managing conflict of interest.

THE ELEMENTS OF CONFLICT OF INTEREST: INTERESTS, CONFLICTS, AND PERCEPTIONS

The concept of conflict of interest adds to notions of public sector integrity rather than merely providing another label for a subset of more generalised problems of misconduct and corruption. However, the evidence in our research suggests that conflict of interest in the public sector is poorly understood and inadequately managed and that the persistence of the problem damages the pursuit of the public good. Although conflict of interest is not in itself corruption, the two are conceptually and practically linked because the improper influence of private interests in the performance of public sector functions may lead to a range of ethical and accountability problems from minor misdemeanours through to major corruption. As a separate category of wrongdoing, conflict of interest is unique in two important respects: (a) it encompasses situations anterior to neglects of duty; and (b) it incorporates the importance of public perceptions of integrity, rather than limiting consideration to narrow or technical readings of propriety. Effective management of conflict of interest issues thus has the potential to both *prevent* neglects of duty, rather than merely reacting to them, and to enhance public confidence in the integrity of the public sector.

    From the perspective of public accountability the ethical concept of conflict of interest ties together three interlinked components: interests, conflicts, and public perceptions (see Boyce and Davids 2009; Davids 2008). First, any public officer would be expected to have many *interests* apart from those associated with the performance of official duties, but some of these interests may pose an inherent risk of interference with the performance of official duties. *Black's Law Dictionary* offers an early but limited definition of a conflict of interest as relating to the "private pecuniary interest of the individual" (cited in Carson 1994, 390), but this narrow conception of pecuniary interests emphasises only a subset of relevant interests and ignores the importance of many non-financial interests, including subjective or ideological biases, associational affiliations, partisan attachments, prejudgements, moral beliefs, and even aesthetic judgements. Interests that are held in common with most other citizens, such as one's general status as home owner/occupier, investor, or taxpayer, are unavoidable and therefore cannot be regarded as sufficiently *personal* interests to come under the aegis of conflict of interest. However, specific home localities, investments, or taxation arrangements could be regarded as interests of concern, as could be the interests of family, friends, and colleagues. As well as affiliations with others, enmity towards individuals or groups could represent an interest of concern if it causes interference with the performance of official duties, for this is the common element in any problematic interest. Such interference may be manifested in preferential treatment for self, family, or friends, or adverse treatment for enemies.

The second element of conflict of interest emphasises how private interests become problematic when they *conflict* with official duties, in particular through the impairment of competent and disinterested judgement. Conflict takes place in the mind, but because it is impossible to definitively determine subjective states of mind, concern focuses on situations that can be directly and objectively perceived as giving rise to conflicts (applying the standard legal perspective of a "reasonable person"). Thus, a conflict is present when there is a *capacity* for a known private interest to affect the performance of official duties and where a reasonable person could conclude that such a capacity existed (see Stark 2000; Davids 2008).

Dealing with *appearances* and *perceptions* is important because conflict of interest relates to "how things look" to a reasonable observer as much as it does to how they actually are. The notion of a "reasonable observer" means that "mere" appearances or uninformed, unreasonable, irrational, or prejudiced perceptions are insufficient to constitute a conflict of interest problem, but if a reasonable person could perceive on the basis of the known facts that a conflict of interest exists, then the conflict of interest so perceived is *ipso facto* a problem because this is in itself sufficient to undermine confidence in the integrity of the public sector.

Formal Definition

Discussion of conflict of interest in prior literature has often been confused by the use of terms such as "real", "apparent", and "potential" conflict of interest (see Davids 2008; cf. Parker 1987; Davis 1982; Kernaghan and Langford 1990; Preston, Sampford, and Connors 2002). The use of these terms is often associated with a failure to clearly distinguish three levels of the problem:

1. having a conflict of interest
2. taking official actions or decisions in a conflict of interest situation
3. wrongly using an official position to actively pursue a private interest at the expense of proper performance of official duties.

The second and third levels involve successively greater degrees of wrongdoing, but all levels are "real" and are problematic for public sector ethics.

Drawing on the preceding discussion and an extensive review of the literature (see Davids 2008; Boyce and Davids 2009), conflict of interest in the public sector context may be defined in the following way:

> A conflict of interest is any conflict between the personal interests of a public officer (including financial and non-financial interests of the individual and family members, friends, associates, and organisations to which the officer belongs) and the officer's duty to act in the public interest. A conflict exists in any situation where a public officer could be influenced, or could be reasonably perceived by an outside observer to be influenced, by a private interest when performing an official function.

Some private interests may, by their very nature, be regarded as inherently incompatible with the holding of an official position in the public sector, while other interests of a more generalised nature may become problematic in the course of day-to-day work if and when they come into conflict with public duties. In the latter case, the focus is not on particular kinds of interest but on the ways that any private interest may conflict with the performance of public duty.

Private Interests

Our research identified four broad areas of private interest that may be regarded as inherently incompatible with employment in the public sector (see Davids 2006). The first area relates to secondary employment and private business interests, including the business interests of family, friends, and associates. Principal concerns relate to the taint that attaches to any official action that favours or is perceived to favour interests associated with an individual's secondary employment arrangements or private business interests. We found that particular problems arise in relation to employment with outside organisations that either compete or interact in an official capacity with the public employer—such as developers, tenderers, private providers of government services, or recipients of government funding, or, in the case of policing, private security operators.

The second category of problematic private interests was post-employment arrangements, where a former public official takes up employment in a private sector organisation that is in some way related to (former) official duties. In relation to government regulatory functions, such as gaming, racing, and liquor licensing, the potential problems and conflicts are obvious, but three main areas of concern are equally applicable across all government functions. First, a public employee may use an official position to enhance or cultivate future employment prospects, possibly by using an official position to favour the interests of a potential future employer. The second concern arises after new employment has commenced, to the extent that a former public official may take improper advantage of previous office by using insider knowledge or confidential information, for example. The third concern relates to the damage that may be done to the ongoing reputation of the public service when a public employee takes up private employment with a party whose private interests the official had the capacity to influence whilst in public employment (even if no such influence was used). Public perceptions in such circumstances mean that even if there was no formal wrongdoing, such post-employment arrangements appear to take private advantage of former public office and may not be trusted by reasonable members of the public.

The third category of problematic private interests relates to a public officer's capacity to affect the interests of external organisations with which the officer is associated, such as civic, social, or political bodies (including local government authorities). The principles of impartiality demand that official decisions and actions in relation to such groups be avoided in order to obviate both material impacts on the performance of public duty and public perceptions of favouritism or partiality, which taint official decisions and actions. For a conflict of interest to be of concern, it is sufficient that a third party might reasonably question the ability of that person to act independently or impartially. Our research found conflict of interest problems in relation to involvement in a range of organisations, including animal welfare groups, sporting and social clubs, school councils, and local government bodies.

The fourth category of problematic private interests involved a range of formal and less formal personal relationships, including relationships between local government council officers and commercial developers, police or prison employees and convicted criminals, and police and proprietors of regulated businesses in areas such as hostelry, gaming, and prostitution.

Public Duties

Day-to-day work in the public sector involves many situations where the application of judgement and discretion represents vulnerability to conflicts of interest because private interests (often of a more generalised nature than those discussed in the section on "Private Interests") may impact on an official's application of discretion, or may reasonably be seen to do so. Our research found that processes involving tendering and contracting, development proposals, local planning applications, child protection, employment of staff, and allocation of grants are particularly vulnerable. The findings suggested that conflict of interest problems are often manifested in allegations of unfair preferential or adverse treatment in these contexts.

As a general problem, preferential treatment involves an official acting in a way that is, or appears to be, partial to particular individuals or groups, such as family members and close associates (see Boyce and Davids 2009). We found that claims of adverse treatment often involved allegations of prejudgement on the basis of personal prejudice or ideological bias on the part of a public official, or that a member of the public had been unfairly treated as a result of their questioning of a public officer's competence or professionalism (such as a local government ratepayer questioning a valuer's judgement of property value for the purpose of levying local property taxes).

An additional area of conflict of interest uncovered by our research related to concerns that a public official may seek to pursue the interests of their organisation, sometimes in the name of "community interest", but against the broader public interest as represented by the rights of individual citizens to fair process. The public interest cannot be regarded as identical with the immediate interests of a government department or agency because over the longer term the public interest cannot be served if individuals have a reasonable basis to perceive that members of the public are not treated fairly and impartially by government authorities (see Boyce and Davids 2009; The Ombudsman 2008).

Understanding Conflict of Interest

Conflict of interest is conceptually simple but in practice it is complex, and our research showed that there are many dimensions that are misunderstood by employees and managers, often extending to senior management and oversight levels. We found general evidence of mistaken beliefs that a conflict of interest is not of particular concern if there is no nefarious intent or a specific breach of duty. There is confusion in practical terms about the distinction between the three levels of the problem outlined earlier:

1. having a conflict of interest
2. acting in a conflict of interest situation
3. using an official position to actively pursue a private interest.

Complainants do not always use the term "conflict of interest" when making allegations of preferential or adverse treatment and complaint investigators do not always recognise the conflict of interest dimensions of a complaint. As a practical matter, the existence of a conflict of interest may become evident at a management or oversight level only at or after the point where a regulatory, ethical, or other breach occurs (a neglect of duty). We found that managers and employees who do not recognise conflict of interest problems when they are not specifically named as such often deal with the manifestations of the problem (the associated neglect of duty), rather than the underlying cause (the conflict of interest).

REGULATION AND MANAGEMENT

Compared to other overt forms of misconduct and corruption, the unique element of conflict of interest as an ethical concern is that conflict of interest focuses on the capacity of a private interest to influence the performance of duty. The key concern is the effect that this capacity has on citizen trust and confidence in the public sector, whether or not the capacity is actualised in a breach of duty. The public trust implicit in the ideals of public service and pursuit of the public good means that private or sectional gain must always be subsumed to the public interest and the public good must always be seen to be paramount. The risks conflicts of interest pose to good governance, public trust, and accountability must be recognised and measures to identify and deal with the problem should be set in the context of a clear commitment to prioritise the public interest over private or sectional interests. In short, the preservation and building of confidence in the integrity, impartiality, and fairness of the public sector and its employees requires that the "political optics" of public sector activity be addressed in a way that maintains public trust (Stark 2000).

Contemporary public sector management activity has been heavily influenced by the practices of New Public Management (see Hood 1995; Pollitt 1993). The attendant infusion of personnel and practices from the private sector results in more complex challenges for managing and enhancing the functions of government (Polidano and Hulme 2001). In this context, processes of regulation, management, and accountability must be carefully designed to ensure that the public good is prioritised. In terms of conflict of interest, effective public management rests on a clear operational understanding of the nature and dimensions of the problem and appropriate means for dealing with it. Practical complexities mean that it is not possible to simply identify and specifically prohibit all specific forms of conflict of interest. Effective regulatory regimes have tended to move from a focus on hortatory (exhortive) approaches that specify appropriate subjective states of mind (independent, disinterested) to greater emphasis on prophylactic (preventive) regulations that prohibit involvement in situations or actions that may lead to impaired judgement or may be reasonably perceived to do so (Stark 2000).

A regulatory approach that prohibits "conflicts of interest" only in a generalised way is likely to be little more effective than an exclusively hortatory approach because it does not address the specific types of circumstances where conflicts of interest tend to arise in day-to-day work. Drawing on our analysis of the nature of conflict of interest, more specific prophylactic approaches are desirable in addition to general hortatory provisions. These involve, first, restrictions on particular sets of private interests that are inherently problematic, thereby preventing conflicts of interest. This recognises that particular kinds of private interests are problematic because of their inherent capacity to interfere with the proper performance of public duty. Prioritisation of the public interest justifies a requirement that individuals surrender the right to freely pursue this limited range of interests. In some areas, the most effective way to avoid conflicts of interest is to prohibit the holding of the particular interests concerned; for other areas, prohibition may not be appropriate but private interests may still need to be managed to prevent conflicts of interest (for example, through approval processes for engaging in secondary employment, notifications and limitations on certain civic involvements, or restrictions on particular forms of post-employment for a defined period after leaving the public sector). Restrictions on secondary employment, post-employment, and involvement with civic and like associations represent sensitive areas of regulation because they limit an individual's present and future right to earn an income and to pursue otherwise legitimate careers and personal interests, and they represent restrictions on individual liberty that are not applied to ordinary citizens.

Although regulatory limitations on particular private interests, such as those associated with employment, business, and organised civic activities, can prevent some conflicts of interest (although enforcement is not necessarily straightforward), a range of other private interests of a more generalised nature, such as relationships involving family, friends, neighbours, and work colleagues, cannot easily be dealt with through regulation. Therefore, a second level of regulation and management relating to the structure and performance of work duties is required to deal with concerns about unfair preferential or adverse treatment based in conflicts of interest. Work roles and the performance of work duties must be structured and undertaken in a way that facilitates the recognition and management of conflicts of interest as they arise in day-to-day operations and ensures that public duties are carried out in a disinterested fashion. This involves the assignment and ongoing management of public officers' duties to ensure that individuals are not involved in decisions or actions where they have a conflict of interest, or where reasonable third-party observers may conclude that such a conflict exists.

A SOCIAL ACCOUNTABILITY FRAMEWORK FOR UNDERSTANDING AND MANAGING CONFLICT OF INTEREST

Accountability, although a complex and sometimes elusive phenomenon, is at the heart of effective democratic governance and the prevention of potential abuses of power (Thomas 1998). As noted earlier, an effective framework for conflict of interest that attends to the three elements identified earlier in the chapter (namely, interests, conflicts, and public perceptions) has become more important for social accountability in the contemporary public sector context. Figure 21.1 outlines the social accountability framework for public sector conflict of interest that was developed as a result of our research. The figure shows how conflict of interest may be managed through a regulatory framework including elements that address each component of the problem. First, limitations on certain categories of private interest that are deemed to be inherently problematic due to incompatibility with public sector roles (addressing interests). Second, the structuring and management of work duties so that individual public officers are not involved in official actions or decisions in matters which may involve the officer in a conflict of interest (addressing conflicts). Finally, decisions in relation to the first two elements, and conflict of interest generally, are made with reference to a "reasonable person" standard, considering how things would look to a reasonable observer (addressing perceptions).

The general approach that underpins this framework transcends the limitations of rule-bound structures by taking a broad perspective on social accountability, seeking to nurture proactive accountability through the development of responsibility as a personal and subjective sense of rightness and good conscience (Sinclair 1995; Bovens 1998; Thomas 1998). In the public sector, as in any other domain, public officials who have power and authority over others must be accountable for the exercise of that power. Accountability operates through organisational structures and hierarchies, but public officers must also be accountable to the broader community. Social accountability is an expansive concept that includes a need

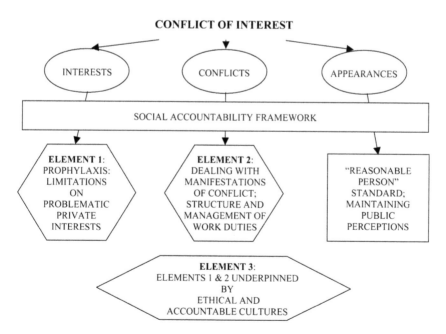

Figure 21.1 A social accountability framework for conflict of interest (adapted from Boyce and Davids 2009).

to account for social as well as technical and financial factors (echoing the broad domain of interests that are included within the concept of conflict of interest) *and* a need to consider both facts and appearances.

The concept of active responsibility (Bovens 1998) within social accountability involves answerability to the self, building outwards to a sense of responsibility towards others, including individuals, groups, organisations, and society at large. It is a form of responsibility that is not limited to the application of particular sets of rules and structures that enforce more passive forms of accountability, which are reactive rather than active in that they focus on accountability for past wrongdoing rather than the prevention of future wrongdoing. However, rules for passive accountability remain necessary both to provide clear and explicit indications of what is expected and to deal with wrongdoing when it occurs, since active responsibility, whilst desirable, is not always effective.

CONCLUSIONS

Public sector employment implies a preparedness and commitment to prioritise the public interest over private interests. To manage this issue effectively, employees and managers must recognise that public perceptions of integrity and impartiality and conflict of interest undermine the effectiveness of the public sector and can arise whether or not a conflict of interest results in an actual breach of official duty and whether or not it results in a private gain to the official. Citizen trust in public institutions cannot be assumed to exist and is not guaranteed to persist in the face of challenges to the public's trust. This trust must be continually and actively generated and nurtured, and ideas and practices of social accountability must be at the core of a framework within which ethical, organisational, and cultural dimensions of management of conflict of interest within the public sector are effectively addressed.

NOTES

1. The term "public officer" or "public official" is used here to refer to any employee who works within the public sector. This includes office- or street-level employees, managers and executives, and government officials.
2. This study examined 377 complaints cases against 539 police officers for the period 1988–1998.
3. Forty-five cases were examined for the period 2003–2006, involving complaints against employees in authorities and agencies dealing with a range of government functions, local and regional councils, authorities and agencies, statutory boards, and higher education providers. This study took the form of an "Own Motion" Enquiry conducted by the authors (as sworn officers of the Ombudsman), under the independent investigation powers of the Victorian Ombudsman (an official report resulting from the Enquiry was presented to the Victorian Parliament in March 2008; see The Ombudsman 2008).

4. Boyce and Davids (2009) provide a detailed overview of the two studies and their findings; individual case studies supporting the analysis are examined in Davids (2008) and The Ombudsman (2008).

REFERENCES

Asian Development Bank and Organisation for Economic Co-Operation and Development. 2006. *Knowledge Commitment Action: Against Corruption in Asia and the Pacific*. Manila: Asian Development Bank.

Bovens, M. 1998. *The Quest for Responsibility: Accountability and Citizenship in Complex Organisations*. Cambridge: Cambridge University Press.

Boyce, G., and C. Davids. 2009. "Conflict of Interest in Policing and the Public Sector: Ethics, Integrity, and Social Accountability." *Public Management Review* 11 (5): 601–640.

Carson, T. L. 1994. "Conflicts of Interest." *Journal of Business Ethics* 13 (5): 387–404.

Cepeda Ulloa, F. 2004. *Forfeiture of Public Office of Members of Congress in Colombia: Conflict of Interest Policy as an Instrument in the Fight against Corruption. Forum on Implementing Conflict of Interest Policies in the Public Service*. Rio de Janeiro: OECD and Inter-American Development Bank.

Davids, C. 2006. "Conflict of Interest and the Private Lives of Police Officers: Friendships, Civic and Political Activities." *Journal of Policing, Intelligence and Counter Terrorism* 1:14–35.

———. 2008. *Conflict of Interest in Policing: Problems, Practices, and Principles*. Sydney: Institute of Criminology Press.

Davis, M. 1982. "Conflict of Interest." *Business and Professional Ethics Journal* 1 (4): 17–32.

Hood, C. 1995. "Contemporary Public Management: A New Global Paradigm?" *Public Policy and Administration* 10 (2): 104–117.

Kernaghan, K., and J. W. Langford. 1990. *The Responsible Public Servant*. Halifax, Nova Scotia: The Institute for Research on Public Policy and the Institute of Public Administration of Canada.

Ombudsman, The. 2008. *Conflict of Interest in the Public Sector*. Melbourne: Office of the Ombudsman.

Organisation for Economic Co-Operation and Development. 2003. *Managing Conflict of Interest in the Public Service: OECD Guidelines and Country Experiences*. Paris: OECD.

———. 2006. *Conflict-of-Interest Policies and Practices in Nine EU Member States: A Comparative Review*. Paris: OECD.

Parker, W. D. 1987. *Commission of Inquiry into the Facts of Allegations of Conflict of Interest Concerning the Honourable Sinclair M. Stephens*. Ottawa: Ministry for Supply and Services.

Polidano, C., and D. Hulme. 2001. "Towards a Post–New Public Management Agenda." *Public Management Review* 3 (3): 297–303.

Pollitt, C. 1993. *Managerialism and the Public Services: Cuts or Cultural Change in the 1990s?* Oxford and Cambridge, MA: Blackwell.

Pope, J. 2000. *Confronting Corruption: The Elements of a National Integrity System*. Berlin: Transparency International.

Preston, N., C. Sampford, and C. Connors. 2002. *Encouraging Ethics and Challenging Corruption: Reforming Governance in Public Institutions*. Sydney: Federation Press.

Raile, E. 2004. *Managing Conflicts of Interest in the Americas: A Comparative Review. Forum on Implementing Conflict of Interest Policies in the Public Service (5–6 May 2004, Rio de Janeiro, Brazil)*. Paris: Organisation for

Economic Co-Operation and Development and Inter-American Development Bank.

Sinclair, A. 1995. "The Chameleon of Accountability: Forms and Discourses." *Accounting, Organizations, and Society* 20 (2/3): 219–237.

Stark, A. 2000. *Conflict of Interest in American Public Life.* Cambridge, MA: Harvard University Press.

Thomas, P. G. 1998. "The Changing Nature of Accountability." In *Taking Stock: Assessing Public Sector Reforms,* ed. B. G. Peters and D. J. Savoie, 348–393. Montreal: Canadian Centre for Management Development and McGill Queens University Press.

Young, M. 2006. *Conflict of Interest Codes for Parliamentarians: A Long Road.* Ottawa: Parliamentary Information and Research Service.

22 Corruption and Accountability in a Globalised World

A Comparative Study of Japan, Hong Kong, and China

Wilson Wong

INTRODUCTION

This chapter applies the analytical framework of global pressure and bureaucratic change developed by Welch and Wong (1998, 2001) in comparative studies of Japan, Hong Kong, and China to explain the divergent responses of national bureaucracies under the global pressure of bureaucratic corruption. It examines some complex interrelations between key concepts of global pressure including corruption, accountability, and institutional change in bureaucracy. The major research questions guiding the investigation in this chapter are: Why is it still so difficult to fight corruption although anti-corruption knowledge and technologies are already widely accessible? How do differences in anti-corruption outcomes reflect the characteristics and nature of a national bureaucracy, particularly its role in the national context and the mode of accountability for holding it responsible?

With the emergence of the global economy, advancement in information and other technologies that link up the globe as one interactive world means bureaucratic corruption has arisen as a major and pressing global concern (Elliot 1997; Glynn, Kobrin, and Naim 1997; Rose-Ackerman 1999). According to the framework of Welch and Wong, the ultimate impact of global pressure on the administrative system of a nation is determined by both the direct influence of the global pressure and the indirect impact as filtered by the domestic context of the nation.

Under the same global pressure of bureaucratic corruption, there is a divergence instead of a convergence of national responses, with some vast differences in the levels of success in eradicating bureaucratic corruption. Bureaucratic corruption, however, is not an organisational pathology with no cure (Klitgaard 1988). Far from it, knowledge about preventing and resolving bureaucratic corruption is widely available and easily accessible to policymakers. It is not the unavailability and inaccessibility of organisational knowledge and technologies on curbing bureaucratic corruption that are leading to the divergence. Bureaucratic corruption is an organisational problem rooted in the domestic context of the national systems that the bureaucracy is imbedded in. The divergent responses to bureaucratic corruption across countries are the manifestations of differences in the domestic context of bureaucracy.

This chapter will first introduce the framework of global pressure and bureaucratic change of Welch and Wong, then discuss how it can be applied to study the research questions concerning public administration in a global environment. It will then apply the framework to the global problem of corruption through the comparative case studies of Japan, Hong Kong, and China to explain how differences in the domestic context can lead to a divergence of responses to the global challenge of corruption.

THE ANALYTICAL FRAMEWORK: GLOBAL PRESSURES AND BUREAUCRATIC CHANGE

Governments and, by extension, bureaucracies are not only increasingly subject to global pressures for change and reform, they are also increasingly making decisions that incorporate global constraints and opportunities into their own domestic agendas (Nye and Donahue 2000; Pollitt 2001). The global environment should not be ignored as an influential force of bureaucratic change and decision-making. However, discussion about the importance of the global environment is not helpful without a theoretical framework that researchers can deploy to examine their related research questions.

Welch and Wong (1998, 2001) developed a framework of global pressure to analyse the impact of the global environment on bureaucratic change (see Figure 22.1). According to this framework, the global system as represented by global pressures acts directly on bureaucracies. However, it also works indirectly on bureaucracies through the filters of political, economic, and social systems of the domestic context of a nation.

Three major global pressures are identified by Welch and Wong: information technology, global institutions, and efficiency and productivity. The global pressure of information technology broadly captures the ongoing impact of information and communication technologies (ICT) on public bureaucracies. The pressure of global institutions is defined as the pressure exerted by a formalised institution with a global jurisdiction that has authority and power over individual countries in the related policy area. The global pressure of public sector efficiency and productivity represents the worldwide pressure on public bureaucracy to cut waste and increase output. These three global pressures are only listed by the authors as examples, and therefore do not preclude the existence and importance of other global pressures, such as corruption.

In terms of the domestic context, this can be classified into three general aspects: economics, political, and social. Dahl and Lindblom (1953) showed that national economies should be classified according to the

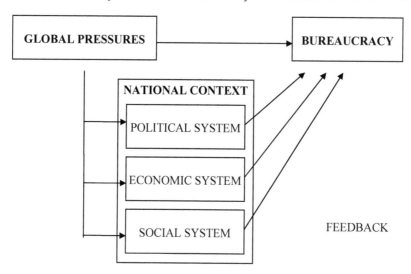

Figure 22.1   Global pressures and bureaucratic change.

degree of influence of market and hierarchy in the economy. Bozeman (1987) agreed that economic context is a major factor that shapes public organisations. Additionally, national economies can be classified in terms of the role of production, degree of dependency, or level of development in the world economy, as emphasised by the dependency theory or world systems theory.

The political context is no less important than the economic context in filtering the effect of global pressure. More centralised political systems (that is, with fewer veto-players) respond more quickly, through policy adjustment, to changes in the global economy. Relating to the political role of bureaucracy, the political context can be classified according to the relationship between the bureaucracy and the political regime (Heady 1996).

There are many different ways to describe the social context of nations, including using variables and concepts such as religion, culture, class, stratification, inequalities, social mobility, ethnicity, and family systems. In studying the politics of Asian countries, Pye (1985) recognised that understanding the social context in which a national bureaucracy was imbedded was important for accessing the role and influence of the bureaucracy in each nation. For example, trust in government and obedience to authority had led to an unusually major role of bureaucracy in policy-making in Asian countries such as Singapore and Japan (Flynn 1999).

While the framework appears to be relatively simple, there are a number of important points for research which could be drawn out. Firstly, global pressures range in significance and impact from minor to major. Their significance depends upon the nations in question. Second, dimensionalisation of the domestic context is an important step toward understanding how global pressures affect public bureaucracy. Under the major dimensions identified, sub-dimensions can also be introduced to enhance the richness of analysis. For example, additional dimensions relating to the socio-economic context of a state bureaucracy can be added for analysis (Heady 1996). Similarly, interfaces among the three dimensions can be studied to further understand how the domestic context alters the impact of the global pressures exerted on public bureaucracies.

It is also important to emphasise that the global environment provides a natural and useful opportunity for developing a more comprehensive theory of public administration. According to Welch and Wong, in the study of the administrative systems around the world, the global environment helps to integrate the knowledge and insights of the traditionalists, who primarily focus on the uniqueness of a single country, and the revisionists, who are mainly interested in building a general theory without appreciating differences across national contexts. By simultaneously taking advantage of the global environment and acknowledging the importance of the domestic context, the theoretical framework can enrich our knowledge about bureaucracies in general and any specific national bureaucracy.

DIVERGENCE UNDER THE GLOBAL PROBLEM OF CORRUPTION

Applying the framework of global pressure and bureaucratic change, this chapter would like to find out how differences in domestic context may help to explain the divergence of bureaucratic corruption. In the analysis, the two dimensions of the domestic context we are particularly interested in are: (a) the role of the bureaucracy in fulfilling the state function of governing the economy; and (b) the mode of accountability imposed on the bureaucracy. Since there can be variations in the definitions of corruption as specified by the laws in different countries, this chapter uses the public office–centred definition of corruption as adopted by many major international organisations including the United Nations Development Program (UNDP) and the World Bank, which is applied in many corruption studies (Klitgaard 1988; Quah 2001). It refers to corruption as "the misuse of public power, office or authority for private benefit—through bribery, extortion, influence, peddling, nepotism, fraud, speed money or embezzlement" (Lambsdorff 2008, 4).

The adoption of this definition does not mean the rejection of corruption as a contested concept with many dimensions. As correctly pointed out by Tanzi (1998), corruption has been defined in many different ways, each lacking in some aspect. For example, the preceding definition, although commonly adopted, does not include corrupt activities in the private sector. It is also possible that the abuse of power is not for private benefit, but for the benefit of one's party, class, tribe, friends, family, and so on. Apart from public office–centred definitions, there are two more typologies of corruption definitions: market-centred definitions and public interest definitions (Brown 2006). Currently, there is no single definition of corruption which can coherently capture all of these aspects. However, it is fully recognised that corruption can have many dimensions and the one adopted in this study is only one of the major ones.

With the rise of a global economy, opportunities for corruption have also become globalised (Elliot 1997; Glynn, Kobrin, and Naim 1997). Nevertheless, there is a divergence in the level of corrupt activities across countries despite exposure to the same kinds and similar levels of global pressure. It is simply not true that countries with the highest potential for corruption in an economic sense, such as having the largest amount of economic activity or the highest economic growth, are the ones experiencing corresponding increases or comparable shares of corruption. Similar to other global pressures, the actual impact of corruption is filtered by the national context of each country, which may either reduce or reinforce the impact.

Table 22.1 shows the levels of corruption in China, Hong Kong, and Japan in three selected years (1998, 2003, and 2008), indicating the level of corrupt activities in these countries over time. Other selected countries are also included in the table for the purpose of comparison. The data is provided by Transparency International (TI), a non-governmental organisation aiming to curb corruption, which is based in Berlin, Germany. As the actual levels of corruption cannot be directly observed (not all corruption cases are caught and prosecuted), TI relies on surveys of businessmen and other participants who have direct knowledge of the countries surveyed to ask their perceptions about the level of corrupt activities in the countries as a proxy for measuring the actual level of corruption. Their perceptions are used to compute the corruption perception index (CPI).

Although CPI is a widely cited and used measure of corruption, its major limitations and criticisms should also be realised. It is a measure of perception, not a measure of actual corruption, and it adopts the public office–oriented definition of corruption, which inevitably ignores the other aspects of corruption (Lambsdorff 2008). By excluding the local people and the general public in the survey sample, CPI is generally biased towards the business community, most of them having a background or sharing the worldview of developed countries. This measurement approach leads to the criticism that CPI has a tendency to overestimate the corrupt activities in the developing world, while underestimating those in the developed world (Miller 2006). Similarly, CPI has been criticised as a one-sided measure as it focuses only on the bribe-taking countries, omitting the bribe-giving countries (Galtung 2006).

In the latest 2008 CPI survey, a total of 180 countries are included, representing a major jump from the eighty-five countries included in the 1998 survey. There is a wide variation of divergence in the level of corruption among the countries. On a scale of zero to ten, a score of ten represents the "cleanest" countries and a score of zero represents the most "corrupted" countries.

Table 22.1   Corruption Perception Index (CPI) by Transparency International on China, Hong Kong, Japan, and Selected Countries

	1998		2003		2008	
	Index	*Rank*	*Index*	*Rank*	*Index*	*Rank*
Denmark	10	1	9.5	3	9.3	1
Sweden	9.5	3	9.3	6	9.3	1
Singapore	9.1	7	9.4	5	9.2	4
Finland	9.6	2	9.7	1	9	5
Switzerland	8.9	10	8.8	9	9	5
Australia	8.7	11	8.8	9	8.7	9
Canada	9.2	6	8.7	11	8.7	9
Hong Kong	**7.8**	**16**	**8**	**14**	**8.1**	**12**
Germany	7.9	15	7.7	16	7.9	14
Norway	9	8	8.8	8	7.9	14
Ireland	8.2	14	7.5	18	7.7	16
United Kingdom	8.7	11	8.7	11	7.7	16
Japan	**5.8**	**25**	**7**	**21**	**7.3**	**18**
United States	7.5	17	7.5	18	7.3	18
France	6.7	21	6.9	23	6.9	23
Spain	6.1	23	6.9	23	6.5	28
Taiwan	5.3	29	5.7	30	5.7	39
South Korea	4.2	43	4.3	50	5.6	40
Malaysia	5.3	29	5.2	37	5.1	47
South Africa	5.2	32	4.4	48	4.9	54
Italy	4.7	38	5.3	35	4.8	55
China	**3.5**	**52**	**3.4**	**66**	**3.6**	**72**
Mexico	3.3	55	3.6	64	3.6	72
Brazil	4	46	3.9	54	3.5	80

Source: Transparency International. *Notes:* 1. Countries are listed according to their rankings in 2008. 2. Number of Countries Surveyed: 85 (1998); 133 (2003); 180 (2008) 8). 3. Scores range between 10 (highly clean) and 0 (highly corrupt).

The three countries we are interested in—China, Japan, and Hong Kong—are relatively stable in their own CPI scores over time, in both their relative rankings and the absolute level of corruption as measured by CPI. Among them, China is the "most corrupted" country. It is still common to see high-ranking officials, including top officials in major cities like Beijing, its capital city, and Shenzhen, a major city in the fast-growing coastal province of Canton, and bosses of major state enterprises, such as the Bank of China, being disciplined by the party or arrested for corruption charges. Although the gap between Hong Kong and Japan has been narrowing over the last decade, there is still a difference between them worthy of our analysis. In Hong Kong, since the establishment of the Independent Commission Against Corruption (ICAC) back in the 1970s, major systemic corruption has been eliminated (Lo 1993; Chan 2001). In the case of Japan, despite the existence of a modern bureaucracy and a high level of economic development, administrative corruption is still systematically imbedded because of the cosy relationship between government and business, including significant problems with the concept of the "revolving door" (Choi 2007). There have been many well-known scandals in the construction and financial sectors in which senior bureaucrats received favours from businesses for leaking them confidential information and awarding them contracts with private deals.

The choice of these three countries represents a balance between controlling the variations in context within a manageable scope and ensuring differences among them in key variables relevant to our analysis. By way of similarities, all of them are Asian countries going through or having gone through rapid industrialisation. In terms of differences, they are different in their levels of corruption. Variations also exist among major independent variables in the domestic context, such as the involvement of state bureaucracy in economic development and the accountability system imposed on the state bureaucracy (Evens 1995; Hopkin and Rodriguez-Pose 2007).

What are the explanations for the divergence of corrupt activities? When both opportunities for corruption and anti-corruption measures are globalised and exerted on our selected countries with similar intensity, it should be the domestic context that serves as the major driving force for divergence. Quah (2001) identified three major patterns of controlling corruption. These were: anti-corruption laws with no independent agency (Pattern One); anti-corruption laws with many agencies (Pattern Two); and anti-corruption laws with independent agencies (Pattern Three). In his study, Quah argued that Pattern Three was the most sufficient mode of corruption control. This pattern is adopted by Hong Kong and Singapore, two of the "cleanest" countries in Asia.

If anti-corruption measures are available and their effectiveness is well demonstrated, why is there still a wide divergence in corruption levels among countries? Why do the more corrupted countries not simply follow the clean countries in adopting anti-corruption measures? In another study, Quah (1999) attempted to answer these questions. In the matrix of two dimensions—anti-corruption measures (adequate versus inadequate) and commitment of political leadership (strong versus weak)—four different scenarios are constructed. An effective strategy will only exist when there

294 *Wilson Wong*

is a combination of strong commitment of political leadership and adequate anti-corruption measures. At the very extreme, a scenario of "hopeless strategy" will come up when there are both inadequate anti-corruption measures and weak commitment of political leadership. Nevertheless, with the availability and enhancement of information technology that facilitates the diffusion of policy solutions and ideas across countries, it can be expected that the scenarios, due to inadequate anti-corruption measures, will be eliminated, leaving weak commitment of political leadership to be the last and ultimate variable for explaining the divergence of bureaucratic corruption across countries.

THE ROLE OF THE STATE AND ACCOUNTABILITY OF BUREAUCRACY: JAPAN, HONG KONG, AND CHINA

Attributing all divergence to the lack of commitment of political leaders can be an oversimplification. Analysing the CPI data from 1980 to 2003, Manion (2004) made two major observations. First, there is a stability of corruption in most countries. Out of the fifty-three countries for which scores are available throughout the study period, 90 percent of them have consistently high, intermediate, or low scores, meaning the level of corruption in many countries remained the same for a long period. Second, there is a persistence of clean and corrupted governments. Intermediate corruption scores are much less common than either high or low scores. According to Manion's study, 70 percent of the countries have high (clean) or low (corrupted) scores.

Even if the lack of political commitment is a cause of corruption, there must still be some institutional reasons behind the persistent lack of commitment. The decision to adopt anti-corruption measures, including the choice of refusing to adopt them, is a reflection of the domestic context, particularly the role and characteristics of the bureaucracy, as corruption is the abuse of official power for personal gain. Table 22.2 introduces the perspective of applying the domestic context as an explanation for the divergence of corruption among the three countries in a global context, focusing on the role of the bureaucracy in the domestic context.

From the table, it does not seem that type of regime or the political context of the three countries is a powerful enough variable to explain most of the divergence. Japan is the most democratic country among the three and, by being an authoritarian country, China is on the other extreme. If democratisation is a key variable, Japan should be the least corrupted country. As it turns out, it is Hong Kong, a partial democracy, which is the least corrupted country. Similarly, it does not seem that economic context is a strong explanatory variable. For instance, both Japan and Hong Kong have experienced a slow growth or even a decline in their economies in recent years, but they have still shown some noticeable differences in their levels of corruption.

Table 22.2   Comparison of the Domestic Context of China, Hong Kong, and Japan

	China	Japan	Hong Kong
Regime Type	*Authoritarian*	*Democratic*	*Partial Democratic*
Economic Context	Semi-reformed market economy. Fast economic growth	Mature market economy. Slow economic growth	Mature market economy. Slow economic growth
Role of Bureaucracy			
Policy-Making Role	Bureaucratic Domination	Strong Bureaucratic Influence	Strong Bureaucratic Influence
Formation of the Bureaucracy	Political loyalty, limited degree of merit	Merit-based	Merit-based
State Autonomy (level of political intrusion)	Weak. Lack of institutional development	High. Powerful and independent bureaucracy. Extended influence to the business sector	High but weakening (due to political and civil service reforms) powerful and independent bureaucracy
Economic Role	State-driven economic development (strong state influence)	State-driven economic development (high state influence)	State-driven economic development (medium state influence)
Bureaucratic Role in Economic Development	Bureaucratic entrepreneurism (direct participation of bureaucrats in economic development)	Developmental State (state formulate industrial policies and direct flow of resources to different industries)	Developmental State (no industrial policy, state involvement in supporting and non-profit sectors)
Bureaucratic Integration with Economic Interests	Almost inseparable	Interconnected and interlocked	Clearly separable
Bureaucratic Incentives for Corruption Control	Low	Medium	High
Nature of Bureaucratic Corruption	Systemic: threatening to slow down the pace of growth and negative impact on the equity in society	Systemic: adversely affecting the economic transformation and restructuring	Non-Systemic
Pattern of Corruption Control	Anti-corruption laws with many agencies	Anti-corruption laws with many agencies	Anti-corruption laws with an independent agency

Source: the author.

It is suggested here that it is the role of the bureaucracy in the domestic context, including its role in governing the economy and the discretionary power it enjoys, which offers a better explanation for divergence. In other words, it is the domestic context under which a bureaucracy is imbedded that takes away the incentive of policymakers, who could be bureaucrats themselves, from introducing widely known anti-corruption reforms. The state bureaucracies in all three countries play a very strong and active role in policy-making, including economic development (Duckett 1998; Evens 1995; Flynn 1999; Johnson 1982). Both Japan and Hong Kong adopt what is widely known as the "developmental state model" for their economic development. That is, the bureaucracies in these two countries play a very active and intervening role in leading the economic development—particularly in the process of industrialisation and economic restructuring.

Despite both of them being developmental in nature, two very different modes of developmental states are adopted in Japan and Hong Kong. The developmental state of Japan is more active in providing directions and guidance to the economy. It actually sets an industrial policy and gives clear directives on how to devote and allocate resources to different sectors and industries in society (Evens 1995; Johnson 1982). Many senior bureaucrats, after their retirement, join the business sector, which is known as *amakudari* (descent from heaven). Together with the school network (*gakubastsu*) and political network (*zoku*), this further enforces the interconnectedness and interlocking of the bureaucracy with business interests (Choi 2007; Lincoln 2001).

In the case of Hong Kong, no industrial policy is set. Despite close government–business relationships, there is still a recognisable separation of interests and clear boundaries between the business sector and the bureaucracy (Chan 2001; Lo 1993). When the state does interfere in the economy it usually participates in policy areas such as housing, welfare, and education, which have a high economic return but relatively loose connections to the business sectors. The distinctive identity of bureaucrats in Hong Kong makes them more willing to adopt anti-corruption measures to shield themselves from opportunities for corruption. On the other hand, in Japan where the line between bureaucrats and the business sector is more blurred and the difference between public and private interests becomes more ambiguous, the bureaucrats, who are also powerful policymakers, are less willing to adopt anti-corruption measures to constrain their own power (Beeson 2003; Choi 2007).

Among the three countries in this study, the most extreme case of state intervention and bureaucrat-driven economy occurs in China. Although China is undergoing rapid economic reform, the growth and expansion of its market economy does not come with the shrinking and retreat of the bureaucracy. A major economic reform strategy devised by Deng Xiaoping, the former Chinese leader and major architect of the economic reform, was to "buy off" or "corrupt" the local bureaucrats (Shirk 1993). The economic model in China is often termed as "bureaucratic entrepreneurism" as many of the new businesses set up under the economic reform are actually businesses owned by bureaucrats themselves or joint ventures with their direct participation (Duckett 1998). This "buying off" strategy is politically ingenious in pushing forward the economic reform. If the bureaucrats know that it is themselves who will get rich as a result of the economic reforms, they would do little to resist the adoption of a market economy. However, a direct consequence of this strategy is to make the interests of the bureaucrats and the businesses essentially inseparable. Effective anti-corruption measures, which would inevitably focus on limiting some of the power of the bureaucracy in influencing the business sector, will be a direct hit to their own interests (Root 1996). As a result, bureaucrats in China, who are also powerful political leaders, are the least interested group among the bureaucrats in the three countries to adopt anti-corruption measures (Gong 1997; Kwong 1997).

A dangerous combination facilitating bureaucratic corruption is the existence of strong bureaucratic roles in guiding the economy and a powerful bureaucracy without a proper accountability system for providing sufficient checks and balances. This should not be difficult to understand as it means no more than exposing bureaucrats to more opportunities for corruption while simultaneously relaxing many formal constraints on their power and behaviour. Using the two dimensions, source of control (internal versus external) and level of control (strong versus weak), Romzek and Dubnick (1987) classified four major modes of accountability systems: bureaucratic (internal and strong), legal (external and strong), political (external and weak), and professional (internal and weak). From an institutional standpoint, professional accountability is the weakest mode as it builds solely on the own self-control of the bureaucracy. There is actually a long and classical debate in the public administration literature on whether trust and confidence could really replace institutional safeguards and external control to provide sufficient checks on bureaucrats. Among the three countries studied, China has the bureaucracy that deviates the most from the traditional and ideal-typed bureaucracy of Max Weber. With the strongest bureaucratic power and the weakest institutional checks in accountability, it should be of no coincidence that China has the highest systemic corruption and the weakest adoption of anti-corruption measures.

CONCLUSION

With the emergence of the global pressure of bureaucratic corruption, there is a divergence instead of a convergence of national responses, with some vast differences in the levels of success in eradicating bureaucratic corruption. In applying the framework of global pressure and bureaucratic change, this chapter attempts to explain the divergent responses through a comparative case study of Japan, Hong Kong, and China. These three countries have some marked differences in their levels of bureaucratic corruption and, importantly, also the role of their bureaucracies. It is argued that it is the degree of integration between the interests of the bureaucrats and the business sector, together with an institutionally weak accountability system giving strong discretional power to state bureaucracy, which explains such a divergence.

The adoption of anti-corruption measures, or their lack of adoption, is a reflection of the characteristics of the domestic context that the bureaucracy is imbedded in. While further research is definitely needed to build a more complete theory, analysis in this chapter does suggest effective anti-corruption measures should incorporate strategies that focus on institutional change with regard to the role of state bureaucracy. As observed by Tanzi (1998) more than a decade ago, the fight against corruption was intimately linked with the reform of the state. Translating our analysis into concrete strategies, this would mean reducing the discretionary power of the bureaucracy in directing the economy by shifting to an economy that is truly directed by market forces instead of bureaucratic directives. In addition, more formal and external accountability measures, which include laws mandating more transparency and eliminating conflict of interests in policy-making, should be introduced to hold the bureaucracy more accountable to the public. However, the true irony and real complexity of fighting corruption is that those strategies are difficult to adopt due to the lack of incentives for key political actors. Many of them are bureaucrats themselves or part of the vested interests of the current corrupted system. Institutional change is always difficult. It is never easy to lessen the role and reduce the power of bureaucracy when bureaucrats themselves are powerful actors in society. All of these factors may in turn explain the persistence and stability of corruption as observed in the CPI data.

REFERENCES

Beeson, M. 2003. "Japan's Reluctant Reformers and the Legacy of the Developmental State." In *Governance and Public Sector in Asia: Paradigm Shifts or Business as Usual?*, ed. A. Cheung and I. Scott, 25–43. New York: Routledge.
Bozeman, B. 1987. *All Organizations Are Public: Bridging Public and Private Organizational Theories.* San Francisco: Jossey-Bass.
Brown, A. J. 2006. "What Are We Trying to Measure? Reviewing the Basics of Corruption Definition." In *Measuring Corruption*, ed. C. Sampford, A. Shacklock, and C. Connors, 57–80. Burlington: Ashgate.
Chan, K. M. 2001. "Uncertainty, Acculturation, and Corruption in Hong Kong." *International Journal of Public Administration* 24 (9): 909–928.
Choi, J. W. 2007. "Governance Structure and Administrative Corruption in Japan: An Organizational Network Approach." *Public Administration Review* 67 (5): 930–942.
Dahl, R., and C. E. Lindblom. 1953. *Politics, Economics and Welfare.* Chicago: University of Chicago Press.

Duckett, J. 1998. *The Entrepreneurial State in China: Real Estate and Commerce Departments in Reform Era*. London: Routledge.

Elliot, K. A. 1997. "Corruption as an International Policy Problem." In *Corruption and the Global Economy*, ed. K. A. Elliot, 175–233. Washington, DC: Institute for International Economics.

Evens, P. 1995. *Embedded Autonomy: States and Industrial Transformation*. Princeton, NJ: Princeton University Press.

Flynn, N. 1999. *Miracle to Meltdown in Asia: Business, Government and Society*. New York: Oxford University Press.

Galtung, F. 2006. "Measuring the Immeasurable: Boundaries and Functions of (Macro) Corruption Indices." In *Measuring Corruption*, ed. C. Sampford, A. Shacklock, and C. Connors, 101–130. Burlington: Ashgate.

Glynn, P., S. J. Kobrin, and M. Naim. 1997. "The Globalization of Corruption." In *Corruption and the Global Economy*, ed. A. E. Elliot, 7–27. Washington, DC: Institute for International Economics.

Gong, T. 1997. "Forms and Characteristics of China's Corruption in the 1990s: Change with Continuity." *Communist and Post-Communist Studies* 30 (3): 277–288.

Heady, F. 1996. "Configurations of Civil Service Systems." In *Civil Service Systems in Comparative Perspective*, ed. H. Bekke, J. Perry, and T. Toonen, 207–226. Bloomington: Indiana University Press.

Hopkin, J., and A. Rodriguez-Pose. 2007. "Grabbing Hand or Helping Hand? Corruption and the Economic Role of the State." *Governance* 20 (2): 187–208.

Johnson, C. 1982. *MITI and the Japanese Miracle*. Stanford, CA: Stanford University Press.

Klitgaard, R. 1988. *Controlling Corruption*. Berkeley: University of California Press.

Kwong, J. 1997. *The Political Economy of Corruption in China*. New York: M. E. Sharpe.

Lambsdorff, J. G. 2008. *The Methodology of the Corruption Index 2008*. Berlin: Transparency International.

Lincoln, E. 2001. *Arthritic Japan: The Slow Pace of Economic Reform*. Washington, DC: Brookings Institution Press.

Lo, T. W. 1993. *Corruption and Politics in Hong Kong and China*. Buckingham: Open University Press.

Manion, M. 2004. *Corruption by Design: Building Clean Government in Mainland China and Hong Kong*. Cambridge, MA: Harvard University Press.

Miller, W. L. 2006. "Perceptions, Experience and Lies: What Measures Corruption and What do Corruption Measures Measure." In *Measuring Corruption*, ed. C. Sampford, A. Shacklock, and C. Connors, 163–187. Burlington: Ashgate.

Nye, J., and J. Donahue, eds. 2000. *Governance in a Globalizing World*. Washington, DC: Brookings Institution Press.

Pollitt, C. 2001. "Convergence: The Useful Myth?" *Public Administration* 79 (4): 933–947.

Pye, L. 1985. *Asian Power and Politics: The Cultural Dimensions of Authority*. Cambridge, MA: Belknap Press.

Quah, J. S. T. 1999. "Corruption in Asian Countries: Can it be Minimized?" *Public Administration Review* 59 (6): 483–494.

———. 2001. "Globalization and Corruption Control in Asian Countries: The Case for Divergence." *Public Management Review* 4 (1): 453–470.

Romzek, B., and M. Dubnick. 1987. "Accountability in the Public Sector: Lessons from the Challenger Tragedy." *Public Administration Review* 47 (3): 227–238.

Root, H. 1996. "Corruption in China: Has It Become Systemic?' *Asian Survey* 36 (8): 741–757.

Rose-Ackerman, S. 1999. *Corruption and Government: Causes, Consequences, and Reform*. New York: Cambridge University Press.

Shirk, S. L. 1993. *The Political Logic of Economic Reform in China*. Berkeley: University of California Press.

Tanzi, V. 1998. "Corruption Around the World: Causes, Consequences, Scope and Cures." *IMF Staff Papers* 45 (4): 559–594.

Welch, E., and W. Wong. 1998. "Public Administration in a Global Context: Bridging the Gaps between Theory and Practice of Western and Non-Western Nations." *Public Administration Review* 58 (1): 40–50.

———. 2001. "Effects of Global Pressures on Public Bureaucracy: Modeling a New Theoretical Framework." *Administration and Society* 32 (4): 371–402.

23 An Accreditation Framework for the Indian Third Sector

Gaurav Patankar and Ashok Jain

INTRODUCTION

Domestic and international contributions to Community-Based Organisations (CBOs) and Voluntary Organisations (VOs) in India grew steadily in the last decade, positively influencing the scope and effectiveness of result-oriented development, especially in rural areas. However, several factors constrain the optimisation of this growth, in particular problems with donors. For example, although charitable giving in the United States totalled around $250 billion in the financial year 2002, CBOs in the state of Maharashtra in western India could not muster more than $25 million—around one hundredth of 1 percent of this total pie.

For the most part, the purse strings of charitable donations are controlled by corporate entities and the foundations they administer. The increasing corporate focus on value optimisation has not left the philanthropic channel untouched. Donor focus on effective and efficient deployment of donated resources is more pronounced than ever before. It becomes the responsibility of the CBOs to ensure that they have a nearly flawless reputation. Thus inspiring donor confidence, CBOs must do everything they can to prevent potential donors from finding excuses, big or small, in a long list of reasons not to donate.

This chapter asks: How can we get past the problem of reluctant donors in Indian CBOs and VOs and continue to see growth, with high donor confidence?

In November 2004, the US Senate Finance Committee Roundtable proposed accreditation of charities nationwide and also established some tenets for international charitable giving. This chapter contends that India should consider the guidelines set forth in the United States as a model for revamping their own system. This chapter proposes an accreditation framework which draws heavily from this proposal, adjusting it to Indian realities.[1]

Drawing on the experience of five CBOs in Maharashtra, this chapter proposes an accreditation framework for increased accountability in CBOs and VOs in India. Our framework uses a balanced scorecard approach to align donor intent with managerial interests, drive corporate governance metrics, and thereby boost donor confidence. This can achieve the intended outcome of improving donor–donee relationships.

The remainder of this chapter is structured as follows. The following section outlines our research approach and the next sets out our findings. The fourth section discusses our proposals for an accreditation framework acclimatised to the emerging world context, including the establishment of a Third Sector Accreditation Council of India (TSACI) and an accreditation assessment model. The fifth section then lists the pillars of our proposed assessment framework, and the final section draws some conclusions.

METHOD

We conducted over thirty interviews with 70 percent of the top fifty donor organisations in the US, including Citigroup, UB Foundation, and the Ford Foundation. We simultaneously met with more than fifteen third sector organisations in western India. This chapter is particularly focused on five such organisations in order to evaluate and understand the challenge of donor aversion. The following provides a snapshot profile of the five organisations that were analysed and evaluated on the basis of our proposed model:

1. Marat Wada Navnirman Lokayat, popularly known as Manavlok, is a registered voluntary organisation, located at Ambajogai in the Beed district of the drought-prone Marathwada region.
2. Yusuf Meherally Centre (YMC) is among the most successful voluntary organisations in Maharashtra, and is engaged in health-related activities in the rural area.
3. Kushtarog Niwaran Samiti Shantivan (KNSS) was founded at Nere village in Panvel Taluka of Raigad district in 1951 for the treatment and rehabilitation of leprosy patients. At present the KNSS oversees the leprosy eradication work in Panvel Taluka, and caters to the needs of a population of over four hundred thousand.
4. Gokul Pratishthan, District Ratnagiri, is an organisation focused on harvesting water resources in Maharashtra.
5. The Nav-Maharashtra Community Foundation (NAVAM) is a non-profit philanthropic organisation working for the development of rural communities in Maharashtra.

FINDINGS

Overview of the CBOs/VOs Space

Our findings indicate that although the CBOs/VOs space in India has become enormous in size, in the absence of an authentic directory of these entities, analysis of this space is a challenging task.

Some of the well-meaning and high-profile organisations (represented by NAVAM in our research) started by well-heeled socialites with wide contacts, reach, and donor power have failed to create an impact due to being disconnected from the needs of the constituents. However, it seems that the third sector is beginning to realise the importance of having a strong brand identity and a modern means of communicating it. The development of the NGO sector in India is in a transition phase; the importance of governance and transparency are well understood, but there is no uniformity when it comes to implementation. At the same time, government policy is shifting in favour of accreditation. Indeed, a recent pronouncement was inspired by the thoughts on common standards and accreditation discussed in this chapter.

The pioneers of the third sector in India, like Manavlok, YMC, and KNSS, are in fine fettle operationally, driven by dedicated social workers. The work of these three organisations has received recognition from the government, and their CEOs have been associated with policy-making activities at the state and local levels. However, they are now at a crossroads when it comes to the generational hand over of the baton.

In spite of decentralised power structures in most CBOs/VOs on paper, we find too much power rests with the CEO, the patriarch, or the largest funding family, which hinders corporate governance. A second line of leadership is lacking, largely driven by an understanding of the unattractive pay rates in a burgeoning commercial economy like India. Moreover, the functioning of governing bodies/committee meetings leaves much scope for improvement.

Donor Perceptions of Third Sector Organisations

Figure 23.1 shows four key areas identified by donors as problems with the current state of charitable institutions in India.

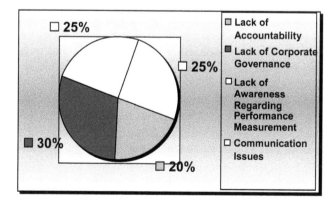

Figure 23.1 Donor issues with Indian charitable institutions.

Our research findings indicate that the single most important issue for donors is a lack of corporate governance in CBOs. All registered non-profit organisations in India are required to have a management structure, varying in scope and function depending on the size of the organisation.[2] Still, there is a perception that the organisations need a stronger governing structure. Without a good system in place to account for how funds are being distributed, donors feel like any funds they give have the potential to be mishandled.

A further key issue for donors is the absence of a structured and standardised performance standard that is measurable, transparent, and mission driven. Such absence has created a sense of scepticism amongst international donors and also allowed preconceived notions to set in and crystallise, which often are a pale shadow of reality. This corresponds to the donors' report that there is not enough communication between CBOs and the donors.

CBOs and VOs Perspectives

Even within the CBOs there is a feeling that there is a lack of proper governance. Process misconduct ranks as one of their primary concerns for why contributions are not higher. This, coupled with the lack of a central governing/accreditation body, indicates that it is time to review the governance structure of CBOs. There are also inefficiencies within the CBOs when it comes to delivering the impact of the donation to those in need. They acknowledge that they have inefficient processes when it comes to managing contributions—getting the most bang for the buck—but they have not come up with an effective method for how to improve this.

However, even once all the tools and guidelines are in place, how does a CBO measure its success? The number of lives impacted/saved? There is an absence of a common performance standard, so it is difficult for a CBO to self-report with any certainty of how well it has met stated goals. The subjectivity of performance evaluation causes frustration among CBOs.

It is vital that CBOs understand what is expected of them so they can better serve not only the people the organisation is trying to help, but so they can also meet the needs of their donors, inspiring confidence that the money they receive is being properly managed and distributed. Many CBOs simply do not understand what the donor expects. This corresponds to the donors' report that there is not enough communication between the CBOs and the donor. Until communication is improved, both the donors and the CBOs will continue to experience frustration and feel they are working at cross-purposes. CBOs want to increase donor confidence, but they are not sure how to do this without knowing what donors expect in return for their donations.

These concerns are illustrated in Figures 23.2 and 23.3.

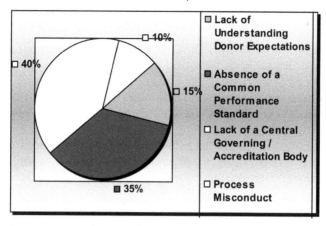

Figure 23.2 What are the issues hindering fund-flow from donor institutions to CBOs?

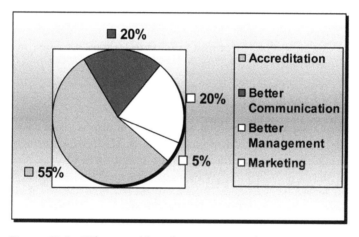

Figure 23.3 What would make you reconsider your view for making grants?

THE WAY FORWARD: PROPOSAL FOR AN ACCREDITATION FRAMEWORK ACCLIMATISED TO THE EMERGING WORLD CONTEXT

Based on our analysis earlier, and keeping the Indian structural context in mind, this section argues for the establishment of a formal body charged with annual accreditation of CBOs and VOs. Accreditation would be based on predetermined criteria that gel with donor objectives; at a broader level, accreditation would correspond with societal good and good governance principles. The two main goals for this proposed accreditation framework model are to increase the amount of foreign donor flows and to optimise the social impact of the flows.

We propose the following to streamline the issues:

1. setting up of the TSACI
2. a corresponding performance measurement—accordingly, we introduce the concept of an "impact ratio" for performance measurement
3. enhancing communication between donors, organisations, and stakeholders, with particular emphasis on beneficiary education and donor awareness

"Third Sector Accreditation Council of India"

The first and key recommendation we have is the creation of a fully functioning autonomous body called the TSACI. We look at this as an expert body with a medley of distinguished academicians and practitioners from the corporate world that has no financial incentive. That being said, we think it is important to arm this high-powered council with clear-cut performance objectives that meet minimum standards as specified in the following in our model.

Proposed Assessment Model

We propose assessment of third sector organisations using a balanced scorecard–based Common Minimum Metric (CMM), which provides comprehensive quantitative and analytical representation of success. The CMM threshold metric is driven in part by a conjoint spectrum analysis, which at a granular level entails in-depth case analyses of organisations at each level of the success spectrum, to include CBOs with:

- increasing international donor inflows
- sustained international donor flows
- failed status

Our proposed Institution Evaluation Model is shown in Table 23.1.

While our model is based on a balanced scorecard model and is inspired by several western accreditation models in the third sector, it is distinct in that it takes into account some of the ground realities innate to the third sector in an emerging country context where the paternalistic influence can be profound. In this institutional context, the nuts and bolts of applying the seven criteria shown in Table 23.1 are as follows:

1. *Institutional Profile*: Within this construct, we focused on clarifying hygiene factors like proper registration documents, vision, mission,

Table 23.1 A Practical Framework Applied for the Assessment of Third Sector
Organisations in India

Criterion Description	Weighting (%)	Marks
Institutional Profile	10	40
Management	10	40
Corporate Governance	20	80
Organisation	15	60
Financial Management	15	60
Activities	20	80
Impact	10	40

linkages, and ideological affiliation. There were ten qualitative criteria across which we divided the ten points.

2. *Management*: Under this criterion, we examined the composition of
the governing body, family affiliation, and ties, if any, management
tenures, removal provisions, management credentials, and board
oversight.

3. *Corporate Governance*: This was one of our highest weighted criterion
and for good reason. Nineteen qualitative and quantitative parameters were applied, with a focus on style as much as on substance.
We focused on communication, operating procedures, accountability,
organisational structure, training, and interconnecting linkages.

4. *Organisation/Structure*: We focused on things like size, tiers, control,
appointments, and some quantitative things like pay packages and
salary parity across sixteen qualitative criteria.

5. *Financial Management*: This was another high-focus criterion for
us. We allocated the fifteen points across fifteen rigorous questions.
We looked at quantitative metrics like turnover, revenue/expenditure
ratio, expenditure/activities, and other expenses/total corpus. We
also looked at qualitative metrics such as account book maintenance,
funding sources, audit, and cash management.

6. *Activities*: Including corporate governance, the actual ground game
aggregated under "activities" got our highest weighting. Here we did
a comprehensive evaluation of the scope, scale, and focus of activities undertaken by the entity. We also examined the horizontal and
vertical linkages in the activities and the proportion of their own programs to government programs, collaboration with other NGOs, and
implementation oversight.

7. *Impact*: Our impact analysis was driven by the spirit if not the definition of the impact ratio we describe in the section on "Corporate Governance" in the following. We quantified the impact metrics in terms

of the number of villages/individuals receiving a positive impact, and also qualitative impact parameters such as poverty alleviation, productivity gains, social justice, empowerment, and environmental protection.

After aggregating the scores on the various parameters under each of our criteria, we assigned a grading to each of the five organisations in our study (see section two above), based on the following rubric in Table 23.2.

Key Qualitative Learning from our Analysis

A number of key lessons emerge from the analysis of our five CBOs/VOs institutions against our evaluation model that can enhance the practicality and applicability of our conclusions.

Overhauling the Organisation Structure

As part of our plan, CBOs would be run like corporations. They would be subject to regular audits, the results of which would be published, creating better and more immediate communication with donors. The CBOs would have target impact ratios to hit, and failure to do so on a continual basis (over two or three years) would result in the CBO either being dissolved or merged in with a more successful, efficient CBO. To help account for funds already coming into the country, we have developed an "impact ratio". This is the second key element of our success model, an effective way to measure performance.

$$\text{Impact Ratio} = \frac{\textit{Economic Value Added to Target Community}}{\textit{Dollars Donated to the Institution}}$$

The impact ratio, in addition to other quantitative measures outlined earlier, allows us to quantify the work of CBOs. The Economic Value Added (EVA) might be measured as Gross Domestic Product (GDP) growth in a target community—savings rate growth, or small business credit growth, for example. It represents a tangible benefit from monies donated.

We also believe it is necessary to bring private sector actors into the system to help run the CBOs, which would mean paying them accordingly. Although they will require higher salaries, the benefit to the community will outweigh the extra internal expenses.

Table 23.2 Grades Assigned to Five Third Sector Organisations Based on Our Evaluation Model

Sr.No.	Criteria	1	2	3	4	5	6	7	Total	Grade
	Weighting (%)	10	10	20	15	15	20	10	100	
	Maximum Marks	40	40	80	60	60	80	40	400	
	Organisation									
1	Manavlok	26	28	40	45	57	61	33	275	A
2	YMC	25	17	41	43	50	36	22	234	B
3	KNSS	26	25	48	41	48	50	20	258	B
4	GP	23	7	18	17	19	24	23	131	D
5	NAVAM	12	24	38	29	14	22	4	143	D

Table 23.2 Key

Total Score	Percent	Grade
260 and above	> 65%	A
220–259	55%–65%	B
200–219	50%–55%	C
Below 200	< 50%	D

Emphasis on Communication

One of our significant findings within CBOs and VOs (in addition to donor perceptions) is that a lot of these organisations have to make considerable progress in terms of their communication strategies if they are to attract donor flows. This includes their communication with donors, constituents, and the government. We firmly believe that organisational effectiveness is driven by the level of education and understanding of the end consumers—beneficiaries in this case.

Keeping an open flow of communication between donors and CBOs will help increase donor confidence and therefore increase the amount donors are willing to contribute. Information is immediately accessible via the Internet and can be updated frequently for very little cost. In today's technological age, there is little excuse for keeping information from donors—especially when that information could substantially increase donor confidence and contributions (Kassam, Handy, and Ranade 2003b).

WHAT WOULD DIFFERENTIATE THE "AS" FROM THE "DS"?

We argue that the primary factor which would make donors reconsider their stance on giving is accreditation. In order to meet the specific needs of the TSACI, we benchmarked our minimum accreditation standards and grading scheme against the principles of the Council on Foundations' *Statement on Ethical Principles* (Council on Foundations n.d.), the *IOWA Principles and Practices for Charitable Nonprofit Excellence* (Iowa Governor's Nonprofit Task Force 2006), and the Better Business Bureaus' *Standards for Charity Accountability* (Better Business Bureau n.d.). The key elements of our proposed assessment framework which differentiate the "As" from the "Ds" are outlined in the rest of this section.

Corporate Governance

Pillar 1: Board Composition and Governance

The board of directors has the ultimate oversight authority for any charitable organisation. TSACI seeks to ensure that the volunteer board is active, independent, and free of self-dealing. To meet these standards, our proposals include:

- A board of directors with a minimum of ten voting members (no political affiliations) that provides adequate oversight of the charity's operations and its staff. A minimum of three evenly spaced meetings per year of the full governing body with a majority in attendance, with face-to-face participation (Drucker 1999).
- At least three members of the board are loaned executives or academics affiliated to an accredited university.
- No transaction(s) in which any board or staff members have material conflicting interests with the charity resulting from any relationship or business affiliation.
- The board should avoid involvement in day-to-day operations of the charitable non-profit.
- If a charitable non-profit wishes to compensate board members, it needs to have significant justification for the expenditure.
- Board and staff interact under a formal communication process.
- The executive director must be evaluated annually. TSACI accredited CBO and VO boards should engage in annual evaluation of their performance, focusing on the effectiveness and dynamics of the board as a whole as well as board committees and their leaders.

Pillar 2: Role of an Executive Director

VOs and CBOs need a strong executive director in place; an individual of impeccable integrity that acts as a liaison between the board and the management team, connecting the intended vision, mission, and execution. The executive director has the day-to-day administrative responsibility for achieving the organisational mission and assuring the efficient and effective operation of the organisation. To accomplish this, we propose the following best practices:

- The executive director has the responsibility to carry out the policies, procedures, and strategic plan adopted by the board.
- The executive director must be effective in the use of the organisation's assets, human resources, and program delivery, and set sufficiently high goals for the organisation to achieve.
- A major responsibility of the executive director is to work closely with the board through the board chair. The executive director must have the intellectual vision to develop the organisation and push the mission of the organisation in seminal directions.
- The executive director must be a communicator who can articulate the non-profit niche to attract and retain public constituencies.
- The executive director assures compliance with legal, financial, accounting, and ethical requirements.
- The executive director performs his or her responsibilities subject to fiduciary duties.

Pillar 3: Prudent Financial Management

TSACI accredited charities should spend funds honestly, prudently, and in accordance with statements made in fundraising appeals. To meet these standards, the charitable organisation should adhere to the following best practices:

- Have 30 percent of the members on the boards' financial review committee from the voluntary pool.
- There should be a balanced budget plan which consists of realistic estimates of income and expenses projected over a timeline (Kassam, Handy, and Ranade 2003a).
- Make available to all, on request, complete annual financial statements prepared in accordance with generally accepted accounting principles.
- Include in the financial statements a breakdown of expenses (for example, salaries, travel, postage) showing what portion of these expenses was allocated to program, fundraising, and administrative activities.

Organisation Building: "Building a Structure and Culture of Excellence"

Pillar 1: Evolving Organisational Mission

The mission statement should be in plain and simple language which can be understood by the general public and can be effectively marketed. Some of the best practices for TSACI accredited organisations include:

- The mission statement should be a rallying point for the organisation's constituencies: board, staff, volunteers, clients, donors, and the general public (Drucker 1999).
- The vision statement should describe what the organisation ultimately desires to achieve by carrying out the mission.
- The values statement should set forth the principles that will guide the organisation in carrying out its mission,

Pillar 2: HR Policies

As one of the key tenets of our proposal, we suggest a complete overhaul of HR policies at CBOs and VOs in India. As things currently stand, on average non-executive employees of third sector organisations make only 18 percent of the average wage of their private sector counterparts. We think that despite best intentions, this does not attract the best talent in the industry and therefore we propose two main tenets:

- Hiring mid-managers at 80 percent of private sector prevailing rates and analysing performance based on EVA added to the community as we discuss in our impact ratio calculation.
- Partnering with the corporate sector and government in designing an "executive loan/rotation" program, wherein top executives in parking lots are loaned to CBOs best practice HR policies.

Pillar 3: Proposed Structure for Volunteer Involvement

Focus is our buzzword in terms of how we want to engage volunteer enthusiasm. Volunteering is the hallmark of charitable non-profit organisations. Volunteers create, govern, fund, and staff charitable organisations. However, their energy needs to be channelled. For example, we are sub-optimising value if a group of volunteers from a Big 4 accounting firm go out on a weekend to paint village walls. While it might still add value, it would only be a small fraction of the value that could be added. To optimise and channel, we propose:

- An Internet-based project database that collates different required tasks from CBOs and VOs on a common database. There would be qualification checklists for each project.
- Give community service credits for each project.
- Work with participating organisations to link community service credits to annual employee development plan at allied companies.
- Work with governments to create incentives for "time" donations from organisations.
- A charitable non-profit should take annual measurement of the impacts of volunteers. A charitable non-profit should regularly supervise and communicate with volunteers.

- A charitable non-profit should have written policies and job descriptions for volunteer involvement.
- A charitable non-profit should provide individual praise for work well done by volunteers and hold group recognition events (Iowa Governor's Nonprofit Task Force 2006).

Pillar 4: Effective Strategic Planning

To achieve its mission and vision, TSACI accredited organisations need comprehensive plans that outline the organisational goals with specific action steps to be taken by specific individuals (Korton 1987). Organisational success depends on execution of this plan, and the following would be the best practices:

- The executive director and staff should be actively involved in the planning process with counsel from other organisational constituencies.
- A comprehensive strategic plan outlines general goals for all aspects of the organisation's operations. Each goal should be broken down into specific actions required to achieve them, including timelines and personnel designated to carry out the action.
- The strategic plan should identify specific management risks and provide for their reduction, elimination, or insurance.
- The strategic planning process should include a Strengths, Weaknesses, Opportunities, and Threats (SWOT) assessment of the organisation's strengths and weaknesses. To be effective, a SWOT analysis needs to incorporate the views of clients served, donors, and other public.

Pillar 5: Effective Performance Measurement

An organisation should regularly assess its effectiveness in achieving its mission. TSACI seeks to ensure that an organisation has defined, measurable goals and objectives in place, and a defined process in place to evaluate the success and impact of its program(s) in fulfilling the goals and objectives that also identifies ways to address any deficiencies. To meet these standards, a charitable organisation should:

- Have a board policy of assessing, no less than every two years, the organisation's performance and effectiveness. Submit a written report to the organisation's governing body that outlines the results of the aforementioned performance and effectiveness assessment.

Pillar 6: Fostering Teamwork

The board and the management committees of TSACI accredited organisations must act and play like a team. They should function as a body rather than as individuals. The board leader is the chair who works closely with the executive director to provide the team with information and involvement.

- Advisory boards and support groups: While the board of directors is the sole governing body of the organisation, it can and should establish advisory groups and friends groups that include staff from different levels and functions, fostering engagement, ownership, visibility, and teamwork.

Communication Strategy

Pillar 1: Constituent Education

The biggest proposition we make within the tenet of communication is a strong undying focus on education of the constituents. We firmly believe that organisational effectiveness and impact are driven by the level of education and understanding of the end consumers so they know what is available, and in worst cases know what they are deprived of. TSACI best practices include:

- There should be regular constituent education seminars with participation from the board, executive director, and management.
- There should be regular measurement of a constituent awareness index driven by independent polls showing how much the target constituents are aware of the organisation's mission and vision.

Pillar 2: Donor Communication and Fundraising

A fundraising appeal is often the only contact a donor has with a charity and may be the sole impetus for giving. This section of the standards seeks to ensure that a charity's representations to the public are accurate, complete, and respectful. CBOs should also be able to substantiate that the timing and nature of its expenditures are in accordance with what is stated, expressed, or implied in the charity's solicitations.

Pillar 3: Communication of the Vision and Mission

Using the Council on Foundations *Statement of Ethical Principles* (Council on Foundations n.d.) as a guide, we propose that TSACI simplify and communicate the following tenets of the mission statement:

- Mission: Members are committed to the public benefit and to their philanthropic purposes and act accordingly.
- Stewardship: Members manage their resources to maximise philanthropic purposes, not private gain, and actively avoid excessive compensation and unreasonable or unnecessary expenses.

- Accountability and transparency: In carrying out their philanthropic activities, members embrace both the letter and the spirit of the law.
- Diversity and inclusiveness: Our members seek diversity and inclusiveness in order to reflect the communities they serve.
- Governance: Our members' governing bodies understand and embrace their responsibility to oversee the mission, strategic direction, finances, and operations (Council on Foundations n.d.).

CONCLUSIONS AND RECOMMENDATIONS

Many CBOs in India are well-intentioned and do good work for the community, but there is little or no tracking of donor money once it reaches India. The money that is already being donated needs to be accounted for and better spent, and donations need to increase. We argue that by thinking about them more as corporations, their performance and impact will improve.

This chapter has recommended the introduction of an accreditation framework for Indian third sector organisations. Our accreditation framework is a model for success derived from international best practice, but tailored to the Indian context to make it practical enough for implementation and measurement. The three key tenets of our framework include: the introduction of an accreditation mechanism; an overhaul of the operating structure of third sector organisations; and a comprehensive upstream and downstream communication strategy.

We proposed the establishment of an independent non-profit body, the TSACI. The key objective of this body would be to evolve common minimum standards, provide accreditation, empower foreign and local donors via education and information, and enforce discipline in case of gross violations of codes and ethics.

Our assessment model uses a balanced scorecard approach to align donor intent with managerial interests and to drive corporate governance metrics in order to boost donor confidence and improve the donor–donee relationship.

To enhance the impact of the organisations we believe that aligning the right talent is crucial. In an economy as dynamic as India's it is difficult to retain talent without paying them close to market in a global context adjusted for purchasing power parity. On this metric, current employees are paid 15 to 20 percent of their global counterparts in the developed world. We propose a change of mindset here, and also advocate holding this new talent accountable for delivering against the proposed "impact ratio".

Effective upstream and downstream communication is vital. We therefore propose a conscious effort and structures which emphasise more effective communication between donors, organisations, and stakeholders with particular emphasis on beneficiary education.

NOTES

1. Notably, Johns Hopkins University provided some leadership in this direction, but excluded India from the discussion.
2. See NGOs of India; www.ngosindia.com.

REFERENCES

Better Business Bureau. n.d. *Standards for Charity Accountability.* http://www. bbb.org/us/Charity-Standards/.

Council on Foundations. n.d. *Statement of Ethical Principles.* Arlington, VA: Council on Foundations. www.cof.org.

Drucker, P. F. 1999. "Lessons in Successful Non-Profit Government." *Nonprofit Management and Leadership* 1 (1): 7–14.

Iowa Governor's Nonprofit Task Force. 2006. *IOWA Principles and Practices for Charitable Nonprofit Excellence.* Des Moines: Iowa Secretary of State. http://publications.iowa.gov/3436/.

Kassam, M., F. Handy, and S. Ranade. 2003a. "Factors Influencing Women Entrepreneurs of NGOs in India." *Nonprofit Management and Leadership* 13 (2): 139–154.

———. 2003b. "Understanding NGO Impact: The Case of Women NGO's in India." *Social Development Issues* 23 (3): 27–36.

Korton, D. C. 1987. "Third Generation NGO Strategy: A Key to People-Centered Development." *World Development* 15:145–159.

24 Conflicts of Interest, Corruption, and Ethics in Public Services

A Public Governance Approach

Andrea Calabrò

INTRODUCTION

Privatisation is an important ingredient of market reform programs (Parker and Saal 2003). These reforms are expected to improve economic efficiency by reducing the role of the state in the economy. Despite examples of improvements (Kikeri and Nellis 2001) there remain concerns about impacts on the public interest (Bayliss 2002; Harper 2002; Manzetti 1999; Stiglitz 2002).

Conflicts of interest and corruption may explain the failure of privatisations. Stiglitz states (2002, 58): "Perhaps the most serious concern with privatization, as it has so often been practiced, is corruption."

This chapter demonstrates that corruption and unethical behaviours related to conflicts of interest are critical considerations in public service firms' governance systems. It contributes to the debate on the effects of privatisation from New Public Management (NPM), New Public Service (NPS), and New Public Governance (NPG) perspectives. We present findings of a case study of partial privatisation and ethical problems in Italian public service firms owned by the Ministry of Economy and Finance (MEF).[1] Key questions are:

- What motivates partial privatisation?
- What are the consequences of partial privatisation for the accountability of public service firms?

We proceed to argue that new modes of governance (joined-up governance, network governance, co-production, and co-operation) provide alternatives (Pestoff 1992, 2008) to privatisation. Indeed, a public governance approach may stimulate more effective public service delivery, assuring the public interest.

The second and third sections of this chapter discuss corruption and conflicts of interest in privatisation. The fourth section presents the privatisation process from NPM, NPS, and NPG perspectives. Methods are shown in the fifth section and results summarised in the sixth. Discussion, findings, and future research directions are presented in the last two sections.

PRIVATISATION AND CORRUPTION

While large privatisation programs have been implemented in some countries, in others, including Italy, the state retains a large presence across many sectors (La Porta et al. 2002). Privatisation has been most apparent in Europe, although experience has been patchy: Telecommunications have largely been privatised; railways are sometimes state owned, sometimes privately owned, sometimes in mixed ownership; and many countries still have state-owned industries.

A major criticism of the privatisation process is that gains in firm profitability are achieved at the expense of society, extracted from consumers through the use of market power (Bayliss 2002). Privatisation may affect consumer welfare through decreased access, worsened distribution, and lower quality of goods and services (Freije and Rivas 2002). The most serious concern is corruption, which is influenced by the choice of privatisation method, the implementation phase, and the legal framework.

Turnovec (1999) demonstrates that privatisation in the Czech Republic was less successful than official statistics indicate, partly as a result of corrupt transactions. Stiglitz (2002, 58) suggests:

> In country after country, government officials have realized that privatization meant that they no longer needed to be limited to annual profit skimming. By selling a government enterprise below market price, they could get a significant chunk of the asset value for themselves rather than leaving it for subsequent officeholders. In effect, they could steal today much of what would have been skimmed off by future politicians.

Shleifer and Vishny (1998) and Laffont and Meleu (1999) discuss the link between corruption and the decision to privatise, and Kaufmann and Siegelbaum (1997) discuss design of privatisation.

Corruption further affects the post-privatisation market structure which in many cases, including Italy, is dominated by the large stake of the state in public service firms.

We do not argue that corruption in the public sector is actually caused by the privatisation process. Privatisation may be no more than a convenient vehicle for corruption (Kaufmann and Siegelbaum 1997). Differing approaches to privatisation can either stimulate or hinder the potential for government officials and their private sector counterparts to engage in corrupt practices. A key issue is the ability of politicians and bureaucrats to create new control rights or to define old control rights, the exercise of which can be sold to extract rents. By maintaining a partial ownership link, government sustains officials' direct control rights, with the special opportunities for rent-seeking that this implies. Where the government retains exceptional governance powers, such as through the use of so-called "golden shares", this risk—and the potential for corruption—increases (Kaufmann and Siegelbaum 1997)

CONFLICTS OF INTEREST

Under partial privatisation, managers of state-owned firms are often political appointees and employees assume a status equivalent to civil servant. The actions of these managers and their employees directly impact citizens (clients or customers).

Public sector employees may face conflicts, especially when personal goals are inconsistent with maximising the benefits of citizens. Public officials may face conflict when they are able to advantage their own position at the expense of other shareholders. The lawful resolution of these conflicts rests on the principle that public officials have an obligation to look after the interests of all shareholders. Yet the simplicity of these goals and principles does not seem to hold sway.

Recent scandals in the public sector highlight the importance of ethical systems. Ministers, agencies, and central and local administrations often share responsibility and involvement in public services provision. Citizens may perceive this distribution of competences as complex, incoherent— even useless. Because legitimacy is in question, issues of ethics, accountability, and governance become imperative for all governments, as does the governance structure of public service firms. The case of partial privatisation is particularly useful for understanding what a conflict of interest is and how it may be avoided in public service firms.

The Organisation for Economic Co-operation and Development (OECD) states: "A 'conflict of interest' involves a conflict between the public duty and private interests of a public official, in which the public official has private interests which could improperly influence the performance of their official duties and responsibilities" (2006, 47). Conflicts of interest often happen without being anyone's fault. If not identified, disclosed, and managed effectively, conflicts of interest may compromise officials' work and create a catalyst for serious misconduct and corruption. Conflicts of interest must be *seen to be* managed in a transparent manner (OECD 2005). A code of ethics with prescriptions on conflict of interest and sanctions may be helpful. There is a growing public perception in western democracies that corruption of public officials is increasing (Chapman and O'Toole 1995; Frederickson 1999). There has been a significant shift in public service ethical standards and in unethical behaviour (Bovens, Schillemans, and Hart 2008; Hondeghem 1998; OECD 2000; Van Wart and Berman 1999).

We argue for strategic consideration of accountability systems in public organisations, especially in state-owned public service firms. In these cases, the adoption of businesslike methods must be accomplished alongside consideration of the public interest and value, and with the right tools for improving effective accountability to the citizens.

NPM, NPS, AND NPG PERSPECTIVES

Privatisation aims to shift functions and responsibilities (wholly or partially) from government to the private sector through such activities as contracting out or asset sales (Bozeman 2007). Privatisation is commonly but incorrectly referred to as a mechanism of the NPM. There are several distinctions between NPM and privatisation. First, privatisation is the older term, entering into common language around 1968, about fifteen years prior to NPM. Second, the NPM has more management strategy trappings than privatisation (Bozeman 2007). While privatisation is about moving public performance and functions to the private sector, NPM includes many other factors, such as viewing the client as a customer. Privatisation is a broad toolkit, whereas NPM is an approach to management reform. Yet we avoid hard-and-fast claims about specific boundaries between NPM and privatisation.

NPM represented a paradigmatic break from the traditional model of public administration (Hood 1991) experienced internationally (Pollitt and Bouckaert 2004). Recently discussed weaknesses in the NPM mean that the public value approach is attracting considerable interest (Bozeman 2002; Hartley 2005; Hefetz and Warner 2004; Smith, Anderson, and Teicher 2004; Stoker 2006). In this new light, the privatisation process assumes a new shape. Scholars examine the negative effects of what are often partial privatisation processes with no improvement in the value of public service. Corruption and ethical problems arising from conflicts of interests are highlighted and privatisation is highly contested (Groot and Budding 2008). Apprehension has been strengthened by highly publicised scandals in many OECD countries. There is increasing concern about the impact of NPM reforms on public officials' ethics and interest in re-regulation (Maesschalck 2004; Frederickson 1999).

The NPS (Denhardt and Denhardt 2000) offers an alternative to the dichotomy between the old public administration and the NPM. It proposes new mechanisms whereby the primary role of the public official is to help citizens, meeting their interests rather than attempting to control or steer society. In contrast to NPM, NPS also recognises that the relationship between government and its citizens is not the same as the business relationships that exist between a firm and customers. Privatisation process is seen as a market-based mechanism, inappropriate in some contexts due to failure and ethical problems.

A reasonable alternative (Pestoff 1992, 2008) to the privatisation process is suggested by the NPG. This perspective includes many modes of governance (for example, joined-up governance, network governance, co-production, and co-operation) as alternatives to privatisation. Issues of corruption, conflicts of interest, and unethical behaviour may be addressed through participatory citizenship in the government of complex issues surrounding public service delivery (Klijn 2008).

In instances of partial privatisation, deregulation in public service delivery, and reorganisation processes, the shape and the power of the governing bodies are constantly changing. Key questions arsing are: Does the accountability system keep up with developments? Would moving from NPM or NPS to NPG approaches better serve the public interest? Can accountability systems address the problems of partial privatisation?

METHODS

We present a case study of privatisation in Italy. The Italian MEF owns many firms involved in public services provision. These public service firms use businesslike methods to improve efficiency and performance. Our focus is their ethical and accountability systems. The aim is to identify whether or not greater risks arise for citizens in terms of public interest and value in cases of partial privatisation processes.

The case analysis is structured in two parts: (a) analysis of the situation pre- and post- privatisation; (b) formal and content analysis of the codes of ethics of all the public service firms controlled by the MEF.

THE MEF: STOP-GO PRIVATISATION AND ACCOUNTABILITY

Privatisation in Italy was characterised by a stop-go dynamic (Marelli and Stroffolini 1998). Privatisations from 1992 to 1999 totalled 185,000 billion lire (more than €95 billion), which accounted for 12.3 percent of the GNP in 1992. This relieved state finances, and it could be considered a success (De Nardis 2000).

However, privatisations did not necessarily translate into a real shift of control over privatised businesses. Privatisations in the industrial sector involved many cases of actual transfer of control, but in other significant cases, the state maintained more than 50 percent of shares. This market-type mechanism may threaten public accountability, creating a split between purchasers (citizens, clients, customers) and service providers which results in corruption, unethical behaviour, and public confusion regarding who is actually responsible for the service delivery.

Pre-privatisation and Post-privatisation

Until the beginning of the 1990s, the state sector in Italy was pervasive. State-owned enterprises (SOEs) were industrial and social policy instruments rather than profit maximising entities, typically operated under strong political interference. Operating and financial performance was very weak in comparison to private firms. Under the pressure of debt and deficits, Italy's fiscal conditions rapidly deteriorated at the beginning of the 1990s. In 1993, Italy embarked on large-scale privatisation aimed at fiscal stabilisation as a requisite to join the European Monetary Union (Goldstein and Nicoletti 2003).

Over a decade, Italy implemented seventy major privatisations, mainly through public offers of shares, placing Italy in the third and fourth position in global ranking by revenues and transactions, respectively (Goldstein and Nicoletti 2003). State entities operating under public law have been transformed into corporations and decision-making concentrated in the hands of the MEF. The control structure of the SOE sector was extremely complex, involving different state holding companies, public entities, ministries, or local government bodies (see Figure 24.1).

Until 1992, the majority of state assets were owned by three large holding companies: IRI,[2] ENI,[3] and EFIM,[4] under the direct control of the Ministry of State Holdings. Important public entities were ENEL, the electricity state monopoly, IMI, a special credit financial institution, and BNL (one of the most important banks). The largest entities owned by ministries were FS, operating in the railway system, and PP.TT, managing the postal and telecommunication services (Goldstein and Nicoletti 2003). Financial and operating performances were generally poor. The objectives of the privatisation program were presented to parliament in November 1992. The MEF had the duty of formulating proposals on privatisation to a committee

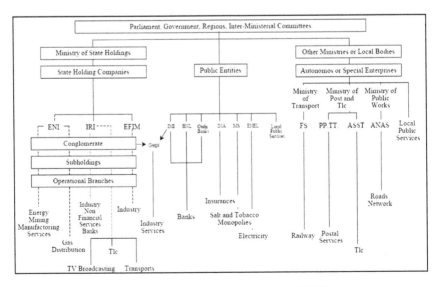

Figure 24.1   The control of state-owned enterprises as of 1992.

of three ministries—MEF, Budget and Planning, and Industry—and final decisions were approved by the Council of the Ministries, chaired by the Prime Ministry. MEF played the role of agenda-setter in privatisation issues, liaising with state holding companies and SOE managers.

Privatisation peaked between 1996 and 2000. This phase was on a much smaller scale. It was characterised by private equity placements (private sales) and, when this was not possible due to international market conditions, blocking transactions to institutional investors.

Figure 24.2 shows public service firms currently owned by the MEF. As in the majority of developed countries, the MEF remains an influential shareholder in several privatised companies, such as ENI, ENEL, Finmeccanica, and Alitalia. The MEF fully owns FS, the railway system operator, and RAI (Italian Radio Television), the television broadcasting company. The MEF is the main shareholder of many Italian public service firms and, importantly, it is the main decision-maker, thus determining the governance system of all these firms. Planning and control functions are performed by the MEF, who also influence the governance structure of public service firms. As shown in Figure 24.2, the Italian privatisation process has now stopped.

We argue that there is an urgent need for accountability infrastructures and ethical behaviour in managing public services, especially if the partial privatisation process remains as it is now. What has already happened and what is going to happen in Italian public service management will be determined by the governance structure of public service firms owned by the MEF.

Questions arising are: What is the role of citizens? Are they citizens, customers, and/or clients? What would be an adequate level of accountability?

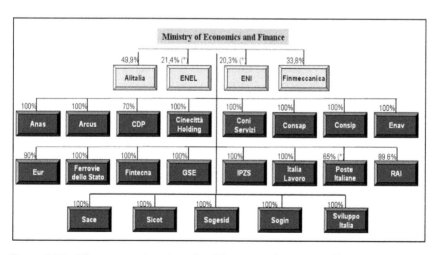

Figure 24.2   The current situation of public service firms owned by the MEF.

How can transparency, ethical prescriptions, and accountability be insured as part of the governance system?

We proceed to discuss the current status of codes of ethics adopted in Italian public service firms (controlled by the MEF). Our focus is on ethical aspects and norms related to corruption and conflicts of interest prevention to assure the public interest.

The Ethical Structure

The term "code of ethics" is defined as: written standards that are reasonably designed to deter wrongdoing and to promote honest and ethical conduct, including the ethical handling of actual or apparent conflicts of interest between personal and professional relationships; full, fair, accurate, timely, and understandable disclosure in reports and documents; compliance with applicable governmental laws, rules, and regulations; the prompt internal report on violations of the code to an appropriate person or person identified in the code; and accountability for adherence to the code (O'Dwyer and Madden 2006).

In public service firms a well-defined ethical structure may help prevent conflicts of interest. Mandatory codes of ethics have only recently been introduced in Italy for public service firms (law no. 231/2001). These new codes outline values and ethical principles that should guide officials in their professional activities.

We used content analysis to analyse the codes of ethics of public service firms owned by the MEF and to identify existing and potential ethical concerns for these firms. We build on earlier content analysis studies of ethical codes internationally (Bondy, Matten, and Moon 2004; O'Dwyer and Madden 2006).

We selected codes of ethics disclosed on the Internet. We analysed current versions and collected codes in English and Italian. The aim was to identify ethical guidelines. We looked for indications of how corruption and conflicts of interest were avoided, emphasising well-defined sanctions.

Despite the new regulations, some of the public service firms in our study have not disclosed their code of ethics on their web sites. Of the twenty-six public services firms owned by the MEF, twenty-two disclosed their code of ethics (84.7 percent).

With regard to sector activity, firms which operate in the same sector are likely to adopt similar patterns in the preparation of an ethics code. In some firms that did not make one (15.3 percent), contrary to the tendency in their sector (employment service and insurance, 7 percent), such a strategy would be adversely interpreted by markets.

Concerning the title of the document, most firms simply use the denomination "Code of Conduct of X" (38.46 percent). Other titles reported are "Ethical Standards" (15.38 percent), "Standards of Ethics and Conduct of" (23.07 percent), and "Code of Ethics" (7.6 percent). The mean length is approximately fourteen pages, with some up to thirty pages. Most codes took effect four or five years ago (36.6 percent from 2001 to 2003, 45.5 percent from 2004 to 2006, and 17.9 percent from 2007 to 2008). The scope of the codes analysed takes in mainly employees and their customers, emphasising the ethical role played by managers, directors, and partially public officials.

Codes are mainly imperative in nature, stating a guide for standards of conduct that firms would like their actors to follow. The structure of the codes usually falls into two sections. There is a first section which states the values and basic principles encouraged by the firm, whereas the second section translates the principles into standards of conduct for the actors in their internal and external relationships. Of the codes analysed, 45.4 percent lack a clear statement of values and principles; 36.4 percent lack an indication of detailed norms of conduct. Tools of promotion and sensitisation to the importance of the public interest and value are present in only 18.2 percent of cases.

The codes analysed included provisions for: use of public resources for personal benefit (31 percent); definition of the target group to which the code is addressed (23.6 percent); duties to the public in confrontation with private interests (22.8 percent); definition of behaviour or conduct constituting violation of the code (13.6 percent); statement of preventing conflicts of interest (9 percent); and sanctions in case of violations (0 percent).

Major deficiencies emerge from this analysis. Many codes are characterised by general content containing few principles, expressed often in terms of "ought" or "should" (and not "must"). Many are ambiguous or unclear. The main ethical concerns have to do with the absence of information on conflicts of interest disclosure. No codes are characterised by a formulation process that includes consultation with citizens or their representatives.

Ethics seem critical in the governance system of the MEF and its public service firms. Accountability, transparency, openness, public officials' duties, complex relationships among actors, public interests, and values are all key aspects. It seems to us that firms' codes of ethics fulfil the role of compulsory documents. They simply suggest guidelines that are quite similar to a code of practice. The analysis clearly shows that the introduction of ethical issues in public service firms is at an early stage.

DISCUSSION AND FINDINGS

Our results indicate that actions on accountability and ethical issues were not considered in detail during privatisations. Codes of ethics were adopted quite recently in the public service firms we analysed. This is partially justified by the complexity of implementing an accountability structure. We argue that now is the right time for "reinventing" privatisation. Conscious of the limits and excessive focus on efficiency and performance in NPM, the emphasis on ethical and accountability aspects of privatisation is more evident in the NPS perspective. Finally, NPG offers a valid alternative to privatisations (Pestoff 1992, 2008), including citizens as key actors in the governance process.

When approaching the privatisation process, a wide host of management techniques and forms of organising social life may be valid alternatives. Recognising that existing service provision by public service firms is lacking in quality and effectiveness provides a further reason to believe that experiments and combinations of accountability and privatisation may be desirable.

In Italy, many public service firms are still state owned and competition is not effective. A major emphasis on accountability is needed. Public service firms have many stakeholders and they are particularly visible to citizens. The use of codes of ethics may legitimise public officials' actions, ensuring that their effects fall within the norms of society.

This point is critical for public service firms owned by the MEF. Our evidence suggests that actions in line with ethical and accountability procedures are sporadic, unstructured, and have been introduced only recently. A lack of accountability is the main weakness of the governance structures. There is also a lack of evidence of increased efficiency following privatisation. Although window-dressing may be likely, the disclosure of codes of ethics on the Internet reveals a public commitment to stakeholders, not just an internal procedure. This seems to be a good starting point.

Governmental reforms are needed in order to introduce market principles and facilitate outsourcing. However, today's public sector with its modern representative democracy can be described as a concatenation of principal–agent relationships (Strøm 2003). Public accountability is an essential precondition for the democratic process to work, providing citizens and their representatives with the information needed for judging the propriety and effectiveness of government.

Our evidence indicates many problems relating to how the fundamental values of public service organisations have been undermined by the partial privatisation process (Lawton 1998). Political and policy considerations are significant and pervade leadership, strategy, and management of public service organisations.

Public services and public services organisations need to be defined, operationalised, measured, and evaluated. The relationship and communication between the government and citizens are fundamental. Citizens are more likely to encourage communication under the new modes of governance associated with the NPG (Klijn 2008; Pestoff 2008; Osborne 2006), with its emphasis on partnership, networking (Klijn 2008), and lateral modes of organising. These new modes of governance may address the accountability deficit in the MEF governance structure. Accountability tools are often introduced through pilots, or incrementally, to build support for more inclusive and transparent governance (Bovens, Schillemans, and Hart 2008).

Mandatory codes of ethics are a good starting point but are not enough. Other means are needed to promote a high level of public service accountability. However, a code imposed from on high will not fit the bill if the goal is to produce a document of shared values. More citizens' participation through a bottom-up process may fulfil the complex process of building codes with shared vision, values, and interests.

CONCLUSIONS

Ethics and accountability are gaining prominence in the governance debate. There is a perception that standards in public life are in decline, raising questions about the costs of misconduct by those who are entrusted with guarding the public interest. These arguments are particularly relevant in public service firms. This chapter has argued that the perception of a decline in public standards is linked to the shifting role of the state, which is undergoing tremendous reform.

Privatisation has been a starting point, but the question now is how to ensure standards of quality and efficiency in public services. As a result, public service firms are under pressure to transform and meet demands for increased accountability. A reduction of public officials' conflicts of interest is paramount and there is a need to implement well-designed accountability mechanisms. Decision-makers in public service firms are thereby provided with the opportunity to explain and justify their actions; and citizens and interest groups may thus ask questions and offer different opinions.

NOTES

1. In many countries, including Italy, firms are still controlled by the state, which constitutes partial privatisation.
2. IRI was a conglomerate with a highly diverse portfolio of assets in the industrial and financial sector.
3. ENI was mainly involved in oil and gas.
4. EFIM was involved in defence, transports, and aluminium.

REFERENCES

Bayliss, K. 2002. "Privatization and Poverty: The Distributional Impact of Utility Privatization." *Annals of Public and Cooperative Economics* 73 (4b): 603–625.
Bondy K., D. Matten, and J. Moon. 2004. "The Adoption of Voluntary Codes of Conduct in MNCs: A Three-Country Comparative Study." *Business and Society Review* 109 (4): 449–477
Bovens, M., T. Schillemans, and P. Hart. 2008. "Does Public Accountability Work? An Assessment Tool." *Public Administration* 86 (1): 225–242.

Bozeman, B. 2002. "Public-Value Failure: When Efficient Markets May Not Do." *Public Administration Review* 62 (2): 145–161.

———. 2007. *Public Values and Public Interest: Counterbalancing Economic Individualism.* Washington, DC: Georgetown University Press.

Chapman, R. A., and B. J. O'Toole. 1995. "The Role of the Civil Service: A Traditional View in a Period of Change." *Public Policy and Administration* 10 (2): 3–20.

De Nardis, S. 2000. "Privatizzazioni, liberalizzazioni, sviluppo: Introduzione e sintesi." In *Le Privatizzazioni Italiane*, ed. S. De Nardis, 9–41. Bologna: Il Mulino.

Denhardt, R. B., and J. V. Denhardt. 2000. "The New Public Service: Serving Rather than Steering." *Public Administration Review* 60 (6): 549–559.

Frederickson, H. G. 1999. "Public Ethics and the New Managerialism." *Public Integrity* 1 (3): 265–278.

Freije, S., and L. Rivas. 2002. "Privatization, Inequality and Welfare: Evidence from Nicaragua." Unpublished manuscript, Caracas, Venezuela, Centro Desarrollo Humano y Organizaciones (IESA).

Goldstein, A., and G. Nicoletti. 2003. "Privatization in Italy 1993–2002: Goals, Institutions, Outcomes and Outstanding Issues." Unpublished manuscript, CESifo Conference on Privatization Experiences in the EU.

Groot, T., and T. Budding. 2008. "New Public Management's Current Issues and Future Prospects." *Financial Accountability and Management* 24 (1): 1–13.

Harper, J. 2002. "The Performance of Privatized Firms in the Czech Republic." *Journal of Banking and Finance* 26:621–649.

Hartley, J. 2005. "Innovation in Governance and Public Services: Past and Present." *Public Money and Management* 25 (1): 27–34.

Hefetz, A., and M. Warner. 2004. "Privatization and Its Reverse: Explaining the Dynamics of the Government Contracting Process." *Journal of Public Administration Research and Theory* 14 (2): 171–190.

Hondeghem, A. 1998. *Ethics and Accountability in a Context of Governance and New Public Management.* Amsterdam: IOS Press.

Hood, C. 1991. "A Public Management for All Seasons?" *Public Administration* 69 (1): 3–19.

Kaufmann, D., and P. Siegelbaum. 1997. "Privatization and Corruption in Transition Economies." *Journal of International Affairs* 50 (2): 419–458.

Kikeri, S., and J. Nellis. 2001. "Privatisation in Competitive Sectors: The Record so Far." Mimeo, Private Sector Advisory Services, World Bank, Washington, DC.

Klijn, E. H. 2008. "Governance and Governance Networks in Europe." *Public Management Review* 10 (4): 505–525.

Laffont, J. J., and M. Meleu. 1999. "A Positive Theory of Privatization for Sub-Saharan Africa." *Journal of African Economics* 60:271–295.

La Porta, R., F. López-de-Silanes, A. Shleifer, and R. Vishny. 2002. "Investor Protection and Corporate Valuation." *Journal of Finance* 57:1147–1170.

Lawton, A. 1998. *Ethical Management for the Public Services.* Buckingham: Open University Press.

Maesschalck, J. 2004. "The Impact of New Public Management Reforms on Public Servants' Ethics: Toward a Theory." *Public Administration* 82 (2): 465–489.

Manzetti, L. 1999. *Privatization South America Style.* Oxford: Oxford University Press.

Marelli, M., and F. Stroffolini. 1998. "Privatization in Italy, a Tale of Capture." In *Privatization in the European Union. Theory and Policy Perspectives*, ed. D. Parker, 22–25. London and New York: Routledge.

O'Dwyer, B., and G. Madden. 2006. "Ethical Codes of Conduct in Irish Companies: A Survey of Code Content and Enforcement Procedures." *Journal of Business Ethics* 63 (3): 217–236.

Organisation for Economic Co-operation and Development. 2000. *Privatisation, Competition and Regulation*. Paris: Centre for Co-operation with Non-Members.

———. 2005. *Managing Conflict of Interest in the Public Sector—A Toolkit*. Paris: OECD.

———. 2006. *Public Ethics and Governance: Standards and Practices in Comparative Perspective*. Oxford: Elsevier Ltd.

Osborne, S. 2006. "The New Public Governance?" *Public Management Review* 8 (3): 377–387.

Parker, D., and D. Saal. 2003. *International Handbook on Privatization*. Cheltenham: Edward Elgar.

Pestoff, V. 1992. "Cooperative Social Services an Alternative to Privatization." *Journal of Consumer Policy* 15:21–45.

———. 2008. "Citizens as Co-Producers of Welfare Services: Childcare in Eight European Countries." *Public Management Review* 8 (4): 503–520.

Pollitt, C., and G. Bouckaert. 2004. *Public Management Reform: A Comparative Analysis*. Oxford: Oxford University Press.

Shleifer, A., and R. W. Vishny. 1998. *The Grabbing Hand, Government Pathologies and Their Cures*. Cambridge, MA: Harvard University Press.

Smith, R. F. I., E. Anderson, and J. Teicher. 2004. "Toward Public Value?" *Australian Journal of Public Administration* 63 (4): 14–15.

Stiglitz, J. 2002. *Globalization and Its Discontents*. London: Allen Lane/Penguin Press.

Stoker, G. 2006. "Public Value Management: A New Narrative for Networked Governance?" *American Review of Public Administration* 36 (1): 41–57.

Strøm, K. 2003. "Parliamentary Democracy and Delegation." In *Delegation and Accountability in Parliamentary Democracies*, ed. K. Strøm, W. Müller, and T. Bergman, 55–107. Oxford: Oxford University Press.

Turnovec, F. 1999. "Privatization, Ownership Structure and Transparency: How to Measure the True Involvement of the State." *European Journal of Political Economy* 15:605–618.

Van Wart, M., and E. M. Berman. 1999. "Contemporary Public Sector Productivity Values." *Public Productivity and Management Review* 22 (3): 326–348.

25 Ethical Audit
Control, Performance, and Review

Alan Lawton, Frédérique Six, and
Michael Macaulay

INTRODUCTION

Audit and inspection regimes have long been a mainstay of public services across the globe, focusing upon key indicators such as financial performance, accountability, quality issues, responsiveness to clients, citizens and consumers, and so on. Ethical audit regimes do not have such a long history, although the last decade has seen considerable growth in this area in the UK and across Europe: standards of behaviour of appointed and elected public officials have been put under ever-increasing scrutiny. In the UK, for example, ethical frameworks have been introduced for both local politicians and parliamentarians.

Despite the introduction of such ethical frameworks, however, it is not obvious that ethical performance has improved. The introduction of the Local Government Act 2000, which laid the foundations for the local government ethical framework in England, saw a rapid increase in the number of complaints of unethical behaviour on the part of local politicians. Yet the number of complaints has thus far been interpreted as a double-edged sword: they may demonstrate the extent of unethical conduct or they may reflect that the new standards framework is successful in rooting out such behaviour. In more recent years local authorities in England are beginning to introduce tools to evaluate the impact of ethical frameworks on the behaviour of individual politicians, on the organisation as a whole, and, tentatively, on their citizens. It is a somewhat moot point, therefore, what ethical improvement might look like, a point to which we will return presently.

By way of contrast, ethical frameworks in the Netherlands have tended to be less centrally imposed. There is little in the way of systematic ethical audits of local or national government. Depending on the commitment of organisational leadership, evaluations of the impact of these frameworks may or may not occur.

This chapter therefore investigates a number of questions regarding the expansion of standards frameworks and ethical audit approaches in recent years:

1. What do ethical frameworks consist of and how are they audited?
2. What definition of *audit* is being used to examine ethics in public service organisations?
3. How is the concept of ethics being defined when examining ethical audit?
4. What is the relationship between the ethical principles that are said to underpin public service and how are these understood in the practice of ethical audit?
5. Are there particular challenges involved in the implementation of ethical audit regimes?

We will address some of the conceptual and philosophical issues associated with ethical audit and then tentatively suggest a process that might be used in practice. The next section thus introduces the nature of ethical issues and the concept of ethical audit. The third section offers a practical guide in carrying out such an audit.

ETHICAL AUDIT IN THEORY

Ethical Issues

The ethical environment of an organisation is complex and strategies to develop such an environment have changed over time. Historically, organisations, at least in the public sector, focused upon detection and punishment of corruption, fraud, and bribery. More recently, there has been as much interest in preventative measures through ethical awareness training and civic education. This approach is often associated with codes of conduct, which can have an aspirational and guidance role as well as a symbolic or regulatory role. Against this background, however, there has been comparatively little discussion of the meaning of ethical performance; indeed, much of the work on ethical audit, by both scholars and practitioners, is strong on audit but weak on ethics (Fleming and McNamee 2005).

There are a number of fundamental issues that need to be considered, focusing upon the nature of moral agency (why do individuals behave unethically?), the organisational context of individual agency (what are the organisational pressures that might force individuals to behave unethically?), and the ethical status of an organisation as an entity in itself (can an organisation have a conscience?).

Increasingly the ethical issues that face organisations are recognised to be much wider in scope than fraud, corruption, and bribery. The UK's Committee on Standards in Public Life (CSPL), for example, developed the seven principles of public life (accountability, honesty, integrity, openness, leadership, objectivity, and selflessness) to which all public bodies must ascribe. It is also recognised that the less obvious ethical issues, such as respect for persons, or civility, are just as important as identifying examples of illegal or improper behaviour and punishing them (although the latter are, of course, more easily recognised and definable in performance measurement terms). Ethics is about the "grey areas" and organisational issues such as mistreatment of staff, discrimination, misuse of office equipment, or harassment, which are sometimes not straightforward.

One increasingly popular way of theorising about organisational misconduct has been the development of integrity violations. Dutch researchers, for instance, commonly use nine varieties of integrity violations (see Table 25.1).

Some integrity violations are primarily connected to processes (for example, accountability of action, transparency of decision-making) whereas others are concerned with outcomes (trust in public officials). Thus the first question an ethical audit needs to address is what exactly is the focus of the audit—processes or outcomes? Added to this is the question of scope: is the focus on individuals within the organisation or the organisation as an holistic entity? This leads on to the nature of ethical standards themselves, that is, what is performance being measured against? It is difficult to argue that there are universal moral values that we can hold as an exact standard, even though there are always broad principles by which we can agree (for example, the seven CSPL principles), and therefore it is difficult to envisage an ethical equivalent of the Generally Accepted Accounting Principles (GAAP) that accountants and auditors subscribe to (see Satava, Caldwell, and Richards 2006).

An ethical audit can only measure what people do, not what they say they would do as reported in, for example, a survey—it cannot measure their intentions. Unethical outcomes often result from a lack of knowledge or incompetence rather than evil intent, but these would still be captured by the audit procedure. Clearly, control is part of any regime that is concerned with performance (Bouckaert and Halligan 2008). However, control is not the only purpose of such a regime; Behn (2003), for example, distinguishes between performance for evaluation, for motivation, for learning and improvement, for promotion and celebration, and as symbolism.

Putting aside these considerations for a moment, an ethical audit must find quantifiable data, and therefore the kinds of questions that might be involved in ethical audit and performance might include:

- Does the act cause more harm than good?
- Were rights protected and obligations fulfilled?
- Was accountability assured?
- Was justice done?
- Were freedoms protected?
- Was consent given?
- Was individual autonomy protected?

Table 25.1   Types of Integrity Violations

1. Corruption; bribing: misuse of public power for private gain, asking, offering, accepting bribes

2. Corruption; nepotism, cronyism, patronage: misuse of public authority to favour friends, family, party

3. Fraud and theft: improper private gain acquired from the organisation (with no involvement of external actors)

4. Conflict of (private and public) interest: personal interest (through assets, jobs, gifts, etc.) interferes (or might interfere) with public interest

5. Improper use of authority (for noble causes): to use illegal/improper methods to achieve organisational goals

6. Misuse and manipulation of information: lying, cheating, manipulating information, breaching confidentiality of information

7. Discrimination and sexual harassment: misbehaviour towards colleagues or citizens and customers

8. Waste and abuse of resources: failure to comply with organisational standards, improper performance, incorrect or dysfunctional internal behaviour

9. Private time misconduct: conduct in one's private time which harms the public's trust in administration and government

Source: Huberts, Pijl, and Steen (1999, 449–451).

Many of these measures are relatively easy to capture (for example, were rights protected?); others are not so straightforward and, therefore, rely on perceptual surveys, a technique that is fast gaining ground in Australasian studies (see Shacklock, Connors, and Gorta 2008). A successful approach must mitigate against the temptation that is available to any performance regime, to evaluate that which is easily measured (for example, structures and processes in terms of Equal Opportunities legislation, or Health and Safety at Work), such as numbers of complaints. Some local authorities have relied upon performance indicators that can be quantified through, for example, the number of employment tribunals or disciplinary actions that could indicate problems with how individuals treat each other in organisations. Other measurable indicators might include the number of challenges to procurement decisions, the number of complaints against officials, or the number of objections to planning decisions (for the problem of the "dark number", see Huberts, Lasthuizen, and Peeters 2006). We have already noted that such measures are open to mixed interpretations and it is crucial that an ethical audit measures outcomes as well as processes. A process-only approach encourages a "low road" to ethics (Rohr 1978) that concentrates upon compliance rather than upon governance in a wider sense, and encourages a belief that if an act is not prescribed in law then it must be acceptable.

Similarly, issues such as procedural fairness can be measured (for instance, time taken to process complaints or consistency of decisions) but others are problematic. How do we measure whether respect for persons is given, for example? Perceptual surveys might help, but they run the risk of bias: are respondents likely to admit that they have treated others with disrespect? There is also an issue of ascribing responsibility and the problem of many hands (Thompson 1980). As public services are delivered through teams and through a multitude of different agencies, where do we ascribe responsibility? Clearly this is a key issue as one of the purposes of an audit is to pinpoint responsibility throughout a chain of decision-making.

Defining Audit

As we suggest in the preceding section, there has been a growth in audit itself. Hood et al. (1998) chronicle the growth in regulation of public bodies in the UK from 1976 to 1995. There appeared to be a belief on the part of legislators that, for example, professionals in the public services could not be trusted to act in the interests of their patients, clients, students, or users. Finding a tension between a commitment towards increased managerial discretion balanced by more explicit and intrusive regulation, Hood et al. (1998) concluded that there are weaknesses in the system of audit used in UK public bodies, with a lack of opportunity for regulators to meet and exchange best practice, a lack of clear central responsibility, and intrusive regulation. At the same time they argued for a systematic exposure of regulators to competition. Too often audit has been used as a control mechanism; as Nutley argues, the faith placed in control by audit is associated with a declining trust in traditional forms of professional self-regulation (Nutley 2000). This is a theme introduced by Power (1997) who found audit valued as an article of faith, with routinised rituals of inspection:

> The audit society is not simply a distrusting society; rather, it reflects a tendency not to trust trust. This means a systemic tendency towards uncritical trust in the efficacy of audit processes, a process which results in the absence of evaluation of the audit process itself. (136–137)

In terms of ethical performance, the definition of *audit* is not that of "attesting to verifiable statements" but can instead be seen in terms of checking the "health" of the organisation (Owen et al. 2000, 92). The ethical health of an organisation may itself be defined narrowly, such as the minimum of compliance with a code of conduct and legal obligations (Skelcher and Snape 2000). Such an approach has been seen to encourage "ritualistic compliance", where organisations "go through the motions" but behaviour does not necessarily change (Ashworth, Boyne, and Walker 2002). A wider interpretation of ethical health sees a much broader view of governance issues with an emphasis on prevention rather than cure or punishment.

Ethical Audit in Action—the Case of English Local Government

Local government in the UK sees different standards and ethics regimes in each of the devolved administrations (England, Scotland, Wales, and Northern Ireland). Since the introduction of the Local Government Act 2000, English local authorities have been subject to a substantial standards framework, including the creation of new codes of conduct; new registers of interests (and gifts and hospitality); the legal requirement for each council to have a standards committee, which investigates complaints against local elected members and which must by law be chaired by an independent (non-political) member of the public; and the creation of a national strategic regulator, Standards for England (formerly the Standards Board for England). Quite naturally, all of this activity has generated considerable interest in the concept of ethical audit. As a result, English local authorities have increasingly begun to develop their own health checks for ethics; to assist them, an ethical governance toolkit has been created. The toolkit has been developed by three national agencies who exercise a major influence upon the ethical framework for local government in the UK: the Audit Commission, the Improvement and Development Agency (IDeA), and Standards for England. The toolkit allows local authorities to conduct their own ethical audit.

The toolkit is designed to be used in two distinct stages. Stage one is diagnosis, and is supervised by the Audit Commission, stage two is development, which is run in conjunction with the IDeA. The toolkit is designed to test knowledge and understanding of the ethical framework adopted by local authorities and can be applied nationally. The diagnostic survey focuses on politicians and key officers and includes some 150 items assessing compliance with rules and regulations, a code of conduct, a register of interests, knowledge of relevant legislation, and declarations of interest. It also asks questions to elicit the quality of leadership, extent of accountability, relations with partners, communications, and team working.

Some problems can be identified with this particular audit tool. National application may provide a useful benchmark, but by its very nature a generic survey will be extremely difficult to assess how an individual organisation is performing against its own stated values and standards of conduct. Furthermore, the issue of knowledge is not straightforward: What does it mean to say that one authority's members have greater knowledge and understanding of ethical issues than another? Even if such knowledge could be gained it does not necessarily correlate to any great extent with respondent's behaviour (nor, indeed, their values and beliefs). On a practical matter, it may not be realistic to expect officers, other than very senior ones, to even have a view on issues that do not impact upon their daily lives.

Perhaps most importantly is the purpose at which the toolkit is aimed. An authority that scores extremely highly on knowledge and understanding may still only be ethically healthy from the narrow perspective identified earlier: as we have already suggested, conformance or compliance may be an essential objective but it cannot alone lead to an ethical culture (Barrett 2004).

DEVELOPING A BROADER APPROACH TO ETHICAL AUDIT

Ethical audits are necessarily more sensitive than other types of audits. When questions about the integrity of individuals are raised, it can have very damaging consequences since integrity is often regarded as part of one's character and very much unchangeable. There has been a tendency to turn competency failures or errors of judgement into ethics violations when not warranted, thus doing more damage. Huberts (2005) has warned about this "integritism".

Nutley (2000) distinguishes between five approaches to audit: systems, compliance, performance, user satisfaction, and strategic contribution. She argues that systems audit, with its emphasis on internal control systems with reference to best practice, is the dominant approach, even though good systems do not necessarily equate with good performance. She argues, therefore, for a hybrid audit that combines both performance and systems audit, thus measuring both outcomes and processes. Indeed, the tension between processes and outcomes is mirrored in attempts to assess ethical performance, as we shall see in the following.

The audit process we propose is just such a hybrid and is very similar to the internal control audit process to assess more general (operational) risk management; it could even be integrated into that process. The auditor can be: (a) an internal auditor, either from the internal control department or from a dedicated integrity department; (b) an external auditor with regulatory oversight powers; or (c) an external auditor hired by the organisation to perform the audit.

Our approach includes perceptual surveys that make clear links between organisational principles and performance. Table 25.2 provides an example of how performance against one principle might be perceived.

The quality of the audit depends on the co-operation and openness of the organisation being audited. The attitude of the auditor will influence the organisation's attitude. If the auditor starts with a distrusting attitude, looking for things going wrong, it is more likely that the organisation will retreat and try to cover up weaknesses. If however, the auditor starts with a more trusting attitude while alert for lapses and weaknesses, a more open and co-operative stance from the organisation is more likely—based on Zand's (1972, 1997) general trust-building process. Whatever the position of the auditor, their ethical conduct should be above reproach, which shows itself foremost in how they go about the audit: treat the audited organisation and its members with respect, deal appropriately with confidential information, follow due process procedures, and conform with the purpose of the audit agreed upon with the organisation. The more the organisation can trust the auditor, the more likely it is that the ethical audit can have a positive contribution to the ultimate aim: improved ethical performance. This holds even for a regulatory oversight auditor.[1]

Table 25.2 Leadership: Does the Leadership of the Organisation Demonstrate and Promote, through Personal Example, Ethical Standards?

Focus	High Performance	Low Performance
Treatment of Staff	-Respect for views of staff -Act as a role model	-Treats staff badly -Does not defend staff -Favours certain individuals
Respect for citizens	-Open communication and co-operation -Listens	-Ignores their views and needs -Does not provide a forum for discussion
Promote the public interest	-Serves the common good	-Seeks to make personal gain through public office -Does not declare conflicts of interest
The vision/values of the organisation	-Has a clear vision of what an ethical organisation looks like	-Ethics are not part of the values of the organisation

Phase I: Planning

The ethical audit process we propose consists of four phases, each with different stages: planning, fieldwork, reporting, and follow-up (Figure 25.1).

Different ethical frameworks focus attention on regulating the behaviour of different groups of people in organisations. For example, in local authorities, the English ethical framework is primarily aimed at politicians, while the Dutch integrity framework is primarily aimed at civil servants. Other Anglo-Saxon cities such as Sydney and Hong Kong follow the English approach of being able to impose sanctions on politicians, while other continental European cities such as Hamburg and Antwerp follow a similar approach as Dutch cities in not being able to sanction politicians apart from through the justice system (Huberts, Anechiarico, and Six 2008). It is therefore important to be explicit about whose ethical framework is audited, since the content of the framework may

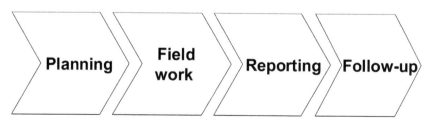

Figure 25.1 Ethical audit process.

vary across groups of officials. Good planning is therefore crucial: it not only addresses the differences in cultural or political context, but it also allows for a standardised audit procedure to be enacted. The planning phase consists of four stages:

1. Notify the organisation that the audit will be taking place.
2. Schedule a pre-audit meeting to discuss purpose of the audit and scope of the audit: Whose ethical standards or integrity are being managed, which ethical issues or risks are included, and which processes are included? Who gets the final report?
3. Prepare pre-audit to determine regulatory context and study documents provided by the organisation.
4. The fourth stage is a preliminary assessment of ethics risks and controls.

The number of "business" processes in each organisation may be vast. Not all carry major ethical risks though and for the purpose of efficiency, a selection may be made of the processes where the largest risks are expected. These may or may not include procurement, financial administration, audit and control, appointments of senior officials, licensing, and elections.

At the same time, the regulatory context within which the audited organisation operates will set the conditions for the ethical framework to be audited. These may include:

• Administrative, penal, and election laws against corruption, theft, and fraud; conflict of interest; sexual harassment and discrimination
• Rules about financial accountability and audit
• Ombudsman obligations
• Ethics policies, such as code of conduct, and integrity watchdog (such as the English Standards Committees)

It is in this first stage that agreement might be reached on which principles should be audited and what is to count as high and low performance (see Table 25.2).

Phase 2: Fieldwork

The aim of the audit is to determine how well the audited organisation is managing the ethical risks present in activities and what controls are operating to help it do this. The fieldwork can consist of several activities, interviews, document analysis, or questionnaire surveys. The output of the fieldwork is a list of significant findings to be used to prepare the draft audit report. During the audit the auditor will look for the degree to which the following is present:

- Can managers ensure that what needs to be done is done in practice and any variations can be explained (are managers "in control")?
- Are problems and ethical risks actively managed?
- Are key controls in place, and do they operate well, to help manage identified risks?
- Is the level of ethical risks left after application of controls acceptable?

A number of factors might influence the auditor's opinion. First, the extent to which management plans are only pieces of paper and not acted upon. Second, what are the reasons for failures and successes and has the organisation identified future learning and improvement? Third, mistakes happen and may arise from, say, indifference, incompetence, or lax controls or processes. How is the organisation proposing to deal with these? Fourth, is there an appropriate level of knowledge and experience of staff in the organisation with regard to ethical management, and is there effective risk management in place?

Ethics risk management consists of different functions that need to be performed:

1. Ethics risk identification: The auditor will look for indications that managers and employees understand the concept of ethics risks and have identified key risks in the organisation.
2. Ethical risk minimisation through policies, procedures, and practices: The auditor will look for indications that the organisation has selected and implemented effective risk-control policies, procedures, and practices.

Investigation, prosecution, restoration, and recovery (after an ethics violation has occurred): the auditor will look for indications that the organisation has developed policies and procedures for when rules are broken.

Phase 3: Reporting

The reporting phase consists of three steps. The first step is the feedback meeting. After the fieldwork the auditor will draft a report and perform an internal quality check. Then a feedback meeting with the organisation will be held with the aim to confirm and inform the draft report content. During the meeting the audit findings, conclusions, and recommendations will be summarised. The organisation will get ample time to respond to these. The higher the commitment of the organisation to the recommendations, the higher the probability of success.

The next step is for the auditor to write the formal draft report incorporating revisions resulting from the feedback meeting and any subsequent work done in light of it. This draft report is then reviewed internally within the auditor organisation. Then the report is sent to the organisation, which is given the opportunity to respond and is asked to complete an action plan.

This action plan will explain how the recommendations will be implemented within the organisation, by whom, and within what time scale. The report will distinguish between different types of recommendations:

- Fundamental: these cover issues that managers must address. They should be resolved immediately.
- Significant: these cover issues that are important but not fundamental. They should be addressed as the next priority.
- Merits attention: these issues are of lesser importance but nevertheless merit attention.

The third step is the final report based on comments by the organisation and any subsequent work done in light of it. Then the final report is sent to all parties agreed upon in the pre-audit meeting. Also, the auditor asks the organisation for feedback on the audit and their performance, so that they can improve the audit quality in the future.

Phase 4: Follow-up

The auditor will make arrangements with the organisation about follow-up reviews. The purpose of these follow-up reviews is to check progress on the implementation of the recommendations. Both parties agree on when and with what scope these reviews will take place. The follow-up reviews use the completed action plan as the basis and use reporting processes similar to Phase 3 of the audit process.

CONCLUSIONS

Research so far has not considered in-depth any unintended consequences of introducing ethical frameworks. Rather, such frameworks have been considered to be intrinsically good, and therefore researchers have focused on seeking to improve ethical performance and to introduce tools that will facilitate this. Yet there may be several consequences that could be perceived in a negative light, including:

- The reporting of unethical acts increases, rather than the number of acts themselves, as there is now a vehicle for complaints.
- The framework is used as a political football, particularly at election time, to traduce political opponents.
- It is possible for individuals to hide behind a code and abrogate responsibility for their actions.
- It may undermine democracy as elected representatives have to stand down from participating in a debate because of perceived prejudicial interests.

- There may be an increase in bureaucracy, in costs, and in time.
- There may be the creation of an ethics industry.
- It could undermine human rights if the distinction between public and private lives of politicians is left in a grey area.

With such considerations hanging over us, what value can an ethical audit actually provide? All the ethical audits in the world will not necessarily stop men and women from acting corruptly and a sceptic might therefore suggest that an ethical audit is another example of how an "industry" around performance measurement has been created.

Our response, in simple cost-benefit terms is: What price can be placed on public trust? The events in the UK over the summer of 2009 regarding MPs expenses have brought public trust in political life to an all time low. Over one-third of parliamentarians are due to resign from their seats at the next general election. It is fair to say that in the UK there has always been a distrust of politicians—they have consistently been ranked at the very bottom of annual public trust surveys since the surveys began many decades ago. The same surveys, however, consistently found that while trust in politicians generally was low, trust in individual local politicians was always considerably higher. The public may not like MPs as a breed but they have always trusted their own local MP. Even this important bond has now been broken.

It is speculative to suggest that an ethical audit of parliament would have prevented these troubles from occurring, but it is difficult to argue against the notion that it would have held parliament up to much greater scrutiny, much earlier. We need to recognise that even after a decade of standards frameworks being introduced, there are significant failings of traditional accountability and that, in our view, these failings are serious enough to warrant concern and that any attempt, no matter how inadequate, to improve ethical performance, is worth it. It is perhaps inevitable and understandable that organisations will want to use an audit.

If the solution is ethical audit, or review, then it needs to be recognised that a "thin" interpretation will not suffice. Review has to be not one task, but several, for example: technical, political, managerial, and ethical, which is part of a wider ethical framework including awareness training, ethical guidelines, and ethical decision-trees (see Lawton 1998).

It is often the case that performance measurement regimes focus upon that which is easily measurable and are often used as control mechanisms. However, there is no reason why a performance regime cannot be used for development and learning through, say, peer review rather than for control, or in the creation of artificial league tables. As always, there is a balance to be struck.

Similarly, there is a concern with ethical standards linked to strategy, as Nutley (2000) suggests, as part of what the organisation stands for: are they "tagged on" and seen as getting in the way of more important financial, political, or service quality considerations? Many organisations might argue that they cannot afford to be ethical (De Vries 2002) but there is evidence to suggest that ethical concerns are taken increasingly into account in terms of reputation, for both public and private sector organisations.

NOTES

1. Based on interviews with Dutch regulatory oversight inspectors during 2009.

REFERENCES

Ashworth, R., G. A. Boyne, and R. M. Walker. 2002. "Regulatory Problems in the Public Sector: Theories and Cases." *Policy and Politics* 30 (2): 195–211.
Barrett, S. M. 2004. "Implementation Studies: Time for a Revival? Personal Reflections on 20 Years of Implementation Studies." *Public Administration* 82 (2): 249–262.
Behn, R. D. 2003. "Why Measure Performance? Different Purposes Require Different Measures." *Public Administration Review* 63:586–606.
Bouckaert, G., and J. Halligan. 2008. *Managing Performance: International Comparisons.* London: Routledge.
De Vries, M. 2002. "Can You Afford Honesty? A Comparative Analysis of Ethos and Ethics in Local Government." *Administration and Society* 34 (3): 309–334.
Fleming, S., and M. McNamee. 2005. "The Ethics of Corporate Governance in Public Sector Organizations: Theory and Audit." *Public Management Review* 7 (1): 135–144.
Hood, C., O. James, G. Jones, and T. Travers. 1998. "Regulation Inside Government: Where New Public Management Meets the Audit Explosion." *Public Money and Management* 18 (2): 61–68.
Huberts, L. W. J. C. 2005. *Integriteit en integritisme in bestuur en samenleving* [*Integrity and Integritism in Governance and Society*]. Amsterdam: VU University Amsterdam.
Huberts, L. W. J. C., F. Anechiarico, and F. E. Six, eds. 2008. *Local Integrity Systems: Fighting Corruption and Safeguarding Integrity in Seven World Cities.* The Hague: BJu.
Huberts, L. W. J. C., K. Lasthuizen, and C. F. W. Peeters. 2006. "Measuring Corruption: Exploring the Iceberg." In *Measuring Corruption*, ed. C. Sampford, A. Shacklock, C. Connors, and F. Galtung, 265–294. Farnham, Surrey: Ashgate Publishing.
Huberts, L .W. J. C., D. Pijl, and A. Steen. 1999. "Integriteit en corruptie" ["Integrity and Corruption"]. In *Politie Studies over haar werking en organisatie*, ed. C. Fijnaut, E. Muller, and U. Rosenthal, 449–451. Alphen aan de Rijn: Samson.
Lawton, A. 1998. *Ethical Management for the Public Services.* Buckingham: Open University Press.
Nutley, S. 2000. "Beyond Systems: HRM Audits in the Public Sector." *Human Resource Management Journal* 10 (2): 21–38.
Owen, D. L., T. A. Swift, C. Humphrey, and M. Bowerman. 2000. "The New Social Audits: Accountability, Managerial Capture or the Agenda of Social Champions?" *European Accounting Review* 9 (1): 81–98.

Power, M. 1997. *The Audit Society: Rituals of Verification.* Oxford: Oxford University Press.

Rohr, J. A. 1978. *Ethics for Bureaucrats: An Essay on Law and Values.* New York: Dekker.

Satava, D., C. Caldwell, and L. Richards. 2006. "Ethics and the Auditing Culture: Rethinking the Foundation of Accounting and Auditing." *Journal of Business Ethics* 64:271–284.

Shacklock, A., C. Connors, and A. Gorta. 2008. "Integrity Assessment Tools: A Preliminary Comparison." In *Promoting Integrity: Evaluating and Improving Public Institutions*, ed. B. W. Head, A. J. Brown, and C. Connors, 221–242. Farnham: Ashgate.

Skelcher, C., and S. Snape. 2000. *Political Executives and the New Ethical Framework.* London: DETR and IDeA.

Thompson, D. F. 1980. "Moral Responsibility of Public Officials: The Problem of Many Hands." *American Political Science Review* 74:905–916.

Zand, D. E. 1972. "Trust and Managerial Problem Solving." *Administrative Science Quarterly* 17 (2): 229–239.

———. 1997. *The Leadership Triad: Knowledge, Trust and Power.* New York: Oxford University Press.

26 Social Accounting and Public Management
Accountability for the Public Good— Conclusions

Victor A. Pestoff

The aim of this book was to address the nexus of issues and disciplines relevant to our growing knowledge of social accounting, and thereby to contribute to the development of both social accounting and public management. It brings together for the first time researchers from a wide range of disciplines, including accounting, economics, management, political science, and sociology. This cross-disciplinary focus makes a unique contribution to the body of knowledge in this field. This is important because accounting, accountability, and social accounting are of growing importance for a number of disciplines and they in turn have unique perspectives on this topic. The presentation of them in a single volume allows for comparing and contrasting these diverse perspectives as well as for combining different theoretical angles in ways that can promote theoretical development.

INTRODUCTION

This volume provides an extensive overview and thorough evaluation of the state of the art in terms of social accounting and public management, as well as their interaction and overlap. It discusses various topics in relation to social accounting and public management, including but not limited to accountability, corporate social resporting (CSR), stakeholders, social capital, sustainability, ethics, semi-autonomous public agencies, third sector organisations (TSOs), assigning a monetary value to some or all of the activities of TSOs, participatory governance, New Public Management (NPM), and New Public Governance (NPG). Providing conclusions to such a rich book on the basis of this vast array of topics is, understandably, no easy task. Such an enterprise clearly implies the risk of emphasising certain aspects of social accounting and public management at the expense of others. In order to write the conclusions to this highly topical subject on the basis of such a vast array of knowledge and varied contributions, all very rich in detail, you must accept that challenge. But, in doing so, I can rely on a certain (pre-) understanding of the subject matter of social accounting and public management. This is based on thirty years of research on the third sector, its role in public policy and providing social services and its potential for re-democratising the welfare state. In a previous book, *Beyond the Market and State* (1998/2005), I devote one chapter to the need to develop social accounting and audit for the third sector, in order to better evaluate and account for the performance of social enterprises. Therefore, I approach this undertaking both with some degree of humility and experience.

Rob Gray, Jesse Dillard, and Crawford Spence's chapter on "A Brief Re-Evaluation of the 'Social Accounting Project': Social Accounting Research as if the World Matters" provides a natural starting point for these conclusions. Gray and his colleagues take stock of the past forty years' experience of the "social audit and accounting project" and its contribution to maintaining an energetic discourse in light of the crisis-ridden social and environmental context and the shortcomings of our current system of accounting and research on it. They start by noting that social accounting is not only a private sector concern, but equally a public and third sector phenomenon, although it has developed differently in these sectors. In the private sector it has nearly always been a voluntary undertaking, typically by large corporations. They have used it to promote image management and legitimise their organisations. Social accounting or CSR is an attempt to demonstrate that they are not purely economic actors. But CSR has been branded cherry-picking and their claims for responsibility and sustainability seem hollow to some, while others will argue that consumer relations management (CRM) is the cousin of CSR. However, as long as there is a major difference between what a corporation is willing to tell society, what they actually do, and what society has a right to know, social accounting will be crucial. By contrast, both the public and third sectors need methods to evaluate their key performance indicators and to capture their principal activities. Thus, social accounting becomes necessary to justify their social and environmental existence and their pursuit of social and environmental goals in economic terms. So the importance and impact of social accounting differs between these three sectors.

Social accounting within the accounting academy has been predominately concerned with developing corporate accountability in the name of some democratic ideal motivated by a concern over the power and influence of corporations and with giving civil society greater control over corporations and their activities. Gray and his colleagues see the emergence of threads of a new conception of what social accounting might become. Many of the ingredients will lie in value-based organisations, NGOs, and community businesses, otherwise known as the third sector and social economy. Finally, they attempt to offer some new directions and conceptions for a newer social accountability in complex institutional situations. Therefore, they propose a range of areas in which social accounting has yet to develop. This includes, among others, new ways to describe, illustrate, and draw out the parameters of less procedural and/or more horizontal accountability mechanisms; developing notions of social bookkeeping and management; developing accounts for specific stakeholder groups, like employees and the unemployed, suppliers, and communities; and accounts focusing on issues such as social justice, human rights, taxation, biodiversity, and natural resources. Gray and his colleagues conclude that social accounting needs to become more vibrant, irreverent, and mischievous, even angry. So there is much work that needs to be done, but it won't be possible if the whims of capital hold sway. Their chapter helps set the tone for many of the contributions of this volume and also facilitates writing these conclusions.

Two underlying yet interrelated themes were touched on by various authors in this volume and need to be emphasised here as they help to provide some structure to these conclusions. The first is the significance of the type of organisational actors being held accountable; that is, are they public services, private for-profit firms, or third sector organisations? As already noted, the social accounting project has developed quite differently in these different sectors and they have different needs. Second, what type of governance regime is envisioned or implied by different authors; that is, is it traditional public administration, NPM, or perhaps NPG? What do these different governance regimes imply for accountability? It could be argued that the traditional public sector is primarily concerned with political accountability through representative democratic channels. However, privatisation and the public–private partnerships typical of NPM complicate and weaken the functioning of traditional political accountability. Many, if not most, of such partnerships are with private for-profit entities, while the third sector usually only plays a marginal role. Efficiency and productivity replace political accountability as key concepts and goals. By contrast, NPG promotes different core values, like pluralistic networks and a greater role for the third sector providers of public services, for example. Here the value-based entities celebrated by Gray, his colleagues, and other contributors have a much greater potential for promoting stakeholder accountability and democratic values.

These two themes contribute two separate dimensions of enquiry that when combined result in a three-by-three table. Not all the cells are touched upon by the authors in this volume; in fact, most of the chapters fall along the diagonal. So, several of the chapters dealing with the traditional public administration naturally focus on various aspects of accountability in the public sector; some of those that discuss relations between public services, private for-profit firms, and CSR also encompass "social" accountability and NPM; while some others that deal with third sector organisations implicitly or explicitly touch on various aspects of NPG (Osborne 2006, 2010). These themes and the underlying dimensions are sketched in Table 26.1.

Superimposed on these two dimensions is a third dimension related to issues of environmental and sustainability accounting and accountability. Most of these chapters focus on the need for greater public sector sustainability. Together these three dimensions cover many of the core topics

Table 26.1   Accountability, Organisational Type, and Governance Regime

	Traditional Public Administration:	New Public Management:	New Public Governance:
Private Non-Profits			Social audit and accounting
For-Profit Firms		Social accountability	
Public Services	Accountability		

Source: the author.

addressed in chapters in this book. Unfortunately, limitations in space and time mean not all of them can be discussed in detail in these conclusions; however, some examples will be provided to illustrate the structure and relations suggested by the dimension in the diagram in Table 26.1. Hopefully, the reader will be able to place additional chapters in relevant cells of the diagram. These conclusions will start by highlighting a few important aspects of traditional public services and accountability, then turn to NPM and social accountability, and finally discuss the third sector and NPG.

Only those chapters that clearly fall on the diagonal of the diagram in Table 26.1 will be discussed in greater detail in the following. Several other chapters are, however, worth noting because of their unique contribution to our understanding of public management and social accounting in this volume. They include two chapters on Central and Eastern Europe and Asia that provide unique insight into important aspects of accountability and public management. They discuss crucial topics such as the interdependency of the role of elites and citizens as parts of a more robust public accountability system in Central and Eastern Europe, and corruption and accountability of the public sector, particularly in the Far East. Such contributions from the new democracies and post-communist societies provide valuable insights to the complexity of accountability and public management. Several other chapters introduce sustainability indicators and social and ethical reporting, both globally as well as among commonwealth and EU member countries. They underline the importance of developing new accountability models that focus on sustainability for the public sector in particular.

Several other chapters on TSOs also make numerous unique contributions to expanding our knowledge of social accounting in diverse social and cultural contexts, including: Anglo-Saxon, traditional European, Central and Eastern European, and Asian countries. They discuss new ways of valuating or monetising some or most of the activities of TSOs; other new accountability models for TSOs, including accreditation; thorny problems related to measuring the social and public value of the social economy; social accounting and audit for social enterprises; and social and environmental reporting in TSOs. Each and every one of these chapters provides valuable insights and is well worth closer attention than is possible here due to the limited space available. Attention will now turn to those chapters that do clearly fall on the diagonal presented in Table 26.1.

TRADITIONAL PUBLIC SERVICE AND ACCOUNTABILITY

First, Amanda Ball, Ian Mason, Suzana Grubnic, Phil Hughes, and S. Jeff Birchall's chapter on "The Carbon Neutral Public Sector: Governmental Accounting and Action on Climate Change" argues for more research into government strategies for a "carbon neutral public sector", but questions whether current strategies constitute meaningful action on climate change. It also discusses the impact, or lack thereof, of sustainability accountability on public policy.

Public sector carbon neutrality is mandated or voluntarily adopted in three commonwealth countries, where climate change is high on the political agenda: New Zealand, Australia, and the United Kingdom. Accounting, including "carbon accounting", while useful, can serve to turn crucial issues into a series of quantifications, resulting in mundane questions about how many?, how much?, at what level?, etc. A key concern then remains whether and how governments can stay focused on building community capacity to mitigate emissions and adapt to climate change. The notion of accounting and accountability for a carbon neutral public sector is arguably at best a necessary but insufficient step in this direction. Much more needs to be done and a focus on accounting can detract from that effort.

Developing more direct methods for civil mobilisation seems necessary in order to curb and prevent carbon emissions. Here researchers can play an important role by focusing their efforts on more relevant questions. They conclude that researchers need to understand the implementation process better, to identify and debate the offset threshold, to critically evaluate the "leading example" rationale, to initiate comparisons across various governmental systems, to understand the relationship between economic and social aspects of sustainability, and to investigate the appropriate unit of analysis. Their suggestions for the research community tie in well with Rob Gray and his colleagues' proposals for more active academic involvement in questions that matter to the world.

Second, Gordon Boyce and Cindy Davids's chapter on "A Social Accountability Framework for Public Sector Conflict of Interest: Private Interests, Public Duties, and Ethical Cultures" delineates the dimensions of the problem of conflict of interest and an appropriate framework for regulation, management, and accountability in public sector services. This is clearly a core concern for traditional public services. Conflicts of interest are key factors in the contemporary decline of trust in government and public institutions, resulting in an erosion of public trust in government and democratic systems. Drawing on two unique empirical studies involving policing and the broader public sector, this chapter examines public complaints about conflict of interest in Victoria, Australia. It provides distinctive insights into the nature of conflict of interest as a problem for public sector ethics. It also analyses and explores appropriate regulatory and management approaches to conflict of interest, focusing on three elements: (a) dealing with conflict of interest that may clash with the duties of public officials; (b) managing conflicts as they occur; and (c) developing ethical and accountable organisational cultures.

The operation of public complaints systems (Ombudsman) provides something of a barometer of the ethical state of the public sector as a whole and of individual organisations and agencies. Adopting a broad rubric of social accountability to examine the problems of conflict of interest draws attention to the relationship between account givers and receivers. Those who are given responsibility in the name of the public are authorised to act in particular ways, but only on condition of accountability for those acts. They conclude that effective and meaningful public sector ethics in the pursuit of public interest must be based on an ethos of social accountability and a commitment to prioritise the public interest in both fact and appearance. The Office of Ombudsman can play an important role in maintaining social accountability in traditional public service settings.

Third, Daphne Rixon and Sheila Ellwood's chapter on "Reporting for Public Sector Agencies: A Stakeholder Model" examines one crucial aspect of the increasing trend of governments to delegate responsibilities for public services to semi-autonomous public sector agencies. Devolution not only increases the complexity of public service accountability, but, as they argue, there is also a need to demonstrate that such organisations are sufficiently accountable to various stakeholders and are meeting their needs. They argue that accountability in the public sector is significantly broader in scope than in the private sector. The private sector can focus on financial results and creation of shareholder value, while the public sector encompasses a more diverse group of stakeholders, which often include most citizens and taxpayers, along with a myriad of accountability expectations. Therefore, the concept of accountability has expanded well beyond the core definition of being called to account for one's actions to include internal responsibility of public servants to professional standards and external responsiveness to the needs of clients and public dialogue. However, such a broad definition of accountability invites numerous complexities and opens various interpretations due to the multidimensional nature of the public sector itself.

Rixon and Ellwood focus their study of stakeholder accountability on the Workers' Compensation Board (WCB) in Newfoundland and Labrador, Canada. A key contribution of this research is to link two different "ladders of stakeholder influence": Stewart's Ladder of Accountability (1984) with Friedman and Miles's Ladder of Stakeholder Management and

Engagement (2006). They arrive at a multidimensional stakeholder reporting model for public sector agencies. Higher rungs of the ladders require
more interaction with stakeholders in order to demonstrate accountability
for outcomes and expected standards. Their study of the WCB demonstrates that stakeholders want to be more involved and have more control
over the direction of the organisation, rather than just provide feedback on
the agency's plans. Their research also clearly shows that some accounting
mechanisms, like financial reports, key performance indicators, balanced
scorecards, and even stakeholder consultations, can be used to achieve
organisational legitimacy, rather than meet the substantive needs of stakeholders. Such mechanisms leave little room for stakeholder participation
and engagement. While their research and findings primarily concern the
complexities of traditional public sector accountability, they also have a
clear bearing on the new directions called for by Gray and his colleagues
and for the development of NPG.

Fourth, Colin Dey, Shona Russell, and Ian Thomson's chapter on
"Exploring the Potential of Shadow Accounts in Problematising Institutional Conduct" argues for a value-driven external account or shadow
account that focuses on undesirable organisational behaviour. Shadow
accounts are a particular form of social accounting produced by external
organisations, including NGOs, on *their* representation of the undesirable
social and environmental impacts of other organisations. Given that these
reports attempt to challenge, problematise, and delegitimise those currently
in a dominant position of power, such accounts will be prepared by or for
less powerful social groups. Shadow accounting is a voluntary activity and
shadow accountants are self-selecting individuals or organisations that seek
to bring about change in society. It intends to reveal contradictions between
what companies choose to report and what they suppress, problematising
their activities and providing new insights into their social and environmental impact. They also explore the extent to which prior examples of
shadow accounting have been effective in the production of new knowledge
and the creation of new visibilities. This is one amongst a number of chapters in this volume that contribute to discussion of important and plausible
new directions for social accounting.

NEW PUBLIC MANAGEMENT AND SOCIAL ACCOUNTABILITY

First, Sandro Brunelli, Alessandro Giosi, and Silvia Testarmata's chapter on
"Agencies as Instruments of New Public Management: Models of Accountability in Italy" explores the growing complexities of public accountability.
They argue that with the introduction of NPM there is a growing need
to develop and adopt suitable models of accountability, in particular after
the introduction of decentralised public service delivery. NPM calls for a
clear division between politics and the administration, where the former

undertakes strategic planning and defines economic targets and the latter is responsible for public service management. The Organisation for Economic Co-operation and Development (OECD) considers public agencies as a means of outsourcing to bodies with specialised operating tasks. This has a major impact on public service accountability, with a shift of responsibility in traditional models of political accountability from the parliament and government to a clear focus on performance results in the market or quasi market for its customers. This implies a change in the principal–agent relations, where the latter is accountable to the former. New models of accountability are necessary to promote coherence between administrative action and political targets. Based on research on the Italian Revenue Agency, the National Social Security Institute, and the National Procurement Agency, they argue that these models require clear definitions of accountability for public agencies and identify the factors that make the public agency accountable. They emphasise the importance of internal control, political leadership, and citizen satisfaction to meet the challenges posed to accountability by NPM.

Second, Marie-Andrée Caron, Alan Lapointe, and Corinne Gendron's chapter on "Prolegomena to Sustainability Reporting: Preventing Premature Closure of Debate Surrounding the Meaning of Sustainability" provides an overview of the debate on sustainability and corporate social responsibility. Previously, Milne and Gray (2007) have argued that social accounting as a discipline helps businesses to mask their socially and ecologically unsustainable practices and to legitimate the ongoing exploitation of people and the environment. This is facilitated by the semi-"objectivity" of social accounting that prevents a public debate about the activities of companies, particularly multinational ones, and also inhibits the emergence of a dialogue about social accounting itself. Moreover, most societal performance reports are not totally "free" to report what they want, since they are subject to constraints imposed on them by the company and anchored in its structures of meaning.

NGOs known as New Social Economic Movements (NSEM) represent groups that have moved from the political to the economic field in order to reinvest socio-political content and meaning into "economic transactions". NSEM preside over new spaces for dialogue and social regulation at the margins of traditional institutional spaces. The Global Reporting Initiative (GRI) successfully penetrated the corporate world in five years, while social accounting still lacks legitimacy in that sector after more than forty years. However, without a robust stakeholder dialogue and reporting process such guidelines may merely be a legitimating exercise by organisations that report only the minimum required but omit all materials not specifically covered by them. This reflects one of the main points made by Rixon and Ellwood's stakeholder model referred to earlier.

Finally, Caron, Lapointe, and Gendron regard social accounting as a collective product obtained through a dialogue. So, they propose to provide a hybrid forum or dialogic space to various social actors with divergent understandings of CSR in order to debate the uncertainties and to reach the compromises that are inherent in the production of societal performance reports. This is necessary in order to avoid prematurely closing the democratic debate about corporate social performance and sustainability. Such a hybrid forum refers to open spaces where social actors can mobilise to debate the technical choices concerning their collective choices. This would allow for the CSR experts "who know" to meet those who favour a more collective and democratic understanding of CSR. Once again, this chapter suggests an important direction for developing social accounting in line with the gaps in the extant literature and practice.

NEW PUBLIC GOVERNANCE AND SOCIAL ACCOUNTING AND AUDIT

First, Taco Brandsen, Mirjan Oude Vrielink, Thomas Schillemans, and Eelco van Hout's chapter on "Non-Profit Organisations, Democratisation, and New Forms of Accountability: A Preliminary Evaluation" examines how different theoretical interpretations of horizontal or social accountability relate to practice in the Netherlands. Their findings rely on extensive comparative research projects in seven policy fields: higher education, health care, elderly care, social housing, welfare, child care, and care for the handicapped, where the services were primarily delivered by non-profit organisations (NPOs). The growth in the size and complexity of public administration has led to a fragmented system of public governance that is ill-adapted to hierarchical models of accountability and has resulted in calls for an accountability regime that is more decentralised. In the Netherlands, many NPOs that work with public funding are subject to accountability mechanisms that are imposed on them by the national or local governments. Here they are accountable to a single financer or principal. However, in recent years new forms of accountability have been introduced that recognise that NPOs are responsible to various principals or stakeholders. These new forms are often seen as more democratic and more in keeping with the non-profit character of the organisations involved. Some of them are thought to give citizens more direct influence on service delivery by NPOs, rather than only indirect influence through representative democratic institutions. The assumption is that new kinds of accountability will empower various stakeholders, including citizens, and provide for a more direct form of democracy.

The evidence suggests that while many new forms of accountability have been adopted with enthusiasm, their effects remain limited in terms of democracy. First, much of the activity associated with accountability is informal, disorganised, and unrecorded. So, attempts to involve stakeholders in institutionalised settings are, at best, only partially successful.

Second, new forms of accountability offer useful input for organisational learning and give clients greater say in day-to-day affairs of service providers, but on the whole they tend to strengthen the influence of the already powerful interests in the service environment. Third, while they provide all stakeholders with greater knowledge, this often leads to intensified efforts by authorities to intervene in the affairs of autonomous service providers or service NPOs. Citizens seldom have the expertise necessary to influence the professionals who run NPOs or social programs and they lack sanction powers necessary to do so. In fact, over time citizens seem to withdraw from engagement due to their disappointment with their limited impact. Their conclusion is that new forms of accountability can have certain benefits for clients, but they also have the capacity to reinforce the existing balance of power within public management. This also suggests that we need to consider closer differences in the role of NPOs in NPM and NPG regimes in order to better understand when greater participation will promote democracy and when it won't.

Second, Andrea Calabrò's chapter on "Conflicts of Interest, Corruption, and Ethics in Public Services: A Public Governance Approach" looks at whether privatising public sector activities might improve or detract from NPM reforms. It starts by noting that privatisation is an important part of market reform programs, which are expected to improve economic efficiency by reducing the role of the state in the economy. Yet, some countries in Europe have only recently begun to privatise, so they may be considered as examples of partial privatisation. The primary aim of this chapter is to show the impact of privatisation on the accountability system for providers of public services. The primary research questions are: What is the main reason for partial privatisation? How can it be related to different regime perspectives, like NPM, NPS, and NPG? How are these different perspectives related to accountability systems of public service firms?

Privatisation is often seen as a tool or mechanism of NPM. However, there are important distinctions between NPM and privatisation. Calabrò argues that privatisation is a broad toolkit, while NPM provides an approach to public management reform. Moreover, privatisation and NPM have both come under growing attack from academics, politicians, and the media. There is an increasing concern about the impact of NPM reforms on public officials' ethics and some now argue for greater rather than less regulation, particularly after the financial debacle in late 2008. New models have recently been proposed that challenge NPM (see Osborne 2006) and new paradigms for government activity, policy-making, and service delivery are emerging that bring with them important implications for public service managers, like NPG (Osborne 2010) and New Public Service (NPS) as alternatives to both the traditional public administration and NPM (Denhardt and Denhardt 2000). They are based on the idea that the relationship between the government and its citizens is not the same as business activity between a firm and its customers.

The NPG perspective includes many modes of governance, like joined-up governance, network governance, co-production, and co-operation, which are seen as alternatives to privatisation of public service provision, particularly for social services. NPG offers a valid alternative to privatisation since it relies on active citizen participation in the governance process of the services they depend on in their daily lives. Given the limits of the current Italian privatisation process, conflicts of interest and corruption require greater public sector accountability. Public accountability is an essential precondition for the democratic process to work, since it provides citizens and their representatives with the information needed for judging the propriety and effectiveness of government.

NPS and NPG may also be able to solve, in part, some of the ethical issues related to interest conflict and corruption, due to greater citizen participation in public service delivery. However, it is important to remember that given different perspectives on privatisation, like NPM, NPS, and NPG, the power of governing bodies is also changing. This gives rise to questions about the capacity of accountability systems to keep up with these developments. Would going from NPM to NPS or NPG help address issues of conflict of interest and corruption and promote the public good? Moreover, how would they impact on partial privatisations, like those so often found in Italy?

Calabrò's conclusions argue for greater citizen involvement in the provision of public services and for developing NPG, rather than more privatisation or NPM. It is necessary to define, operationalise, measure, and evaluate public services and public service organisations to make them accountable. However, communications between the government and its citizens become fundamental. New modes of governance that are more citizen oriented go in that direction. This focuses attention on NPG with its emphasis on partnerships, networking, and the lateral modes of organising rather than the vertical command and control forms typical of NPM. It also takes a more pragmatic view of public services that can be delivered both publicly and privately. These new modes of governance can help to address the accountability deficit in the Italian Ministry of Economy and Finance governance structure. The lack of accountability is a growing concern, particularly with regard to privatisation. Mandatory codes of ethics are not enough, but they provide a good starting point. Surely, other means are needed to promote a high level of public service. However, a code imposed from above will not work if the goal is to produce a document of shared values. Only more citizens' participation through a bottom-up process can help to fill the complex process of building codes with shared values, vision, and interests. Calabrò's chapter not only reflects concerns about the limits of current accountability systems in both the traditional public administration and NPM expressed by several of the authors discussed thus far, it also clearly points to new developments and the need for new models of social accounting proposed by several contributors to this volume.

Third, Giulio Citroni and Sabina Nicolella's chapter on "Participatory Governance and Social Audit in the Third Sector" analyses the role that participation and participatory governance can have in social audit and accounting for third sector organisations. They argue that the third sector is playing an increasingly important role in a variety of fields in society today. In addition, third sector organisations are progressively contributing to a greater "welfare mix" due to their ability to provide high-quality services in areas where welfare systems are not adequately covered by governments, especially concerning minority needs. Moreover, due to their proximity to social and environmental concerns, they are emerging as valid representatives of such needs in the global debate on the inclusiveness and democratisation of globalisation. However, their emerging roles and growing significance raises important questions about their transparency and representativeness, especially given an often narrow focus that prevents them from acting as representatives of wider societal needs. Opening up an organisation to stakeholder contributions and scrutiny can provide an effective solution to issues of representativeness, transparency, and accountability. Engaging both external and internal stakeholders in the formulation of organisational strategies, policies, and actions that affect them brings the concept of representativeness to a more concrete level.

The debate on social accounting concerns the values and ethics governing the actions of organisations of all types. Both sustainability reporting and stakeholder engagement can serve this purpose. Participatory governance brings stakeholders to the centre of strategic and functional planning and promotes greater stakeholder engagement and empowerment by involving them in the definition of the organisation's goals, in the evaluation of how well these goals were met, and the planning and carrying out of specific tasks to meet these goals, for example. Citroni and Nicolella employ data from three TSOs in north-eastern Italy that implement a participatory governance approach to social accounting and audit in the third sector. In each of these three organisations a process was designed and implemented that led to the publication and diffusion of a Social Report (*Bilancio Sociale*). A very narrow line separates participation and manipulation in politics and the market, where implications of power relations may affect the way participation is perceived and implemented. However, in the third sector participation takes on a different meaning. Here a balance must be struck between the organisation's idea of sustainability or social good and that of its stakeholders. Commitment of the top management in the organisation is a necessary but not sufficient condition to implement an effective auditing process. The administration and other staff must also be committed to the underlying logic of the participatory approach to social auditing so that information can be gathered and processed effectively and the process carried out smoothly.

In the absence of an established chain of political accountability or market mechanisms to promote greater consumer choice, which can be measured either by votes or by consumer decisions, accountability in the third sector must find its own way and tools, so that its corporate actions and its economic, social, and environmental impacts can be measured against the declared values of an organisation and individual or collective stakeholder expectations. The participatory governance approach to social auditing and reporting underlines the importance of stakeholder engagement and leaves the content and structure of the audit and report to negotiation and deliberation between stakeholders. This may help to construct a shared definition of the goals and capabilities of the organisation and may help to overcome eventual problems. However, some problems remain unresolved, like the definition of the boundaries of the organisation, which stakeholders to include, and the credibility of using a previously untried and unknown process. Once again we find the outlines and elements of a common effort to develop new directions for social accounting, and more horizontal accountability mechanisms, based on stakeholder participation. This fits well with the tone and focus of several of the chapters discussed earlier and concerns throughout the book with future direction.

Fourth, Guenther Lorenz and Alan Kay's chapter, "Social Accounting and Auditing: Assessing the Contribution of Social Capital to Social Enterprise and the Social Economy", reports the findings from the CONSCISE Project. It was a fifth EU framework research project in four countries (Germany, Spain, Sweden, and the UK) on the implementation of social capital features in social accounting procedures. They used social accounting and audit to see how social capital contributes to the growth of social enterprise, how local social enterprises generate social capital, and finally how social enterprises can generate social capital by working together, and thereby develop the local social economy. The CONSCISE Project adopted the five-stage social accounting process as described in the *Social Audit and Accounting Manual*. This research demonstrated that the social accounting process is capable of looking at certain issues in a uniform way across a number of social enterprises, at the same time allowing for the enterprises to explore and report on their own values, objectives, and activities.

Lorenz and Kay illustrate how social accounts assisted social enterprises in measuring performance against its own social objectives and its impact on the development of the locality. At the same time, social accounts explored how the enterprise used and generated social capital in its development and the development of the local area. Social enterprises often emerge from the social capital of groups responding to socio-economic problems such as industrial decline, youth unemployment, and rural isolation. Social capital is therefore a crucial resource where a social enterprise is formed to tackle such problems, and often the starting point of the setting up of a social enterprise. Responding to a crisis may be the stimulus for a community to begin to work together and, by doing so, to begin to create the social capital to help tackle the crisis. The potential of this approach is to facilitate the measurement and comparison of the social performance of social enterprises in terms of the social capital they generate. By demonstrating the connection between social accounting, social capital, and social enterprise, Lorenz and Kay provide yet another example of developing new techniques and methodologies that permit us to speak about new directions and conceptions for a newer social accountability in complex institutional situations. They share this developmental work with several of the other chapters noted earlier.

Finally, Cynthia and Thomas Lynch's chapter on "Budget and Social Capital System Theory: Empirical Research Tools" proposes to add intervening variables and feedback loops to the established budget systems model and then to extend a similar logic to develop a social capital system model. The budget model is based on the four components—inputs, process, outputs, and outcomes—while system dynamics are provided by the three intervening variables and their feedback loops—evaluation reports, progress reports on program accomplishments, and accounting and financial information related to the program. The main components of the social capital systems model are trust, relationships, norms, and oneness, while the intervening variables and feedback loops that provide system dynamics are participation, civility, and growth.

Both systems models enable those who do research to greatly strengthen their understanding of how to achieve greater accountability and trust in government and third sector organisations. Both require researchers to develop performance indicators of the elements in their respective system models if they wish to move beyond broad generalisations to more specific causal understanding. In the case of the social capital systems model, researchers can go beyond resource allocation to see if social interactions among sets of participants are essentially working. Beyond monitoring the viability of social interactions, researchers can investigate what policymakers can do to improve social interactions so that the joint efforts are more likely to be successful. Once again we find new directions for promoting the development of new social accounting techniques and mechanisms.

SOME FINAL COMMENTS

Rob Gray and his colleagues lament the lack of progress in the "social accounting project" during the past forty years, but note different rates of development of social accounting in different sectors of society. In the private sector, where it is most developed, CSR has been branded as cherry-picking, while the claims of major corporations appear hollow and seem motivated mainly by gaining legitimacy. By contrast, both the public and third sectors need to develop techniques and methods to evaluate their key performance indicators and to capture their principal activities in order to justify their social and environmental existence. So the importance and impact of social accounting differs understandably between these three sectors.

This book sees the emergence of the threads of a new conception of what social accounting might become. The third sector and social enterprises can provide the ingredients of a more value-based orientation for social accounting. Ethics, stakeholder accountability, participative governance, horizontal accountability, sustainability reporting, shadow accounts, stakeholder dialogue spaces, negotiations and compromises on social performance reports, and NPG—all of them provide threads for a new fabric of social accounting, particularly in the public and third sectors. Many of the chapters in this book provide profound insights into new directions and conceptions for a newer social accounting project in the complex institutional settings of NPM, and more clearly so of NPG. Gray's conclusion that social accounting needs to become more vibrant, irreverent, and mischievous, even angry, seems to be fulfilled, at least in part, by many of the chapters in this excellent book. Together these chapters provide important, exciting, and contrary views of social accounting. Better yet, they point to the future, rather than the past, and to the public and third sector rather than the private for-profit sector. This bodes well for a revival of and the future growth of the social accounting project and for its positive impact on public management.

Finally, in addition to emphasising the threads for a new conception of social accounting, some of the chapters herein also touch on what might prove to be the threads for a new fabric of public management; not one just based on public–private partnerships between the public sector and private for-profit firms, but one that also leaves ample space for an active and growing third sector. It would rely to a much greater extent on value-based non-profit organisations, co-operatives, and social enterprises (for example) that do not primarily seek to maximise their profit in the name of efficiency, but rather see their surplus as a means to effectively achieve their social and political goals and to promote the public good. Such a view of the public good, of course, includes both an effective public sector and efficient private sector, but it does not stop there.

Public management also encompasses a dynamic and thriving third sector as a major provider of goods and services. Thus, it would include many more features of NPG than NPM. It would be based on a new paradigm that was comprised not only of big government and big business, but numerous modes of governance like co-production and co-operation. It would rely on active citizen participation in the provision and governance processes of some of the services they are dependent upon in their daily lives. It would involve partnerships with the third sector, networking, and lateral modes of organising, rather than vertical command and control forms typical of NPM. Such new modes of governance could help to address many of the shortcomings discussed in the current deficit in accountability in all three sectors. Greater stakeholder participation in a bottom-up social accounting and audit process, like those discussed herein, can help to fulfil the complex processes of building common codes, shared values, and a vision of the public good. NPG would also help to strengthen the ties between social accounting and public management, and they would both be linked together by active citizens and democratic processes.

REFERENCES

Denhardt, R. B., and J. V. Denhardt. 2000. "The New Public Service: Serving Rather than Steering." *Public Administration Review* 60 (6): 549–559.
Milne, M. J., and R. Gray. 2007. "Future Prospects for Corporate Sustainability Reporting." In *Sustainability Accounting and Accountability*, ed. J. Unerman, J. Bebbington, and B. O'Dwyer, 184–207. London and New York: Routledge.
Osborne, S. 2006. "The New Public Governance?" *Public Management Review* 8 (3): 377–387.
———, ed. 2010. *The New Public Governance*. London and New York: Routledge.
Pestoff, V. 1998/2005. *Beyond the Market and State. Social Enterprises and Civil Democracy in a Welfare Society*. Aldershot, UK, and Brookfield, NJ: Ashgate.

Contributors

Amanda Ball is Professor of Accounting at the University of Canterbury, New Zealand.

S. Jeff Birchall is a PhD candidate and Royal Society of New Zealand Marsden Researcher in the Department of Accounting and Information Systems, University of Canterbury, Christchurch.

Gordon Boyce is an Associate Professor in the School of Accounting at LaTrobe University, Melbourne, with research expertise in social, environmental, and critical perspectives on accounting.

Taco Brandsen is Associate Professor at the Nijmegen School of Management, Radboud University Nijmegen, the Netherlands.

Sandro Brunelli is a doctoral student in Public Management and Governance at the University of Rome "Tor Vergata". His prevalent research interests are accounting and accountability.

Andrea Calabrò is a doctoral student in Public Management and Governance at the University of Rome "Tor Vergata", Faculty of Economics, Department of Business Administration.

Marie-Andrée Caron is Professor in Accounting at the University of Quebec in Montreal (ESG-UQAM). Her special interests include corporate social responsibility, sustainability reporting, and sociology of professions.

Giulio Citroni is a researcher in Political Science at the University of Florence (Research Unit on Local Governance) and teaches Political Science and Public Policy Analysis at the University of Calabria, Italy.

Ram A. Cnaan is Professor, Associate Dean for Research, and Chair of the Doctoral Program in Social Welfare at the University of Pennsylvania, School of Social Policy and Practice.

Cindy Davids is Senior Lecturer in the School of Law at Deakin University, Melbourne. She has extensive research experience in examining complaint case files in relation to policing and the public sector.

Colin Dey is a Lecturer at the School of Accounting and Finance at the University of Dundee. His research projects have explored accountability issues with a particular focus on social accounting and reporting.

Jesse Dillard is Professor of Accounting at Portland State University, Oregon.

Sheila Ellwood is Professor of Financial Reporting at the University of Bristol, UK. Her research interests are public sector accounting, financial management, and audit.

Federica Farneti is Assistant Professor at the Alma Mater Studiorum University of Bologna, Faculty of Economics and Business, Italy.

Pavol Frič is a Senior Researcher in the Centre for Social and Economic Strategies and also Lecturer at the Institute of Sociological Studies, both at the Charles University in Prague, Czech Republic.

Corinne Gendron is a Professor in the Department of Strategy, Social and Environmental Responsibility at the Business School of the University of Quebec in Montreal.

Alessandro Giosi is Assistant Professor of Accounting at the Department of Business Administration at the University of Rome "Tor Vergata", and a public administration consultant, especially health care agencies.

Rob Gray is Professor of Social and Environmental Accounting at the University of St. Andrews and Director of the Centre for Social and Environmental Accounting Research.

Suzana Grubnic is Lecturer in Accounting and Finance at Nottingham University Business School. Her current research focuses on performance management in local government and sustainability in the public sector.

James Guthrie is an Honorary Porfessor at the University of Sydney and a Professor at the University of Bologna. He is also the Head of Academic Relations for the Institute of Chartered Accountants in Australia.

Femida Handy is a Professor in the School of Social Policy and Practice, University of Pennsylvania. She is an economist whose research interests include non-profits, volunteering, and non-government organisations.

Phil **Hughes** is a principal consultant in sustainability and water management with Halcrow Pacific Pty. Ltd. in Melbourne, Australia. Phil has worked sustainability-related topics for some fifteen years.

Magdalena Hunčová is Head of Department of Finance and Accounting at the Faculty of Social and Economic Studies, University J. E. Purkyně in Ústí nad Labem, Czech Republic.

Ashok Jain is one of the leading architects of rural development research and social economics in India. He is a Professor at Tilak Maharashtra University and a Professor Emeritus at the University of Mumbai.

Meenaz Kassam is Assistant Professor at the American University of Sharjah, UAE. She is a sociologist whose research interests include sociological theory and international non-governmental organisations.

Alan Kay is a freelance researcher who has experience in community development, social accounting, and social capital. He is based in Edinburgh and is a Director of CBS Network and the Social Audit Network.

Tony Kinder is Senior Lecturer in Public Services Management at the University of Edinburgh Business School. He has spent two decades leading public services reform in Scottish local authorities.

Alain Lapointe is a Professor of Corporate Social Responsibility at the Business School of the University of Quebec in Montreal. He is the co-chair of the "Chaire de responsabilité sociale et de développement durable".

Alan Lawton is Professor of Public Sector Management at the Business School, University of Hull, and also Professor of Integrity of Governance at the VU University, Amsterdam.

Guenther Lorenz is co-ordinator of R&D, Technologie-Netzwerk Berlin e.V. He has been project co-ordinator of numerous national and transnational R&D projects.

Cynthia E. Lynch is an Associate Professor in the MPA program at the University of Texas Pan American. She is the Texas Director of International Academy for Interfaith Studies http://interfaithacademy.org.

Thomas D. Lynch is Professor Emeritus, Louisiana State University, and Research Professor at the University of Texas Pan American. He founded and was editor of *The Public Manager* for ten years.

Michael Macaulay is a Reader in Governance and Public Ethics at Teesside University Business School. With a research background in political philosophy, Michael has written extensively on ethics and ethical leadership.

Ian Mason is a Research Fellow in Environmental and Energy Engineering and a Senior Fellow in Carbon Management at the University of Canterbury in New Zealand.

Dianne McGrath is the Accounting and Law Discipline Leader in the School of Accounting, Thurgoona Campus, Charles Stuart University. Her current research includes social and environmental reporting in credit unions.

Monika Molnár is an Associate Professor of Management at the College of Dunaujvaros, Hungary. Her current research interests include general management issues of third sector organisations.

Laurie Mook is Co-Director of the Social Economy Centre, University of Toronto. She specialises in alternative models of accounting for nonprofit and other social economy organisations.

Sabina Nicolella is a Project Manager for CSR at Ecosistemi and a founder member of Associazione Sinapsi. She is a former researcher of Fondazione Eni Enrico Mattei and has expertise in CSR mainstreaming.

Dick Osborn spent four decades advising Australia's local, state, and national governments. He is a doctoral student within the Centre for the Public Awareness of Science at the Australia National University.

Stephen P. Osborne is Professor of International Public Management within the University of Edinburgh Business School in Scotland, editor of the journal 'Public Management Review' and President of the International Research Society on Public Management.

Gaurav Patankar, in addition to being a doctoral student in Political Science at TMV in India, is a leading practitioner in free market economics in New York.

Victor A. Pestoff is Professor Emeritus in Political Science and currently Guest Professor at the Institute for Civil Society Studies at Ersta Skondal University College in Stockholm, Sweden.

Daphne Rixon is Assistant Professor of Accounting at Saint Mary's University, Halifax, Nova Scotia, Canada. Her area of research includes public sector stakeholder accountability and financial and performance reporting.

Shona Russell completed her PhD at the University of Strathclyde and is now a Researcher at Landcare Research Manaaki Whenua in New Zealand.

Thomas Schillemans is Assistant Professor in Public Administration at the Utrecht School of Governance, Utrecht University, and Visiting Fellow at the Centre for Social Impact, University of New South Wales, Sydney.

Benedetta Siboni is Assistant Professor and Lecturer of Management and Accounting at the Alma Mater Studiorum University of Bologna, Faculty of Economics and Business, Italy.

Frédérique Six is Senior Lecturer at the VU University Amsterdam Research Group Integrity of Governance, Department of Governance Studies, Amsterdam, the Netherlands.

Crawford Spence is Assistant Professor of Accounting at Concordia University.

Silvia Testarmata is a postdoctoral Research Fellow in Public Administration at the University of Rome "Tor Vergata". She has a PhD in Public Management and Governance.

Ian Thomson is Reader in Accounting in the Department of Accounting and Finance at the University of Strathclyde.

Eelco van Hout is Senior Research Fellow at the TiasNimbas Business School, Tilburg University, the Netherlands. He specialises in developing and leading hybrid, public–private, governance networks.

Mirjan Oude Vrielink is Assistant Professor at the Tilburg School of Politics and Public Administration, Tilburg University, the Netherlands, and Senior Researcher at Twente University, the Netherlands.

Wilson Wong is an Associate Professor of Department of Government and Public Administration and Associate Director of the Public Policy Research Center, the Chinese University of Hong Kong.

Index